INTELLI 2016

The Fifth International Conference on Intelligent Systems and Applications

InManEnt 2016

International Symposium on Intelligent Manufacturing Environments

November 13 - 17, 2016

Barcelona, Spain

INTELLI 2016 Editors

Antonio Martin, Universidad de Sevilla, Spain

Gil Gonçalves, Faculty of Engineering, University of Porto, Portugal

Leo van Moergestel, Utrecht University, the Netherlands

Printed from e-media with permission by:

Curran Associates, Inc.
57 Morehouse Lane
Red Hook, NY 12571

Some format issues inherent in the e-media version may also appear in this print version.

Printed by Curran Associates, Inc. (2016)

International Academy, Research, and Industry Association (IARIA)
412 Derby Way
Wilmington, DE 19810

Phone: (408) 893-6407
Fax: (408) 527-6351

petre@iaria.org

Additional copies of this publication are available from:

Curran Associates, Inc.
57 Morehouse Lane
Red Hook, NY 12571 USA
Phone: 845-758-0400
Fax: 845-758-2633
Email: curran@proceedings.com
Web: www.proceedings.com

Table of Contents

Norbert Link, Jurgen Pollak, and Alireza Sarveniazi

INTELLI 2016

Foreword

The Fifth International Conference on Intelligent Systems and Applications (INTELLI 2016), held between November 13-17, 2016 - Barcelona, Spain, was an inaugural event on advances towards fundamental, as well as practical and experimental aspects of intelligent and applications.

The information surrounding us is not only overwhelming but also subject to limitations of systems and applications, including specialized devices. The diversity of systems and the spectrum of situations make it almost impossible for an end-user to handle the complexity of the challenges. Embedding intelligence in systems and applications seems to be a reasonable way to move some complex tasks form user duty. However, this approach requires fundamental changes in designing the systems and applications, in designing their interfaces and requires using specific cognitive and collaborative mechanisms. Intelligence became a key paradigm and its specific use takes various forms according to the technology or the domain a system or an application belongs to.

We take here the opportunity to warmly thank all the members of the INTELLI 2016 Technical Program Committee, as well as the numerous reviewers. The creation of such a high quality conference program would not have been possible without their involvement. We also kindly thank all the authors who dedicated much of their time and efforts to contribute to INTELLI 2016. We truly believe that, thanks to all these efforts, the final conference program consisted of top quality contributions.

Also, this event could not have been a reality without the support of many individuals, organizations, and sponsors. We are grateful to the members of the INTELLI 2016 organizing committee for their help in handling the logistics and for their work to make this professional meeting a success.

We hope that INTELLI 2016 was a successful international forum for the exchange of ideas and results between academia and industry and for the promotion of progress in the field of intelligent systems and applications.

We are convinced that the participants found the event useful and communications very open. We also hope the attendees enjoyed the charm of Barcelona, Spain.

INTELLI 2016 Chairs:

INTELLI Advisory Committee

Michael Negnevitsky, University of Tasmania, Australia
Roy George, Clark Atlanta University, USA
Pradeep Atrey, University of Winnipeg, Canada
Jerzy Grzymala-Busse, University of Kansas, USA
Daniël Telgen, HU University of Applied Sciences Utrecht, The Netherlands
Zoi Christoforou, Ecole des Ponts-ParisTech, France

Jiho Kim, Chung-Ang University, Korea
Ingo Schwab, Karlsruhe University of Applied Sciences, Germany
Firas B. Ismail Alnaimi, Universiti Tenaga Nasional, Malaysia
Giuseppe Salvo, Università degli studi di Palermo, Italy
Nittaya Kerdprasop, Suranaree University of Technology, Thailand
Susana Vieira, IDMEC/LAETA, Instituto Superior Técnico, Technical University of Lisbon, Portugal

INTELLI Industry/Research Chairs

Matjaž Gams, Jožef Stefan Institute - Ljubljana, Slovenia
Haowei Liu, INTEL Corporation, USA
Michael Affenzeller, HeuristicLab, Austria
Paolo Spagnolo, Italian National Research Council, Italy
Pieter Mosterman, MathWorks, Inc. - Natick, USA
Paul Barom Jeon, Samsung Electronics, Korea
Kiyoshi Nitta, Yahoo Japan Research, Japan
Wolfgang Beer, Software Competence Center Hagenberg GmbH, Austria
András Förhécz, Multilogic Ltd., Hungary
Pierre-Yves Dumas, THALES, France

INTELLI Publicity Chairs

Frederick Ackers, Towson University, USA
Stephan Puls, Karlsruhe Institute of Technology, Germany
Paulo Couto, GECAD - ISEP, Portugal
Yuichi Kawai, Hosei University, Japan

InManEnt Co-Chairs

Ingo Schwab, University of Applied Sciences Karlsruhe, Germany
Gil Gonçalves, Faculty of Engineering, University of Porto, Portugal
Juha Röning, University of Oulo, Finland

INTELLI 2016

Committee

INTELLI Advisory Committee

Michael Negnevitsky, University of Tasmania, Australia
Roy George, Clark Atlanta University, USA
Pradeep Atrey, University of Winnipeg, Canada
Jerzy Grzymala-Busse, University of Kansas, USA
Daniël Telgen, HU University of Applied Sciences Utrecht, The Netherlands
Zoi Christoforou, Ecole des Ponts-ParisTech, France
Jiho Kim, Chung-Ang University, Korea
Ingo Schwab, Karlsruhe University of Applied Sciences, Germany
Firas B. Ismail Alnaimi, Universiti Tenaga Nasional, Malaysia
Giuseppe Salvo, Università degli studi di Palermo, Italy
Nittaya Kerdprasop, Suranaree University of Technology, Thailand
Susana Vieira, IDMEC/LAETA, Instituto Superior Técnico, Technical University of Lisbon, Portugal

INTELLI Industry/Research Chairs

Matjaž Gams, Jožef Stefan Institute - Ljubljana, Slovenia
Haowei Liu, INTEL Corporation, USA
Michael Affenzeller, HeuristicLab, Austria
Paolo Spagnolo, Italian National Research Council, Italy
Pieter Mosterman, MathWorks, Inc. - Natick, USA
Paul Barom Jeon, Samsung Electronics, Korea
Kiyoshi Nitta, Yahoo Japan Research, Japan
Wolfgang Beer, Software Competence Center Hagenberg GmbH, Austria
András Förhécz, Multilogic Ltd., Hungary
Pierre-Yves Dumas, THALES, France

INTELLI Publicity Chairs

Frederick Ackers, Towson University, USA
Stephan Puls, Karlsruhe Institute of Technology, Germany
Paulo Couto, GECAD - ISEP, Portugal
Yuichi Kawai, Hosei University, Japan

INTELLI 2016 Technical Program Committee

Syed Sibte Raza Abidi, Dalhousie University - Halifax, Canada
Witold Abramowicz, The Poznan University of Economics, Poland
Michael Affenzeller, HeuristicLab, Austraia
Zaher Al Aghbari, University of Sharjah, UAE

Angel P. del Pobil, Universitat Jaume-I, Spain
Vincenzo Deufemia, Università di Salerno - Fisciano, Italy
Tadashi Dohi, Hiroshima University, Japan
Andrei Doncescu, LAAS-CNRS - Toulouse France
Elena-Niculina Dragoi, "Gheorghe Asachi" Technical University of Iasi, Romania
Sourav Dutta, Max Planck Institute for Informatics, Germany
Marcos Eduardo Valle, University of Campinas, Brazil
Bernard Espinasse, Aix-Marseille Université, France
Shu-Kai S. Fan, National Taipei University of Technology, Taiwan
Alena Fedotova, Bauman Moscow State Technical University, Russia
Aurelio Fernandez Bariviera, Universitat Rovira i Virgili, Spain
Edilson Ferneda, Catholic University of Brasília, Brazil
Manuel Filipe Santos, Universidade do Minho, Portugal
Adina Magda Florea, University "Politehnica" of Bucharest, Romania
Juan J. Flores, Universidad Michoacana, Mexico
Gian Luca Foresti, University of Udine, Italy
Rita Francese, Università di Salerno - Fisciano, Italy
Santiago Franco, University of Auckland, New Zealand
Kaori Fujinami, Tokyo University of Agriculture and Technology, Japan
Naoki Fukuta, Shizuoka University, Japan
Simone Gabbriellini, University of Brescia, Italy
Matjaž Gams, Jožef Stefan Institute - Ljubljana, Slovenia
Sasanko Sekhar Gantayat, GMR Institute of Technology, India
Leonardo Garrido, Tecnológico de Monterrey - Campus Monterrey, Mexico
Alexander Gelbukh, Mexican Academy of Sciences, Mexico
David Gil, University of Alicante, Spain
Berio Giuseppe, Université de Bretagne Sud, France
Lorraine Goeuriot, LIG | Université Grenoble Alpes, France
Anandha Gopalan, Imperial College London, UK
Sérgio Gorender, UFBA, Brazil
Victor Govindaswamy, Concordia University - Chicago, USA
Manuel Graña, Facultad de Informatica - San Sebastian, Spain
David Greenhalgh, University of Strathclyde, UK
Jerzy Grzymala-Busse, University of Kansas, USA
Bin Guo, Northwestern Polytechnical University, China
Sung Ho Ha, Kyungpook National University, Korea
Maki K. Habib, The American University in Cairo, Egypt
Sami Habib, Kuwait University, Kuwait
Belal Haja, University of Tabuk, Saudi Arabia
Sven Hartmann, Technische Universität Clausthal, Germany
Fumio Hattori, Ritsumeikan University - Kusatsu, Japan
Jessica Heesen, University of Tübingen, Germany
Enrique Herrera Viedma, DECSAI - University of Granada, Spain
Pilar Herrero, Universidad Politecnica de Madrid, Spain
Benjamin Hirsch, Khalifa University - Abu Dhabi, United Arab Emirates
Didier Hoareau, University of La Réunion, France
Tetsuya Murai Hokkaido, University Sapporo, Japan
Wladyslaw Homenda, Warsaw University of Technology, Poland

Katsuhiro Honda, Osaka Prefecture University, Japan
Tzung-Pei Hong, National University of Kaohsiung, Taiwan
Samuelson Hong, Management School - Hangzhou Dianzi University, China
Bin Hu, Birmingham City University, UK
Yo-Ping Huang, National Taipei University of Technology - Taipei, Taiwan
Carlos A. Iglesias, Universidad Politecnica de Madrid, Spain
Fodor János, Óbuda University – Budapest, Hungary
Jayadeva, Indian Institute of Technology - Delhi, India
Yanguo Jing, London Metropolitan University, UK
Maria João Ferreira, Universidade Portucalense - Porto, Portugal
Diala Jomaa, Dalarna University, Sweden
Janusz Kacprzyk, Polish Academy of Sciences, Poland
Epaminondas Kapetanios, University of Westminster - London, UK
Nikos Karacapilidis, University of Patras - Rion-Patras, Greece
Panagiotis Karras, Rutgers University, USA
Sang-Wook Kim, Hanyang University, South Korea
Sungshin Kim, Pusan National University- Busan, Korea
Abeer Khalid, International Islamic University Islamabad, Pakistan
Shubhalaxmi Kher, Arkansas State University, USA
Alexander Knapp, Universität Augsburg, Germany
Sotiris Kotsiantis, University of Patras, Greece
Ondrej Krejcar, University of Hradec Kralove, Czech Republic
Natalia Kryvinska, University of Vienna, Austria
Satoshi Kurihara, Osaka University, Japan
Tobias Küster, Technische Universität Berlin, Germany
Hak-Keung Lam, King's College London, UK
K.P. Lam, University of Keele, UK
Antonio LaTorre, Universidad Politécnica de Madrid, Spain
Frédéric Le Mouël, INRIA/INSA Lyon, France
Alain Léger, Orange - France Telecom R&D / University St Etienne - Betton, France
George Lekeas, City Universty – London, UK
Omar Lengerke, Autonomous University of Bucaramanga, Colombia
Carlos Leon, University of Seville, Spain
Haowei Liu, INTEL Corporation, USA
Lei Liu, HP Labs, USA
Abdel-Badeeh M. Salem, Ain Shams University - Cairo, Egypt
Giuseppe Mangioni, University of Catania, Italy
Antonio Martin, Universidad de Sevilla, Spain
Gregorio Martinez, University of Murcia, Spain
George Mastorakis, Technological Educational Institute of Crete, Greece
Constandinos X. Mavromoustakis, University of Cyprus, Cyprus
Pier Luigi Mazzeo, Institute on Intelligent System for Automation - Bari, Italy
Michele Melchiori, Università degli Studi di Brescia, Italy
Radko Mesiar, Slovak University of Technology Bratislava, Slovakia
John-Jules Charles Meyer, Utrecht University, The Netherlands
Angelos Michalas, TEI of Western Macedonia, Greece
Hamid Mirisaee, LIP6 | UPMC, Paris, France
Veronica S. Moertini, Parahyangan Catholic University, Indonesia

Dusmanta Kumar Mohanta, Maharaj Vijayaram Gajapathi Raj College of Engineering, India
Felix Mora-Camino, ENAC, Toulouse, France
Fernando Moreira, Universidade Portucalense - Porto, Portugal
Pieter Mosterman, MathWorks, Inc. - Natick, USA
Bernard Moulin, Université Laval, Canada
Debajyoti Mukhopadhyay, Maharshtra Institute of Technology, India
Isao Nakanishi, Tottori University, Japan
Tomoharu Nakashima, Osaka Prefecture University, Japan
Nayyab Zia Naqvi, iMinds - Distrinet | KU Leuven, Belgium
Michael Negnevitsky, University of Tasmania, Australia
Filippo Neri, University of Naples "Federico II", Italy
Mario Arrigoni Neri, University of Bergamo, Italy
Hongbo Ni, Northwestern Polytechnical University, China
Cyrus F. Nourani, akdmkrd.tripod.com, USA
Kenneth S. Nwizege, Swansea University, UK
Joanna Isabelle Olszewska, University of Gloucestershire, United Kingdom
Hichem Omrani, CEPS/INSTEAD Research Institute, Luxembourg
Frank Ortmeier, Otto-von-Guericke Universitaet Magdeburg, Germany
Sanjeevikumar Padmanaban, Ohm Technologies, India
Jeng-Shyang Pan, Harbin Institute of Technology, Taiwan
Endre Pap, University Novi Sad, Serbia
Marcin Paprzycki, Systems Research Institute / Polish Academy of Sciences - Warsaw, Poland
Yonghong Peng, University of Bradfrod, UK
Dana Petcu, West University of Timisoara, Romania
Leif Peterson, Methodist Hospital Research Institute / Weill Medical College, Cornell University, USA
Diego Pinheiro-Silva, University of Pernambuco, Brazil
Alain Pirott, Université de Louvain - Louvain-la-Neuve, Belgium
Agostino Poggi, Università degli Studi di Parma, Italy
Radu-Emil Precup, Politehnica University of Timisoara, Romania
Anca Ralescu, University of Cincinnati, USA
Sheela Ramanna, University of Winnipeg, Canada
Fano Ramparany, Orange Labs Networks and Carrier (OLNC) - Grenoble, France
Martin Randles, Liverpool John Moores University, UK
Zbigniew W. Ras, University of North Carolina - Charlotte & Warsaw University of Technology, Poland
José Raúl Romero, University of Córdoba, Spain
Danda B. Rawat, Georgia Southern University, USA
David Riaño, Universitat Rovira i Virgili, Spain
Daniel Rodríguez, University of Alcalá - Madrid, Spain
Agos Rosa, Technical University of Lisbon, Portugal
Alexander Ryjov, Lomonosov Moscow State University, Russia
Gunter Saake, University of Magdeburg, Germany
Ozgur Koray Sahingoz, Turkish Air Force Academy, Turkey
Shigeaki Sakurai, Toshiba Corporation, Japan
Demetrios G. Sampson, University of Piraeus, Greece
Daniel Schang, Groupe Signal Image et Instrumentation - ESEO, France
Ingo Schwab, Karlsruhe University of Applied Sciences, Germany
Florence Sedes, IRIT | Université de Toulouse, France
Amal El Fallah Seghrouchni, University of Pierre and Marie Curie (Paris 6) - Paris, France

Hao Lan Zhang, NIT - Zhejiang University, China
Yongfeng Zhang, Tsinghua University, China
Si Q. Zheng, The University of Texas at Dallas, USA
Jose Jacobo Zubcoff Vallejo, University of Alicante, Spain

InManEnt 2016

Symposium Co-Chairs

Ingo Schwab, University of Applied Sciences Karlsruhe, Germany
Gil Gonçalves, Faculty of Engineering, University of Porto, Portugal
Juha Röning, University of Oulo, Finland

Program Committee Members

Dirk Berndt, Fraunhofer IFF, Germany
Eisse Jan Drewes, AWL, Netherlands
Michael Emmerich, University of Leiden, The Netherlands
Björn Hein, University of Karlsruhe, Germany
Adel Hejaaji, ESM LTD Essex, UK
Martin Kasperczyk, Fraunhofer IPA, Germany
Norbert Link, University of Applied Sciences Karlsruhe, Germany
Niels Lohse, Loughborough University, UK
Giorgio Pasquettaz, CRF, Italy
Marcello Pellicciari, University of Modena and Reggio Emilia, Italy
Marius Pflueger, IPA, Germany
Franz Quint, University of Applied Sciences Karlsruhe, Germany
João Reis, Faculty of Engineering, University of Porto, Portugal
Steffen Scholz, Institute for Applied Computer Science/Karlsruhe Institute of Technology, Germany
Vassilis Spais, Inos Hellas, Greece
Leo van Moergestel, Utrecht University of Applied Sciences, The Netherlands

Copyright Information

For your reference, this is the text governing the copyright release for material published by IARIA.

The copyright release is a transfer of publication rights, which allows IARIA and its partners to drive the dissemination of the published material. This allows IARIA to give articles increased visibility via distribution, inclusion in libraries, and arrangements for submission to indexes.

I, the undersigned, declare that the article is original, and that I represent the authors of this article in the copyright release matters. If this work has been done as work-for-hire, I have obtained all necessary clearances to execute a copyright release. I hereby irrevocably transfer exclusive copyright for this material to IARIA. I give IARIA permission or reproduce the work in any media format such as, but not limited to, print, digital, or electronic. I give IARIA permission to distribute the materials without restriction to any institutions or individuals. I give IARIA permission to submit the work for inclusion in article repositories as IARIA sees fit.

I, the undersigned, declare that to the best of my knowledge, the article is does not contain libelous or otherwise unlawful contents or invading the right of privacy or infringing on a proprietary right.

Following the copyright release, any circulated version of the article must bear the copyright notice and any header and footer information that IARIA applies to the published article.

IARIA grants royalty-free permission to the authors to disseminate the work, under the above provisions, for any academic, commercial, or industrial use. IARIA grants royalty-free permission to any individuals or institutions to make the article available electronically, online, or in print.

IARIA acknowledges that rights to any algorithm, process, procedure, apparatus, or articles of manufacture remain with the authors and their employers.

I, the undersigned, understand that IARIA will not be liable, in contract, tort (including, without limitation, negligence), pre-contract or other representations (other than fraudulent misrepresentations) or otherwise in connection with the publication of my work.

Exception to the above is made for work-for-hire performed while employed by the government. In that case, copyright to the material remains with the said government. The rightful owners (authors and government entity) grant unlimited and unrestricted permission to IARIA, IARIA's contractors, and IARIA's partners to further distribute the work.

Intelligent MagLev Slider System by Feedback of Gap Sensors to Suppress 5-DOF Vibration

Yi-Ming Kao, Nan-Chyuan Tsai*, Hsin-Lin Chiu
Department of Mechanical Engineering,
National Cheng Kung University
Tainan City 70101, Taiwan (ROC)
email: *nortren@mail.ncku.edu.tw

***Abstract*—This paper is focused at position deviation regulation upon a slider by Fuzzy Sliding Mode Control (FSMC). Five Degrees Of Freedom (DOFs) of position deviation are required to be regulated except for the direction (i.e., X-axis) in which the slider moves forward and backward. At first, the system dynamic model of slider, including load uncertainty and load position uncertainty, is established. Intensive computer simulations are undertaken to verify the validity of proposed control strategy. Finally, a prototype of realistic slider position deviation regulation system is successfully built up. According to the experiments by cooperation of pneumatic and magnetic control, the actual linear position deviations of slider can be regulated within (-40, +40)μm and angular position deviations within (-2, +2)mini-degrees. From the viewpoint of energy consumption, the applied currents to 8 sets of MAs are all below 1A. To sum up, the closed-loop levitation system by cooperation of pneumatic and magnetic control is capable to account for load uncertainty and uncertainty of the standing position of load to be carried.**

Keywords- Position Deviation Regulation; Fuzzy Sliding Mode Control (FSMC); Magnetic Levitation (MagLev).

I. INTRODUCTION

In recent years, a few types of active non-contact slider systems were proposed. An air-driven slider was presented by Denkena *et al.* [1]. Based on their study, the compressed air not only can levitate the slider but also can drive the slider back and forth. Unlike pneumatic actuators, a 5-DOF (5 Degrees of Freedom) active magnetic levitation slider was reported by Kim *et al.* [2]. However, the applied currents to the magnetic actuators are up to 10A to counterbalance the weight of the slider.

In comparison to the air-driven actuator, in general the required force by magnetic actuator is relatively much larger. Hence, the bending phenomenon on thinner portion of slider would become easier to occur if the applied magnetic force exceeds over a certain level. Not only the heat dissipation problem has to be considered but also the electronic circuit of power amplifier is more complicated than the other low-power actuators. Among the available research reports regarding active levitation sliders, the most acceptable design by industries was proposed by Ro *et al.* [3]. In their work, four magnetic actuators are allocated at the corners of the slider to account for external disturbance. The weight of the slider and load is supported by the force component by air actuator. Additionally, a linear motor, to drive the slider back and forth, is equipped at the middle of the guide rail. Nevertheless, there exists a common disadvantage: both uncertainties of load to be carried and the standing position of load during the loading/unloading process onto the slider are not counted into consideration of the corresponding control stratagy at all.

For high-precision machines and production, it often needs a slider system, which can account for load uncertainty and suppress undesired vibration effectively. However, no matter contact-type slider or aerostatic slider is employed, the slider systems are lack of the capability against load uncertainty and multi-degree-of-freedom vibration during the transportation of carried load. Therefore, an active robust slider levitation system is proposed by this paper to deal with the induced position deviation of the slider due to load uncertainty and load position uncertainty.

The rest of this article is organized as follows. In Section 2, the dynamic model of slider levitation system is developed. In Section 3, the fuzzy sliding mode control law is proposed. In Section 4, the experiments to examine the capability of the maglev slider to account for load uncertainty and uncertainty of the standing position are undertaken. Finally, conclusions are presented in Section 5.

II. DYNAMIC MODEL OF SLIDER LEVITATION SYSTEM

The mechanical structure of the proposed slider levitation system by cooperation of pneumatic and magnetic control is schematically shown in Fig. 1. In Fig. 1, "S" is the mass center of the slider. "S" is also the origin of the coordinate system. ϕ , θ and ψ are angular position deviations along X-axis, Y-axis and Z-axis respectively. y and z are the linear position deviations along Y-axis and Z-axis respectively. Eight sets of Magnetic Actuators (MAs) and an Electro-Pneumatic Transducer (EPT) are employed together to regulate both angular and linear position deviations of the slider. The four sets of magnetic actuators, Vertical Magnetic Actuators (VMAs), along with the EPT, are employed to together regulate the angular position deviations along X- and Y-axes and the linear position deviation along Z-axis. Another four sets of magnetic actuators, i.e., Horizontal Magnetic Actuators (HMAs), are employed to regulate the angular position deviation along Z-axis and position deviation along Y-axis. Three Vertical Gap Sensors (VGSs) are equipped to measure the linear position deviation along Z-axis. Besides, the angular position deviations along X-axis and Y-axis can be estimated by the linear position deviations measured by these 3 VGSs at the same time. On the other hand, two Horizontal Gap Sensors (HGSs) are equipped to measure the linear position deviation along Y-axis. It is noted that the angular position deviation along Z-axis can be evaluated by the linear position deviations measured by the aforesaid HGSs.

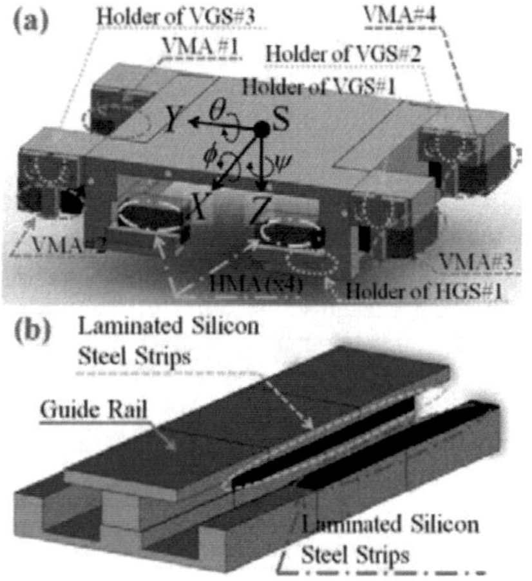

Figure 1. Schematic diagram of proposed levitation slider: (a) Slider, (b) Guide Rail.

The dynamic equations in terms of force/moment at equilibrium of the slider dynamics can be described as follows:

$$(m+\Delta m)\ddot{y}-\frac{A_u\mu_A}{g_u}\dot{y}=F_y^{MA} \tag{1a}$$

$$(m+\Delta m)\ddot{z}-A_s\mu_A\left(\frac{1}{g_l}+\frac{1}{g_r}\right)\dot{z}=F_z^{MA}-F_a+\Delta mg \tag{1b}$$

$$(I_x+\Delta md_x^2)\ddot{\phi}-A_s l_{sx}\mu_A\left(\frac{l_{sx}}{g_l}+\frac{l_{sx}}{g_r}\right)\dot{\phi}=M_x^{MA}+\Delta mgd_x \tag{1c}$$

$$(I_y+\Delta md_y^2)\ddot{\theta}-A_s\mu_A\left(\frac{\int_0^{l_{sy}}rdr}{g_l}+\frac{\int_0^{l_{sy}}rdr}{g_r}\right)\dot{\theta}=M_y^{MA}+\Delta mgd_y \tag{1d}$$

$$(I_z+\Delta md_z^2)\ddot{\psi}-A_u\mu_A\frac{\int_0^{l_{sy}}rdr}{g_u}\dot{\psi}=M_z^{MA} \tag{1e}$$

where m is the mass of the slider, and Δm the mass of load. I_x, I_y and I_z are the moments of inertia of the slider along X-axis, Y-axis and Z-axis respectively. d_x, d_y and d_z are the distances between the centroid of load and X-axis, Y-axis and Z-axis respectively. A_u and A_s are the area of the upper surface and side surface of guide rail respetively. μ_A is viscosity coefficient of air. l_{sx} is the distance between the inner-side wall of slider and X-axis, l_{sy} the distance between Y-axis and the front/tail of slider. g_u, g_l and g_r are the air gaps between the slider and guide rail on the upper side, left side and right side of guide rail respectively. $\tau_{\phi l}$ and $\tau_{\phi r}$ are the shear stresses induced by the air on the inner wall of slider as the slider rotates along X-axis. In similar fashion, $\tau_{\theta r}$ and $\tau_{\theta l}$ are the shear stresses induced by the air on the inner wall of slider as the slider rotates along Y-axis. By same arguments, τ_{ψ} is the shear stress induced by the air on the inner wall of slider as the slider rotates along Z-axis. As long as the velocity component along +Z-axis of slider is present, two types of shear stresses, i.e., τ_{zl} and τ_{zr} are generated. Likewise, the shear stress τ_y emerges as long as the velocity component along +Y-axis of slider is not zero. M_x^{MA}, M_y^{MA} and M_z^{MA} are the moments induced by magnetic actuators along X-axis, Y-axis and Z-axis respectively. F_y^{MA}, F_z^{MA} and F_a are the resultant force by HMAs, the resultant force by VMAs and the applied force by EPT respectively.

III. FUZZY SLIDING MODE CONTROL

For a slider, in general the mass of carried load and the standing location of the load are not fixed all the time. This implies that a certain degree of uncertainties is embedded in the dynamic model of the slider system. Therefore, the basic concept of Sliding Mode Control (SMC) [4]-[6] is adopted by our work. Moreover, fuzzy logic [7]-[11] is additionally applied to adjust slope of the corresponding sliding surface, based on the real-time trajectory tracking error and error rate, such that superior system response can be achieved. That is, FSMC (Fuzzy Sliding Mode Control) is proposed to replace the standard SMC by this research.

A. *Design of Controller*

Before FSMC is synthesized, the dynamic equations of the slider system, i.e., (1), are deduced into another form to aim at uncertainties of load and load position:

$$\ddot{q}=f+u \tag{2}$$

where

$$q=[y \quad z \quad \phi \quad \theta \quad \psi]^T \tag{3a}$$

$$f=\begin{bmatrix} \dfrac{A_u\mu_A\dot{y}}{(m+\Delta m)g_u} \\ \dfrac{A_s\mu_A\dot{z}}{m+\Delta m}\left(\dfrac{1}{g_l}+\dfrac{1}{g_r}\right)+\dfrac{\Delta mg}{m+\Delta m} \\ \dfrac{A_s\mu_A l_{sx}^2\dot{\phi}}{I_x+\Delta md_x^2}\left(\dfrac{1}{g_l}+\dfrac{1}{g_r}\right)+\dfrac{\Delta mgd_x}{I_x+\Delta md_x^2} \\ \dfrac{A_s\mu_A\int_0^{l_{sy}}rdr}{I_y+\Delta md_y^2}\left(\dfrac{1}{g_l}+\dfrac{1}{g_r}\right)\dot{\theta}+\dfrac{\Delta mgd_y}{I_y+\Delta md_y^2} \\ \dfrac{A_u\mu_A\int_0^{l_{sz}}rdr}{(I_z+\Delta md_z^2)g_u}\dot{\psi} \end{bmatrix} \tag{3b}$$

$$u=\left[\frac{F_y^{MA}}{m+\Delta m} \quad \frac{F_z^{MA}-F_a}{m+\Delta m} \quad \frac{M_x^{MA}}{I_x+\Delta m d_x^{\,2}} \quad \frac{M_y^{MA}}{I_y+\Delta m d_y^{\,2}} \quad \frac{M_z^{MA}}{I_z+\Delta m d_z^{\,2}}\right]^T \quad (3c)$$

Since the mass of load and the standing location of load are not fixed all the time, d_x, d_y, d_z and Δm are all variables in this system. For the uncertain system dynamics, its nominal model, f_0, is defined as follows:

$$f_0=\begin{bmatrix} \frac{A_u\mu_A}{m\cdot g_u}\dot{y} \\ \frac{A_s\mu_A}{m}\left(\frac{1}{g_l}+\frac{1}{g_r}\right)\dot{z} \\ \frac{A_s\mu_A l_{sx}^{\,2}}{I_x}\left(\frac{1}{g_l}+\frac{1}{g_r}\right)\dot{\phi} \\ \frac{A_s\mu_A\int_0^{l_{sy}} r dr}{I_y}\left(\frac{1}{g_l}+\frac{1}{g_r}\right)\dot{\theta} \\ \frac{A_u\mu_A\int_0^{l_{sz}} r dr}{I_z g_u}\dot{\psi} \end{bmatrix} \quad (4)$$

Consequently, the system uncertainty, $f-f_0$, is assumed to be bounded by a functional, W^{smc}:

$$|f-f_0|\le W^{smc} \quad (5)$$

The sliding functional, S, can be defined as follows:

$$S=\lambda e+\dot{e}=\lambda(q_r-q)+(\dot{q}_r-\dot{q}) \quad (6)$$

where e represents the vector of differences between the actual state and the desired state, q the actual state vector, q_r the vector of desired state trajectory, λ the slope of phase plot of the state tracking error and its error rate. In order to ensure the system remains on the sliding surface, the sliding condition, i.e., $S=0$, has to be imposed. Based on the sliding condition [4]-[6] and (2), the equivalent control component can be obtained:

$$u_{eq}=-f_0+\ddot{q}_r+\lambda\dot{e} \quad (7)$$

On the other hand, to satisfy the reaching condition, i.e., $S\dot{S}<0$, the switching control component can be designed as follows:

$$u_{sw}=-K^{smc}\cdot Sgn(S) \quad (8)$$

where K^{smc} is a positive definite matrix and " Sgn " represents the symbol operator. Explicitly, K^{smc} and Sgn are defined as follows:

$$K^{smc}=diag(K_1^{smc} \;\; K_2^{smc} \;\; K_3^{smc} \;\; K_4^{smc} \;\; K_5^{smc}) \quad (9a)$$

$$Sgn(S)=\begin{cases} 1 & if \;\; S>0 \\ 0 & if \;\; S=0 \\ -1 & if \;\; S<0 \end{cases} \quad (9b)$$

where the parameters $K_1^{smc} \sim K_5^{smc}$ are named as reaching factors. They can dominate the reaching speed of the deviated state, off the sliding surface, approaching towards the sliding surface. Finally, the composite control input by SMC policy, u, is added up as follows:

$$u=u_{eq}+u_{sw} \quad (10)$$

As usual, the Lyapunov direct method is employed to examine the stability for the proposed control policy. The Lyapunov candidate is defined as follows:

$$V=\frac{1}{2}S^T S>0, \text{ where } \forall S\neq 0 \quad (11)$$

The derivative of Lyapunov candidate can be obtained as follows:

$$\dot{V}=(f-f_0)S-K^{smc}|S|\le(W^{mc}-K^{smc})|S|\equiv-\eta|S| \quad (12)$$

To satisfy (12), K^{smc} can be chosen as follows:

$$K^{smc}=W^{smc}+\eta \quad (13)$$

By substituting (13) into (8), the composite control, u, can be described as follows:

$$u=u_{eq}-[W^{smc}+\eta]Sgn(S) \quad (14)$$

By adding FLA (Fuzzy Logic Algorithm) to adjust the slope of the sliding surface is the main concept to adopt FSMC, instead of standard SMC alone. The schematic configuration of the closed-loop slider system is shown in Fig. 2. The transformation matrix α is utilized to convert the measurements from the 5 sets of gap sensors into the form of changes of state variables. The slope of the sliding surface, λ_i, $i=$ y, z, ϕ, θ or ψ, is adaptively altered by the real-time fuzzy algorithm based on state tracking error and rate of state tracking error. The transformation matrix β is employed to convert the controller outputs into the required control current/voltage with respect to the corresponding actuators.

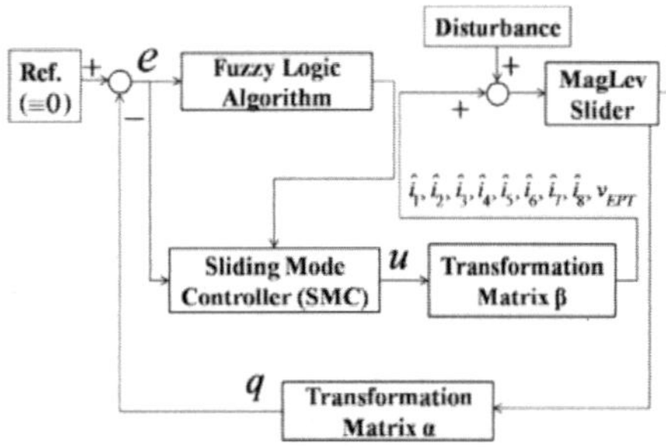

Figure 2. Schematic configuration of closed-loop slider system under FSMC.

The interested rules of FLA are summarized and listed in Table 1. e_i, $\dot{e}_i$ and c_i are the state tracking error, rate of the state tracking error and the output of FLA respectively. Seven fuzzy sets with triangle membership functions (NB, NM, NS, ZE, PS, PM, PB) are set for e_i, $\dot{e}_i$ and c_i. The subscript, i, denotes y, z, ϕ, θ or ψ. $\mu(e_i)$, $\mu(\dot{e}_i)$ and $\mu(c_i)$ are the corresponding membership functions of e_i, $\dot{e}_i$ and c_i. Finally, by using the method based on Center Average Defuzzification (CAD)[12], the corresponding output of FSMC, u_{crisp}, can be obtained by the defuzzification interface. The crisp control command can be evaluated as follows:

$$u_{crisp} = [\mu_{PB}(c_i)\cdot 1 + \mu_{PM}(c_i)\cdot(2/3) + \mu_{PS}(c_i)\cdot(1/3) + \mu_{NS}(c_i)\cdot(-1/3) + \mu_{NM}(c_i)\cdot(-2/3) + \mu_{NB}(c_i)\cdot(-1)] / [\mu_{PB}(c_i) + \mu_{PM}(c_i) + \mu_{PS}(c_i) + \mu_{ZE}(c_i) + \mu_{NS}(c_i) + \mu_{NM}(c_i) + \mu_{NB}(c_i)] \quad (15)$$

TABLE I. RULE BASE FOR FLA

c_i \ e_i, $\dot{e}_i$	NB	NM	NS	ZE	PS	PM	PB
NB	NB	NB	NB	NB	NM	NS	ZE
NM	NB	NB	NB	NM	NS	ZE	PS
NS	NB	NB	NM	NS	ZE	PS	PM
ZE	NB	NM	NS	ZE	PS	PM	PB
PS	NM	NS	ZE	PS	PM	PB	PB
PM	NS	ZE	PS	PM	PB	PB	PB
PB	ZE	PS	PM	PB	PB	PB	PB

NB Negative Big
NM Negative Medium
NS Negative Small
ZE Zero
PS Positive Small
PM Positive Medium
PB Positive Big

B. *Computer Simulations*

At the stage of computer simulations, two cases are to be studied:

Caes I: Load (1kg) added onto slider
Case II: Load (1kg) subtracted out of slider

*1) Load added onto slider **(Case I)***

An additional load of 1 kg, is put onto the slider at the position, $(x, y, z) = (5\,cm, 5\,cm, 0)$ at $Time = 2s$, for ***Case I***. However, the mass center of the slider is at $(x, y) = (0, 0)$. Since the load is not put onto the position of mass center of the slider, the angular position deviations are hence induced. The corresponding computer simulations are shown in Fig. 3(a). It is observed that an outstanding linear position deviation along +Z-axis occurs at $Time = 2s$. Besides, most often the load is not exactly thrown at the position of mass center of the slider, the angular position deviations along X-axis and Y-axis are hence induced as the load is added onto the slider. In similar fashion, the applied currents to VMA#1~VMA#4 are all increased to account for the angular position deviations along X-axis and Y-axis.

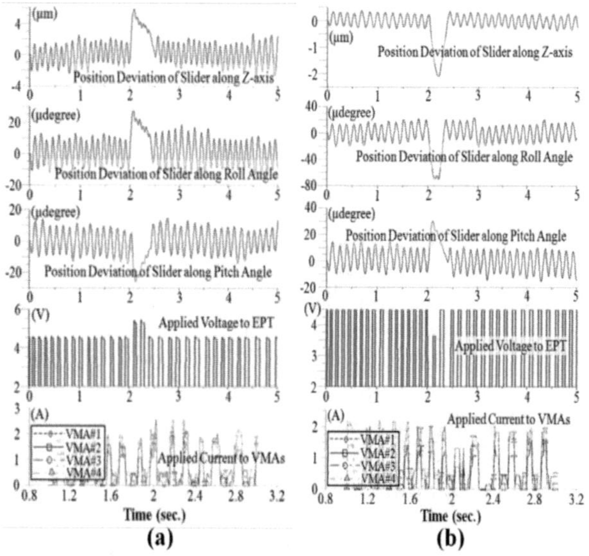

Figure 3. Position deviations regulation on slider: (a) load added onto slider at position $(x, y, z) = (5\,cm, 5\,cm, 0)$, (b) load subtracted at position $(x, y, z) = (5\,cm, 5\,cm, 0)$.

*2) Load subtracted out of slider **(Case II)***

A carried load, with weight quantity 1kg, is subtracted out of the slider at position $(x, y, z) = (5\,cm, 5\,cm, 0)$ at $Time = 2s$, for ***Case II***. The corresponding computer simulations are shown in Fig. 3(b). Accordingly, an outstanding linear position deviation along –Z-axis is induced at the same time. In addition, the currents applied at VMA#1~VMA#4 are all reduced but still have to cooperate with EPT. On the other hand, since the load subtracted is hardly located exactly at the position of mass center of the slider, the corresponding currents applied at VMA#1~VMA#4, to suppress the angular position deviations along X-axis and Y-axis, are usually necessary.

IV. EXPERIMENTAL VERIFICATION

The photograph of proposed MagLev slider system by cooperation of pneumatic and magnetic actuators is shown in Fig. 4. A set of pneumatic cylinder and air pump is equipped to generate the power to move the slider forwards and backwards along X-axis. The schematic diagram of the experimental setup is shown in Fig. 5. Two categories of experiments are to be undertaken, namely, ***PART I*** and ***PART II***. For ***PART I***, an additional load, with weight 1kg, is added onto the slider at $(x, y, z) = (5\,cm, 5\,cm, 0)$ at $Time = 0.1s$. The aforesaid additional load is later-on substracted out of the slider for ***PART II***.

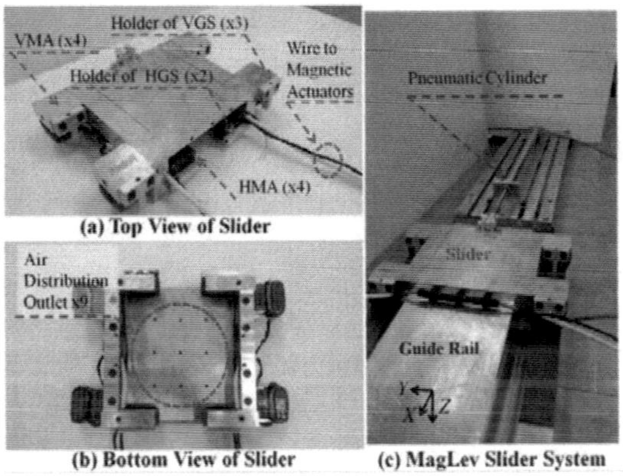

Figure 4. Photograph of MagLev slider system

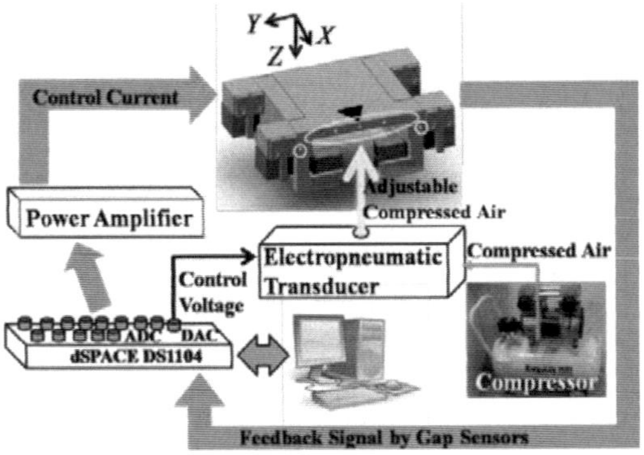

Figure 5. Schematic diagram of experimental setup

A. *PART I: Additional Load Added*

An additional load, with weight 1kg, is put onto the slider at position $(x, y, z) = (5\,cm, 5\,cm, 0)$ at $Time = 0.1s$. It is noted that the mass center of the slider on the horizontal plane is at $(x, y) = (0, 0)$. Obviously, the standing location of the added load does not coincide with the mass center of the slider so that outstanding angular position deviations due to this applied moment by load weight are hence induced. The experimental results for position deviation regulation on slider in 5 DOF are shown in Fig. 6. The maximum linear position deviations along Z-axis and Y-axis induced by the additional load are 80μm and 130μm respectively. The linear position deviations along Z-axis and Y-axis can be suppressed to ± 20μm and ± 40μm respectively within 0.1sec. In addition, the maximum angular position deviations along X-axis, Y-axis and Z-axis are 4.5×10^{-3} degree, -3×10^{-3} degree and 5×10^{-3} degree respectively. The angular position deviations along X-axis, Y-axis and Z-axis can be all regulated within $\pm2\times10^{-3}$ degree in 0.1sec. It is concluded that both of the linear position deviations and angular position deviations can be completely suppressed within a very short time interval (about 0.1sec). On the other hand, the applied currents to the magnetic actuators, shown in Fig. 7, are jointly adjusted accordingly so that the induced tilt about X-axis and the induced pitch about Y-axis can be suppressed. Since most of the weight of the slider and load is supported by the supportive force by the high pressurized air, the applied currents to VMAs are not increased much to counterbalance the weight of the additional load newly put on. It is observed that the average applied currents to VMAs are all below 0.2A. The applied currents to VMAs in the undertaken experiments are much lower than that in computer simulations stated in previous section. The reason might be stemmed from the actual viscosity and friction in vertical direction being more serious in real world but neglected in computer simulations under over-simplified assumptions for interconnection between any two components in motion.

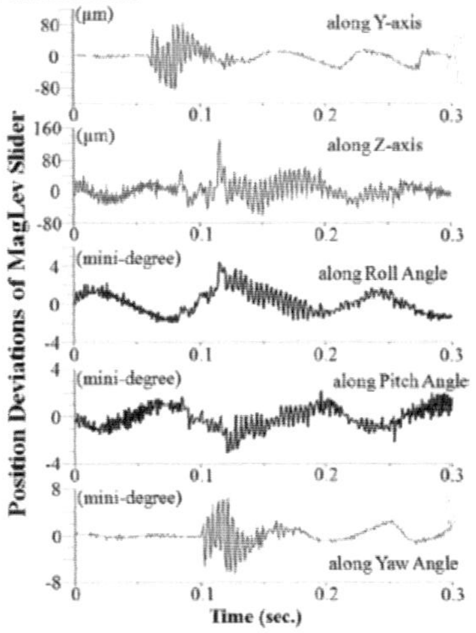

Figure 6. Position deviations regulation on slider by experiments (***Part I***)

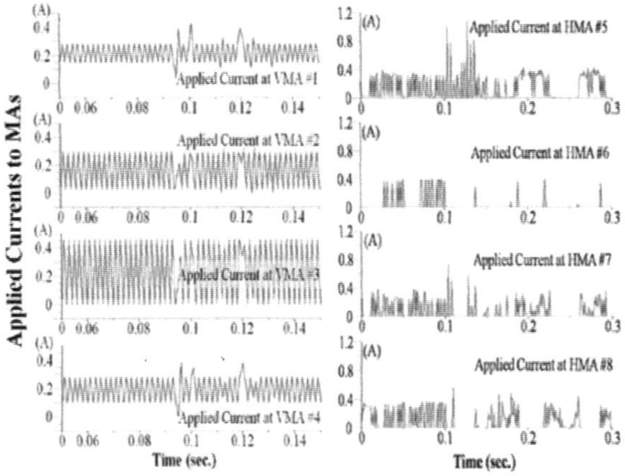

Figure 7. Applied currents at MAs by experiments (***Part I***)

B. *Part II: Partial Load Subtracted*

A partial load, with weight 1kg, is subtracted out of the slider at position $(x, y, z)=(5\,cm, 5\,cm, 0)$ at $Time=0.05s$. The experimental results for position deviations regulation on slider in 5 DOF are shown in Fig. 8. The position deviations along 5-axes can be completely suppressed within a very short time interval (about 0.15sec). In similar fashion, the applied currents to the magnetic actuators, shown in Fig. 9, are jointly adjusted as well to regulate the induced tilt and pitch motions. Since partial load is taken off the slider, the average applied currents to VMAs become only half of those in ***Part I***. Besides, the maximum applied currents to HMAs are all below 0.5A. Nevertheless, the currents applied to VMAs and HMAs are still required and absolutely necessary in order to counterbalance the external disturbance, particularly for the transient time period as the partial load suddenly removed, no matter how significantly the quantities of consumed electricity at magnetic actuators are reduced.

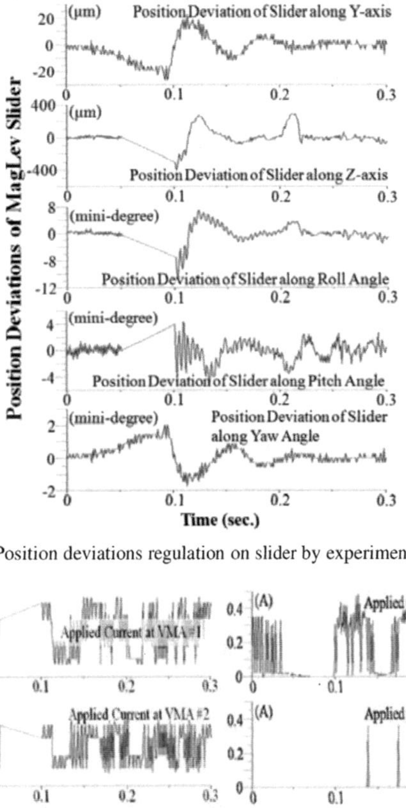

Figure 8. Position deviations regulation on slider by experiments (***Part II***).

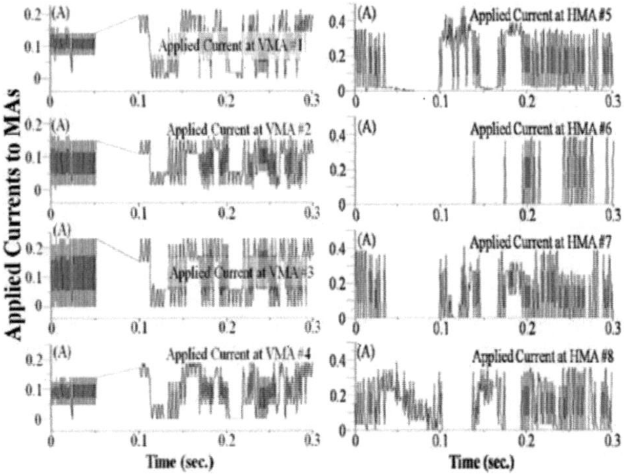

Figure 9. Applied currents at MAs by experiments (***Part II***)

V. CONCLUSION

An active robust MagLev slider system is proposed to deal with the induced position deviations of the slider due to load uncertainties and load position uncertainties. By cooperation of pneumatic and magnetic actuators, efficient regulations of the position deviations of slider in 5 DOF can be achieved. According to the experiments undertaken, the actual linear position deviations of slider can be regulated within ± 40μm and angular position deviations within ± 2mini-degrees. Besides, the applied currents to the 8 sets of MAs are all below 1A. The closed-loop slider levitation system is fairly capable to account for load uncertainties and load position uncertainties. To sum up, by the cooperation of pneumatic and magnetic actuators, the proposed closed-loop slider system exhibits the merits of stabilization to the inherently unstable system, capability for simultaneous position regulation in 5 DOF and outstanding reduction of energy consumption.

ACKNOWLEDGMENT

This research was partially supported by Ministry of Science and Technology (Taiwan) with Grant MOST 103-2221-E-006-046-MY3. The authors would like to express their appreciations.

REFERENCES

[1] C. H. Kim, K. J. Kim, J. S. Yu, and H. W. Cho, "Dynamic Performance Evaluation of 5-DOF Magnetic Levitation and Guidance Device by Using Equivalent Magnetic Circuit Model", *IEEE Transactions on Magnetics*, vol. 49, no. 7, pp. 4156-4159, 2013.

[2] B. Denkena, H. C. Möhring, and H. Kayapinar, "A novel fluid-dynamic drive principle for desktop machines", *CIRP Journal of Manufacturing Science and Technology*, vol. 6, no. 2, pp. 89-97, 2013.

[3] S. K. Ro, S. Kim, Y. Kwak, and C. H. Park, "A linear air bearing stage with active magnetic preloads for ultraprecise straight motion", *Precision Engineering*, vol. 34, no. 1, pp. 186-194, 2010.

[4] W. Perruquetti and J. P. Barbot, Sliding Mode Control in Engineering. New York, NY: Marcel Dekker. 2002.

[5] V. I. Utkin and V. Ivanovich, Sliding Mode Control in Electromechanical Systems, London: Taylor&Francis, 1999.

[6] Y. Shtessel, Sliding Mode Control and Observation, Birkhäuser, New York:Control Engineering, 2014.

[7] M. Jamshidi, N. Vadiee, and T. J. Ross, "Fuzzy logic and control : software and hardware applications", 1993.

[8] D. Driankov, "An Introduction to Fuzzy Control," 1996.

[9] C. C. Lee, "Fuzzy Logic in Control Systems: Fuzzy Logic Controller-Part I, II", *IEEE Transactions on Systems, Man, and Cybernetics: Systems includes the fields of systems engineering*, vol. 20, issue 2, pp. 404-435, 1990.

[10] N. F. Al-Muthairi and M. Zribi, "Sliding Mode Control of a Magnetic Levitation System", *Mathematical Problems in Engineering*, vol. 2, pp. 93-107, 2004.

[11] A. K. Ahmad, Z. Saad, M. K. Osman and S. K. Abdullah, "Control of Magnetic Levitation System Using Fuzzy Logic Control", *Second International Conference on Computational Intelligence, Modelling and Simulation*, 2010.

[12] K. M. Passino and S. Yurkovich, "Fuzzy Control," Addison Wesley, 1998.

Pre-curved Beams as Technical Tactile Sensors for Object Shape Recognition

Carsten Behn
Dept. of Mechanical Engineering
Technische Universität Ilmenau
Ilmenau, Germany, 98693
Email: carsten.behn@tu-ilmenau.de

Joachim Steigenberger
Institute of Mathematics
Technische Universität Ilmenau
Ilmenau, Germany, 98693

Anton Sauter
and Christoph Will
Dept. of Mechanical Engineering
Technische Universität Ilmenau
Ilmenau, Germany, 98693

***Abstract*—Recent research topics in bionics focus on the analysis and synthesis of animal spatial perception of their environment by means of their tactile sensory organs: vibrissae and their follicles. Using the vibrissae, these mammals (e.g., rats) are able to determine an obstacle shape using only a few contacts of the vibrissa with the object. The investigations lead to the task of creating models and a stringent exploitation of these models in form of analytical and numerical calculations to achieve a better understanding of this sense. The sensing lever element vibrissa for the stimulus transmission is frequently modeled as an Euler-Bernoulli bending rod. We assume that the rod is one-sided clamped and interacts with a rigid obstacle in the plane. But, most of the literature is limited to the research on cylindrical and straight, or tapered and straight rods. The (natural) combination of a cylindrical and pre-curved shape is rarely analyzed. The aim is to determine the obstacles contour by one quasi-static sweep along the obstacle and to figure out the dependence on the pre-curvature of the rod. To do this, we proceed in several steps: At first, we have to determine the support reactions during a sweep. These support reactions are equate with the observables an animal solely relies on and have to be measured by a technical device. Then, the object shape has to be reconstructed in using only these generated observables. The consideration of the pre-curvature makes the analytical treatment a bit harder and results in numerical solutions of the process. But, the analysis of the problem results in an extension of a former decision criterion for the reconstruction by the radius of pre-curvature. Is is possible to determine a formula for the contact point of the rod with the profile, which is new in literature in context of pre-curvature.**

Keywords–Vibrissa; Sensing; Object scanning; Contour reconstruction; Pre-curved beam.

I. INTRODUCTION

In recent years, the development of vibrissae-inspired tactile sensors gain center stage in the focus of research, especially in the field of (autonomous) robotics, see e.g., [1] – [5]. These tactile sensors complement to and/or replace senses like vision, because they provide reliable information (object distance, contour and surface texture) in a dark and noisy environment (e.g., seals detect freshet and turbulence of fish in muddy water [6] [7] [8]), and are cheaper in fabrication.

Most mammals exhibit such vibrissae, in a variety of types and located in various areas of the skin/fur. Vibrissae differ from typical body hairs: they are thicker, longer, embedded in an own visco-elastic support (the so-called "follicle-sinus complex" (FSC)), see also [9] for some illustrations. Moreover, they feature a pre-curvature, a conical shape, cylindrical cross-section and are made of different material with hollow parts (like a multi-layer system) [10] [11] [12]. The vibrissa mainly serves as a force transmission (due to an obstacle contact) to its support. Hence, movement and deformation of the vibrissa can only be detected by mechanoreceptors in the FSC [1] [13]. It is hypothesized, that changing the blood-pressure in the FSC allows the animal to adjust the stiffness of the tissue to control the movement of the vibrissa [10] [12]. Furthermore, the surrounding tissue (fibrous band) and muscles (intrinsic and extrinsic musculature) enable the animal to actively move the vibrissa (active mode for surface texture detection) or to passively return the vibrissa to a rest position after deflection (due to a obstacle contact in passive mode) [14]. The pre-curvature is due to a kind of protection role: purely axial forces are prevented and, including the conical shape, the area of the tip of the vibrissa is limp. This results in a tangential contact to an object [10] [15].

In this paper, the investigations focus the influence of the *pre-curvature* to the static bending behavior of a vibrissa in context of obstacle contour detection and reconstruction. We describe a quasi-static scanning process of obstacles: 1. analytical/numerical generation the observables in the support which an animal solely relies on, 2. reconstruction of the scanned profile contour using only these observables, and 3. verification of the working principle by means of experiments. These steps were done in [5], [16] and [17] for cylindrical vibrissae. Therefore, we extend these results to pre-curved vibrissae in this paper.

The paper is arranged as follows: In Section II, a short overview of the related literature is given. Based on these information, Section III deals with aspects of setting up a mechanical model for the object sensing and presenting the describing equations. These equations are exemplarily solved in Section IV – considering only a constant pre-curvature radius of the bending rod. The results governed by numerical simulations are verified by experiments in Section V. Section VI concludes the paper.

II. SOME STATE OF ART OF PRE-CURVED VIBRISSAE

From the biological point of view, there are a lot of works focussing on the determination of vibrissae parameters. Towal et al. [12] pointed out an important fact that the mostly vibrissae are curved in a plane. The deviation of the vibrissa from this plane (referred to the length) is less than

0.1%. In [12], [15] and [18] – [22], a vibrissa is described using a polynomial approximation of 2nd-, 3rd- and 5th-order, which is rather low. In contrast to this references, we present numerical results using one of order 10. In [15], it is stated that approximately 90% of rat vibrissae exhibit a pre-curvature $\kappa_0 \in (0.0065/mm, 0.074/mm)$, and in [20] that extremely curved vibrissa provide $\kappa_0 > 0.25/mm$. The authors of [11], [15], [20] publish the following dimensionless parameters

$$\frac{L}{d} \approx 30\,, \quad \frac{r_0}{d} \approx 90\,,$$

whereas L is the length, d is the base diameter, and r_0 is the pre-curvature radius of the vibrissa.

From the technical point of view, pre-curved vibrissae are rarely used in applications. In [15], [21], [22], experimental and theoretical investigations concerning the distance detection to a pole are presented, using a pre-curved artificial vibrissa, also incorporating the conical shape. The pros and cons of a positive (curvature forward, CF) and negative (CB) curved vibrissae are stated in [15] whereas the vibrissa is used for tactile sensing of a pole. The CF-scanning results in low axial forces, but higher sheer ones; CB the inverse results. Summarized, the pre-curvature influences mainly the support forces instead of the support moment.

III. Modeling

This section shall serve as an introduction to the profile scanning procedure.

Beam Deflection Formula: The deflection of a largely deformed beam with pre-curvature is described in using the so-called *Winkler-Bach-Theory*. A detailed derivation of the equations can be found in [23] and [24]. Furthermore, the authors in [24] pointed out, that – assuming, that the radius of pre-curvature is much greater than the dimensions of the cross-section – the influence of the normal force can be neglected. Hence, the describing equations can be simplified to

$$\frac{d\varphi(s)}{ds} = \frac{1}{r_0(s)} + \frac{M_{bs}(s)}{EI_z}\,, \tag{1}$$

with second moment of area

$$I_z := \int_A \eta^2 dA\,,$$

and Young's modulus E, cross-section A, bending moment M_{bs}, and radius of pre-curvature r_0.

Scanning Procedure: Here, we describe the scanning procedure of *strictly convex profile contours* using pre-curved technical vibrissae *in a plane*. This is done in two steps:

1. Because of analytical interest, we firstly generate the observables (support reactions) during the scanning process. Since our intension is from bionics, we simply model the support as a clamping (being aware that this does not match the reality). Hence, the support reactions are the clamping forces and moment $\vec{M}_{Az}$, $\vec{F}_{Ax}$, $\vec{F}_{Ay}$, which an animal solely relies on.
2. Then, we use these observables in an algorithm to reconstruct the profile contour.

Fig. 1 sketches the scanning process of a plane, strictly profile. For this scanning process, several assumptions are made:

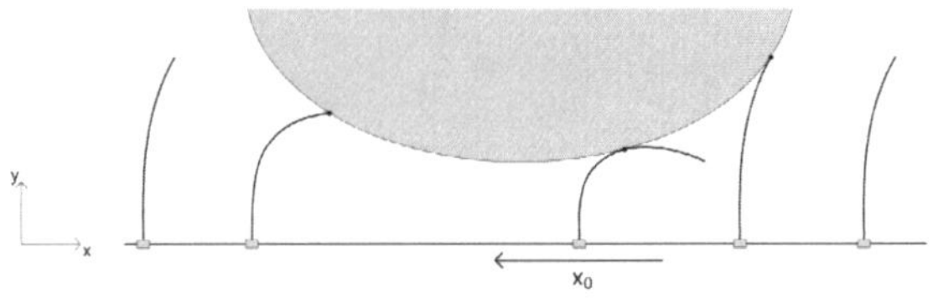

Figure 1. Scanning procedure using an artificial vibrissa; adapted from [5].

- The technical vibrissa is moved from *right to the left* (negative x-direction), i.e., the base point is moved.
- The problem is handled *quasi-statically*, i.e., the vibrissa is moved incrementally (and presented in changes of the boundary conditions). Then, the elastically deformed vibrissa is determined.
- Since we do not want to deal with friction at the beginning, we assume an *ideal contact*, i.e., the contact force is *perpendicular* to the contact point tangent of the profile.

The scanned profile is given by a function $g : x \mapsto g(x)$, where $g \in C^1(\mathbb{R};\mathbb{R})$. Since the graph of g is convex by assumption, the graph can be parameterized by means of the slope angle α in the xy-plane. Then we have, [5]:

$$\begin{aligned} \frac{dg(x)}{dx} &= g'(x) = \tan(\alpha) \\ \longrightarrow x &= \xi(\alpha) := g'^{-1}(\tan(\alpha)) \\ y &= \eta(\alpha) := g(\xi(\alpha)) \end{aligned}$$

Therefore, each point of the profile contour is given by $(\xi(\alpha), \eta(\alpha))$, $\alpha \in (-\frac{\pi}{2}, \frac{\pi}{2})$. For generality, we introduce dimensionless variables, starting with the arc length s with $s = Ls^*$, $s^* \in [0,1]$. Then, all lengths are measured in $\mathbf{L}$, all moments in $\mathbf{EI_zL^{-1}}$, and all forces in $\mathbf{EI_zL^{-2}}$, whereby we omit the asterisk "$*$" for brevity from now on.

Boundary-value Problem in Step 1: The system of differential equations (ODEs) describing the deformed pre-curved, technical vibrissa in a plane in dimensionless quantities is:

$$\left.\begin{aligned} \frac{dx(s)}{ds} &= \cos(\varphi(s)) \\ \frac{dy(s)}{ds} &= \sin(\varphi(s)) \\ \frac{d\varphi(s)}{ds} &= \frac{1}{r_{0L}(s)} + f\Big(\big(y(s)-\eta(\alpha)\big)\sin(\alpha) \\ &\qquad + \big(x(s)-\eta(\alpha)\big)\cos(\alpha)\Big) \end{aligned}\right\} \tag{2}$$

Observing Figs. 1 and 2 gives the hint to distinguish two phases of contact between the vibrissa and the obstacle:

- *Phase A – tip contact:* We have still ODE-system (2) with the boundary conditions (BCs)

$$\begin{aligned} y(0) = 0\,, \quad \varphi(0) = \frac{\pi}{2}\,, \\ x(1) = \xi(\alpha)\,, \quad y(1) = \eta(\alpha) \end{aligned} \tag{3}$$

- *Phase B – tangential contact:* Only the BCs change:

$$\begin{aligned} y(0) = 0\,, \quad \varphi(0) = \frac{\pi}{2}\,, \\ x(s_1) = \xi(\alpha)\,, \quad y(s_1) = \eta(\alpha)\,, \quad \varphi(s_1) = \alpha \end{aligned} \tag{4}$$

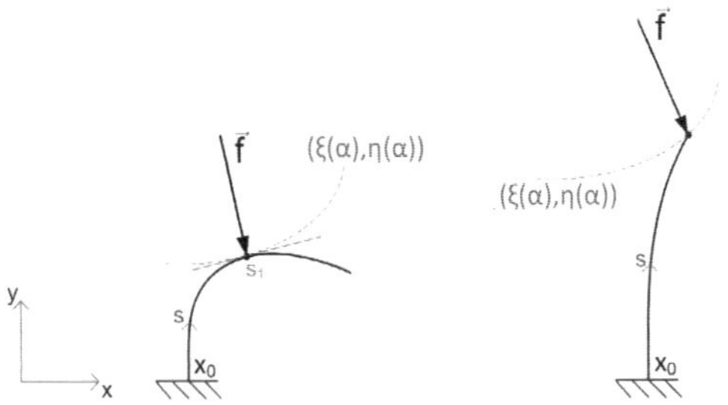

Figure 2. Contact of vibrissa and obstacle in *Phase A* (left) and in *Phase B* (right) during scanning process.

A direct inspection of the occurring problems (2) & (3) and (2) & (4) yield the choice of a shooting method to determine the parameters f and s_1, and finally with f the clamping reactions $\vec{M}_{Az}$, $\vec{F}_{Ax}$, $\vec{F}_{Ay}$.

Initial-value Problem in Step 2: Here, we use only the generated observables (measured in experiments) $\vec{M}_{Az}$, $\vec{F}_{Ax}$, $\vec{F}_{Ay}$ and known base of the vibrissa x_0 to reconstruct the scanned profile. Due to [2], we determine the bending moment, see Fig. 3, to formulate the initial-value problem (IVP) in this step:

$$\left.\begin{aligned} \frac{dx(s)}{ds} &= \cos(\varphi(s)) \\ \frac{dy(s)}{ds} &= \sin(\varphi(s)) \\ \frac{d\varphi(s)}{ds} &= \frac{1}{r_{0L}(s)} - M_{Az} - F_{Ax}y(s) + F_{Ay}\big(x(s) - x_0\big) \end{aligned}\right\} \quad (5)$$

with initial conditions (ICs)

$$x(0) = x_0\,, \quad y(0) = 0\,, \quad \varphi(0) = \frac{\pi}{2} \quad (6)$$

Now, it is necessary – for each input $\{M_{Az}, F_{Ax}, F_{Ay}, x_0\}$

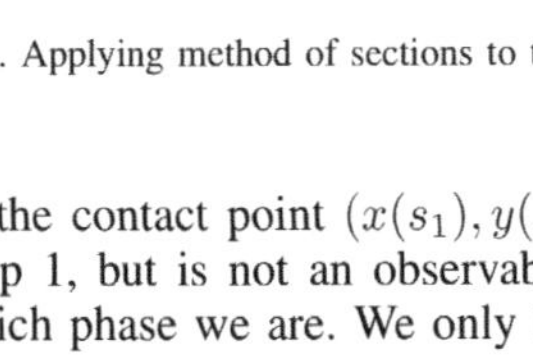

Figure 3. Applying method of sections to the vibrissa.

– to determine the contact point $(x(s_1), y(s_1))$ (note, that s_1 is known in step 1, but is not an observable). But, it is still unknown in which phase we are. We only have

$$M_{bz}(s_1) = 0$$

In accordance to [5], we determine a decision criterion to distinguish both phase. The vibrissa is in Phase B, iff it holds:

$$\boxed{M_{Az}^2 + \frac{2M_{Az}}{r_{0L}} - 2F_{Ay} = 0} \quad (7)$$

In comparison to the condition in [5], we get one new term $\frac{2M_{Az}}{r_{0L}}$. And, in a limiting case for $r_{0L} \longrightarrow \pm\infty$, condition (7) forms the condition in [5], which serves as a validation.

IV. Profile Scanning Using a Constant Pre-curvature Radius

Here, we present numerical simulations of the described profile scanning algorithm (based of two steps). At first, we focus on a *constant* pre-curvature radius $r_{0L} \neq r_{0L}(s)$. Referring to [5], we consider a profile described by $g_1 : x \mapsto \frac{1}{2}x^2 + 0.3$. Exemplarily, two scanning processes are presented in Figs. 4 and 5. Note, that the vibrissae in Phase B are only plotted to the contact point, just for clarity. One can clearly see, that the smaller the pre-curvature radius is no Phase A occurs, i.e., no tip contact, which might explain the protective role of the pre-curvature of vibrissae.

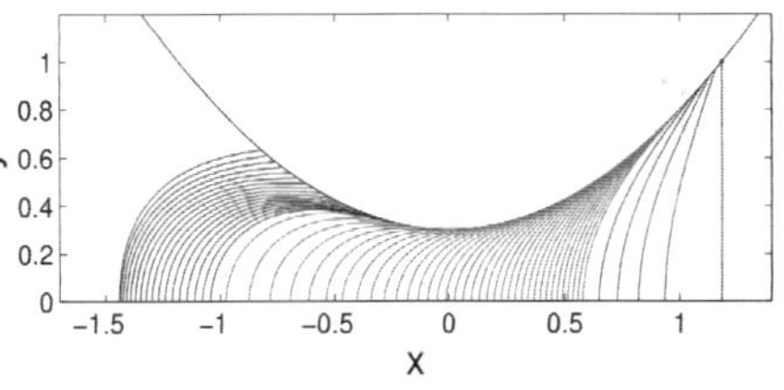

Figure 4. Profile scanning using a pre-curved vibrissa with $r_{0L} = -1000$: in blue *Phase A*, in red *Phase B*.

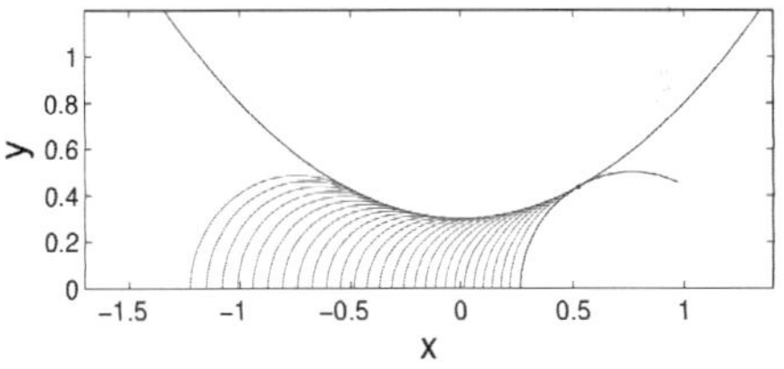

Figure 5. Profile scanning using a pre-curved vibrissa with $r_{0L} = -0.5$: in red *Phase B*, no Phase A.

Figs. 6, 7 and 8 show the observables during a scanning process in dependence on the pre-curvature radius. The transition between both phases is marked with a "+". It becomes clear: the smaller the pre-curvature radius the smaller the bending behavior of the vibrissa, the smaller the observables, but the smaller the scanning area. Therefore, a small pre-curvature radius results in poor scanning results. The error of the reconstruction between the given and reconstructed profile is defined for single points according to [5]:

$$error = \sqrt{\big(x_k(s_{1k}) - \xi(\alpha_k)\big)^2 + \big(y_k(s_{1k}) - \eta(\alpha_k)\big)^2}\,, \quad (8)$$

whereby $(\xi(\alpha_k), \eta(\alpha_k))$ represent a point of the given profile and $(x_k(s_{1k}), y_k(s_{1k}))$ is the corresponding one of the

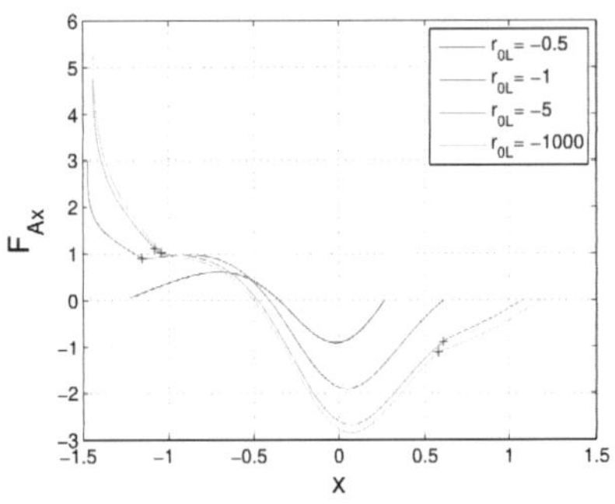

Figure 6. Clamping force F_{Ax} for varying pre-curvature radius r_{OL}.

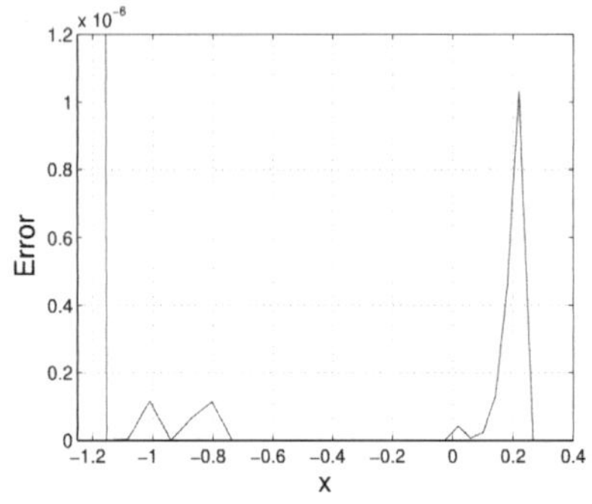

Figure 9. Error of given and reconstructed profile for $r_{OL} = -0.5$.

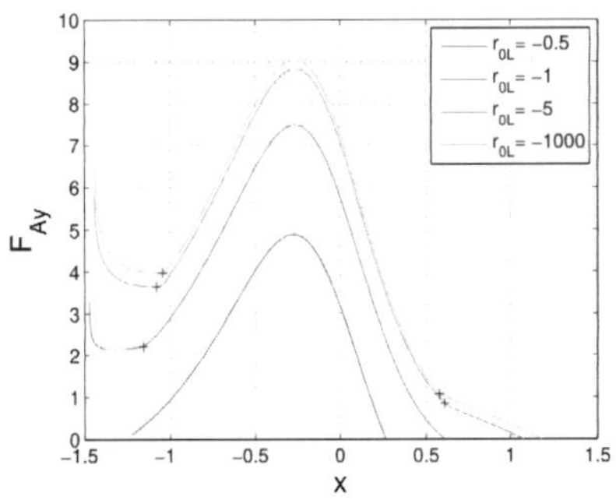

Figure 7. Clamping force F_{Ay} for varying pre-curvature radius r_{OL}.

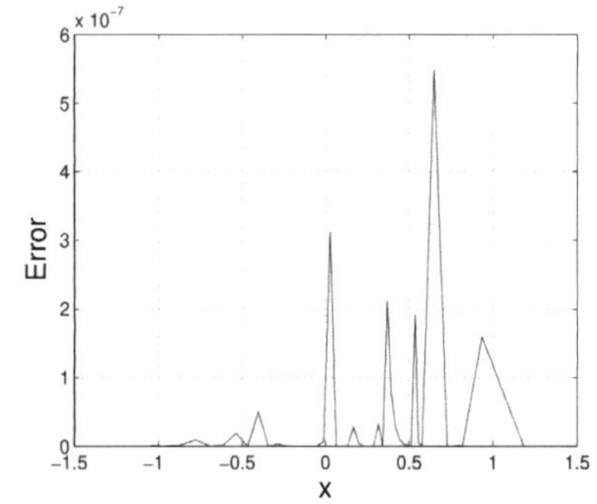

Figure 10. Error of given and reconstructed profile for $r_{OL} = -1000$.

reconstructed profile. Figs. 9 and 10 exemplarily present the reconstruction errors of two reconstruction simulations. The magnitude of the error is from 10^{-7} to 10^{-6}.

V. Experiments in Scanning with Variable Pre-curvature Radius

To verify the algorithms, we present numerical investigations of scanning vibrissae with variable pre-curvature and experimental results, using a parabola profile $g_1(x) = 2x^2+0.55$. Three different technical vibrissae with different pre-curvature are used in an experiment. Fig. 11 shows that the first vibrissae is straight, the second and the third one have a variable pre-curvature radius. With the help of a computer-aided evaluation of the graphic representation of the vibrissae in Fig. 11, their pre-curvature radius $r_{OL}(s)$ is determined in dependence of the arc length s as polynomials of order 10. This is rather new in literature, because a lot of works from literature restrict to a representation of the pre-curvature only to s^2-terms.

The simulated scanning processes are shown in Figs. 12 and 13 for vibrissa 1 and 3. Figs. 14, 15 and 16 show exemplarily the observables (simulation vs. experiment) of the experiment using vibrissa 3. An easy inspection confirms prior results, that the maximal values of M_{Az}, F_{Ax} and F_{Ay} decrease the bigger the pre-curvature and the smaller the pre-curvature radius are. These figures show a good coincidence of the simulated and measured curves of the observables.

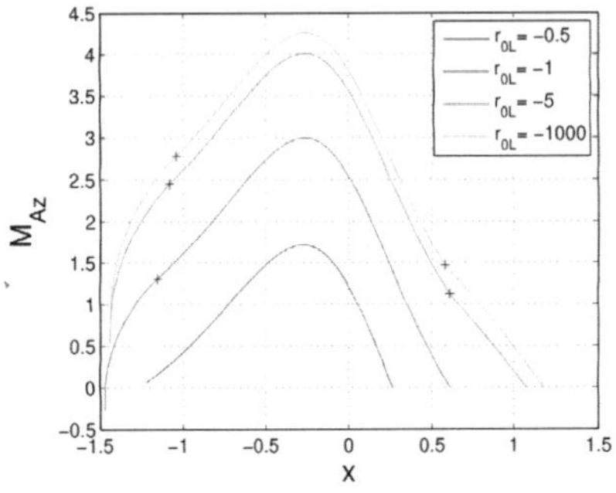

Figure 8. Clamping moment M_{Az} for varying pre-curvature radius r_{OL}.

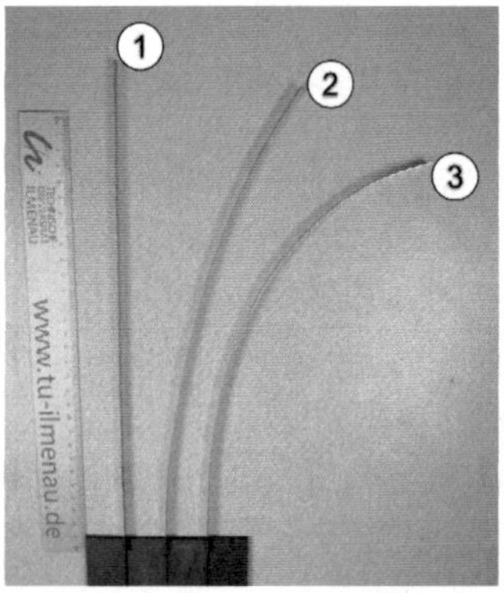

Figure 11. Three different pre-curved vibrissae for the experiment.

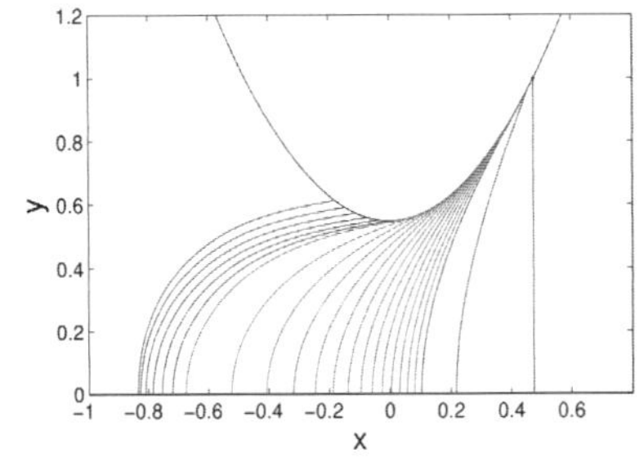

Figure 12. Scanning process using vibrissa 1 – in blue *Phase A*; in red *Phase B*.

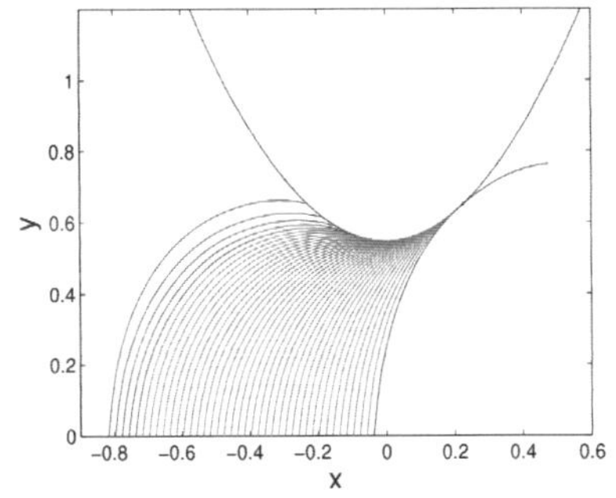

Figure 13. Scanning process using vibrissa 3 – in blue *Phase A*; in red *Phase B*.

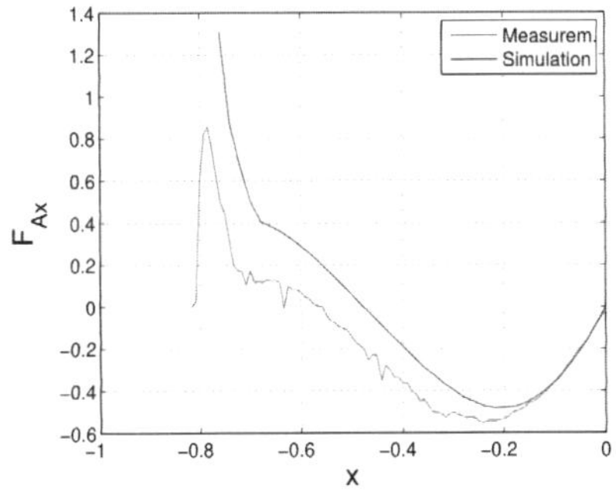

Figure 14. Experiment using vibrissa 3: clamping force F_{Ax} of a simulation and the experiment.

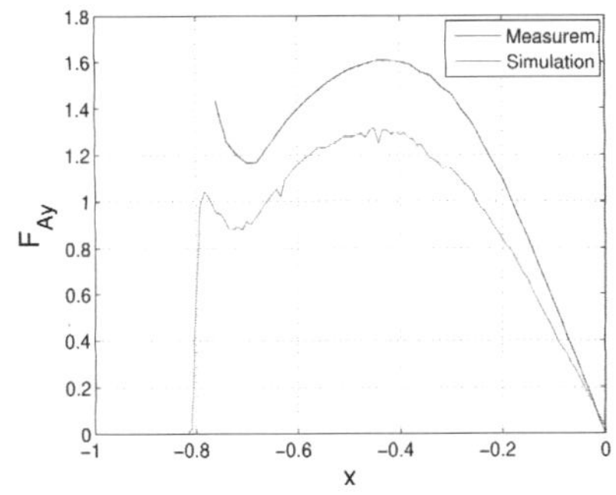

Figure 15. Experiment using vibrissa 3: clamping force F_{Ay} of a simulation and the experiment.

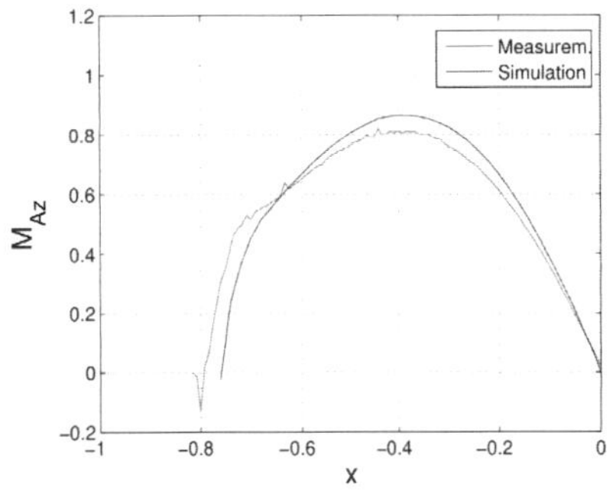

Figure 16. Experiment using vibrissa 3: clamping moment M_{Az} of a simulation and the experiment.

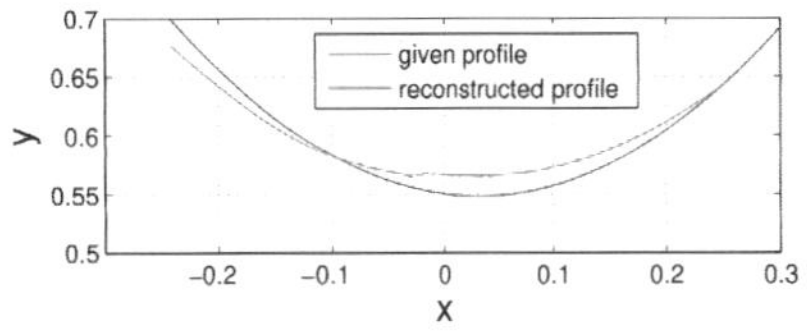

Figure 17. Experiment using vibrissa 3: reconstruction error of a simulation and the experiment.

Fig. 17 presents the reconstruction of the profile. Compared to further simulations, we point out that the smaller the pre-curvature radius is the smaller is the reconstruction error.

Summarizing, we show that it is promising to use pre-curved vibrissae for object contour scanning and reconstruction. The simulated and measured curves of the observables show up a good coincidence. The presented algorithms work effectively.

VI. CONCLUSION

Due to the functionality of animals vibrissae, the goal was to set up a model for an object scanning and shape reconstruction algorithm. For this, the only available information are the observables (support reaction which an animal solely relies on) governed by one single sweep along the profile. Based on these observables, the object boundary has to be reconstructed. It was possible to illustrate the characteristics and influences of pre-curved technical vibrissae in view of profile scanning. Based on the Winkler-Bach-Theory for pre-curved beams we set up the equations for a deformed vibrissa during a scanning process. We presented an algorithm to reconstruct the scanned profile in using the generated observables (which an animal is supposed to solely rely on) via shooting methods. The reconstruction then was based on solving initial-value problems on contrast to the generation procedure where we solved boundary-value problems. The investigations respective the scanning of a strictly convex profile with a pre-curved vibrissae showed noticeable differences to the profile scanning with a straight vibrissa. The extrema of the bending reactions and the size of the scanned profile area depends on the pre-curvature radius of the vibrissa. Using a smaller radius, the tangential contact *phase B* in the scanning process could be enlarged. Experiments confirmed the numerical results and algorithms in this paper. Moreover, the investigation showed that the profile reconstruction works better with a pre-curved vibrissa.

ACKNOWLEDGMENT

This work was supported by the Deutsche Forschungsgemeinschaft (DFG), Grant ZI 540-16/2.

REFERENCES

[1] R. Berg and D. Kleinfeld, "Rhythmic Whisking by Rat: Retraction as Well as Protraction of the Vibrissae Is Under Active Muscular Control," Journal of Neurophysiology, vol. 89, no. 1, pp. 104-117, 2002.

[2] G.R. Scholz and C.D. Rahn, "Profile Sensing With an Actuated Whisker," IEEE Transactions on Robotics and Automation, vol. 20, no. 1, pp. 124–127, 2004.

[3] M.J. Pearson et al., "A Biologically Inspired Haptic Sensor Array for use in Mobile Robotic Vehicles," Proceedings of Towards Autonomous Robotic Systems (TAROS), pp. 189-196, 2005.

[4] M.J. Pearson, A.G. Pipe, C. Melhuish, B. Mitchinson, and T.J. Prescott, "Whiskerbot: A Robotic Active Touch System Modeled on the Rat Whisker Sensory System," Adaptive Behavior, vol. 15, no. 3, pp. 223-240, 2007.

[5] C. Will, J. Steigenberger, and C. Behn, "Object Contour Reconstruction using Bio-inspired Sensors," in: Proceedings 11th International Conference on Informatics in Control, Automation and Robotics (ICINCO 2014), September 0103, 2014, Vienna, Austria. IEEE, pp. 459-467, ISBN: 978-989-758-039-0, 2014.

[6] G. Dehnhardt, "Tactile size discrimination by a California sea lion (Zalophus californianus) using its mystacial vibrissae," Journal of Comparative Physiology A, vol. 175, no. 6, pp. 791-800, 1994.

[7] G. Dehnhardt and A. Kaminski, "Sensitivity of the mystacial vibrissae of harbour seals for size differences of actively touched objects," The Journal of Experimental Biology, vol. 198, pp. 2317-2323, 1995.

[8] G. Dehnhardt, B. Mauck, and H. Bleckman, "Seal whiskers detect water movements," Nature, vol. 394, pp. 235-236, 1998.

[9] C. Behn, C. Will, and J. Steigenberger, "Effects of Boundary Damping on Natural Frequencies in Bending Vibrations of Intelligent Vibrissa Tactile Systems," International Journal On Advances in Intelligent Systems, vol. 8, no. 3&4, pp. 245-254, ISSN: 1942-2679, 2015.

[10] K. Carl et al., "Characterization of Statical Properties of Rats Whisker System," IEEE Sensors Journals, vol. 12, no. 2, pp. 340-349, 2012.

[11] D. Voges et al., "Structural Characterization of the Whisker System of the Rat," IEEE Sensors Journals, vol. 12, no. 2, pp. 332-339, 2012.

[12] R.B. Towal, B.W. Quist, V. Gopal, J.H. Solomon, and M.J.Z. Hartmann, "The Morphology of the Rat Vibrissal Array: A Model for Quantifying Spatiotemporal Patterns of Whisker-Object Contact," PLoS Computational Biology, vol. 7, no. 4, pp. 1–17,e1001120, 2011.

[13] A. Ahl, "The role of vibrissae in behavior: A status review," Veterinary Reserarch Communications, vol. 10, pp. 245-268, 1986.

[14] J. Dörfl, "The musculature of the mystacial vobrissae of the white mouse," Journal of Anatomy, vol. 135, no. 1, pp. 147-154, 1982.

[15] B.W. Quist and M.J.Z. Hartmann, "Mechanical signals at the base of a rat vibrissa: the effect of intrinsic vibrissa curvature and implications for tactile exploration," Journal of Neuophysiology, vol. 107, pp. 2298-2312, 2012.

[16] C. Will, J. Steigenberger, and C. Behn, "Quasi-static object scanning using technical vibrissae," in: Proceedings 58. International Colloquium Ilmenau (IWK), September 0812, 2014, Ilmenau, Germany. ilmedia, URL: http://nbn-resolving.org/urn:nbn:de:gbv:ilm1-2014iwk:3 [accessed: 2016-06-10], 2014.

[17] C. Will, J. Steigenberger, and C. Behn, "Bio-inspired Technical Vibrissae for Quasi-static Profile Scanning," Springer International Publishing Switzerland, J. Filipe et al. (eds.), ISBN: 978-3-319-26453-0, pp. 277-295, 2016.

[18] M. Knutsen, D. Derdikman, and E. Ahissar, "Tracking Whisker and Head Movements in Unrestrained Behaving Rodents," Journal of Neurophysiology, vol. 93, pp. 2294-2301, 2004.

[19] M. Knutsen, A. Biess, and E. Ahissar, "Vibrissal Kinematics in 3D: Tight Coupling of Azimuth, Elevation, and Torsion across Different Whisking Modes," Neuron, vol. 59, pp. 35-42, 2008.

[20] N.G. Clack et al., "Automated Tracking of Whiskers in Videos of Head Fixed Rodents," PLoS Computational Biology, vol. 8, no. 7, e1002591, pp. 1–8, 2012.

[21] S.A. Hires, L. Pammer, K. Svoboda, and D. Golomb, "Tapered whiskers are required for active tactile sensation," eLife, 2013, e01350, pp. 1–19, 2013.

[22] L. Pammer et al., "The mechanical variables underlying object lokalisation along the axis of the whisker," The Journal of Neuroscience, vol. 33, no. 16, pp. 6726-6741, 2013

[23] P. Gummert and K.-A. Reckling, "Mechanik (Mechanics)," 3rd edition, Vieweg, Braunschweig, Germany, 1994.

[24] A. Sauter, C. Will, J. Steigenberger, and C. Behn, "Artificial tactile sensors with pre-curvature for object scanning," in: Proceedings 13th Conference on Dynamical Systems – Theory and Applications (DSTA), Lódz, Poland, 7-10 December 2015, Volume "Mathematical and numerical approaches", ISBN: 978-83-7283706-6, pp. 425–436, 2015.

Laser-based Cooperative Estimation of Pose and Size of Moving Objects using Multiple Mobile Robots

Yuto Tamura, Ryohei Murabayashi
Graduate School of Science and Engineering
Doshisha Unversity
Kyotanabe, Kyoto 610-0394 Japan

Masafumi Hashimoto, Kazuhiko Takahashi
Faculty of Science and Engineering
Doshisha Unversity
Kyotanabe, Kyoto 610-0394 Japan
e-mail: {mhashimo, katakaha}@mail.doshisha.ac.jp

Abstract—**This paper presents laser-based tracking (estimation of pose and size) of moving objects using multiple mobile robots as sensor nodes. Each sensor node is equipped with a single-layer laser scanner and detects moving objects, such as people, cars, and bicycles, in its own laser-scanned images by applying an occupancy-grid-based method. Each sensor node then estimates the objects' poses (positions and velocities) and sizes using Bayesian filtering and sends these estimates to a central server. The central server combines the estimates to improve the tracking accuracy and then feeds the information back to the sensor nodes. In this cooperative-tracking method, the sensor nodes share their tracking information, allowing tracking of invisible or partially visible objects. The hierarchical architecture of cooperative tracking also makes the system scalable and robust. Experimental results using two sensor nodes confirm the performance of our tracking method.**

Keywords—moving-object tracking; cooperative tracking; pose and size estimation; laser scanner; mobile robot; sensor node

I. INTRODUCTION

Tracking of multiple moving objects is an important issue in the safe navigation of mobile robots and vehicles. The use of laser scanners, radars, or stereo cameras in mobile robotics and vehicle automation has attracted considerable interest [1]–[7]. The term "tracking" means estimating the pose (position and velocity) and size of moving object throughout this paper.

Recently, numerous studies have been conducted on multirobot coordination and cooperation [8][9]. When multiple robots are located near each another, they can share their sensing data through communication network. The multirobot team can then be considered a multisensor system. Even if moving objects locate outside the sensing area of the robot are occluded, they can be found using tracking data from other robots in the team. Hence, multi robot system can improve the accuracy and reliability with which moving objects are tracked [10]–[16].

Such cooperative tracking or cooperative object localization can also be applied to vehicle automation, including intelligent transportation systems (ITS) and systems for personal mobility devices, as shown in Fig. 1. Cooperative tracking enables the detection of moving objects in the blind spot of each vehicle and can be used to detect sudden changes in a crowded urban environment such as people appearing on roads or vehicles making unsafe lane changes. It can therefore prevent traffic accidents.

Our previous works presented a cooperative people-tracking method in which multiple mobile robots or vehicles were used as mobile sensor nodes and equipped with laser scanners [17][18]. The covariance intersection method [19] was applied to operate the tracking system effectively in a decentralized manner without any central server. In cooperative people tracking, each person could be assumed to be a mass point because of the small size, and mass-point tracking (only the pose estimation) was then performed.

In the real world, several types of moving objects, such as people, cars, bicycles, and motorcycles, exist. Therefore, we should design a cooperative-tracking system for moving objects. In vehicle (car, motorcycle, and bicycle) tracking, we have to consider moving objects as rigid bodies and estimate both the poses and sizes to avoid the collisions in a crowded environment.

Figure 1. Example of cooperative tracking in urban environments.

Tracking of a rigid body is known as extended-object tracking, and many related studies have been conducted [20]–[24]. However, to the best of our knowledge, cooperative tracking using multiple mobile sensor nodes covers only mass-point tracking under the assumption that the tracked object is small. It estimates only the object's pose but does not estimate its size.

Therefore, we presented a laser-based cooperative-tracking method for rigid bodies that estimates both poses and sizes of people and vehicles using multiple mobile sensor nodes [25]. In a crowded environment, a vehicle is occluded or rendered partially visible by each sensor node. To correctly estimate the size of the vehicle, the laser measurements captured by sensor nodes in the team have to be merged. Our previous cooperative-tracking method for rigid bodies applied a centralized architecture. Each sensor node detected laser measurements related to the moving objects in its sensing area and transmitted the measurement information to a central server, which then estimated the poses and sizes of the objects. Such a centralized architecture imposes a computational burden upon the central server. Moreover, the architecture has a weakness for fault of communication system between sensor nodes and central server.

To address this problem, in this paper, we present a hierarchical method of cooperative tracking by which the poses and sizes of moving objects are locally estimated by the sensor nodes. Moreover, these estimates are then merged by a central server. The rest of the paper is organized as follows. Section II gives an overview of our experimental system. In Sections III and IV, cooperative tracking is discussed. In Section V, we describe an experiment in moving-object tracking using two mobile sensor nodes in an outdoor environment. We present our conclusions in Section VI.

Figure 2. Overview of the mobile sensor node.

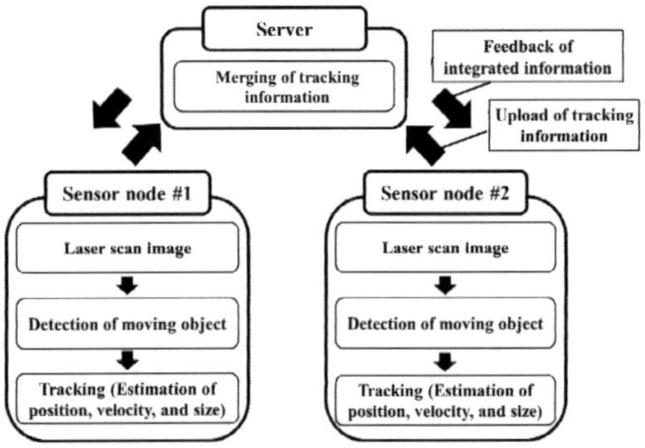

Figure 3. System overview of cooperative tracking.

II. EXPERIMENTAL SYSTEM AND COOPERATIVE TRACKING OVERVIEW

Fig. 2 shows the mobile-sensor node system used in our experiments. Each of the two sensor nodes has two independently driven wheels. A wheel encoder is attached to each drive wheel to measure its velocity. A yaw-rate gyro is attached to the chassis of each robot to sense the turning velocity. These internal sensors calculate the robot's pose using dead reckoning.

Each sensor node is equipped with a forward-looking laser scanner (SICK LMS100) to capture laser-scanned images that are represented by a sequence of distance samples in a horizontal plane of 270°. The angular resolution of the laser scanner is 0.5°, and each scan image comprises 541 distance samples. Each sensor node is also equipped with RTK–GPS (Novatel ProPak-V3 GPS). The sampling frequency of the sensors is 10 Hz.

We use broadcast communication over a wireless local area network to exchange information between the central server and the sensor nodes. The computer used in the sensor nodes and the central server is an Iiyama 15X7100-i7-VGB with a 2.8 GHz Intel core i7-4810MQ processor, and the operating system used is Microsoft Windows 7 Professional.

Fig. 3 shows the sequence of moving-object tracking. Each sensor node independently finds the moving objects in its own laser-scanned images using an occupancy-grid method [26]. The sensor node then tracks the moving objects (estimates their poses and sizes), and the information is uploaded to the central server. The information includes the time stamp, the number of the objects tracked, and their pose and size. The central server merges the information. It estimates the poses and sizes of the moving objects using a Bayesian filter. The estimated information is then fed back to the sensor nodes.

To map the laser-scanned images onto the world coordinate frame (on which the grid map is represented), each sensor node accurately identifies its own position based on dead reckoning and GPS information using an extended Kalman filter [18].

III. TRACKING BY SENSOR NODE

In this section, we describe the process of estimating the poses and sizes of moving objects using Bayesian filter in conjunction with data association.

A. Pose and Size Estimation

We represent the shape of the moving object by a rectangle of width W and length L. We detail the size-estimation method in Fig. 4, where red circles indicate laser measurements of the moving object (hereafter, moving-object measurements), green lines are the feature lines extracted from those measurements, the green dashed rectangle is the estimated rectangle, and the green star is the centroid of that rectangle. As shown in Fig. 4, an $x_v y_v$-coordinate frame is defined, on which the y_v-axis aligns with the heading (orange arrow) of the tracked object. From the clustered moving-object measurements, we extract the width W_{meas} and length L_{meas}.

When a moving object is perfectly visible, its size can be estimated from these measurements. In contrast, when the object is partially occluded by other objects, its size cannot be accurately estimated. Therefore, the size of the partially occluded object is estimated by the following equation [20]:

$$\begin{cases} W_k = W_{k-1} + G(W_{meas} - W_{k-1}) \\ L_k = L_{k-1} + G(L_{meas} - L_{k-1}) \end{cases} \quad (1)$$

where W and L are estimates of width and length, respectively, and k and $k-1$ are time steps. G is the filter gain, given by $G = 1 - \sqrt[k]{(1-p)}$ [20], and p is a parameter. As the value of p increases, the reliabilities of the current measurements of W_{meas} and L_{meas} increase. We assume that a vehicle passes at 60 km/h in front of the sensor node. After the vehicle enters the surveillance area of the sensor node, we aim to estimate 99% of the size (p = 0.99) within 10 scans (1 s) of the laser scanner. We can then determine G as follows:

$$G = \begin{cases} 1 - \sqrt[k]{(1-0.99)} & \text{for } k \le 10 \\ 1 - \sqrt[10]{(1-0.99)} = 0.369 & \text{for } k > 10 \end{cases} \quad (2)$$

For a perfectly visible object, we set G = 1 in (1) and estimate its size.

The estimated size of the tracked object is used to classify the object as a person or a vehicle. If the estimated size in length or width is larger than 0.8 m, the object is assumed to be a vehicle. However, if the size is smaller than 0.8 m, it is assumed to be a person.

We then define the centroid position (green star in Fig. 4) of the rectangle estimated by (1). From the centroid position, the pose of the tracked object, position and velocity $(x, y, \dot{x}, \dot{y})$ on the world coordinate frame, is estimated using the Kalman filter under the assumption that the object is moving at an almost constant velocity.

To extract W_{meas} and L_{meas} from the moving-object measurements, we have to obtain the heading of the tracked object. As shown in Fig. 4, we extract two feature lines (green lines in Fig. 4) from the moving-object measurements using the split-and-merge method [27] and RANSAC [28] and determine the heading of the object from the orientations of the feature lines. When the two feature lines cannot be extracted, we determine the heading from the estimated velocity $(\dot{x}, \dot{y})$ of the object.

B. Data Association

To track objects in multi-object and multi-measurement environments, we apply data association (i.e., one-to-one matching of tracked objects and moving-object measurements). As shown in Fig. 5, a validation gate (validation region) is set around the predicted position (black circle) of each tracked object. The validation gate is rectangular, with a length and width 0.5 m greater than those of the object estimated at the previous time step (green dashed rectangle).

We refer to a representative point of grouped moving-object measurements (red and blue circles) as the representative measurement (light blue triangles). Representative measurements inside the validation gate are assumed to originate from the tracked object and are used to update the pose of the tracked object with the Kalman filter. Measurements outside the validation gate are identified as false and discarded.

Figs. 6 and 7, respectively, show an exemplary laser image and data association for a case in which two people move close to a car. In these figures, red circles indicate moving-object measurements, light blue triangles indicate representative measurements, black circles indicate tracked

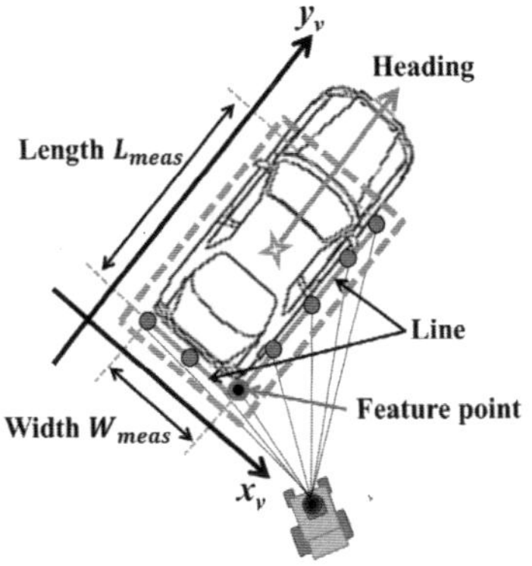

Figure 4. Size estimation of a vehicle.

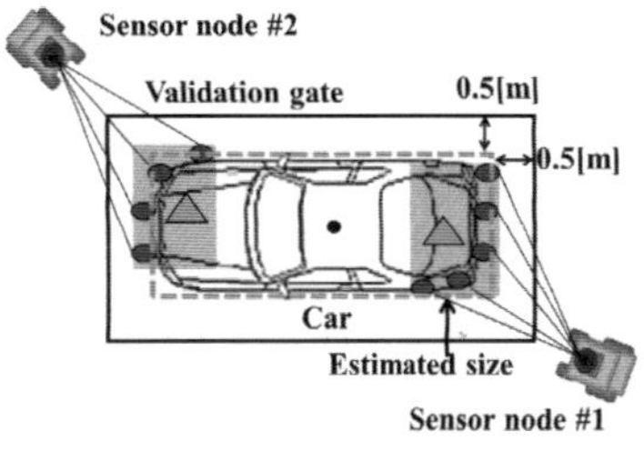

Figure 5. Laser images and data association.

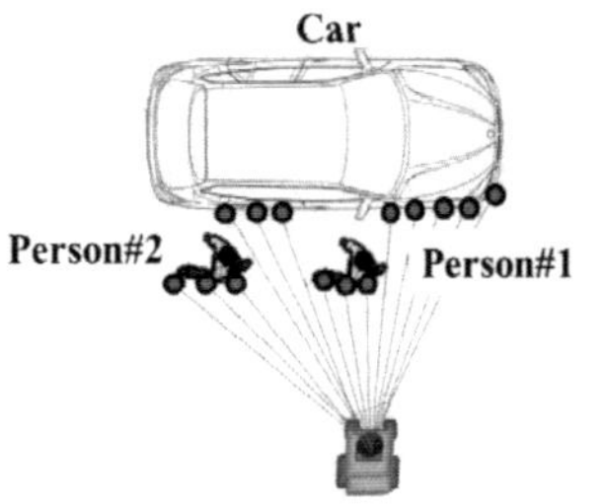

Figure 6. Laser images of a case in which two people are moving close to a car.

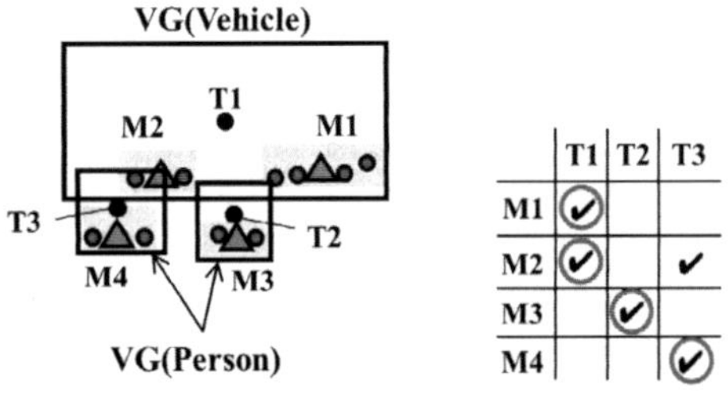

Figure 7. Data association for the laser images in Fig. 6.

objects, and VG stands for validation gate. The right table in Fig. 7 shows the correspondence between tracked objects and representative measurements.

As shown in Fig. 7, multiple representative measurements are often obtained inside a validation gate in the real world, and multiple tracked objects also compete for representative measurements. To achieve a reliable data association, we introduce the following rules:

a) Person: Because a person is small, he/she usually result in one representative measurement. Thus, if a tracked object is assumed to be a person, one-to-one matching of the tracked person and a representative measurement is performed.

b) Vehicle (car, motorcycle, or bicycle): Because a vehicle is large, as shown in Fig. 7, it often produces multiple representative measurements. Thus, if a tracked object is assumed to be a vehicle, one-to-many matching of the tracked vehicle and representative measurements is performed.

As shown in Fig. 6, on urban streets, people often move close to vehicles, whereas vehicles move far away from each other. Thus, when representative measurements of people exist in the validation gate of a tracked vehicle, they might be matched to the tracked vehicle. To avoid this, we begin data association for people.

We illustrate our data-association method from Fig. 7, in which the validation gates of a person and a car overlap. If tracked objects T2 and T3 are determined to be people, the representative measurement M3 is matched with T2 and the representative measurement M4 nearest to T3 is matched with T3, both through one-to-one matching. Subsequently, if the tracked object T1 is determined to be a vehicle, the two representative measurements M1 and M2 in the validation gate are matched with T1 through one-to-many matching. If the validation gates of several people overlap, one-to-one matching is performed using the global nearest neighbor method [18][29].

A representative measurement that is not matched with any tracked objects is assumed either to originate from a new moving object or to be a false alarm. Therefore, we tentatively initiate tracking of the measurement with the Kalman filter. If the measurement remains visible, it is assumed to originate from a new object and tracking is continued. If the measurement disappears quickly, it is treated as a false alarm, and tentative tracking is terminated.

Moving objects appear in and disappear from the sensing area of the laser scanner. They also occlude each other and are occluded by other objects in the environment. To maintain reliable tracking under such conditions, we implement a rule-based tracking-handling system [18].

IV. MERGING OF TRACKING DATA BY A CENTRAL SERVER

The information concerning objects tracked by the sensor nodes is combined using data association. We present an example of our data-association procedure in Figs. 8 and 9, in which two sensor nodes are tracking a car. In Fig. 8, red and blue rectangles indicate the sizes of the tracked objects #A (TA) and #B (TB), as estimated by sensor nodes #1 and #2, respectively. Orange arrows indicate the headings of the objects.

If TA and TB originate from the same object, their position, velocity, and heading estimates will have similar values. If the tracked object is a vehicle, the size estimated by sensor nodes will be large. If it is a person, the estimated size will be small. Therefore, we set a validation gate with a constant radius of 3 m around the TA position (red star in Fig. 8) and introduce the following rules to match TB with TA:

a) Same or different object: When the estimated position of TB (blue star) is located within the validation gate, and the

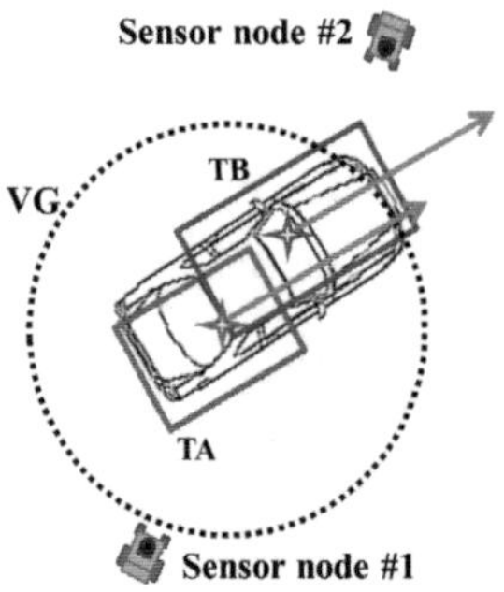

Figure 8. Data association of tracking information related to objects TA and TB.

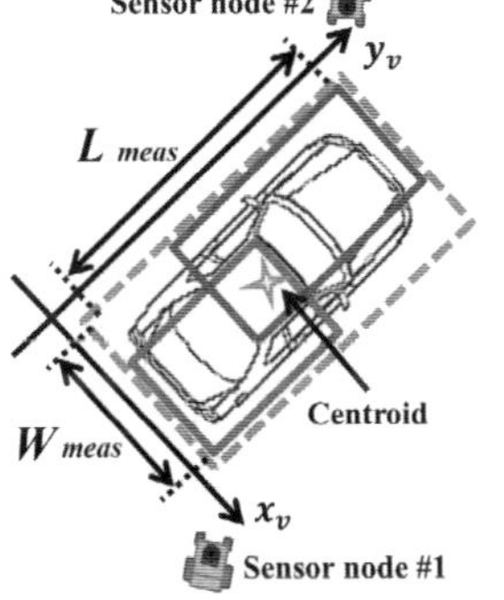

Figure 9. Integration of tracking information.

differences in the velocity and heading estimates of TA and TB are less than 0.8 m/s and 15°, respectively, the objects TA and TB are determined to originate from the same object. Otherwise, the objects TA and TB are determined to be different objects.

b) Vehicle or person: When the width and/or length estimates of the matched objects TA and TB are larger than 0.8 m, their objects are determined to originate from the same vehicle. When their width and length estimates are less than 0.8 m, the objects TA and TB are determined to originate from the same person.

When more than two tracked objects (e.g., TB and TC) are present in the validation gate of TA, the similar data association rules are applied.

After the two tracked objects TA and TB have been matched, their tracking information is combined. As shown in Fig. 9, we select the tracked object TB, which has a larger rectangle (blue rectangle) than TA (red rectangle), and define an $x_v y_v$-coordinate frame on which the y_v-axis aligns with the heading of TB. A rectangle (the green dashed rectangle) is then generated that encloses the two rectangles of TA and TB using positional information on their vertices. We then estimate the size of the integrated object using (1) based on the width and length of the new rectangle.

From the centroid position (green star) of the new rectangle, the position and velocity of the integrated object are estimated using the Kalman filter under the assumption that the object is moving at an almost constant velocity.

V. EXPERIMENTAL RESULTS

We evaluated our cooperative-tracking method by conducting an experiment in a parking environment, as shown in Fig. 10. Two mobile sensor nodes tracked a car (vehicle #1), a motorcycle (vehicle #2), and two pedestrians (persons #1 and #2). Fig. 11 shows the movement paths of the sensor nodes (black dashed lines), vehicles #1 and #2 (blue and green lines), and persons #1 and #2 (red and black lines). The moving speeds of the sensor nodes, car, motorcycle, and people were approximately 1.5, 15, 20, and 6 km/h, respectively.

Fig. 12 (a) shows the position and size results estimated by cooperative tracking. We plot estimated rectangles every 1 s (10 scans). For comparison, individual tracking by each sensor node was also conducted. The tracking results for sensor nodes #1 and #2 are shown in Figs. 12 (b) and (c), respectively.

The estimated size of car (vehicle #1) using cooperative and individual tracking is shown in Figs. 13 (a), (b), and (c). In these figures, red and blue lines indicate the estimated length and width, respectively. Two dashed lines indicate

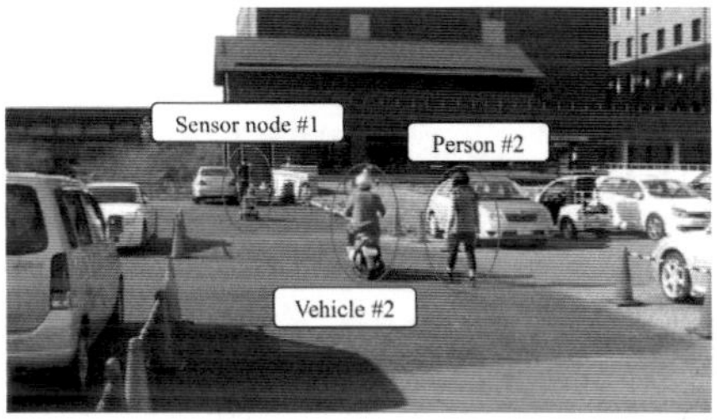

(a) Photo by camera #A

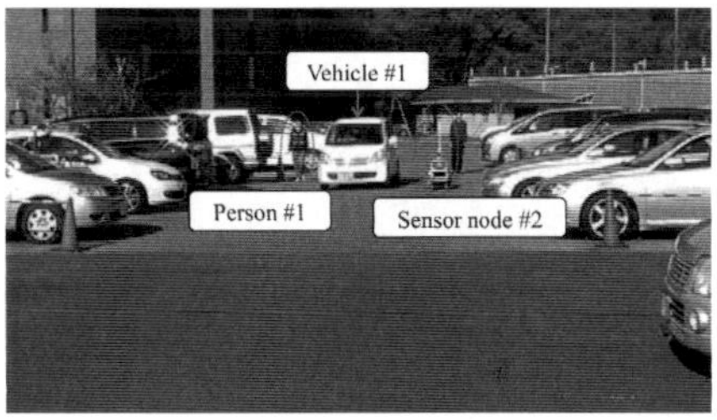

(b) Photo by camera #B

Figure 10. Photo of the experimental environment.

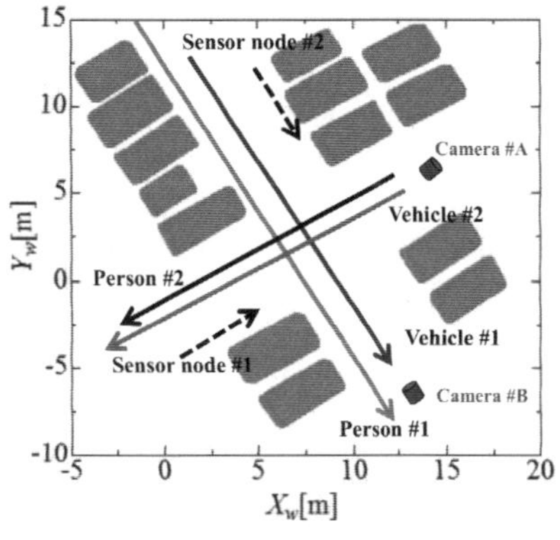

Figure 11. Movement paths of sensor nodes and moving objects

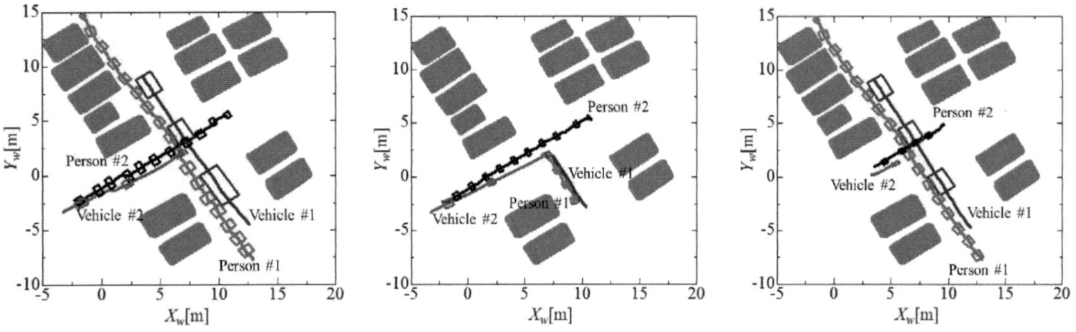

(a) Cooperative tracking (b) Individual tracking by sensor node #1 (c) Individual tracking by sensor node #2

Figure 12. Tracks and sizes of moving objects estimated by cooperative- and individual-tracking methods.

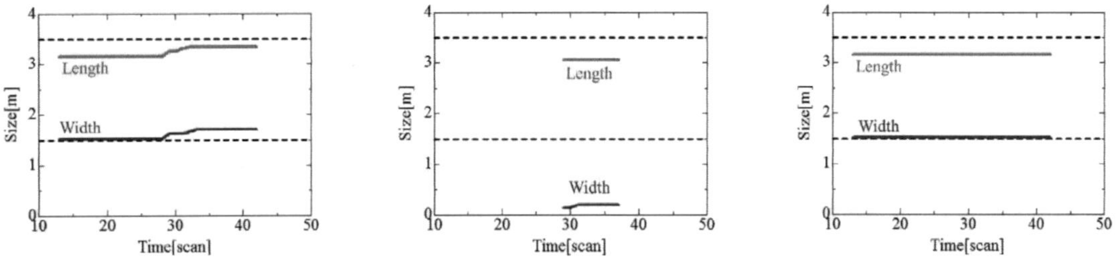

(a) Cooperative tracking (b) Individual tracking by sensor node #1 (c) Individual tracking by sensor node #2

Figure 13. Size of car (vehicle #1) estimated by cooperative- and individual-tracking methods.

TABLE I. PROCESSING TIME OF PROPOSED HIERARCHICAL COOPERATIVE TRACKING

	Maximum [ms]	Minimum [ms]	Mean [ms]
Central server	2.3	0.1	0.8
Sensor node #1	47.9	36.8	41.7
Sensor node #2	49.8	39.3	43.0

TABLE II. PROCESSING TIME OF PREVIOUS CENTRALIZED COOPERATIVE TRACKING

	Maximum [ms]	Minimum [ms]	Mean [ms]
Central server	23.8	2.2	7.9
Sensor node #1	41.5	36.1	38.2
Sensor node #2	45.7	36.5	38.8

the true length and width of the car.

In individual tracking, each sensor node partially tracks moving objects because the objects leave from the sensing area of the sensor nodes and are blocked by parked cars. In contrast, cooperative tracking always tracks the moving objects, because the two sensor nodes share the tracking data. It is clear from Figs. 12 and 13 that cooperative tracking offers better tracking accuracy than individual tracking.

We examined the processing times of the sensor nodes and the central server in the experiment. Tables I and II show the results of our proposed hierarchical tracking scheme and the previous centralized cooperative-tracking scheme, respectively.

In our previous method [25], the central server estimated the poses and sizes of moving objects based on the moving-objects measurements sent from the sensor nodes. Conversely, in our proposed method, the sensor nodes locally estimate the poses and sizes of moving objects, and the central server merges these estimates. Therefore, the hierarchical cooperative-tracking scheme reduces the computational burden on the central server.

VI. CONCLUSIONS

This paper presented a laser-based cooperative-tracking for moving objects using multiple mobile robots as sensor nodes. The moving objects were assumed to be rectangular rigid bodies, and the poses (positions and velocities) and sizes were locally estimated by the sensor nodes. These estimates were then merged by a central server. The effectiveness of such a hierarchical cooperative-tracking method was demonstrated by an experiment in which a car, a motorcycle, and two pedestrians were tracked using two sensor nodes.

In this study, single-layer laser scanners on mobile sensor modes were used to sense the surrounding environments. Multilayer laser scanners provide richer information than single-layer laser scanners and thus improve recognition of the surrounding environment. Research is currently being conducted on the design of cooperative-tracking system using multiple sensor nodes equipped with multilayer laser scanners.

ACKNOWLEDGMENT

This study was partially supported by the Scientific Grants #26420213, the Japan Society for the Promotion of Science (JSPS), and the MEXT-Supported Program for the Strategic Research Foundation at Private Universities, 2014–2018, Ministry of Education, Culture, Sports, Science and Technology, Japan.

REFERENCES

[1] K. O. Arra and O. M. Mozos, Special issue on: People Detection and Tracking, Int. J. of Social Robotics, vol.2, no.1, 2010.

[2] C. Mertz, et al., "Moving Object Detection with Laser Scanners," J. of Field Robotics, vol.30, pp. 17–43, 2013.

[3] T. Ogawa, H. Sakai, Y. Suzuki, K. Takagi, and K. Morikawa, "Pedestrian Detection and Tracking using In-vehicle Lidar for Automotive Application," Proc. of IEEE Intelligent Vehicles Symp. (IV2011), pp. 734–739, 2011.

[4] A. Mukhtar, L. Xia, and T.B. Tang, "Vehicle Detection Techniques for Collision Avoidance Systems: A Review," IEEE Trans. on Intelligent Transportation Systems, vol. 16, pp. 2318–2338, 2015.

[5] H. Cho, Y. W. Seo, B.V.K. V. Kumar, and R. R. Rajkumar, "A Multi-sensor Fusion System for Moving Object Detection and Tracking in Urban Driving Environments," Proc. of Int. Conf. on IEEE Robotics and Automation (ICRA2014), pp. 1836–1843, 2014.

[6] D. Z. Wang, I. Posner, and P. Newman, "Model-free Detection and Tracking of Dynamic Objects with 2D Lidar," Int. J. of Robotics Research, vol.34, pp. 1039–1063, 2015

[7] D. Z. Wang, I. Posner, P. Newman, "What could move? Finding cars, pedestrians and bicyclists in 3D laser data," Proc. of IEEE Int. Conf. on Robotics and Automation (ICRA2012), pp. 4038–4044, 2012.

[8] Z. Yan, N. Jouandeau, and A. A. Cherif, "A Survey and Analysis of Multi-Robot Coordination," Int. J. of Advanced Robotic Systems, vol. 10, pp. 1–18, 2013.

[9] S. Nadarajah and K. Sundaraj, "A Survey on Team Strategies in Robot Soccer: Team Strategies and Role Description," Artificial Intelligence Review, vol. 40, pp. 271–304, 2013.

[10] Z.Wang and D. Gu, "Cooperative Target Tracking Control of Multiple Robots," IEEE Trans. on Industrial Electronics, vol. 59, pp. 3232–3240, 2012.

[11] K. Zhou and S. I. Roumeliotis, "Multirobot Active Target Tracking with Combinations of Relative Observations," IEEE Trans. on Robotics, vol. 27, pp. 678–695, 2011.

[12] A. Ahmad and P. Lima, "Multi-robot Cooperative Spherical-Object Tracking in 3D Space based on Particle Filters," Robotics and Autonomous Systems, vol. 61, pp. 1084–1093, 2013.

[13] P. U. Limaa, et al., "Formation Control Driven by Cooperative Object Tracking," Robotics and Autonomous Systems, vol. 63, Part 1, pp. 68–79, 2015.

[14] C. Robin and S. Lacroix, "Multi-robot Target Detection and Tracking: Taxonomy and Survey," Autonomous Robots, vol. 40, pp. 729–760, 2016.

[15] C. T. Chou, J. Y. Li, M. F. Chang, and L. C. Fu, "Multi-Robot Cooperation Based Human Tracking System Using Laser Range Finder," Proc. of IEEE Int. Conf. on Robotics and Automation (ICRA2011), pp. 532–537, 2011.

[16] N. A. Tsokas and K. J. Kyriakopoulos, "Multi-robot Multiple Hypothesis Tracking for Pedestrian Tracking," Autonomous Robot, vol. 32, pp. 63–79, 2012.

[17] K. Kakinuma, M. Hashimoto, and K. Takahashi, "Outdoor Pedestrian Tracking by Multiple Mobile Robots based on SLAM and GPS Fusion," Proc. of IEEE/SICE Int. Symp. on System Integration (SII2012), pp. 422–427, 2012.

[18] M. Ozaki, K. Kakinuma, M. Hashimoto, and K. Takahashi, "Laser-based Pedestrian Tracking in Outdoor Environments by Multiple Mobile Robots," Sensors, vol. 12, pp. 14489–14507, 2012.

[19] S.J. Julier and J.K. Uhlmann, "A Non-divergent Estimation Algorithm in the Presence of Unknown Correlations," Proc. of the IEEE American Control Conf., pp. 2369–2373, 1997.

[20] F. Fayad and V. Cherfaoui, "Tracking Objects using a Laser Scanner in Driving Situation based on Modeling Target Shape," Proc. of the 2007 IEEE Int. Vehicles Symp. (IV2007), pp. 44–49, 2007.

[21] T. Miyata, Y. Ohama, and Y. Ninomiya, "Ego-Motion Estimation and Moving Object Tracking using Multi-layer LIDAR," Proc. of IEEE Intelligent Vehicles Symp. (IV2009), pp. 151–156, 2009

[22] K. Granstrom, C. Lundquist, F. Gustafsson, and U. Orguner, "Radom Set Methods, Estimation of Multiple Extended Objects," IEEE Robotics & Automation Magazine, pp. 73–82, June 2014

[23] L. Mihaylova, et al., "Overview of Bayesian Sequential Monte Carlo Methods for Group and Extended Object Tracking," Digital Signal Processing, vol. 25, pp.1–16, 2014.

[24] J. Lan and X. R. Li, "Tracking of Extended Object or Target Group using Random Matrix Part I: New Model and Approach," Proc. of 15th Int. Conf. on Information Fusion (FUSION2012), pp.2177–2184, 2012.

[25] M. Hashimoto, R. Izumi, Y. Tamura, and K. Takahashi, "Laser-based Tracking of People and Vehicles by Multiple Mobile Robots," Proc. of the 11th Int. Conf. on Informatics in Control, Automation and Robotics (ICIT2014), pp. 522–527, 2014.

[26] M. Hashimoto, S. Ogata, F. Oba, and T. Murayama, "A Laser-based Multi-Target Tracking for Mobile Robot," Intelligent Autonomous Systems 9, pp. 135–144, 2006.

[27] V. Nguyen, A. Martinelli, N. Tomatis, and R. Siegwart, "A Comparison of Line Extraction Algorithms using 2D Laser Rangefinder for Indoor Mobile Robotics," Proc. of 2005 IEEE/RSJ Int. Conf. on Intelligent Robots and Systems (IROS2009), pp. 1929–1934, 2009.

[28] M. Fischler and R. Bolles, "Random Sample Consensus: A Paradigm for Model Fitting Applications to Image Analysis and Automated Cartography," Proc. of Image Understanding workshop, pp. 71–88, 1980.

[29] P. Konstantinova, A. Udvarev, and T. Semerdjiev, "A Study of a Target Tracking Algorithm Using Global Nearest Neighbor Approach," Proc. of Int. Conf. on Systems and Technologies, 2003.

Verification and Configuration of an Intelligent Lighting System Using BACnet

Daichi Terai, Mitsunori Miki, Ryohei Jonan and Hiroto Aida

Graduate School of Science and Engineering, Doshisha University, Kyoto, Japan
email: dterai@mikilab.doshisha.ac.jp, mmiki@mail.doshisha.ac.jp, rjonan@mikilab.doshisha.ac.jp, haida@mail.doshisha.ac.jp

Abstract—**We have been engaged in the development and research of an intelligent lighting system, which allows both improving comfort of office workers and reducing power consumption. The results of our demonstration experiments in a real office environment showed that an intelligent lighting system is effective. Consequently, it is required to consider the introduction and operation of an intelligent lighting system. In a current intelligent lighting system, it has to be constructed for each office as it needs to be configured by creating a unique network. In addition, lighting control methods differ by vendors and a system needs to be configured differently for each vendor. For these reasons, there are problems in introducing and operating an intelligent lighting system in a large-scale environment. We thus propose an intelligent lighting system configured by using the BACnet communication protocol, which has increasingly spread in recent years, for the purpose of making it easier to introduce and operate an intelligent lighting system. Our verification experiments and simulation showed that an intelligent lighting system configuration using BACnet was effective.**

Keywords–office lighting; lighting control; BACnet.

I. INTRODUCTION

In recent years, many researches have been conducted about the effects of the lighting of the office building on office workers [2]. It is expected that office worker's intellectual productivity, creativity and comfort are improved by working in their preferred light brightness[1].

In addition, energy conservation of office buildings have been promoted. However, in many cases, the lighting is brighter than what the office workers prefer, or unnecessary places are lit. It is possible to reduce the power consumption by improving the lighting environment. Against such a backdrop, we have focused on office lighting environment and proposed an intelligent lighting system that provides illuminance to individual office workers which they request, in minimal power consumption [4]. An intelligent lighting system is recognized as being useful and demonstration experiments have been carried out at 10 locations in Japanese office [3]. When an intelligent lighting system has been introduced, we confirmed that the power consumption is reduced by about 50% compared to the nomal office. In the future, we need to consider the spread of an intelligent lighting system and the operation and deployment in large-scale environment. A current intelligent lighting system is connecting to the dimmable lighting fixtures and a control computer in the network of each office.

Further, the control method of the lighting is different for each vendor. It is necessary to configure the suitable system of lighting control method for each vendor. In addition, with such a system configuration, a control computer is required for each office in which the system is installed. From these things, a current intelligent lighting system has issues in its diffusion to common offices, as well as in its implementation and operation in a large-scale environment. In order to solve these issues, we propose an intelligent lighting system using BACnet, which has been spreading increasingly to office buildings in recent years.

BACnet is a network protocol for office buildings. BACnet provides mechanisms for computerized building automation devices to exchange information, regardless of the particular building service they perform. Constructing an intelligent lighting system via BACnet enables centralized control without dependance on lighting control methods of different vendors. As it eliminates the necessity to install and individually control a control computer in each office, it makes the implementation and operation of an intelligent lighting system easy. Also, BACnet has already been used to control lighting in advanced office buildings. Therefore, it is possible to utilize the lighting apparatus in the office. For that reason, it is not necessary to do the improvement work when when we introduce an intelligent lighting system. This study thus constructed an intelligent lighting system using BACnet that can be implemented in an office building already controlling lighting by BACnet and examined its effectiveness and issues.

In Section 2, we describe an intelligent lighting system that we have proposed. In Section 3, we describe an intelligent lighting system using BACnet. In Section 4, we describes the issues of BACnet type intelligent lighting system. In Section 5, we build the BACnet type intelligent lighting system and perform an operation experiment. In Section 6, we perform a simulation assuming the large scale office environment to solve the issues shows in Section 4.

II. INTELLIGENT LIGHTING SYSTEM

In this section, we describe an intelligent lighting system that we have proposed. First, we describes the outline of an intelligent lighting system. Second, we describes the algorithm of an intelligent lighting system. Finally, we describe the issues of an intelligent lighting system in a large scal office environment.

A. Outline and Configuration of an Intelligent LIghting System

An intelligent lighting system realizes illuminance desired by each worker while minimizing energy consumption by changing the luminous intensity of lighting fixtures. An intelligent lighting system, as indicated in Fig. 1, is composed of a control computer, illuminance sensors, and electrical power meter, with each element connected via a IP network. A Control computer varies the luminance of each lighting fixture using an optimization method on the basis of the illuminance information and the power consumption information. It is thereby possible to achieve the illuminance desired by each worker with low power consumption.

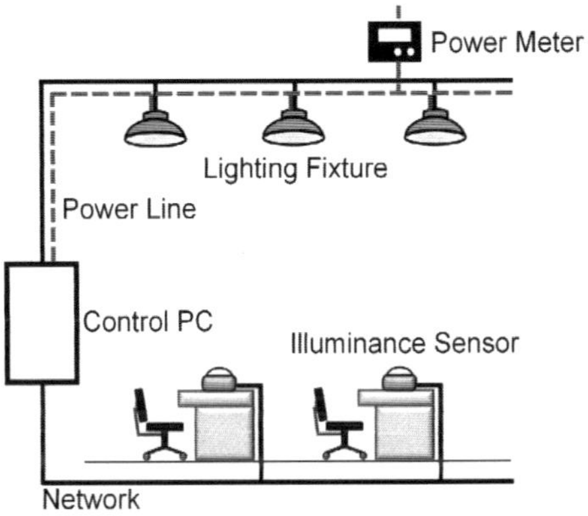

Figure 1. Configuration of The Intelligent Lighting System

B. Control Algorithm of Intelligent Lighting System

In an intelligent lighting system, the ANA/RC(Adaptive Neighborhood Algorithm using Regression Coefficient) which is improved algorithm of SA(Simulated Annealing) for lighting control is used to control luminance intensity for each lighting fixture [5].

It is possible with ANA/RC to provide the target illuminance with minimum power consumption by making luminance intensity for lighting fixtures the design variable and by using the difference between the current illuminance and target illuminance as well as power consumption as objective functions. Furthermore, by learning the influence of each lighting fixture on each illuminance sensor using the regression analysis and by changing the luminance intensity depending on the results, rtly change to the optimal luminance intensity. This algorithm is effective to solve the problem, which the objective function is near monomodal function and changes in real time. The objective function is indicated in the (1).

As indicated in (1), the objective function f consists of power consumption and illuminance constraint. Also, changing weighting factor w enables changes in the order of priority for electrical energy and illuminance constraint. The illuminance constraint brings current illuminance to target illuminance or greater, as indicated by formula.

$$f_i = P + \omega \times \sum_{j=1}^{n} g_{ij} \quad (1)$$

$$g_{ij} = \begin{cases} 0 & (Ic_j - It_j) \geq 0 \\ R_{ij} \times (Ic_j - It_j)^2 & (Ic_j - It_j) < 0 \end{cases}$$

$$R_{ij} = \begin{cases} r_{ij} & r_{ij} \geq T \\ 0 & r_{ij} < T \end{cases}$$

i:lighting ID , j:illuminance sensor ID, P:power consumption [W], ω:weight[W/lx^2]
Ic:current illuminance [lx], It:target illuminance [lx], r:regression coefficient, T:threshold

C. Issues in Introducing the System in a Large Scale Environment

While the effectiveness of an intelligent lighting system has been demonstrated in an actual office, its verification experiments have been all conducted in a small environment (a single office) and following three issues remain in a large-scale environment. The first issue is that lighting control methods in office buildings differ by vendors. For this reason, it is necessary to consider the optimal configuration of an intelligent lighting system for each vendor in implementing it. The second issue is that due to the configuration of a current intelligent lighting system, a control computer is required for each office in which it is implemented and each vendor. Namely, in a large-scale environment, there are problems with the installation cost, installation area, and operating cost of control computer for an intelligent lighting system. The third issue is that improvement work for enabling the individual control of lightings in each vendor's lighting system by using the control computers of an intelligent lighting system is executed for each vendor. This makes the implementation cost of an intelligent lighting system high. Assuming that the number of an intelligent lighting system to be implemented and its scale are expected to expand, it is necessary to solve these issues.

III. An Intelligent Lighting System Using BACnet

In this section, we describe an intelligent lighting system using BACnet. First, we describe the outline of BACnet. Second, we described the configuration of an intelligent lighting system using BACnet. Finally, we described the advantage of an intelligent lighting system using BACnet.

A. Outline of BACnet

BACnet is a communication protocol for networks which is equipped in buildings, and it is a standard protocol specified by ASHRAE, ANSI, ISO, etc. Unlike with common communication protocols, BACnet standardizes control devices connected to it as a set of objects. This method ensures interconnectivity between systems, various vendor's system is able to interconnect the systems which are constructed by different vendors. In recent years, BACnet has been used in an increasing number of office buildings to manage and control centrally systems in those buildings as doing so enables streamlined building management.

B. Outline and Configuration of an Intelligent LIghting System Using BACnet

As noted in Section 2, an intelligent lighting system, as it is has problems in implementing and operating it in a large-scale environment. In order to solve those problems, we propose a new intelligent lighting system using BACnet (hereinafter referred to as "BACnet-type intelligent lighting system").

In recent years, BACnet has been used in an increasing number of office buildings to control lighting in offices centrally. In those buildings, however, individual lighting is not centrally controlled by using BACnet, and lighting in each vendor's system is controlled only by turning them on or off at once. Furthermore, the individual control of lighting in each vendor's system is performed by the method unique to each vendor by using ceiling illuminance sensors or infrared sensors, apart from the central control via BACnet. On the other hand, under the configuration of the new intelligent lighting system proposed by authors, lighting in each vendor's system is individually controlled by the central control computer via BACnet.

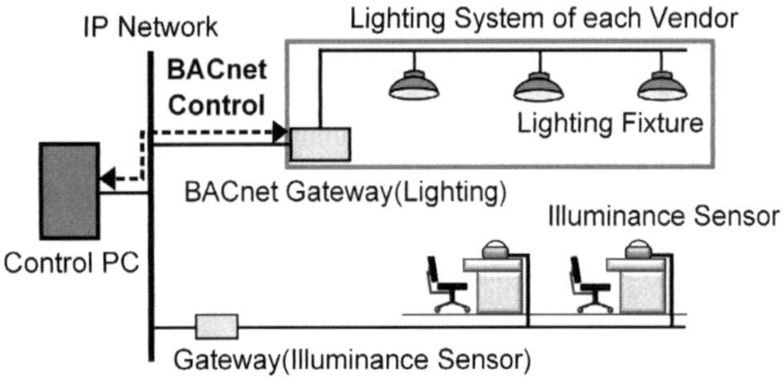

Figure 2. BACnet Type Intelligent Lighting System Configuration

Fig. 2 is the system configuration diagram for the proposed system. The system composed by connecting the control computer of an intelligent lighting system (central control computer) and illuminance sensors to the IP network inside an office building. The control computer controls the lighting individually in each vendor's system in offices on the basis of illuminance values obtained from vendor's systems in offices. As illuminance sensors that can communicate over an IP network are installed, they need not be controlled via BACnet.

C. Advantages of an Intelligent Lighting System

There are two advantages to the BACnet-type intelligent lighting system. The first one is that it makes the design, implementation, and operation of an intelligent lighting system easy. From the system configuration diagram given in Fig. 2, by using BACnet to construct the system, an intelligent lighting system can be implemented and managed just by connecting the central control computer and illuminance sensors to the IP network in a building. Furthermore, as control is performed from outside vendors' systems using a standard protocol, it does not depend on the lighting control system in each vendor's system. In addition, as centralized control is possible, there is no need to install a control computer in each office, which able to reduce cost.

The second advantage is that the proposed system enables realizing the further optimization of an office space by controlling lighting in coordination with air-conditioning and blind instead of controlling it alone. This is because, as the integrated protocol makes different systems interconnectable with each other, various systems can be controlled in coordination with each other. There are, however, two issues with the BACnet-type intelligent lighting system, which are described in the following section.

IV. Issues of an Intelligent Lighting System Using BACnet

In this section, we describe the two issues of intelligent lighting system using BACnet.

A. Limit of the number of possible dimming levels

In controlling a dimmable lighting fixtures, the number of possible dimming levels varies by how lighting is controlled. The lighting control method in an existing intelligent lighting system had 256 dimming levels by 8-bit PWM control or 1000 dimming levels by digital control. On the other hand, lighting control via BACnet has from 0 to 100 dimming levels in accordance with the BACnet protocol. Namely, the BACnet-type intelligent lighting system has 100 dimming levels irrespective of the lighting control methods of vendors. For this reason, the BACnet-type intelligent lighting system offers a smaller number of dimming levels compared with an existing intelligent lighting system. This difference in the number of dimming levels, however, only means the difference in luminance between adjacent levels of approximately 6 cd (for existing 256 levels) and approximately 15 cd (for 100 levels under BACnet) even if with a lighting whose maximum luminance is 1,500 cd. In other words, even on a desktop directly under a lighting, the illuminance value corresponding to one level only differs by approximately 2 lx. Therefore, the same control as exercisable by an existing intelligent lighting system (256 levels) is considered to be possible by 100-level lighting control using BACnet. For the operation verification of the BACnet-type intelligent lighting system, which has a smaller number of dimming levels, it is necessary to construct the BACnet-type intelligent lighting system actually, verify its operation, and compare its operation with that of an existing intelligent lighting system. The verification experiment is described in Section 5.

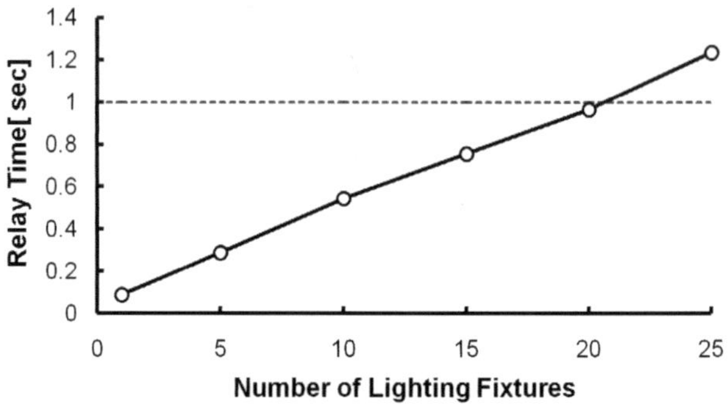

Figure 3. The Time of Sending Control Signal to Starting All Lighting's Luminous Intensity Increase

B. Delay of Lighting Control

As it takes time from transmitting control signals to starting to boost all lightings under lighting control via BACnet, an impact of the delay needs to be examined. AN intelligent lighting system controls lighting at a certain interval (1 or 2 seconds) in consideration of the time required for lighting luminance to stabilize after a sharp change in the lighting environment and a change in lighting luminance. If, however, the lighting control interval becomes longer due to a delay in lighting control, it takes more time for illuminance to converge to the target illuminance. Therefore, it is required to maintain the current lighting control interval (1 or 2 seconds). In consideration of this, the BACnet-type intelligent lighting system sets the lighting control interval to 2 seconds. That is, in order to ensure time for lighting luminance to stabilize (1 second per step), the boosting of all lightings needs to be completed within 1 second. Thus we measured time required to start boosting all lightings by individual lighting control using BACnet. In this measurement, lighting luminance was changed from 40% to 50%.

Fig. 3 shows a graph indicating time from transmitting control signals to lighting fixtures via BACnet to starting to boost all lighting fixtures. The vertical axis denotes time required to boost all lighting fixtures and the horizontal axis denotes the number of lighting fixtures controlled. Fig. 3 shows that individual lighting control using BACnet can only control approximately 20 lighting fixtures per second. In other words, in order to maintain the same convergence time to the target illuminance as the existing intelligent lighting system has, the BACnet-type intelligent lighting system is limited to an office with 20 or less lighting fixtures. This delay in control is considered to be caused by the fact that control signals transmitted by the central control computer control lighting fixtures via various equipments including the IP network (media for BACnet communication), BACnet gateways located on each floor or in each office, and lighting control equipments in each vendor's system.

Groups of 20 lighting fixtures individually controlled per second can be controlled in parallel if they are on different floors or in different offices supporting a BACnet gateway. Time required for controlling this number of lighting fixtures is considered to differ somewhat by the performance of the control PC and BACnet supporting equipments. If all lighting fixtures are controlled at the same luminance instead of being individually controlled, as an effective instruction is sent once to all lighting fixtures then, lighting control via BACnet does not take time in controlling. On the other hand, in an office where the number of lighting fixtures is more than 20, the number of lighting fixtures to be controlled simultaneously needs to be 20 or less in order to control them without a delay. This is covered in Section 6.

V. Verification Experiment of an Intelligent Lighting System Using BACnet

In this section, we build the BACnet type intelligent lighting system and perform an operation experiment. First, we describe the outline and environment of experiment. Second, we describe the result of the experiment.

A. *Outline of Experiment*

This section examines the limitation of dimming levels of lighting fixtures mentioned in Section 4.1. This verification experiment verifies the operation of the BACnet-type intelligent lighting system with a smaller number of dimming levels and examines the difference in performance between this type of system and an existing intelligent lighting system. A BACnet-type intelligent lighting system was constructed to perform verification. This experiment used a BACnet-ready transceiver, gateways, and lighting equipment made by Mitsubishi Electric Corporation as a lighting system inside a vendor's system. Fig. 4 shows a part of system constructed. The gateway is connected to IP network (BACnet communication media) and further to the central control computer.

This experiment was conducted in a small room with 20 or less lighting fixtures (the number of lighting fixtures was 9) in order to verify the operation of a BACnet-type intelligent lighting system. That is, the delay time in lighting control via BACnet does not affect the control time of an intelligent lighting system. This experiment was intended to verify that an intelligent lighting system can operate normally by lighting control via BACnet with a smaller number of dimming levels and to compare its operation with that of an existing intelligent lighting system. An experiment was thus conducted on convergence to the target illuminance to verify the operation of the BACnet-type intelligent lighting system and compare the results of control by an existing intelligent lighting system and the BACnet-type intelligent lighting system.

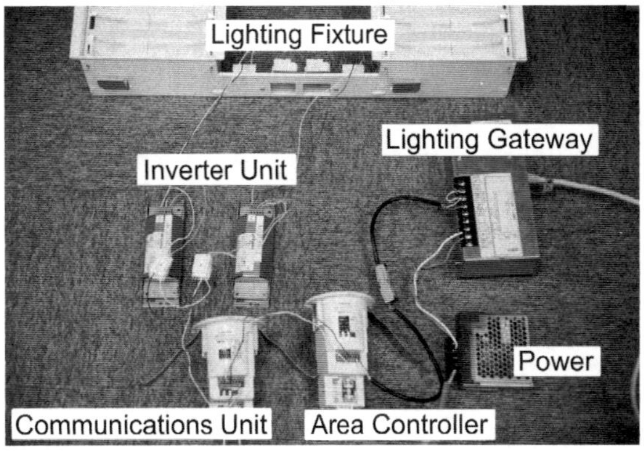

Figure 4. BACnet Corresponding Signal Transceiver of Mitsubishi Electric Corporation

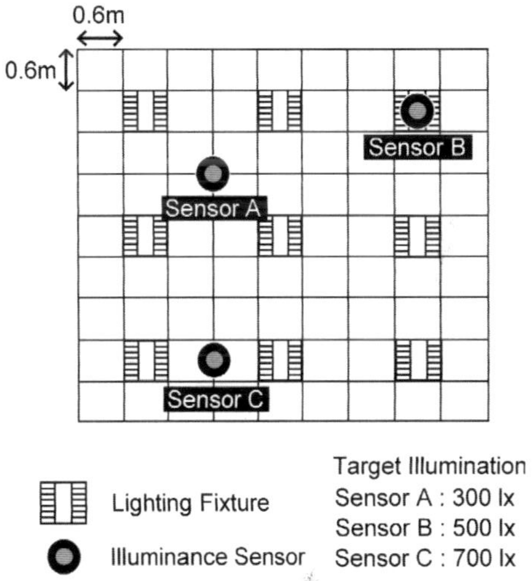

Figure 5. Illuminance Sensor Layout Plan and LED Lighting

The experimental environment was composed of 9 dimmable LED lighting fixtures and 3 illuminance sensors made by Mitsubishi Electric Corporation. Fig. 5 gives the layout of illuminance sensors relative to LED lighting fixtures and the target illuminance of each illuminance sensor. As shown in Fig. 5, the target illuminance of Illuminance Sensors A, B, and C is, respectively, 300 lx, 500 lx, and700 lx.

B. *Result of Experiment*

As stated above, this section shows the result of the target illuminance convergence experiment of the BACnet-type intelligent lighting system and the comparison experiment with an existing intelligent lighting system. First, we indicate the result of the target illuminance convergence experiment.

Fig. 6 shows the result of convergence to the target illuminance by the BACnet-type intelligent lighting system. The horizontal axis denotes the number of steps taken by the BACnet-type intelligent lighting system, and the vertical axis denotes illuminance obtained from illuminance sensors.

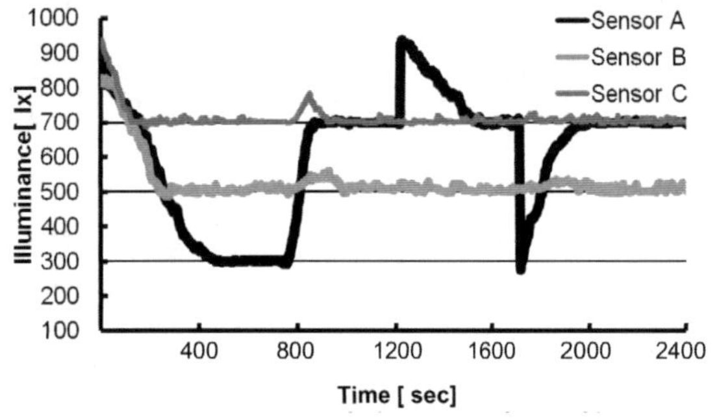

Figure 6. Illumination Convergence of BACnet Type Intelligent Lighting System

As Fig. 6 shows, in approximately 100 steps (approximately 400 seconds) after an intelligent lighting system started up, the illuminance obtained by every illuminance sensors converged to the respective target illuminance.

In this case, approximately 100 steps (approximately 400 seconds) were required to reach convergence. This is because an intelligent lighting system changes the luminance of lighting so slightly as to be not perceived by workers in order not to disturb their work. Furthermore, an intelligent lighting system performs a regression analysis to obtain the positional relationship between lighting fixtures and illuminance sensors during the first 50 steps from its start-up. For this reason, since luminance cannot be efficiently changed during the regression analysis, convergence to the target illuminance takes time. As this regression analysis, however, needs to be performed only at the start-up of the system, convergence to the target illuminance in about 50 steps (approximately 200 seconds) is possible purely in terms of illuminance convergence.

Next, the target illuminance of illuminance sensor A was changed from 300 lx to 700 lx at around 200th step. It is shown that, as a result, the illuminance of the illuminance sensor A converged to 700 lx while the target illuminance of each of other two illuminance sensors was satisfied. It is shown that illuminance convergence in several steps was possible as this was illuminance convergence to greater illuminance and the regression analysis had been completed.

Next, the light of a task light was cast on illuminance sensor A in order to simulate natural light. A sharp rise in the illuminance of illuminance sensor A in approximately 300 steps was due to the light from a task light. As desktops near Illuminance Sensor A became brighter than necessary, an intelligent lighting system lowered the luminance of ceiling lighting fixtures around the illuminance sensor to make illuminance converge to the target illuminance. As a result, illuminance converged to the target illuminance again as shown in Fig. 6. As described above, it was confirmed that an intelligent lighting system was able to operate normally even if lightings were individually controlled by the BACnet-type intelligent lighting system.

Next, in order to verify the performance of the BACnet-type intelligent lighting system, the convergence results of the BACnet-type intelligent lighting system and an existing intelligent lighting system were compared by focusing on illuminance sensor B. Fig 7 shows the graph comparing the histories of target illuminance convergence for both systems. The result of comparison shown in Fig 7 indicates that there

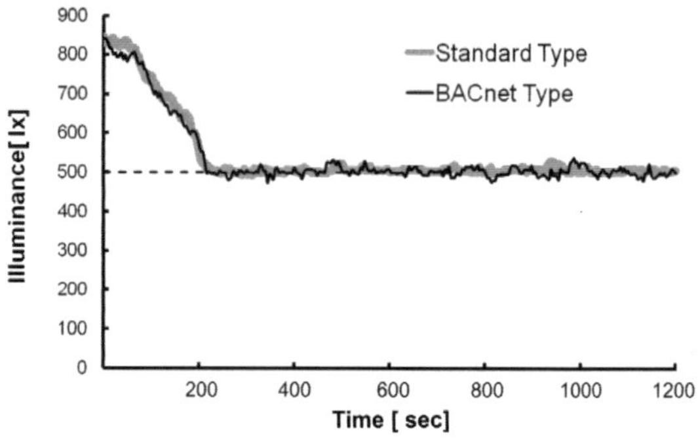

Figure 7. Comparison of Convergence History in The Sensor B

was no difference in the convergence time of illuminance between standard type and BACnet type of an intelligent lighting system. The verification results show that an intelligent lighting system can be normally controlled by individually controlling lighting fixtures via BACnet.

It also turned out that there were hardly any differences between the BACnet-type intelligent lighting system and an existing intelligent lighting system in terms of convergence time and error. It follows from this that the BACnet-type intelligent lighting system can have the same performance as an existing intelligent lighting system and that it is an effective system for making the development, implementation, and operation of an intelligent lighting system easier.

It is, however, necessary to conceive a method to deliver the same performance as an existing intelligent lighting system even if the number of lightings in each office is greater than the number of controllable lightings (20). A method is thus proposed to prioritize lightings in controlling them instead of controlling them in an equal manner. This method is considered to enable controlling the BACnet-type intelligent lighting system without delay in an office in which the number of lighting fixtures is more than 20. This is described in the next section.

VI. Verification of an Intelligent Lighting System Using BACnet in an Large Scale Environment

In this section, we perform a simulation assuming the large scale office environment to solve the issues shows in Section 4. First, we describe the outline of simulation. Second, we describe the result of simulation.

A. *Outline of Simulation*

In this section, we verified using simulation whether an intelligent lighting system to work conventional equivalent without delay in the number of lighting fixtures more than 20 room described in section 4.2. In Fig. 8 shows the simulation environment. The number of dimmable lighting fixtures without delay at the same time in the lighting control using a BACnet is 20 units. Therefore, it is necessary to operate an inttelijent lighting system to control lighting fixtures to below 20 units in an office in which the number of lighting fixtures is more than 20. In this simulation, it compares the realization rate of the target illuminance in a conventional intelligent

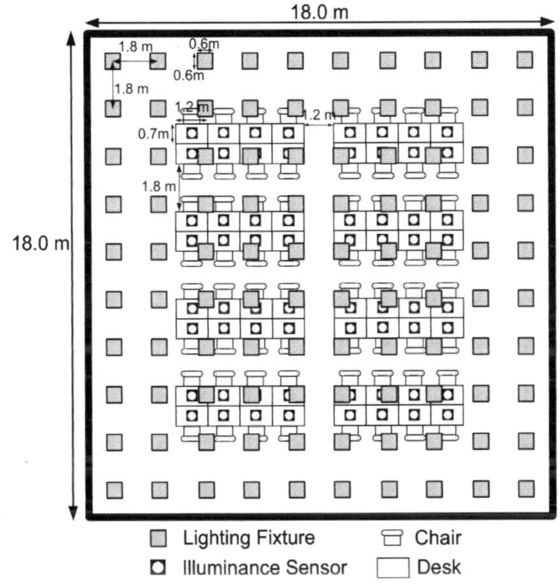

Figure 8. Simulation environment

lighting system without using BACnet (conventional method) and proposed method using BACnet.

Fig 9 shows the simulation environment. Simulation will assume the day from 7:00 to 22:00 and workers come to the office from 7:00 to 8:30 and leave the office from 17: 30 to 22:00 and that number of workers increases and decreases linearly during those periods of time. In addition, workers leave their seat for 1 hour once a day. The target illuminance of each worker is random and ranges from 300 lx to 700 lx.

B. Result of Simulation

In this section, we verify the realization rate of the target illuminance in the proposed method. Realization rate of the target illuminance shall be realization if the illuminance in the range ± 10 % of the realizable illuminance. Realizable illuminance represents a value that illuminance is converged using the conventional method. This is to verify whether even if the target illuminance can not be achieved by physical factors, there is no difference in illuminance to provide the conventional method.

Fig 9 shows the result of simulation. The average of the illuminance realization rate was 91.5 % in the proposed method. As shown Fig 9, even when using the proposed method, it was possible to realize the illuminance as in the conventional method.

In the control algorithm of an intelligent lighting system, each lighting is linked to extract the illuminance sensor is greatly affected by the luminance changes. The number of lighting each illuminance sensor is linked depend on the location, and the illuminance sensor is linked to the lighting of the 4 or 5 lights. Lighting that is linked to the illuminance sensor is luminance change amount increases when the illuminance sensor is significantly different value as the target illuminance. Therefore, If the illuminance sensor doesn't converge to the target illuminance, the target illuminance is achieved by controlling the lighting of 4 or 5 lights near the illuminance sensor. Thus by preferentially control the lighting

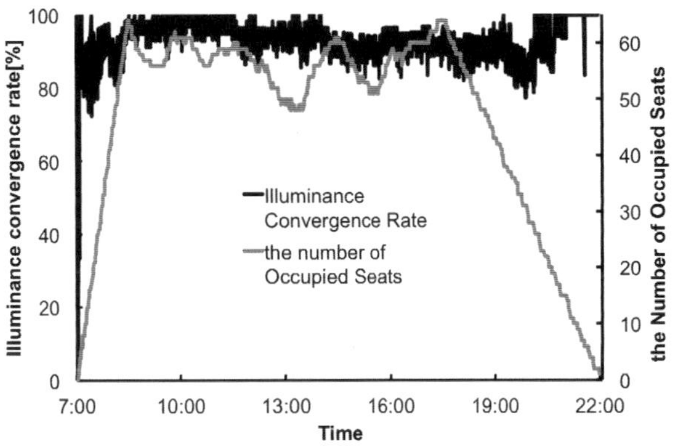

Figure 9. Simulation result

which the luminance changes greately, the proposed method can exhibit conventional method the same performance.

VII. CONCLUSION

A current intelligent lighting system has issues in its diffusion to common offices as well as in its implementation and operation in a large-scale environment. In order to solve these issues, we proposed an intelligent lighting system using BACnet. The result of verification experiment showed the BACnet-type intelligent lighting system can have the same performance as an existing intelligent lighting system and that it is an effective system for making the development, implementation, and operation of the Intelligent Lighting System easier.

REFERENCES

[1] P. R. Boyce, N. H. Eklund and S. N. Simpson, "Individual Lighting Control: Task Performance, Mood and Illuminance", Journal of the Illuminating Engineering Society, vol.29, pp.131-142, 2000

[2] O. Seppanen and W.J. Fisk, "A model to estimate the cost effectiveness of indoor environment improvements in office work", ASHRAE Transactions, vol.111, pp.663-679, 2005

[3] F. Kaku, et al., "Construction of Intelligent Lighting System Providing Desired Illuminance Distributions in Actual Office Environment", Artifical Intelligence and Soft Computing, vol.6114, pp.451-460, 2010

[4] M. Miki, T. Hiroyasu and K. Imazato, "Proposal for an Intelligent Lighting System and verification of control method effectiveness", Cybernetics and Intelligent Systems, 2004 IEEE Conference on, vol.1, pp.520-525, 2004

[5] S. Tanaka, M. Miki, T. Hiroyasu, M. Yoshikata, "An Evolutional Optimization Algorithm to Provide Individual Illuminance in Workplaces", Systems, Man and Cybernetics, 2009. SMC 2009. IEEE International Conference on, vol.1, pp.941-947, 2009

Individual Identification Using EEG Features

Mona F. M. Mursi Ahmed
email: monmursi@yahoo.com

May A. Salama
email: msalama@megacom-int.com

Ahmed Abdullah Hussein Sleman
email: mindhunter74@gmail.com

Electrical Engineering Dept.
Faculty of Engineeringat Shoubra, Benha Univ.
Cairo, Egypt

***Abstract*— Electroencephalography (EEG) is a method of monitoring electrical activity along the scalp by measuring voltage variations resulting from neural activity of the brain. A number of published research papers have indicated that there is enough individuality in the EEG recording, rendering it suitable as a tool for person authentication. In recent years there has been a growing need for greater security for person authentication and one of the potential solutions is to employ the innovative biometric authentication techniques. In this research paper, we investigate the possibility of person identification based on features extracted from person's measured brain signals electrical activity (EEG) with different classification techniques; Radial Basis Functions (RBF), Support Vector Machines (SVM) and Backpropagation (BP) neural networks. The highest identification accuracy was achieved using modular backpropagation neural network for classification.**

Keywords—EEG; identification; biometrics; brain-waves;

I. INTRODUCTION

The brain is one of the largest and most complex organs in the human body. It is involved in every thought and movement produced by the body, which allows humans to interact with their environment, communicating with other humans and objects. It consists of several parts as indicated in Figure 1 [1] and every part is responsible for certain functions and activities.

There are several different methods used for measuring the activity of the brain such as positron emission tomography (PET), functional magnetic resonance imaging (FMRI), Magnetoencephalography (MEG), and EEG.

EEG is the recording of electrical activity along the scalp. EEG measures voltage fluctuations resulting from ionic current flows within the neurons of the brain [2]. In recent years there has been a growing need for greater security for person authentication. Using EEG as a biometric has some advantages over other biometrics like fingerprint and iris image. Unlike other biometrics, we find that brain-waves are almost impossible to be mimicked; even similar activities produce different brain-waves per person, can't be easily stolen – requires special equipment touching the scalp and can't be produced by forcing the person to do so being sensitive to the person's mental state.

EEG data could be collected with single or multi-electrodes device. This depends on the EEG device and the number of signals needed to be processed. All electrode names mentioned hereafter are based on the 10-20 system for EEG electrodes locations [3]. An overview of this system is shown in Figure 2.

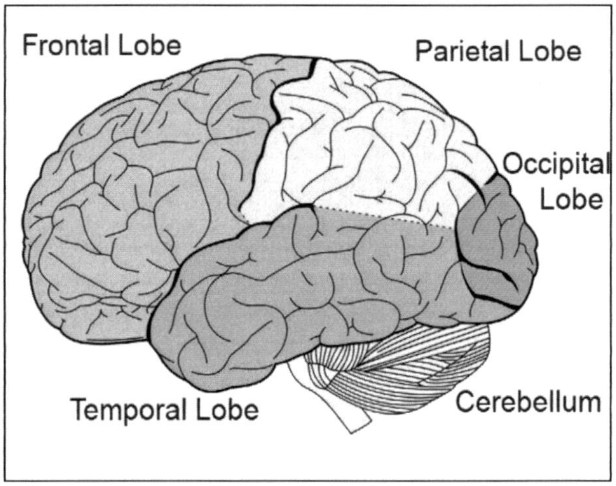

Figure 1. Brain Structure

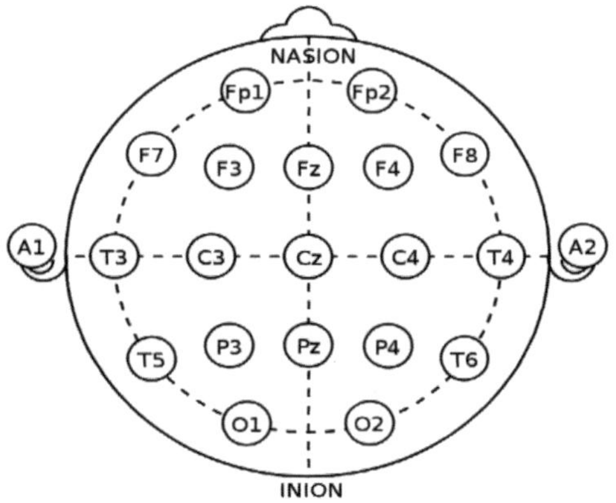

Figure 2. 10-20 Standard System for EEG electrodes locations

One of the potential solutions to identify individuals is to employ the innovative biometric authentication techniques. In this paper, we present a biometric authentication system based on EEG and using offline dataset. After presenting an overview of the previous work (Section II) in this area of research, we first describe the used dataset (Section III) and what the feature vector is composed of. Then we elaborate on using 3 different classification techniques: Radial Basis Function, Support Vector Machines and modular backpropagation neural networks (Section IV). Finally, a conclusion of our work and future work are discussed (Section V). We use MATLAB in all our experiments.

II. PREVIOUS WORK

Different methods have been applied for EEG based person identification. Based on our survey, different methods differ in data collection and Brain Computer Interface (BCI), Preprocessing and feature extraction, and/or classification techniques.

Both Autoregressive (AR) and Power Spectral Density (PSD) were used in [4] and [5] to produce the input feature vector of collected EEG data. AR model of order 19 was selected after testing the orders 10 – 50 as being the optimal order. PSD of frequency range 4 Hz – 32 Hz has been applied and added to the feature vector to produce a final vector of 127 features. A maximum identification accuracy of 97.5% was reported in [4] using K-nearest neighbor (KNN) and Fisher's Discriminant Analysis (FDA) as classifiers while [5] reported a 95.4% accuracy for a consistent person state and 84.5% for persons on diet using same classification techniques. Arguing that autoregressive model coefficients may not have a remarkable effect on the system performance as a feature extraction method, as mentioned in [6], relying only on PSD for the frequency range (5 Hz to 32 Hz) enabled them to an obtain identification accuracy of 90% and 93.7% using dual space Linear Discriminant Analysis (LDA) based on simple regularization and KNN for classification. Independent Component Analysis (ICA) was used in [7] by separating multi-channels EEG data into independent sources. After testing different ICA algorithms using ICALAB Signal Processing Toolbox [8], JADEop ICA algorithm was found to give the highest percentage of identification accuracy (100%) with 5, 10, and 20 subjects using backpropagation neural networks for classification and in order to find the minimum number of relevant channels for person identification, all possible combinations of 4, 3, and 2 channels were tested to find that the best combination of channels to use is {ch1, ch11, ch14} i.e., {FP1, T5, C4}.

Instead of determining a set of features for classification, [9] uses convolutional neural networks to select the most distinctive features that can be used for classification leading to an identification accuracy of 80% with a dataset of 10 subjects that are in a resting state with their eyes open.

III. DATASET AND FEATURE VECTOR

The dataset used in our work is the large version of the KDD Dataset [10], which contains EEG recording for 10 alcoholic subjects and 10 control subjects. A subject's sample is a 1-second recording of EEG. The dataset contains measurements from 64 electrodes placed on the scalp sampled at 256 Hz. Statistics about this KDD dataset are shown in **Error! Reference source not found.**.

TABLE I. KDD Dataset Statistics

Subjects	20 subjects
Sample length	1 second
Samples per subject	60 samples
Dataset size	20 x 60 = 1200 samples

Although this dataset examines EEG correlation of genetic predisposition to alcoholism, we used the EEG data for person identification regardless of the state of the person. First, we derived the feature vector, which had four types:

- AR Coefficients (order 6)
- Spectral Power
- Power Spectral Entropy
- Approximate Entropy

We started by finding out the best combination of features to use by attempting every different valid combination of the suggested features while choosing backpropagation neural networks for classification being it used in many previous of the researches and giving good results. The results indicated in Figure 3 show that using all 4 types of features together gives the best classification accuracy (87%).

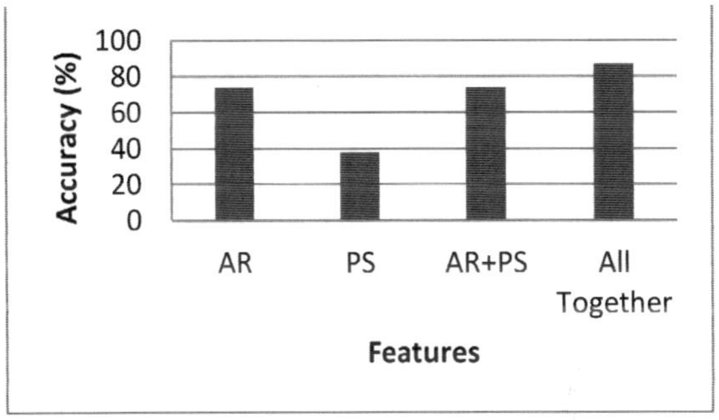

Figure 3. Results of using different combination of proposed features

Principal Component Analysis (PCA) was then applied to reduce the dimensionality of the obtained feature vector to a length of 36 to speed up the classification process.

IV. CLASSIFICATION

Various classification techniques have been experimented. The results of classification using RBF, SVM, and modular backpropagation neural networks are discussed below. In all classification techniques, we use 2/3 of the mentioned dataset for training the test its accuracy against the remaining 1/3 of it.

A. RBF

Different dataset sizes (number of subjects and samples per subject) and different numbers of centers were tested for classification. The results are shown in Table II.

TABLE II. RBF CLASSIFIER RESULTS

#	Subjects	Samples	Max Training Accuracy		Max Testing Accuracy	
			%	*Centers*	%	*Centers*
1	10	10	82	6	50	2
2	10	20	83	6	60	2
3	10	30	82	13	66	5
4	20	10	70	4	38	9
5	20	20	69	9	40	19
6	20	30	68	16	44	18

The best classification accuracy obtained was 44% with the whole dataset and using 18 centers.

B. SVM

Different SVM model types and kernel functions - mentioned in **Error! Not a valid bookmark self-reference.** - were tested.

TABLE III. DIFFERENT SVM MODEL TYPES THAT WILL BE TESTED

Model Types	Weston and Watkins (WW)
	Crammer and Singer (CS)
	Lee, Lin, and Wahba (LLW)
	Guermeur and Monfrini (MSVM2)
Kernel Functions	Linear kernel
	Gaussian RBF kernel
	homogeneous polynomial kernel
	non-homo. polynomial kernel

First, the results of testing different model types with half of the dataset (2/3 of the half for training and 1/3 of the same half for testing) shows that CS model type is the best one to use as indicated in Figure 4.

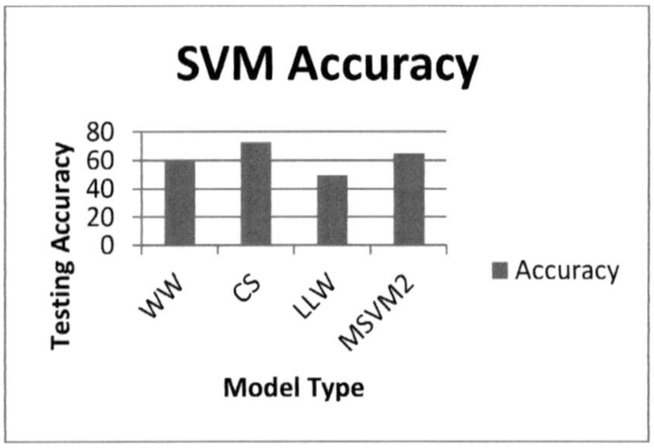

Figure 4. Results of using different SVM model types for classification

Second, testing different kernel functions with the CS model but now with the whole dataset shows that the non-homogenous polynomial kernel function gives the best classification accuracy (63%) as shown in Figure 5.

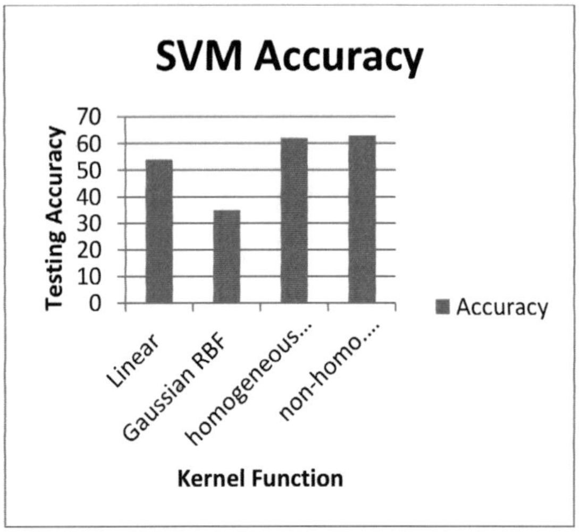

Figure 5. Results of using SVM CS model type with different kernel functions

C. Modular Neural Network

In attempt to achieve better accuracy for identification taking into consideration that being an individual alcoholic affects his EEG measurement, a modular backpropagation neural network is used for classification as follows. A separate BP network, BP2, is used to classify control subjects while BP1 is used to classify alcoholic subjects.

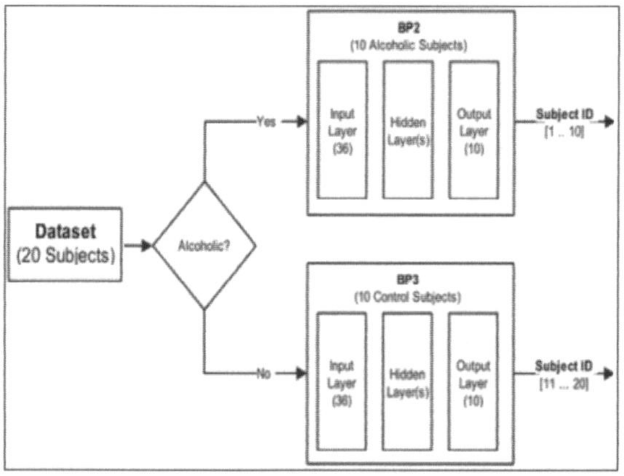

Figure 6. Modular Neural Network design for classification

The property of a subject being alcoholic or not is fed into BP1 to decide onto which network to use to identify that person. The result of the design shown in Figure 6 was 93.5% for the whole dataset.

V. DISCUSSION

After testing different combinations of the four proposed feature types, using them all together was shown to give best accuracies. Moreover, the lower the number of channels used to extract the features, the less the identification accuracy we get, which was the reason we have chosen to use all the 64 channels used in the dataset to extract the proposed features. Finally, after attempting different classification techniques to identify the 20 subjects in the dataset, the best obtained result (93.5%) was using a modular backpropagation neural network at which there is a separate network for identifying alcoholic subjects and another for identifying control subject where the property of being alcoholic or not was a pre-given property to the whole network design. Although being an alcoholic subject has a noticeable effect on its EEG, we found that separating alcoholic and control subjects yielded better identification results – having a single classifier for all subjects yielded accuracies of 44%, 63%, and 87% using RBF, SVM and backpropagation neural network while the modular design yielded 93.5% identification accuracy. The best accuracy we have got (93.5%) is lower than that obtained in [7] while it used a different dataset and used ICA instead of PCA that was used in our system. In comparison to [9] that used Convolutional Neural Networks for classification to get an identification accuracy of 80% with a dataset of 10 subjects, our system outperformed that yielding better 93.5% identification accuracy with a dataset of 20 subjects. Keeping in mind the particularity of the dataset used (EEG of alcoholic/control subjects), we could better improve the accuracy of the final proposed classification network by having alcoholic and control group of subjects each identified by a separate network. The latter piece of information might not be generally available in practice and we would have to use a single network for classification regardless of the subject state.

VI. CONCLUSION

In this paper, it was shown that EEG can be used effectively for individual identification. A combination of 4 feature types were used to construct the feature vector; Autoregressive model of order 6, Spectral Power, Power Spectral Entropy, and Approximate Entropy, which was found to give best accuracy results. Different approaches were proposed that yielded identification accuracies of 44%, 63%, and 93.5% using RBF, SVM and modular backpropagation neural network respectively. In future work, we would consider measuring EEG from volunteering individuals to construct the EEG dataset. Also, the measurements would be performed in different mental states so that it would be more efficient to identify individuals when they are doing certain activities.

REFERENCES

[1] "Structure of the Brain," [Online]. Available: http://controlmind.info/human-brain/structure-of-the-brain. [retrieved: 10, 2016].

[2] E. Niedermeyer and F. H. L. d. Silva, Electroencephalography: Basic Principles, Clinical Applications, and Related Fields., Lippincott Williams & Wilkins, 2005.

[3] "10-20 System," 05 2015. [Online]. Available: http://www.wikiwand.com/en/10-20_system_(EEG) [retrieved: 10, 2016].

[4] F. Su, L. Xia, A. Cai, Y. Wu, and J. Ma, "EEG-based Personal Identification, from Proof-of-Concept to A Practical System," in *International Conference on Pattern Recognition*, 2010.

[5] F. Su, L. Xia, and A. Cai, "Evaluation of Recording Factors in EEG," in *Systems Man and Cybernetics (SMC), IEEE International Conference*, 2010.

[6] F. Su, H. Zhou, Z. Feng, and J. Ma, "A Biometric-based Covert Warning System Using EEG," in *Biometrics (ICB), 5th IAPR International Conference*, 2012.

[7] P. Tangkraingkij, C. Lursinsap, S. Sanguansintukul, and T. Desudchit, "Selecting Relevant EEG Signal Locations for Personal Identification Problem Using ICA and Neural Network," in *Eigth IEEE/ACIS International Conference on Computer and Information Science*, 2009.

[8] "ICALAB for Signal Processing," 05 2015. [Online]. Available: http://www.bsp.brain.riken.jp/ICALAB/ICALABSignalProc/ [retrieved: 10, 2016].

[9] L. Ma, J. W. Minett, and T. Blu, "Resting State EEG-Based Biometrics for Individual Identification Using Convolutional Neural Networks," in *37th Annual International Conference of the IEEE EMBC*, 2015.

[10] KDD Dataset [Online]. Available: https://kdd.ics.uci.edu/databases/eeg/eeg.html [retrieved: 10, 2016].

Species Pattern Analysis in Long-Term Ecological Data Using Statistical and Biclustering Approach

Hyeonjeong Lee
Bio-Intelligence & Data Mining Laboratory, Graduate School of Electronics,
Kyungpook National University,
Republic of Korea
e-mail: dic1224@naver.com

Miyoung Shin
School of Electronics Engineering,
Kyungpook National University,
Republic of Korea
e-mail: shinmy@knu.ac.kr

Abstract—**Analyzing long-term ecological data and appropriate visualization techniques are important for understanding biodiversity mechanisms and predicting effects of environmental changes. In this study, we applied an unconventional approach of finding species pattern, the tendency of species abundance monthly and annually in long-term ecological data, by using statistical and biclustering methods. We tended to find out the similarity between each species after summarizing long-term dataset, and then visualized a correlation matrix and network, which exhibit significant statistical association with each other. For detecting species sets frequently appearing together or showing similar variation in abundance, we also employed a clustering based association mining. For experiments, we used weekly abundance butterfly data from the Environmental Change Network (ECN) in the UK. We could find out how often sets of species show the repeated pattern in long-term species abundance data. The approaches we have described can enable researchers to gain insight of many other relationships like between various species and environmental factors. In addition, combining our methods with detailed analyses or assumptions, such as genetic associations between species and functional subsystems may especially be effective in further analysis.**

***Keywords-** long-term ecological data; association mining; visualization; species set; species abundance pattern.*

I. Introduction

Analyzing long-term ecological data is important for understanding biodiversity mechanisms and predicting effects of environmental changes. Several long-term environmental monitoring projects, such as Terrestrial Ecosystem Research Network (TERN), National Ecological Observatory Network (NEON), and Long-Term Ecological Research (LTER) have attempted to manage and share records of climate and species in international networks [1]-[3]. Accordingly, appropriate data analyses and visualization methods play a significant role in providing more insights into underlying trends in long-term ecological data. Many studies have attempted to search various patterns or trends of species, mostly plotting abundance of individual species across time, without regarding for associations between species [4][5]. In this study, we aim to find sets of species showing similar abundance pattern in long-term ecological data. The rest of this paper is organized as follows. In Section Methods, our proposed methodology is represented. Section Results and Discussion draws the experimental results and discussion.

II. Methods

In this study, we applied an unconventional approach of finding species pattern, the tendency of species abundance monthly and annually in long-term ecological data, by using statistical and biclustering methods. We first summarized the long-term dataset, and then tended to detect the presence of interesting trend by calculating the similarity between each species statistically. After that we visualized a correlation matrix and network, which exhibit significant statistical association with each other.

For detecting species sets frequently appearing together or showing similar variation in abundance, we also employed a clustering based association mining. Association rule mining finds interesting itemsets (in this case, sets of species) that occur frequently in a dataset [6][7], and biclustering clusters rows and columns of a data matrix simultaneously [8]. We applied the BiMax clustering algorithm which is relatively faster than traditional approaches like Apriori algorithm, since Apriori often create too many rules and is time consuming. For performing the BiMax clustering to find associated species under certain condition, we first constructed experimental data in a such way that rows and columns represent species and samples (all months in 18 years), respectively. After that we utilized discretization to assign either 0 (less than average abundance) or 1 (more than average abundance) to each value of monthly species abundance. That is, we only focused on species sets that appearing more than average abundance in every months. By doing so, we could find out interesting species-sets in the rule form of {species set} ⇒ {major month and its abundance percentage}. We also visualized the species sets into species abundance heatmap illustrating monthly and annually repeated abundance pattern of species sets.

III. Results and Discussion

For experiments, we used butterfly data from the Environmental Change Network (ECN) in the UK [9]. Weekly abundance records of 29 kinds of butterflies from

1994 to 2012 are analyzed, showing several possible species sets. We visualized the overall trend of dataset as shown in Fig.1. Correlation between each species in long-term data are shown in Fig.2. The color and width of boxes in Fig.2 (a) and edges in Fig. 2 (b) represent how much two species show the similar abundance in long-term data. The size of node in Fig. 2 (b) is proportional to its degree or the number of edges. We could also find out how often sets of species show the repeated pattern in long-term species abundance data by applying biclustering based association mining on month-species summarized dataset (Fig.3). We represented species sets as association rule forms, for example, {"Red admiral", "Meadow brown"} ⇒ {JUN 5.6%, JUL 61.1%}, which indicates that a species set including two species "Red admiral" and "Meadow brown" is appearing in June and July as a percentage of 5.6 and 61.1, respectively. Fig. 4 illustrates top 100 interesting species sets at a glance. Relationships between species and climate, i.e., temperature and wind speed are however not found in this experiment. Nevertheless, the results show that our approach have general use in finding the species sets for addressing species abundance patterns of interest. It might be showing better performance if more ecological data are accumulated in recent years or near future.

The approaches we have described can enable researchers to gain insight of many other relationships, for example, between various species and environmental factors. In addition, combining our methods with detailed analyses or assumptions, such as genetic associations between species and functional subsystems may especially be effective in further analysis.

ACKNOWLEDGMENTS

This subject is supported by Korea Ministry of Environment (MOE) as "Public Technology Program based on Environmental Policy (2014000210003)."

REFERENCES

[1] Terrestrial Ecosystem Research Network: TERN. [Online]. Available from: http://www.tern.org.au/

[2] M. Keller, D. S. Schimel, W. W. Hargrove, and F. M. Hoffman, "A continental strategy for the National Ecological Observatory Network," The Ecological Society of America, pp. 282-284, 2008.

[3] J. T. Callahan, "Long-term ecological research," BioScience, vol. 34, pp. 363-367, 1984.

[4] S. Benham, "The Environmental Change Network at Alice Holt Research Forest," Forestry Commission, pp. 1-12, 2008, ISSN: 1756-5758, ISBN: 973-0-85538-762-4.

[5] B. J. McGill, et al., "Species abundance distributions: moving beyond single prediction theories to integration within an ecological framework," Ecology letters, vol. 10, pp. 995-1015, 2007, doi: 10.1111/j.1461-0248.2007.01094.x.

[6] A. Mukhopadhyay, U. Maulik, and S. Bandyopadhyay, "A novel biclustering approach to association rule mining for predicting HIV-1-human protein interactions," PLoS One, vol. 7, e32289, 2012.

[7] R. Giugno, A. Pulvirenti, L. Cascione, G. Pigola, and A. Ferro, "MIDClass: Microarray data classification by association rules and gene expression interfals," PLoS One, vol. 8, e69873, 2013.

[8] A. Prelić, et al. "A systematic comparison and evaluation of biclustering methods for gene expression data," Bioinformatics, vol. 22, pp. 1122-1129, 2006.

[9] M. D. Morecroft, et al., "The UK Environmental Change Network: emerging trends in the composition of plant and animal communities and the physical environment," Biological Conservation, vol. 142, pp. 2814-2832, 2009.

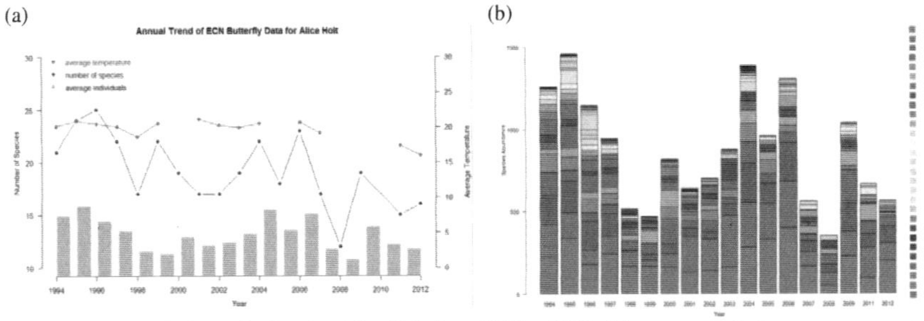

Figure 1. Overall trend of long-term ECN butterfly data for Alice Holt from 1994 to 2012: (a) annual trend of average temperature, number of species, and average individuals of butterflies (b) bar graph of butterfly species abundance and ratio at each year.

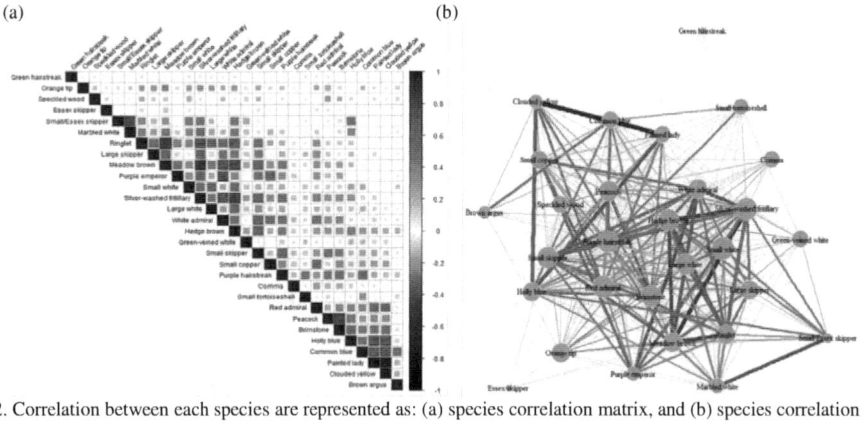

Figure 2. Correlation between each species are represented as: (a) species correlation matrix, and (b) species correlation network.

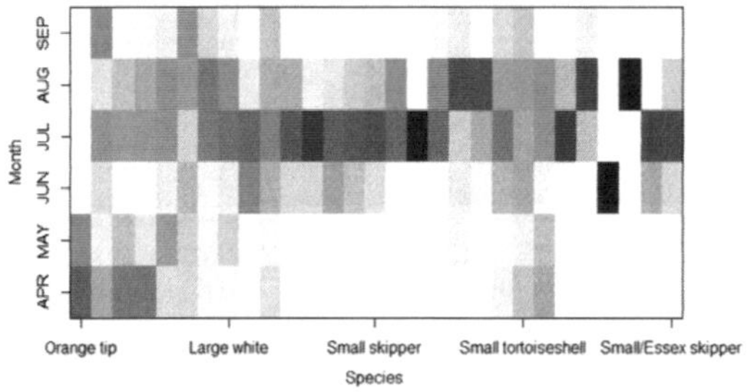

Figure 3. Species-month Summarized data with rows indicating months and columns indicating species of butterflies. The color represents how much individuals of each species are shown in each month on average from 1994 to 2012. This summarized data are used for further analysis.

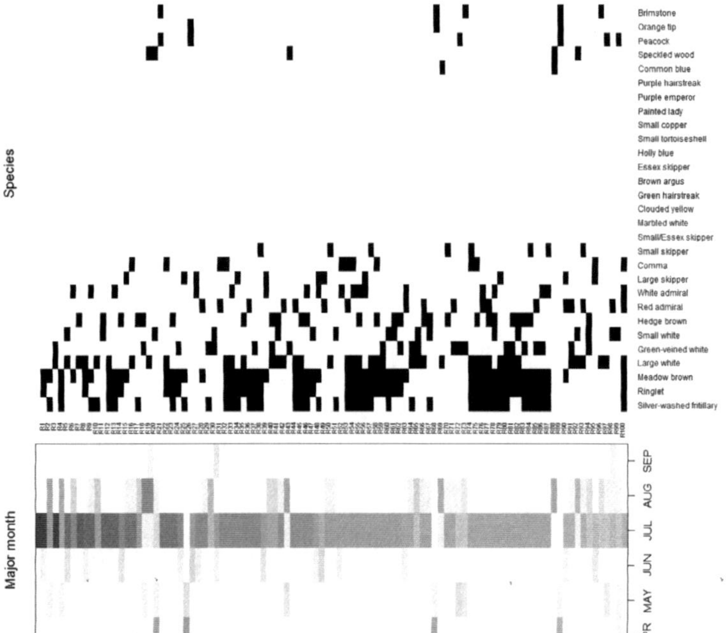

Figure 4. Top 100 interesting species sets frequently shown in each months among the datasets

Towards the Development of Tactile Sensors for Surface Texture Detection

Moritz Scharff, Carsten Behn
Technical Mechanics Group
Department of Mechanical Engineering
Technische Universität Ilmenau
Max-Planckring 12
98693 Ilmenau, Germany
Email: Moritz.Scharff@TU-Ilmenau.de

Joachim Steigenberger
Institute of Mathematics
Technische Universität Ilmenau

Jorge Alencastre
Department of Engineering
Section Mechanical Engineering
Pontifical Catholic University of Peru

Abstract—**Adapting the principle of natural vibrissae, artificial tactile sensors are designed to fulfill the functions: object distance detection, object shape recognition and surface texture scanning. To realize the process of surface texture detection with an artificial sensor, firstly a theoretical approach is done. Replacing the natural vibrissa by an Euler-Bernoulli bending beam and modeling the vibrissa-surface contact with respect to Coulomb's Law of Friction, a quasi-static scenario is performed. In this, the support of the vibrissa moves in a way that the tip of the beam gets pushed. Starting the movement of the support, the tip of the beam is sticking to the surface until the maximal stiction force is reached. It follows a period of sliding and after this a period of stiction again. In dependence on the shape of the beam, the relation between the quasi-static movement and the present coefficient of static friction is analyzed.**

Keywords–Surface detection; vibrissae; friction; mechanical contact; beam; taper.

I. Introduction

Animals, e.g., rodents and cats collect information about the environment in various ways. They could transduce stimulus of light and sound as well as tactile signals. While light and sound are related to eyes and ears, tactile signals are recorded by tactile hairs. The tactile stimulus represents information about the distance to an object, as well as information about the shape and the surface of the object. The capability of the somatosensory system, including, i.a., the vibrissa, of rodents etc. is high and allows to fulfill the mentioned functions excellent. The concept of a vibrissa is already adapted in several technical devices like sensor systems [1]–[3] or robots [4]–[7]. But, the majority of existing concepts could only differ between different surface textures. The task to detect and classify a surface texture with a technical, vibrissa like sensor is still challenging.

The present work focuses on the theoretical, mechanical background of surface texture detection. Section II gives a brief summary about the morphology of a vibrissa, the biological view of surface texture detection and different mechanical approaches concerning this topic. The details of the used mechanical model are introduced in Section III. The results of the numerical simulation are discussed in Section IV and Section V contains an evaluation of the current state together with an outlook.

II. State of the Art

There are different types of vibrissae, e.g., the carpal vibrissae are located at the paws and the mystacial vibrissae around the snout of the animal [8]. Because this study concentrates on mystacial vibrissae, the general term *vibrissa* is used for this kind in this paper.

The base of a vibrissa is embedded in the follicle-sinus complex. The follicle-sinus complex is a sophisticated structure that includes, i.a. muscles, mechanoreceptors and elastical tissue. It enables an active movement and control of the vibrissa. The vibrissa itself is characterized by various properties. From in- to outside, there are three layers of different thickness and material properties. The outer layer is covered with scales. Starting from the base of the vibrissa, its diameter gets smaller. In comparison to the length of the vibrissa, the diameter is much smaller. Along the complete length of the vibrissa there is a natural (unstressed) pre-curvature [9]. With the combination of the follicle sinus complex and the vibrissa, the animal could extract information about the distance, the shape and the surface texture while an object is scanned [10].

The authors of [11] and [12] focus on the behavior of the animal while surface texture detection. Using the example of a rat, it is reported that if the vibrissae get into contact with an object respectively surface, the rat will attempt to minimize the deformation of the vibrissae by changing the position of its head. Out of this state, the rat starts to move its head, following a special motion pattern. The authors of [13] observed that the rat repeats the scan three to five times.

There are different hypothesizes how the animals transduce the surface properties via a tactile stimulus into meaningful information. The *vibrissa resonance hypothesis* relates the frequency of a vibrissa to a vibration that is, e.g., caused by surface roughness while the vibrissa is swept along the surface [14]. Analyzing a simillar idea, the authors of [15] and [16] describe the *kinetic signature hypothesis*. The kinetic signature is a temporal pattern of the vibrissa velocity that contains information about the surface texture. A further theory is formulated in [17]. The authors observed that the frequency and the amplitude of the *Stick–Slip* occurrences vary with different surface textures.

From the mechanical point of view, the theoretical background of these hypotheses is not well analyzed. In [18], the vibrissa is assumed as an *Euler-Bernoulli* beam, with and without a conical beam shape. This model is limited by linear bending theory and not usable for larger deflections. There is no relation between any surface property and the used theory, only a distinction of surfaces is possible. In [19], a flexible probe represents the vibrissa and a spatial distribution of spaces and gaps of macroscopic size the surface. Analyzing this scenario, by using the finite element method and considering only small deflections of the probe, the varying distances of the spaces and gaps are determined. So, the surface texture is classified by a finite number of distance determinations of macroscopic obstacles, this ignores many effects and do not match with smooth surfaces. Determining forces and moments at the base of the virbissa, the initial contact with an object is analyzed in [20]. In this case, the mechanical model adapts various geometrical properties of a real vibrissa, e.g., it considers a tapered and pre-curvature (stress free) shape. The vibrissa is quasi-statical moved, until is touches the object. This model is advanced in [21], where dynamical properties like damping and effects of inertia are added. But, both versions of the model are formulated as multi-body system and do not analyze any surface properties besides the initial contact. Again, supposing that a surface is a spatial distribution of spaces and gaps surface textures are investiagted in [22]. In comparison to [19], there are several differences: The deformation of the straight, conically shaped Euler-Bernoulli beam is a combination of a large deformation (non-linear theory) due to a quasi-static displacement and a small deformation (linear theory) resulting from dynamical effects. Furthermore, the influence of friction (*Coulomb's Law of friction*) is considered in the contact point. Like in the previous models, a relation between surface properties and mechanical is still missing. Only macroscopic effects caused by the spaces and gaps are analyzed.

The authors of [23] form a *first* approach to analyze the connection between surface texture properties and mechanical reactions of the vibrissa in an complete analytical way. Fig. 1

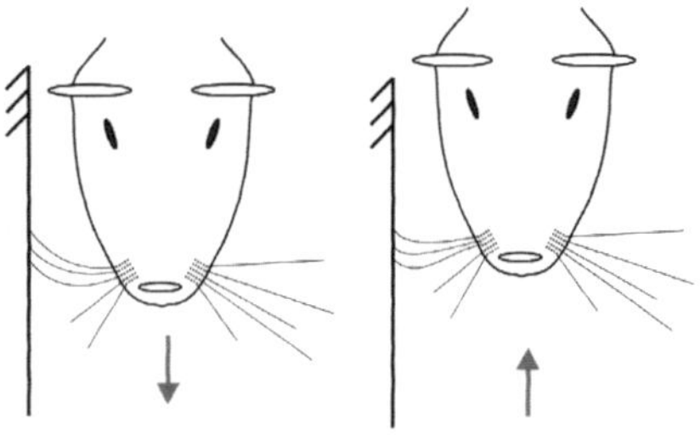

Figure 1. The green arrow represents the direction of motion of the head of the rat.

illustrates the assumed scenario. A rat is scanning a surface by getting in touch with it and moving its head. First, it moves forward (left) and afterwards it starts to move backward (right). The vibrissae are non-stop in touch with the surface, they are sticking to it. While the rat is moving backward the vibrissae gets further deformed, until the coefficient of static friction μ_0 is reached. After this period of sticking, it is sliding until it sticks again. As reaction to the deformation, forces and moments act at the follicle-sinus complex. The follicle-sinus complex is able to encode these stimuli, in a way that the present μ_0 could be determined. Besides that, there is a specific frequency of stick-slip events in dependence on μ_0 if the rat scans a defined length of the surface. This scenario could be adapted for artificial tactile sensor concepts. The following simulations show the described procedure of a surface scan and the influence of a change of the sensor shape with respect to the natural vibrissa morphology.

III. MODELING

Taking over some of the described structural properties in a mechanical model, the following assumptions are done:

- The vibrissa is modeled as an Euler-Bernoulli beam, with respect to large deflections.
- The beam is straight and has a tapered shape.
- The follicle-sinus complex is firstly represented by a clamping.
- The contact between surface and vibrissa is an ideal point contact within the limits of Coulomb's Law of Friction.
- The displacement of the support is quasi-statically.

To simplify the mathematical treatment and to be independent of exact values for, e.g., geometrical parameters or material properties, a nondimensionalization is performed:

$$\text{units:} \quad [\text{length}] = L\,, \; [\text{force}] = \frac{E\,I_{z0}}{L^2}\,, \; [\text{moment}] = \frac{E\,I_{z0}}{L}\,,$$

where L as the length, E as the Young's Modulus, $I_{z0} = \frac{\pi\, d_0^4}{64}$ as the second moment of area and d_0 as the diameter at the base of the beam are the representation of the basic parameters. Using the example of a beam consisting of steel and characterized by the following basic parameters: $E = 2.10 \cdot 10^5$ MPa, $d_0 = 5\,\text{mm}$, $L = 100\,\text{mm}$, than the dimensionless force $f = 10.86$ corresponds to a real force F:

$$F = f \cdot [\text{force}] = f \cdot \frac{E\,I_{z0}}{L^2} = 7000\,\text{N}$$

Furthermore, the beam length is given by L with $L = s \cdot [\text{length}]$, whereby s is the arc length:

$$s \in [0, 1]$$

The tapered shape of the beam is defined by the diameter $d(s)$ as function of s, see Fig. 2:

$$d(s) = -\frac{d_0 - \frac{d_0}{\theta}}{L} s + d_0 \tag{1}$$

with the taper factor θ as quotient of d_0 to the diameter of the tip of the beam d_1:

$$\theta := \frac{d_0}{d_1}$$

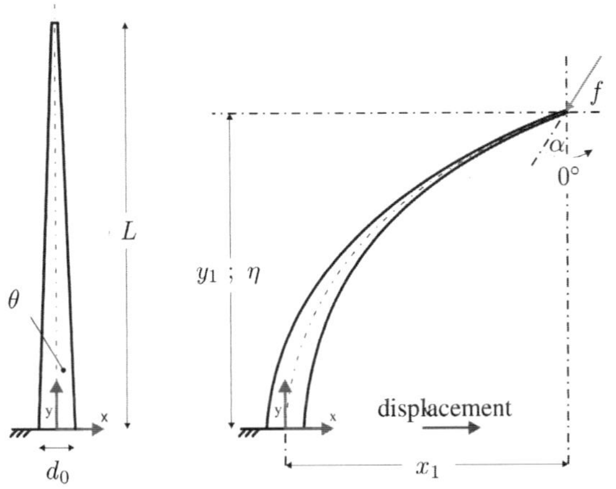

Figure 2. The straight shape of the unloaded tapered beam is shown on the left and the loaded beam on the right.

The position of the tip of the deformed beam is located at (x_1, y_1). The tip is loaded by the force f that is inclined in dependence on the angle of static friction α (counter clockwise counted). The distance between clamping and contact surface is given by η. Using [23] and (1), the set of modeling equations is given by (2):

$$\left.\begin{aligned} x'(s) &= \cos(\varphi(s)) \\ y'(s) &= \sin(\varphi(s)) \\ \varphi'(s) &= \frac{f\,\theta^4}{(\theta\,s - \theta - s)^4}\left[\cos(\alpha)(x(s) - x_1)\right. \\ &\qquad \left. + \sin(\alpha)(y(s) - y_1)\right] \end{aligned}\right\} \quad (2)$$

with boundary conditions (3):

$$\left.\begin{aligned} x(0) &= x_0 \quad ; \quad x(1) = x_1 \\ y(0) &= 0 \quad ; \quad y(1) = y_1 \\ \varphi(0) &= \frac{\pi}{2} \quad ; \quad \varphi(1) = \varphi_1 \end{aligned}\right\} \quad (3)$$

The derivatives of $x(s)$, $y(s)$ and the slope $\varphi(s)$ results in a non-linear system of differential equations (2) and forms together with the boundary conditions (3) a free boundary value problem with two unknown quantities.

To solve this problem, a *shooting method* is used incorporated into MATLAB R2016a. Starting with a guess for the two initial values for the unknown quantities, the resulting system of equations is solved by the *Runge-Kutta-Method 4th order* using MATLAB function *ode45()* and an optimization process begins. This $2d$-optimization is realized by applying the function *fminsearch()* integrated in MATLAB.

IV. Results & Discussion

Using the mentioned algorithm, different simulations are performed. It is assumed that the beam in the initial state is only loaded by a vertical force. Therefore, α is equal to zero. When the quasi-static footpoint displacement starts, α takes negative values and the frictional force loads the tip of the beam, too. Continuing the movement, the beam gets further deformed. When the maximal stiction force is reached respectively passed, the tip of the beam starts to slip.

The traveled distance between the position of the clamping in the initial state and the last state of stiction gives the maximal footpoint displacement $x_{0_{max}}$. So, this group of different states of deformation of the beam is one period of stiction. Fig. 3 shows the movement of the clamping in positive x-direction, with a step size for the footpoint displacement of $x_0 = 0\,(0.001)\,x_{0_{max}}$ and a fixed distance between surface and clamping of $\eta = 0.85$. For a given $\theta = 2$ and $\mu_0 = 0.4$, $x_{0_{max}}$ is determined. At every footpoint position, the forces and moments at the clamping are determined. For a real application, these reactions will be measured with force and torque sensors. Out of these information, it are possible to determine the μ_0 between sensor and surface.

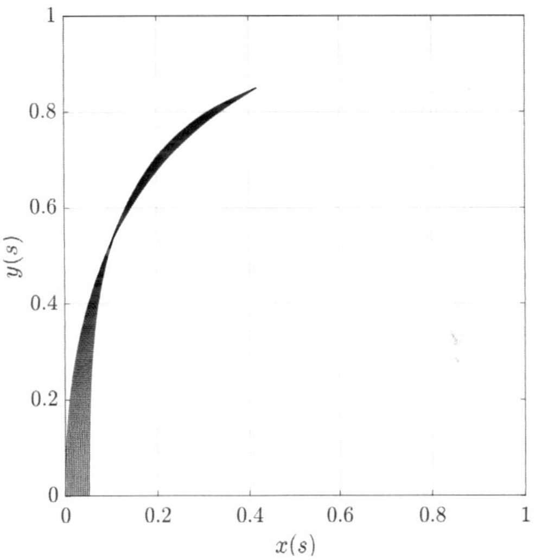

Figure 3. For each position of the clamping the resulting deformed shape of the beam is illustrated.

Like in the previous simulation, the footpoint displacement is set to an increment of $\Delta x_0 = 0.001$ and the distance between surface and clamping to $\eta = 0.85$. The simulation stops after nine stick-slip cycles, see Figs. 4 and 5.

Remark: To describe stick-slip cycles, it is assumed that the period of slipping goes on until the initial condition $\alpha = 0$ is reached again. In this state, a new period of sticking begins.

For each μ_0, a larger θ leads to a larger distance between start and end point of the clamping movement for one period of sticking and also to a stronger deformation of the beam. The comparison of $\mu_0 = 0.3$ and $\mu_0 = 0.4$ indicates a smaller distance of the footpoint displacement and lower deformations of the shape of the beam, for one period of sticking in the case of $\mu_0 = 0.3$.

The distance between start and end point of the footpoint displacement is directly influenced by the values of μ_0 and θ. This influence is important for an artificial sensor. For example, the cylindrical shape ($\theta = 1$) of the beam reacts very sensitive to the footpoint displacement, see Fig. 4a.

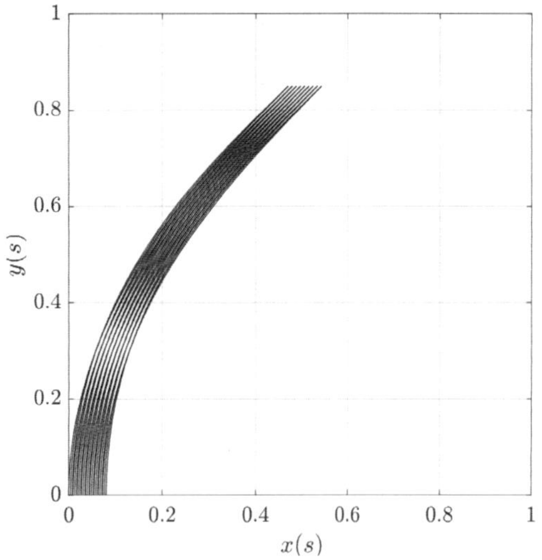

(a) $\theta = 1$

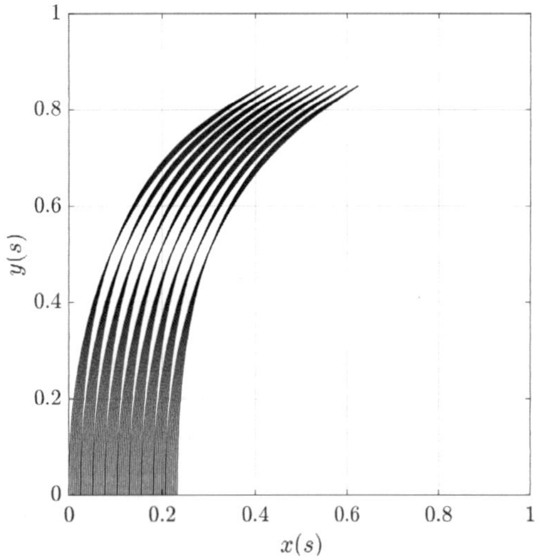

(b) $\theta = 2$

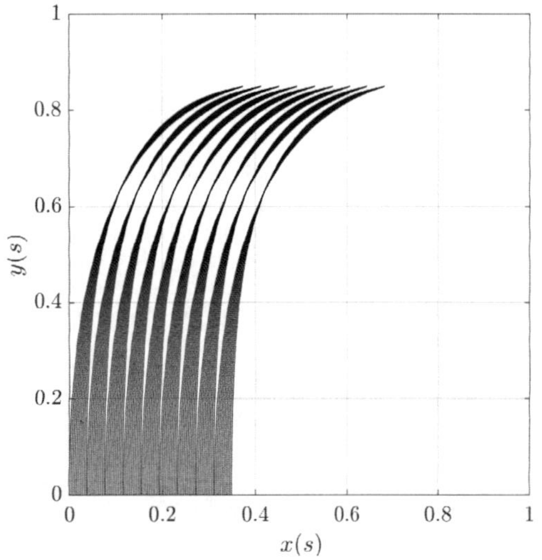

(c) $\theta = 3$

Figure 4. The plots 4a to 4c show the deformed shapes of the beam for different values of θ, a fixed $\mu_0 = 0.3$ and distance between clamping and surface of $\eta = 0.85$.

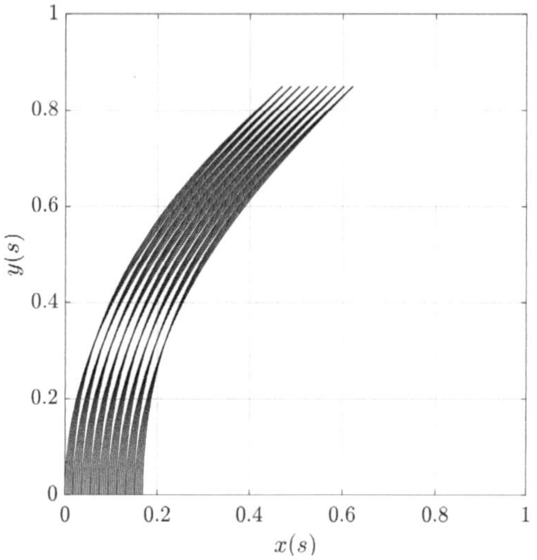

(a) $\theta = 1$

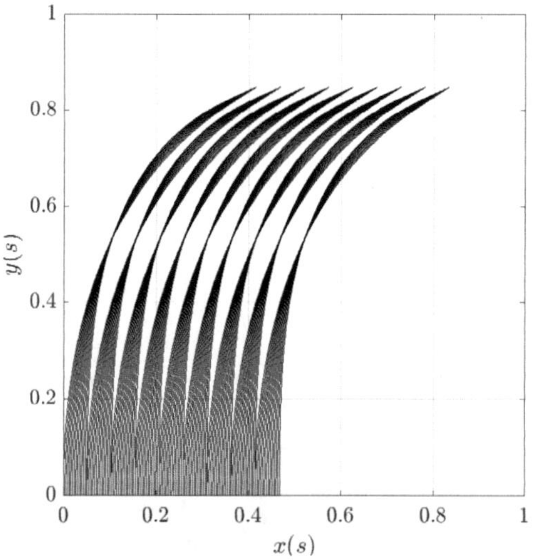

(b) $\theta = 2$

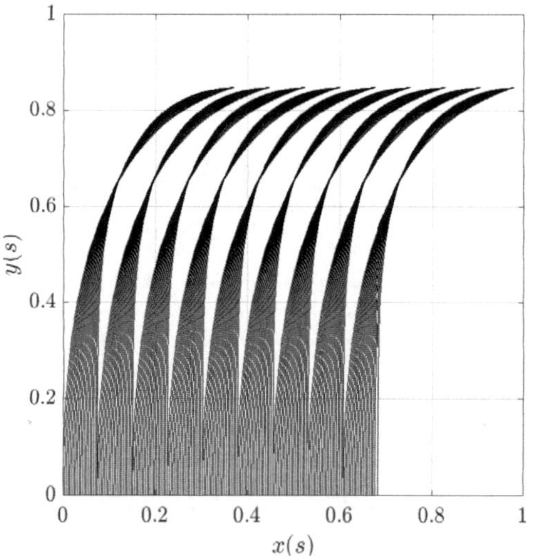

(c) $\theta = 3$

Figure 5. The plots 5a to 5c show the deformed shapes of the beam for different values of θ, a fixed $\mu_0 = 0.4$ and distance between clamping and surface of $\eta = 0.85$.

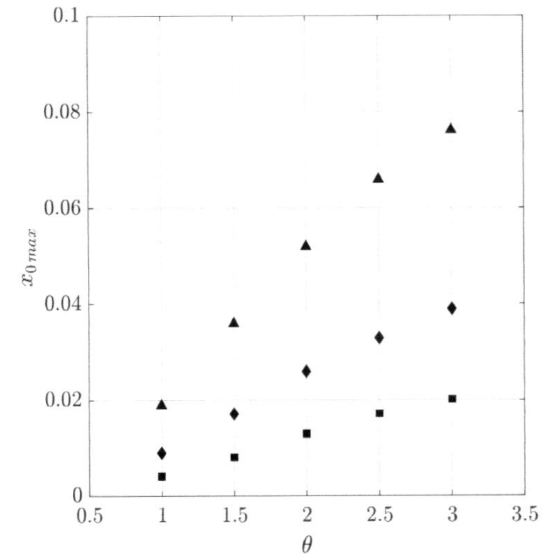

Figure 6. The ordinate shows values for the maximal footpoint displacement of one period of sticking and the abscissa different values of θ.The squares correspond to $\mu_0 = 0.2$, the diamonds to $\mu_0 = 0.3$ and the triangles to $\mu_0 = 0.4$.

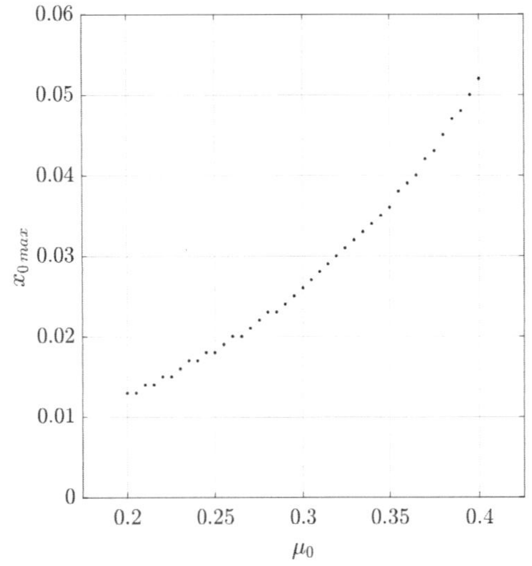

Figure 7. The ordinate shows values for the maximal footpoint displacement of one period of sticking and the abscissa different values of μ_0, with $\theta = 2$.

Already, after a few steps there is a period of sliding. This property is problematic for an artificial sensor because the sensor drive has to be very accurate, else it will be impossible to detect the periods of sticking.

When there is a tapered shape of the beam, this effect is compensated, this is illustrated by the Figs. 4b, 4c and 5b, 5c. A disadvantage of the tapered shape of the beam is the tendency to larger periods of sliding. For an equal quantity of stiction periods, a larger length on a surface has to be scanned. The relation between the maximal displacement of the footpoint $x_{0_{max}}$, θ and μ_0 is summarized for one period of sticking, see Fig. 6. There seems to be a linear correlation between $x_{0_{max}}$ and θ for each value of μ_0. But in contrast, for larger values of μ_0 the effect of a taper shape gets stronger.

This effect is analyzed in Fig. 7. There are different levels of groups of points. Each point is equal to one combination of $x_{0_{max}}$ and μ_0. The different levels are caused by the step size of x_0. The resolution of the step size of x_0 is too large to consider the fine change of the values of μ_0. Based on this result, it is not possible to determine an exact trend of $x_{0_{max}}$ over μ_0, but it seems to be non-linear.

V. CONCLUSION

The presented mechanical model of a vibrissa includes some typical features of the natural vibrissa, like the conical shape. Also, the approach compromises a model for the contact between vibrissa and touched surface. With in the limits of the Euler-Bernoulli beam theory and Coulomb's Law of Friction, the relations between the tapering factor θ, the maximal footpoint displacement $x_{0_{max}}$, the step size Δx_0 and the coefficient of static friction μ_0 are analyzed by numeric simulations of a quasi-static scenario.

Studying one period of sticking, a larger μ_0 leads to a larger footpoint displacement and stronger deformation of the beam. If the maximal friction force is reached respectively passed, the beam starts to slip. Out of the last state before the slipping starts, the current forces and moments, acting on the support of the beam, can be used to determine the present coefficient of static friction. The influence of θ and μ_0 on stick-slip events is analyzed. For the period of slipping, it is assumed that it goes on until the initial state is reached again. The initial state is characterized by the condition that the angle of static friction α is equal to zero.

A larger θ and μ_0 correspond to longer periods of sticking and sliding. So, for the same quantity of stick-slip events, a longer distance on the contact surface becomes necessary. Also, the total number of steps of the footpoint rises. In short: in dependence on θ a larger μ_0 leads to more stick-slip events.

These findings have to be validated by an experiment in future. Especially, the assumption in the context of the period of slipping is critical. An experiment could also show if there is any relation between other surface properties like roughness, the lay or the waviness.

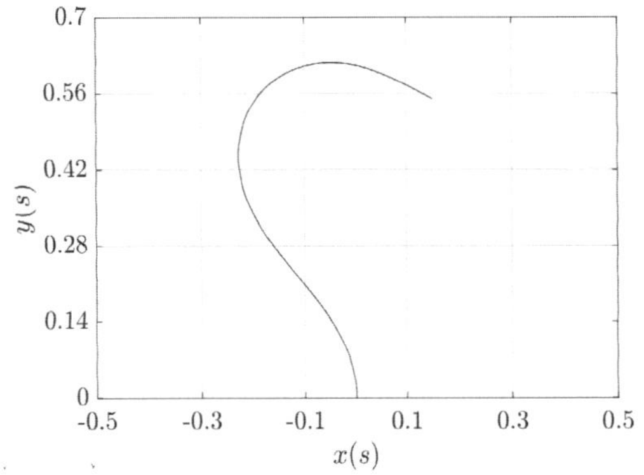

Figure 8. For the values of $x_0 = 0$, $x_1 = 0.15$, $y_1 = 0.55$ and $\theta = 1$ results a deformed shape with a negative value for φ_1.

The mechanical model has to be improved, too. Fig. 8 illustrates the problem. In theory, this result is correct but in reality the shape of the beam penetrates the contact surface. That means the present approach and numeric simulation are not able to analyze every situation in an realistic way. It is necessary to consider a complete contact surface, respectively, line for future simulations.

REFERENCES

[1] M. Lungarella, V. V. Hafner, R. Pfeifer, and H. Yokoi, "An artificial whisker sensors in robotics," in *Proceedings of the IEEE/RSJ International Conference on Intelligent Robots and Systems (IROS) September 30–October 4, 2002, Lausanne, Switzerland.* IEEE, Oct. 2002, pp. 2931–2936, doi: 10.1109/IRDS.2002.1041717.

[2] C. Tuna, J. H. Solomon, D. L. Jones, and M. J. Z. Hartmann, "Object shape recognition with artificial whiskers using tomographic reconstruction," in *Proccedings of theIEEE International Conference on Acoustics, Speech and Signal Processing (ICASSP) March 25–30, 2012, Kyoto, Japan.* IEEE, Mar. 2012, pp. 2537–2540.

[3] F. Ju and S.-F. Ling, "Bioinspired active whisker sensor for robotic vibrissal tactile sensing," *Smart Materials and Structures*, vol. 23, no. 12, pp. 1–9, 2014, doi: 10.1088/0964-1726/23/12/125003.

[4] M. Fend, S. Bovet, H. Yokoi, and R. Pfeifer, "An active artificial whisker array for texture discrimination," in *Proceedings of the IEEE/RSJ International Conference on Intelligent Robots and Systems (IROS) October 27–31, 2003, Las Vegas, USA.* IEEE, Oct. 2003, pp. 1044–1049, doi: 10.1109/IROS.2003.1248782.

[5] D. Kim and R. Möller, "Biomimetic whisker experiments for tactile perception," in *Proceedings of the 3rd International Symposium on Adaptive Motion in Animals and Machines (AMAM) September 25–30, 2005, Ilmenau, Germany.* ISLE, Sep. 2005, pp. 1–7.

[6] S. N'Guyen, P. Pirim, and J.-A. Meyer, *Texture Discrimination with Artificial Whiskers in the Robot-Rat Psikharpax.* Springer Berlin Heidelberg, Jan. 2011, pp. 252–265, Fred, A. et al., Biomedical Engineering Systems and Technologies.

[7] M. J. Pearson, A. G. Pipe, C. Melhuish, B. Mitchinson, and T. J. Prescott, "Whiskerbot: A robotic active touch system modeled on the rat whisker sensory system," *Adaptive Behavior*, vol. 15, no. 3, pp. 223–240, 2007, doi: 10.1177/1059712307082089.

[8] T. Helbig, D. Voges, S. Niederschuh, M. Schmidt, and H. Witte, *Characterizing the Substrate Contact of Carpal Vibrissae of Rats during Locomotion.* Springer International Publishing, Aug. 2014, pp. 399–401, Duff, A. et al., Biomimetic and Biohybrid Systems.

[9] D. Voges et al., "Structural characterization of the whisker system of the rat," *IEEE Sensors Journal*, vol. 12, no. 2, pp. 332–339, 2012, doi: 10.1109/JSEN.2011.2161464.

[10] K. Carl et al., "Characterization of statical properties of rat's whisker system," *IEEE Sensors Journal*, vol. 12, no. 2, pp. 340–349, 2012, doi: 10.1109/JSEN.2011.2114341.

[11] B. Mitchinson, C. J. Martin, R. A. Grant, and T. J. Prescott, "Feedback control in active sensing: rat exploratory whisking is modulated by environmental contact," *Proceedings of the Royal Society B: Biological Sciences*, vol. 274, no. 1613, pp. 1035–1041, 2007, doi: 10.1098/rspb.2006.0347.

[12] R. A. Grant, B. Mitchinson, C. W. Fox, and T. J. Prescott, "Active touch sensing in the rat: Anticipatory and regulatory control of whisker movements during surface exploration," *Journal of Neurophysiology*, vol. 101, no. 2, pp. 862–874, 2009, doi: 10.1152/jn.90783.2008.

[13] G. E. Carvell and D. J. Simons, "Biometric analyses of vibrissal tactile discrimination in the rat," *The Journal of Neuroscience*, vol. 10, no. 8, pp. 2638–2648, 1990.

[14] C. I. Moore and M. L. Andermann, *The Vibrissa Resonance Hypothesis.* CRC Press, 2005, chaper 2, pp. 21–60, Ebner, F., Somatosensory Plasticity.

[15] E. Arabzadeh, E. Zorzin, and M. E. Diamond, "Neuronal encoding of texture in the whisker sensory pathway," *PLoS Biology*, vol. 3, no. (1):e17, pp. 1–11, 2005, doi: 10.1371/journal.pbio.0030017.

[16] J. Hipp et al., "Texture signals in whisker vibrations," *Journal of Neurophysiology*, vol. 95, no. 3, pp. 1792–1799, 2006, doi: 10.1152/jn.01104.2005.

[17] J. Wolfe et al., "Texture coding in the rat whisker system: Slip-stick versus differential resonance," *PLoS Biology*, vol. 6, no. (8):e215, pp. 1–17, 2008, doi: 10.1371/journal.pbio.0060215.

[18] A. E. Schultz, J. H. Solomon, M. A. Peshkin, and M. J. Z. Hartmann, "Multifunctional whisker arrays for distance detection, terrain mapping, and object feature extraction," in *Proccedings of the IEEE International Conference on Robotics and Automation (ICRA) April 18–22, 2005, Barcelona, Spain.* IEEE, Apr. 2005, pp. 2588–2593, doi: 10.1109/ROBOT.2005.1570503.

[19] A. Vaziri, R. A. Jenks, A.-R. Boloori, and G. B. Stanley, "Flexible probes for characterizing surface topology: From biology to technology," *Experimental Mechanics*, vol. 47, no. 3, pp. 417–425, 2007, doi: 10.1007/s11340-007-9046-8.

[20] B. W. Quist and M. J. Z. Hartmann, "Mechanical signals at the base of a rat vibrissa: the effect of intrinsic vibrissa curvature and implications for tactile exploration," *Journal of Neurophysiology*, vol. 107, no. 9, pp. 2298–2312, 2012, doi: 10.1152/jn.00372.2011.

[21] B. W. Quist, V. Seghete, L. A. Huet, T. D. Murphey, and M. J. Z. Hartmann, "Modeling forces and moments at the base of a rat vibrissa during noncontact whisking and whisking against an object," *The Journal of Neuroscience*, vol. 34, no. 30, pp. 9828–9844, 2014, doi: 10.1523/JNEUROSCI.1707-12.2014.

[22] Y. Boubenec, L. N. Claverie, D. E. Shulz, and G. Debrégeas, "An amplitude modulation/demodulation scheme for whisker-based texture perception," *The Journal of Neuroscience*, vol. 34, no. 33, pp. 10 832–10 843, 2014, doi: 10.1523/JNEUROSCI.0534-14.2014.

[23] J. Steigenberger, C. Behn, and C. Will, "Mathematical model of vibrissae for surface texture detection," 2015, preprint No. M 15/03 19 pages, Technische Universität Ilmenau, Germany.

Bagged Extended Nearest Neighbors Classification for Anomalous Propagation Echo Detection

Hansoo Lee
School of Electrical and Computer Engineering
Pusan National University
Busan, Republic of Korea, 46241
Email: hansoo@pusan.ac.kr

Hye-Young Han
Weather Radar Center
Korea Meteorological Administration
Seoul, Republic of Korea, 07062
Email: hyhan98@gmail.com

Sungshin Kim
School of Electrical and Computer Engineering
Pusan National University
Busan, Republic of Korea, 46241
Email: sskim@pusan.ac.kr

***Abstract*—Radar is one of essential and popular devices in weather prediction process because of its wide array of advantages. Unfortunately, the observation results contains lots of unwanted radar signals and they disrupt forecasting process. The representative non-precipitation echoes are permanent, spurious, and anomalous propagation echoes. Among them, the anomalous propagation echo can be a source of severely negative influences in a quantitative precipitation estimation. Therefore, a reliable automatic systems for identifying the anomalous propagation echo is needed. In this paper, we suggest a novel k-nearest neighbors algorithm, by combining the Hamamoto's bootstrap II method and the extended nearest neighbors for improving performance of the classifier. Using the actual appearance cases of the anomalous propagation echo, it is confirmed that the suggested method is better than the k-nearest neighbors and the extended nearest neighbors.**

Keywords*–Extended nearest neighbors; Hamamoto's bootstrap II; Anomalous propagation echo; Weather prediction; Classification.

I. INTRODUCTION

Weather radar is an essential device in weather forecasting process because of its wide array of advantages. For example, the weather radar is capable of near-real time observation with high resolution monitoring over a wide area. Also, the radar can observe development, movement of precipitation areas, and calculate rainfall intensity [1]. By virtue of its advantages, the weather radars are installed in many places of the world and actively involved in various kinds of weather-related fields such as estimating precipitation, disaster management, and so on. Unfortunately, the weather radar has no function to make meteorological observation selectively. Namely, the observation results contains lots of unwanted radar signals inevitably, which disrupt weather prediction process and make low prediction accuracy. Therefore, a quality control process is an indispensable part to remove these unwanted radar signals, so-called non-precipitation echoes [2].

The representative non-precipitation echoes are permanent, spurious, and anomalous propagation echoes. The permanent echoes are caused by mountains, skyscrapers, or other kinds of surface obstacles blocking the radar beam inside the observation area [3]. The spurious echoes are caused by various reasons such as chaff in use of military exercises, jamming by other radars, and so on [4] [5]. And the anomalous propagation echoes are caused by refracted radar beam. It appears in certain conditions of non-standard refraction in the atmosphere when the radar beam passes through air of varying density. The resultant echo represents reflection of the ground or not a meteorological target, and it can be misinterpreted as a heavy precipitation [6].

Considering that the anomalous propagation echo can be a source of significantly negative influences in a quantitative precipitation estimation, a reliable automatic systems for identifying the anomalous propagation echo is needed. Unless, there is a chance to make erroneous calculations of quantitative precipitation estimation or other types of mislead forecasting results.

To classify the anomalous propagation echo in the radar data automatically, several researches using data mining techniques have been studied: fuzzy logic [7] [8]; Bayesian approaches [9] [10]; artificial neural networks [11] [12]; support vector machine [13]; and so on. According to these researches, two important things can be derived. First, the previous researches consider selecting the most efficient classifier for implementing the automated anomalous propagation echo identification system with serious consideration. Second, these researches are focused on a single classification methods.

There are various types of classification methods in machine learning, and used to solve a variety of practical problems. Among them, the k-nearest neighbors [14] algorithm has been a successful choice under many circumstances because of its advantages, such as easy implementation and a good performance without requiring knowledge of a probability distribution function. This decision rule provides a simple nonparametric procedure for the assignment of a class label to the input pattern based on the class labels represented by the k-closest neighbors of the vector [15].

However, the k-nearest neighbors algorithm has some drawbacks. One of representative drawbacks is that k-nearest neighbors algorithm is sensitive to the scale or variance of the distributions of the pre-defined class data. In other words, the nearest neighbors of an unknown sample will tend to be dominated by the class with the highest density [16] [17]. Fortunately, the novel kind of k-nearest neighbors algorithm is suggested, called as the extended nearest neighbors that uses the generalized class-wise statistics [18].

Furthermore, we consider a bagging method in order to improve performance of the extended nearest neighbors. By generating an artificial training samples from the original training samples and obtaining classification results from majority vote, it is possible to improve performance of the extended nearest neighbors algorithm. However, taking into account that small changes in the training sample generated by sampling with replacement do not lead to significantly different classification results of k-nearest neighbors algorithm due to its stable characteristics [19], we consider Hamamoto II bootstrap method [20], which generates a new training sample by resampling and locally transforming.

Consequently, we suggest a novel type of nearest neighbors algorithm by combining Hamamoto's bootstrap II method and extended nearest neighbors in this paper. The rest of the paper is organized as follow. Section 2 explains the bagged extended nearest neighbors with its essential components, extended nearest neighbors and bagging method. And in Section 3, the anomalous propagation echo is briefly elucidated. After that, the experimental results with actual radar observation data are described in Section 4. Finally, the conclusion and future works are showed in Section 5.

II. METHODS

To illustrate the principles of the bagged extended nearest neighbors, fundamental algorithms should be described. This section explains extended nearest neighbors, bagging and Hamamoto's bootstrap II, and the suggested bagged extended nearest neighbors.

A. Extended Nearest Neighbors

k-nearest neighbors algorithm is a popular nonparametric method used for both classification and regression [21]. The input consists of the k closest training samples measured by distance in feature space, and the output indicates a class. An object is classified by a majority vote of its neighbors, with the object being assigned to the class most common among its nearest neighbors.

k-nearest neighbors classifier has remarkable advantages, such as easy implementation, competitive performance, independent of the underlying data distribution, and so on. However, it also has some disadvantages. One of typical weaknesses is that k-nearest neighbors method is sensitive to the scale or variance of distributions of the pre-defined classes. In other words, the nearest neighbors of an unknown object will tend to be dominated by the class with the highest density. This has been a long-standing limitation of the classic k-NN method [16] [17].

In order to solve the problem, a novel nearest neighbors algorithm is suggested, namely extended nearest neighbors. The extended nearest neighbors makes a prediction in a "two-way communication" style using the generalized class-wise statistics T_i^j: it considers not only who are the nearest neighbors of the test sample, but also who consider the test sample as their nearest neighbors [18].

The entire process of the extended nearest neighbors is described in Fig. 1, which considers a two-class problem. The first step of the extended nearest neighbors is applying k-nearest neighbors to the training samples. Let's assume S is an entire training data set, $\mathrm{S} = \mathrm{S}_1 \cup \mathrm{S}_2$, S_1 and S_2 indicate the samples in class 1 and class 2, respectively. Each training sample saves its k nearest neighbors and distances. The second step is getting one sample $\mathbf{z}$ from testing data $\mathbf{Z}$, $\mathbf{z} \in \mathbf{Z}$.

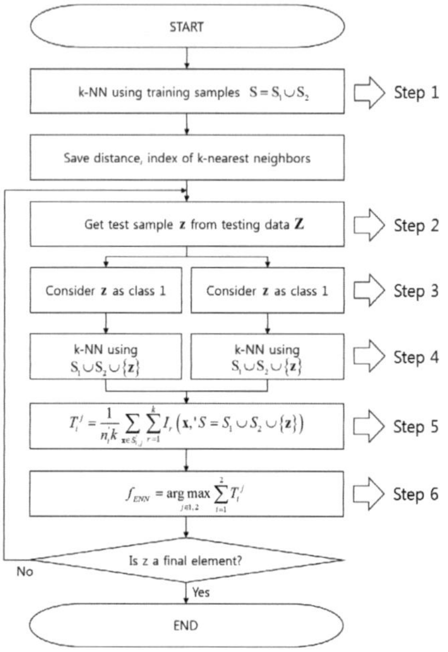

Figure 1. Principles of extended nearest neighbors

The third step is a core step. The obtained testing sample $\mathbf{z}$ is considered as class 1 and class 2, simultaneously and individually. And the fourth step is applying k-nearest neighbors again to union set of the training data set and the testing sample, $\mathrm{S} = \mathrm{S}_1 \cup \mathrm{S}_2 \cup \{\mathbf{z}\}$. In the fifth step, the generalized class-wise statistics is applied to estimate the influences of given $\mathbf{z}$ using (1).

$$T_i^j = \frac{1}{n_i^{'} k} \sum_{\mathbf{x} \in \mathrm{S}_{i,j}^{'}} \sum_{r=1}^{k} I_r \left(\mathbf{x}, \mathrm{S}^{'} = \mathrm{S}_1 \cup \mathrm{S}_2 \cup \{\mathbf{Z}\}\right) \qquad i,j = 1,2 \tag{1}$$

where $\mathbf{x}$ denotes one of samples in $\mathrm{S}_1 \cup \mathrm{S}_2 \cup \{\mathbf{z}\}$. And k is the user-defined parameter of the number of the nearest neighbors. $n_i^{'}$ is the size of $\mathrm{S}_{i,j}^{'}$ and $\mathrm{S}_{i,j}^{'}$ is defined as

$$\mathrm{S}_{i,j}^{'} = \begin{cases} \mathrm{S}_i \cup \{\mathbf{Z}\}, & \text{when } j = i \\ \mathrm{S}_i, & \text{when } j \neq i \end{cases} \tag{2}$$

The indicator function indicates whether both the sample $\mathbf{x}$ and its r-th nearest neighbor belong to the same class as shown in (3)

$$I_r(\mathbf{x}, \mathrm{S}) = \begin{cases} 1, & \text{if } \mathbf{x} \in \mathrm{S}_i \text{ and } \mathrm{NN}_r(\mathbf{x}, \mathrm{S}) \in \mathrm{S}_i \\ 0, & \text{otherwise} \end{cases} \tag{3}$$

where $\mathrm{NN}_r(\mathbf{x}, \mathrm{S})$ denotes the r-th nearest neighbor of $\mathbf{x}$ in S. This equation means for either class, if both the sample $\mathbf{x}$ and its r-th nearest neighbor in the pool of S belong to the same class, then the outcome of the indicator function $I_r(\mathbf{x}, \mathrm{S})$ equals 1; otherwise, it equals 0.

In sixth step, the generalized class-wise statistics are derived. Given two-class classification problem, we have four generalized class-wise statistics: T_1^1, T_2^1, T_1^2 and T_2^2. The extended nearest neighbors classifier predicts its class membership according to the following target function

$$f_{\text{ENN}} = \arg\max_{j \in 1,2} \sum_{i=1}^{2} T_i^j \tag{4}$$

Using (4), the class of unknown sample $\mathbf{z}$ is defined. And it is repeated until all the testing elements are went through the processes, from the second to sixth step.

B. Bagging

Bagging (Bootstrap aggragating) is a type of ensemble method, which uses bootstrap to improve the performance of the classifier [19]. With bootstrap, many new training samples are generated from the original training set. Then, for each bootstrap training set, the test object is classified using k-nearest neighbors. As a result of this process, a series of classification results for each object are obtained. The test object is finally assigned to the class where it was classified by majority vote.

There are several possible setups for bootstrap [19] [22] [20]. The classical bootstrapping uses random sampling with replacement. This was already used with k-nearest neighbors but without satisfactory results due to the "stability" of the k-nearest neighbors [19]. k-nearest neighbors is "stable" because small changes in the training data do not lead to significantly different classification results.

However, Hamamoto's bootstrap method [20] is considerable because all the objects in the original training set participate in creating the bootstrap training set using locally weighted sum as shown in (5). Fig. 2 explains the principles of Hamamoto's bootstrap II method when $k = 3$ in a two-class problem. The given data is separated by class and applied k-nearest neighbors individually including selected sample itself. The generated class data is derived using locally weighted sum, and the process is repeated until all the data is processed. The entire process is shown below.

1) Select one sample $\mathbf{x}_i$ from $\mathbf{X}_c$.
2) Using Euclidean distance, find the r nearest neighbors $\mathbf{x}_{i,1}, \mathbf{x}_{i,2}, \cdots, \mathbf{x}_{i,r}$ from $\mathbf{X}_c$.
3) Compute a new bootstrap sample $\mathbf{x}_i^b$ as a weighted average of r nearest neighbors, including the selected object i itself ($\mathbf{x}_{i,0}$):

$$\begin{aligned} \mathbf{x}_i^b &= \sum_{j=0}^{r} \omega_j \mathbf{x}_{i,j} \\ &= \omega_0 \mathbf{x}_{i,0} + \omega_1 \mathbf{x}_{i,1} + \cdots + \omega_r \mathbf{x}_{i,r} \end{aligned} \tag{5}$$

The weight ω_j is given by

$$\omega_j = \frac{\Delta_j}{\sum_{c=0}^{r} \Delta_c}, \qquad 0 \le j \le r \tag{6}$$

where Δ_j is chosen from a uniform distribution on $[0, 1]$ and $\sum_{j=0}^{r} \omega_j = 1$.
4) Step 1) to 3) are run for all the objects $i = 1, \cdots, l_c$ of $\mathbf{x}_c$, thus obtaining a new matrix $\mathbf{X}_c^b$ for class $c = 1$.
5) Step 1) to 4) are repeated for the other classes $c = 2, \cdots, C$.
6) The bootstrap matrices $\mathbf{X}_c^b$ generated for all the classes are then adjoined to obtain the bootstrap training set $\mathbf{X}^b$ and $\mathbf{X}^b$ is used to classify the test object.
7) Step 1) to 5) are repeated B times and the results are finally combined.

C. Bagged Extended Nearest Neighbors

Combining the Hamamoto's II bootstrap method and the extended nearest neighbors, we suggest the bagged extended nearest neighbor as shown in Fig. 3. The operating principle is as follow. First, the training data is divided into r number of data by Hamamoto's II bootstrap method. The samples inside the divided data is not identical to the original training data, because it is derived by (5). Second, each generated data is applied to extended nearest neighbors classifier respectively. Third, the testing data is applied each trained extended nearest neighbors. Fourth, the results are gathered for voting using (7).

$$f_{\text{Bagged\_ENN}}(\mathbf{X}) = \arg\max_{i} \sum_{j=1}^{r} I(f_{ENN_j}(\mathbf{x}_j) = i) \tag{7}$$

where $I(f_{ENN_j}(\mathbf{x}_j) = i)$ is an indicator function, which derives 1 when they are matched, 0 otherwise.

III. Anomalous Propagation Echo

For ground-based radar propagation at quasi-horizontal beam elevation, the sensitive terms are the vertical gradient of temperature distribution and water vapor. The quantity used to describe the radar beam propagation is the refractivity N, a particular form of the refractive index n used because n is close to unity for the atmosphere [23]. The refractivity can be approximated with the simplified expression in (8)

$$(n-1) \times 10^6 = N = \frac{0.776p}{T} + \frac{3730e}{T^2} \tag{8}$$

where p is the total atmospheric pressure, e is the water vapor partial pressure, and T is the temperature [24].

Let's assume α is the angle of the radar ray with the surfaces of constant N, and let's consider an arc ∂s along a radar ray. And assume that $\partial \alpha$ is the corresponding variation of the angle of the tangent to this ray. The curvature of the ray is C and the radius of curvature ρ with $C = 1/\rho = d\alpha/ds$. From geometrical consideration, the radius of curvature is related to the vertical gradient of refractivity $\partial N/\partial z$ where z is the vertical coordinate, as shown in (9)

$$\frac{1}{\rho} = -\frac{1}{n}\frac{\partial N}{\partial z} \cos\alpha \times 10^6 \tag{9}$$

where ρ in meters if z is in meters. For an elevation close to zero, it can be re-written as shown in (10)

$$\frac{1}{\rho} \approx -\frac{\partial N}{\partial z} \times 10^6 \tag{10}$$

There are four types of propagation: subrefraction, normal refraction, superrefraction, and ducting as follows. [25].

- Subrefraction
  - The radar beam bends less than usual

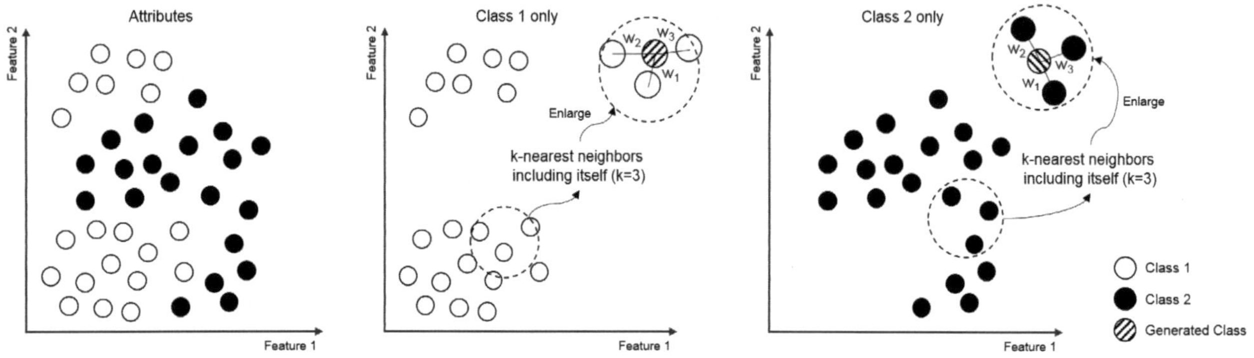

Figure 2. Principles of Hamamoto's bootstrap II method

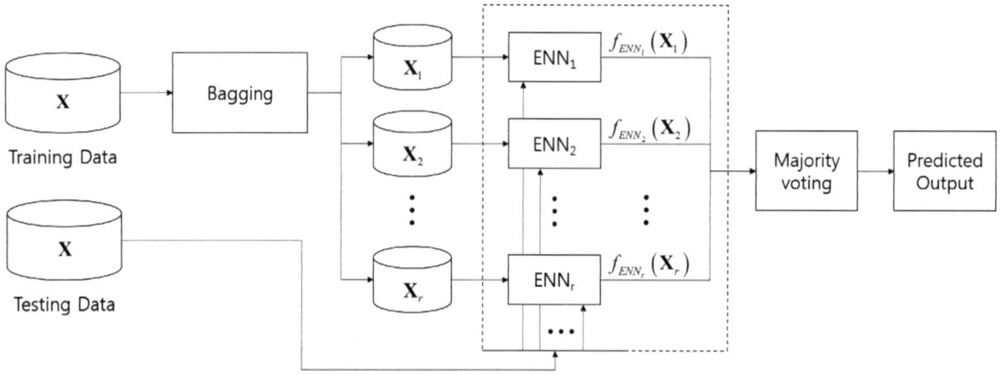

Figure 3. Overall structure of suggested method

- $\frac{\partial N}{\partial z} > 0$
- Normal refraction
  - Considered as standard radar beam trajectory
  - Corresponding to rays bending downward with $\rho \geq \rho_e$
  - $\rho_e \approx 6371km$: the radius of curvature of the Earth's surface
  - $\frac{\partial N}{\partial z} = 0$
- Superrefraction
  - The radar beam bends more towards the ground surface
  - $-0.157 \leq \frac{\partial N}{\partial z} \leq -0.0787m^{-2}$
- Ducting
  - Extreme case of superrefraction
  - The ground surface can be observed as objects in the atmosphere
  - $\frac{\partial N}{\partial z} \leq -0.157m^{-2}$

The subrefraction, superrefraction, and ducting are categorized as the anomalous propagation echoes. The echoes can be lead to erroneous calculations of quantitative rainfall estimation. Therefore, reliable automatic detection and removal of anomalous propagation echoes is one of the essential problems in this area. In the weather forecasting process, there are some complicated expert's knowledge for removing the anomalous propagation echo in the radar data as shown below.

1) The echo moves with near zero Doppler velocity $\approx 0m/s$
2) The maximum altitude of the echo is low
3) The reflectivity distribution is discontinuous in vertical and horizontal way

IV. Experimental Results

In order to evaluate and compare the nearest neighbors classifiers, this paper selected actual appearance cases of the anomalous propagation echo. According to the expert's knowledge described in previous section, it is confirmed that Doppler velocity, reflectivity, and altitude are essential input variables for classification. Therefore, we use five features as inputs in this paper: centroid altitude of the cluster, average reflectivity, maximum reflectivity, average Doppler velocity, and minimum Doppler velocity.

Considering that the suggested system is a type of binary classifier, we applied accuracy, sensitivity and specificity as verifications of each classifier performance as shown in (11), (12), and (13).

$$\text{Accuracy} = \frac{TP + TN}{TP + TN + FP + FN} \tag{11}$$

$$\text{Sensitivity} = \frac{TP}{TP + FN} \tag{12}$$

$$\text{Specificity} = \frac{TN}{TN + FP} \tag{13}$$

TABLE I. PERFORMANCE COMPARISON OF k-NN, ENN, AND BAGGED ENN

		Accuracy		Sensitivity		Specificity	
		Average	StDev	Average	StDev	Average	StDev
k=3	k-NN	0.8075	0.0237	0.8335	0.0325	0.8431	0.0381
	ENN	0.8055	0.0195	0.8258	0.0318	0.8325	0.0397
	BENN	**0.8794**	**0.0075**	**0.8690**	**0.0114**	**0.8638**	**0.0137**
k=5	k-NN	0.8022	0.0183	0.8151	0.0245	0.8195	0.0313
	ENN	0.8029	0.0145	0.8375	0.0355	0.8496	0.0417
	BENN	**0.8593**	**0.0079**	**0.8598**	**0.0106**	**0.8585**	**0.0122**
k=7	k-NN	0.8000	0.0148	0.8205	0.0158	0.8297	0.0195
	ENN	0.8063	0.0238	0.8399	0.0360	0.8520	0.0411
	BENN	**0.8516**	**0.0078**	**0.8560**	**0.0132**	**0.8561**	**0.0156**
k=9	k-NN	0.8051	0.0187	0.8343	0.0302	0.8455	0.0350
	ENN	0.8059	0.0248	**0.8481**	0.0409	**0.8536**	0.0591
	BENN	**0.8399**	**0.0050**	0.8422	**0.0091**	0.8415	**0.0113**

where TP is true positive, TN is true negative, FP is false positive, and FN is false negative. Also, in this paper, the true means the anomalous propagation echo, and the false indicates the non-anomalous propagation echo, respectively.

As shown in Table I, we compared the suggested method, BENN which is a written abbreviation for bagged extended nearest neighbors, to other nearest neighbors classifiers, the k-nearest neighbors and the extended nearest neighbors. To avoid a tie vote, we selected the number of nearest neighbors as odd numbers under 10. In bagged extended nearest neighbors, the number of k for bagging is set to 5. The experiments are conducted 30 times in each case. The average and standard deviation values of accuracy, sensitivity, specificity are shown in Table I.

The bagged extended nearest neighbors shows the best accuracy regardless of the number of k. And it shows the best sensitivity and specificity in most of cases. In $k = 9$ case, the sensitivity and specificity of the bagged extended nearest neighbors are slightly lower than the extended nearest neighbors. However, considering that its standard deviations of those factors are small, it seems more stable than the extended nearest neighbors.

Fig. 4 shows the performances of nearest neighbors classifiers in a form of boxplot: the first, fourth, seventh, and tenth indicates the k-nearest neighbors; the second, fifth, eighth, and eleventh indicates the extended nearest neighbors; and the third, sixth, ninth, and twelfth indicates the bagged extended nearest neighbors, respectively. Fig. 4 (a) describes that the suggested method, bagged extended nearest neighbors, shows impressive accuracy distribution than others when $k = 3$. From Fig. 4 (b) to (d), even though the accuracy of the bagged extended nearest neighbors is gradually decreased, it shows better result than other results. Consequently, it is confirmed that the bagged extended nearest neighbors classifier has the best performance in most cases.

Fig. 5 shows one of graphically described experiment results using the bagged extended nearest neighbors. Fig. 5 (a) indicates a mixed case of precipitation echo and anomalous propagation echo that the upper area is represented as the anomalous propagation echo. Fig. 5 (b) describes the identified anomalous propagation echo, and Fig. 5 (c) shows the radar image without anomalous propagation echo. As a result, it is also confirmed that the bagged extended nearest neighbors can detect the anomalous propagation echo successfully.

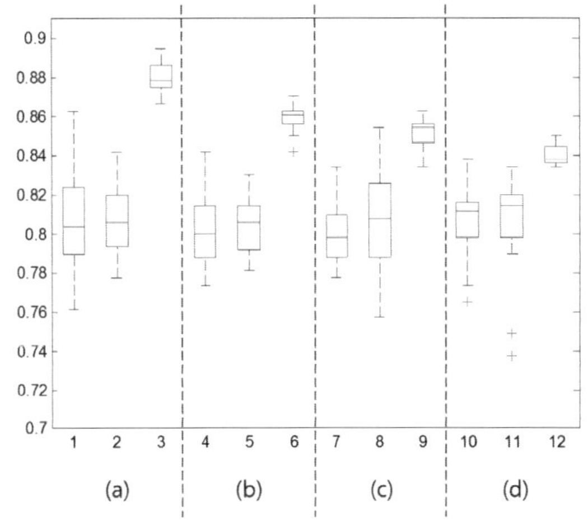

Figure 4. Accuracy comparison of k-NN, ENN, and Bagged ENN methods: (a) k=3, (b) k=5, (c) k=7, (d) k=9

V. CONCLUSION

The anomalous propagation echo occurs frequently and has similar characteristics to precipitation echoes. And it should be removed because it has a serious effect on the quantitative precipitation estimation. Therefore, we suggest a novel nearest neighbors classifier by combining bagging method and extended nearest neighbors for identifying anomalous propagation echo in radar data. Using the actual appearance cases of the anomalous propagation echo, it is confirmed that the suggested method is better than other nearest neighbors classifiers.

In the future work, we will continue to study not only for enhancing classification performance using parameter optimization but also for applying to other representative non-precipitation echoes such as chaff and sea clutter. Furthermore, based on the fact that the classification technique is one of the most important of the data mining method, the proposed method in this paper is expected to be able to perform an important role in various fields.

ACKNOWLEDGMENT

This research was supported by Basic Science Research Program through the National Research Foundation of Korea (NRF) funded by the Ministry of Education (NRF-2014R1A1A2056958).

REFERENCES

[1] S. Jebson, "Fact sheet number 15: Weather radar," 2007.

[2] S. Moszkowicz, G. J. Ciach and W. F. Krajewski, "Statistical detection of anomalous propagation in radar reflectivity patterns," Journal of Atmospheric and Oceanic Technology, vol. 11, no. 4, pp. 1026-1034, 1994.

[3] U. Germann, G. Galli, M. Boscacci and M. Bolliger, "Radar precipitation measurement in a mountainous region," Quarterly Journal of the Royal Meteorological Society, vol. 132, no. 618, pp. 1669-1692, 2006.

[4] Y. H. Kim, S. Kim, H.-Y. Han, B.-H. Heo and C.-H. You, "Real-time detection and filtering of chaff clutter from single-polarization doppler radar data," Journal of Atmospheric and Oceanic Technology, vol. 30, no. 5, pp. 873-895, 2013.

[5] J. Sugier, J. P. du Chatelet, P. Roquain and A. Smith, "Detection and removal of clutter and anaprop in radar data using a statistical scheme based on echo fluctuation," Proceedings of ERAD (2002), pp. 17-24, 2002.

[6] J. Pamment and B. Conway, "Objective identification of echoes due to anomalous propagation in weather radar data," Journal of Atmospheric and Oceanic Technology, vol. 15, no. 1, pp. 98-113, 1998.

[7] Y.-H. Cho, G. W. Lee, K.-E. Kim and I. Zawadzki, "Identification and removal of ground echoes and anomalous propagation using the characteristics of radar echoes," Journal of Atmospheric and Oceanic Technology, vol. 23, no. 9, pp. 1206-1222, 2006.

[8] M. Berenguer, D. Sempere-Torres, C. Corral and R. Sánchez-Diezma, "A fuzzy logic technique for identifying nonprecipitating echoes in radar scans," Journal of Atmospheric and Oceanic Technology, vol. 23, no. 9, pp. 1157-1180, 2006.

[9] J. R. Peter, A. Seed and P. J. Steinle, "Application of a Bayesian classifier of anomalous propagation to single-polarization radar reflectivity data," Journal of Atmospheric and Oceanic Technology, vol. 30, no. 9, pp. 1985-2005, 2013.

[10] S. Rennie, M. Curtis, J. Peter, A. Seed, P. Steinle and G. Wen, "Bayesian Echo Classification for Australian Single-Polarization Weather Radar with Application to Assimilation of Radial Velocity Observations," Journal of Atmospheric and Oceanic Technology, vol. 32, no. 7, pp. 1341-1355, 2015.

[11] R. B. Da Silveria and A. R. Holt, "An automatic identification of clutter and anomalous propagation in polarization-diversity weather radar data using neural networks," IEEE Transactions on Geoscience and Remote Sensing, vol. 39, no. 8, pp. 1777-1788, 2001.

[12] M. Grecu and W. F. Krajewski, "An efficient methodology for detection of anomalous propagation echoes in radar reflectivity data using neural networks," vol. 17, no. 2, pp. 121-129, 2000.

[13] H. Lee, E. K. Kim and S. Kim, "Anomalous Propagation Echo Classification of Imbalanced Radar Data with Support Vector Machine," Advances in Meteorology, vol 2016, pp. 1-13, 2016.

[14] T. Cover and P. Hart, "Nearest neighbor pattern classification," IEEE transactions on information theory, vol. 13, no. 1, pp. 21-27, 1967.

[15] J. M. Keller, M. R. Gray and J. A. Givens, "A fuzzy k-nearest neighbor algorithm," IEEE transactions on systems, man, and cybernetics, no. 4, pp. 580-585, 1985.

[16] S. Har-Pelec, P. Indyk and R. Motwani, "Approximate nearest neighbor: Towards removing the curse of dimensionality," Theory of computing, vol. 8, no. 1, pp. 321-350, 2012.

[17] J. H. Friedman, S. Steppel and J. Tukey, A nonparametric procedure for comparing multivariate point sets, Stanford Linear Accelerator Center Computation Research Group Technical Memo, no. 153, 1973.

[18] B. Tang and H. He, "ENN: Extended nearest neighbor method for pattern recognition [research frontier]," IEEE Computational Intelligence Magazine, vol. 10, no. 3, pp. 52-60, 2015.

[19] L. Breiman, "Bagging predictors," Machine learning, vol. 24, no. 2, pp. 123-140, 1996.

[20] Y. Hamamoto, S. Uchimura and S. Tomita, "A bootstrap technique for nearest neighbor classifier design," IEEE Transactions on Pattern Analysis and Machine Intelligence, vol. 19, no. 1, pp. 73-79, 1997.

[21] J. MacQueen, "Some methods for classification and analysis of multivariate observations," in Proceedings of the fifth Berkeley symposium on mathematical statistics and probability, vol. 1, no. 14, pp. 281-297, 1967.

[22] R. Wehrens, H. Putter and L. M. Buydens, "The bootstrap: a tutorial," Chemometrics and intelligent laboratory systems, vol. 54, no. 1, pp. 35-52, 2000.

[23] F. Mesnard and H. Sauvageot, "Climatology of anomalous propagation radar echoes in a coastal area," Journal of Applied Meteorology and Climatology, vol. 49, no. 11, pp. 2285-2300, 2010.

[24] B. R. Bean and E. Dutton, Radio meteorology, Dover Publications, 1966.

[25] P. Lopez, "A 5-yr 40-km-resolution global climatology of superrefraction for ground-based weather radars," Journal of applied meteorology and climatology, vol. 48, no. 1, pp. 89-110, 2009.

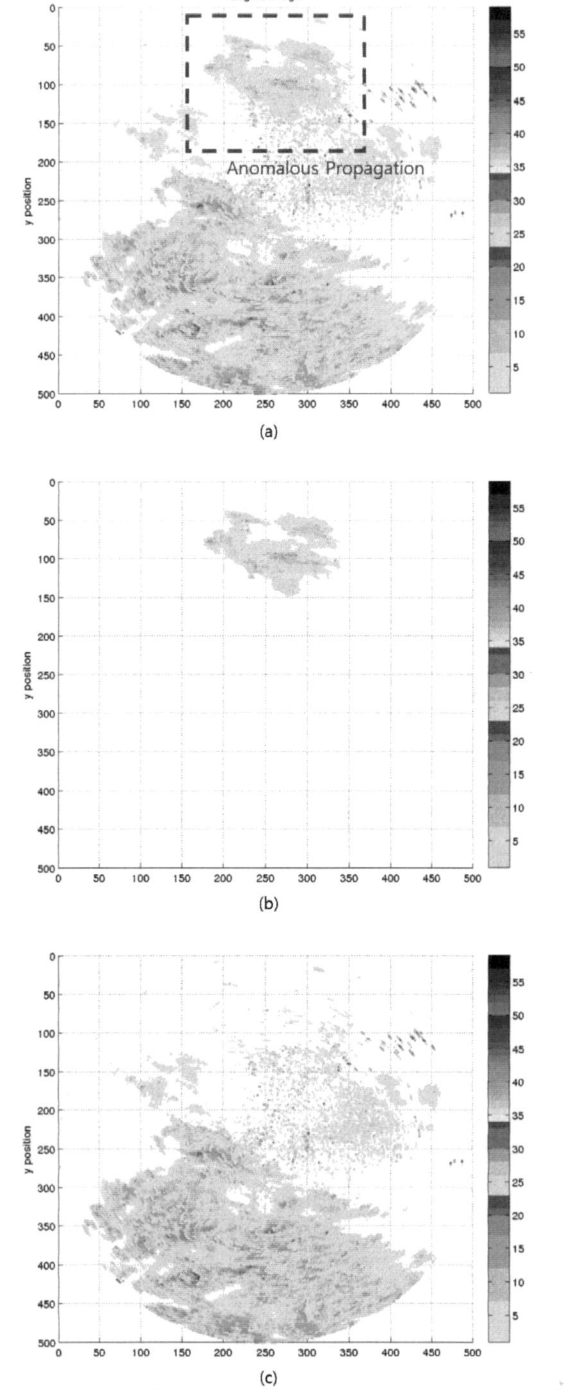

Figure 5. Experimental result: (a) Original radar image, (b) Identified anomalous propagation echo image, (c) Modified radar image

Analysis of Semantically Enriched Process Data for Identifying Process-Biomarkers

Tobias Weller*, Maria Maleshkova*, Martin Wagner†, Lena-Marie Ternes† and Hannes Kenngott†
*Institute of Applied Informatics and Formal Description Methods (KIT), Germany
Email: {tobias.weller,maria.maleshkova}@kit.edu
†Department of General, Visceral and Transplant Surgery, University Hospital Heidelberg, Germany
Email: {Martin.Wagner,Lena-Marie.Ternes,Hannes.Kenngott}@med.uni-heidelberg.de

Abstract—**Intelligent data analysis is used in multiple domains to find new insights in data that has not been known before. Among others, intelligent data analysis is used in the health-care sector to analyse patient and process data for discovering conclusions and supporting the decison-making process. Besides this, Semantic Web Technologies are currently finding new and broader application areas, including the medical domain. We want to use the advantages of semantic technologies in our data analysis for identifying Process-Biomarkers in medical treatment processes. The semantics allow for a more efficient retrieval of arduous and complex requests, which enables a more intelligent data analysis. This allows for identifying and quantifying effects between different performed tasks and events, in medical treatment processes, in a more detailed way. To address this we 1) extracted information from different data sources; 2) applied Semantic Web Technologies on the extracted information and integrated them into a collaborative platform and enriched them with further semantic background knowledge; 3) performed different statistical methods on the semantically enriched data to identify Process-Biomarkers.**

Keywords–Data Analysis;Healthcare;Semantic Technologies; Semantic MediaWiki

I. Introduction

Intelligent data analysis uses techniques from Knowledge Discovery and Data Ming to predict the outcome and find patterns in the data. There are approaches available that extend these existing techniques in order to include semantic information about the data [1][2]. This shows among others that Semantic Web Technologies find their way in new application areas, including the medical domain. Hereby, one can use the advantages of Semantic Web Technologies including data integration, data retrieval and intelligent data analysis [3][4]. Semantics enables a machine-readable description of data. Thereby, context information can be included that can be used by machines and in analysis. We want to contribute towards an intelligent data analysis by using Semantic Web Technologies in the medical domain by presenting our approach for identifying Process-Biomarkers.

In the medical domain, Biomarkers [5] are used as indicators to determine a biological condition and to make clinical estimates. Thus Biomarkers are, among others, used to assess the medical condition of an individual. The National Institutes of Health (NIH) defined in 1998 Biological Markers (Biomarkers) as "a characteristic that is objectively measured and evaluated as an indicator of normal biologic processes, pathogenic processes, or pharmacologic responses to a therapeutic intervention" [5].

Although Biomarkers are well-established in the biomedicine, there are no such indicators for medical treatment processes. Therefore, we want to make a first step towards establishing this term as part of a medical treatment process analysis. We introduce in this context "Process-Biomarkers" and use the term as a process related measurement that reflects a coherence between a performed task and event in a medical treatment process.

The considered problem that we want to tackle is to identify and quantify coherences of performed tasks and events in medical treatment processes. We are interested if specific events, like a surgical complication, occurred during a surgery, effects the length of stay of a patient or if the fact that a patient is smoker influences the occurrence of complications during a surgery. Thus, we aim to identify correlations between different parameters in medical treatment processes.

In order to address this problem, we present an approach to identify correlations in medical treatment processes. For this purpose, we exported process and patient data from a Hospital Information System (HIS) and semantified them. We integrated the data with other available data, such as medical treatment flow schema, ontologies to structure the process and other meta-information, into a collaborative platform. All available information in this collaborative platform can be queried and analyzed in order to identify Process-Biomarkers. This semantically enriched data allows not only to analyse the data itself but also include background knowledge in our data analysis.

We demonstrate the applicability of our approach by modeling a concrete medical treatment process and considering information extracted from the Hospital Information System (HIS) for rectal surgeries. Information include habits of the patient, timestamps of different performed tasks, if different complications occurred during the surgery, loss of blood during the surgery and length of stay in the hospital. Overall, we address the following research questions:

1) How can we use different information from multiple sources?
2) How can we implement an infrastructure necessary for storing, accessing, and processing information?
3) Which methods can we apply to identify Process-Biomarkers and enable intelligent data analyis?

The paper is structured as follows. First, we present state of the art in the field of integrating data and applying Semantic Web Technologies on data in section II. In addition, we will show similar approaches to identify correlations in data. Afterwards, we will introduce the goals and the significance of our contributions in Section III. Section IV introduces our proposed methodology to identify correlations in the medical treatment processes and quantify the results. This Section includes the enrichment of the medical data with semantics, handling different scales of measurements in the data and introducing methods, which we used to identify Process-Biomarkers. We applied multiple methods to identify Process-Biomarkers in order to compare the results and receive multiple views on the process data. After that, we will describe the results of the proposed methodology in Section V. Finally, in Section VI, we will conclude the paper.

II. Related Work

Our approach is addressed by roughly two kinds of work: 1) integrating data from different sources and applying Semantic Web Technologies 2) performing statistical methods to identify correlations in the data.

Previous works covered the aspects of data integration [6][7][8][9]. Hereby, the Biomedical and Live Science domain used Semantic Web Technologies in order to structure and integrate data from different sources [10][11]. Data from different data sources is usually represented in different formats. Therefore, in order to integrate the data from different data sources in one data store, an ETL approach is needed to extract the data and transform them into a common representation. Hereby, approaches that converts the data and structure them in an ontology already exists [12][13]. Usually, the data is only on a local machine available. It is hard for domain experts to contribute to a semantic enrichment. A collaborative approach and providing the possibility to domain experts to enrich the data with their knowledge is preferable. This additional information can be exploited in subsequent data analysis.

For the purpose of capturing and structuring medical treatment processes in BPMN, we had to find suitable ontologies and approaches that allowed to model all considered aspects. There are many ontologies for BPMN 2.0 available [14][15][16] that allows to capture the semantics in processes and include meta-information. However, not all ontologies are online available and follow the latest BPMN 2.0 version. We used a BPMN Ontology from the Data & Knowledge Management (DKM) research unit [17][18] to structure processes. This ontology has a very detailed formalization in OWL 2 DL of the BPMN 2.0 specification. However, we abstract from the ontology and the process modeling, so that the ontology can also be changed in future. This approach enables a flexible representation of knowledge.

Patient related aspects, like, e.g., the type of surgery, were modeled by using OPS Code [19], which provides medical classifications and terminologies for health care systems.

The second aspect that we addressed with our approach is the application of statistical methods on the integrated semantic data in order to identify Process-Biomarkers. In the medical domain are Biomarkers identified by performing experiments, recording the data and applying Student's t-test on the recorded data [20][21][22]. However, we could not perform experiments during a process. Therefore, we used historical data and applied a similar hypothesis test and correlation analysis on the data. Similar approaches were used to identify tumor perfusion related parameters [23], cardiac and metabolic markers in visceral and abdominal subcutaneous [24] and impacts of clinical and genetic features on the clinical progression of Huntington's Disease [25]. In all these approaches could no experiments be performed. They mostly used Spearman's rank correlation to find correlations, however, they did not use other correlation coefficients like, e.g., Kendall in order to compare their results with other statistical methods.

III. Motivation

We want to use Data Science analysis and Semantic Web Technologies and apply them in the medical domain to address our research questions and tackle the raised problems of identifying Process-Biomarkers.

The information, which we will use for Process-Biomarker identification, is distributed across different data sources. In order to use them, we will first integrate the information into one SPARQL store and semantically enrich them with additional information. Afterwards, we can take advantage from the Semantic Web Technologies by efficiently querying the data and easily integrate further information. Our approach to identify Process-Biomarkers is shown in fig. 1. We extracted information such as process data, medical treatment process and patient data. Afterwards, we structured it according to existing ontologies (1). All available information is integrated into a SPARQL store, which was enriched with additional semantic information (2). Afterwards, we queried the data (3) and analyzed it (4) in order to identify Process-Biomarkers.

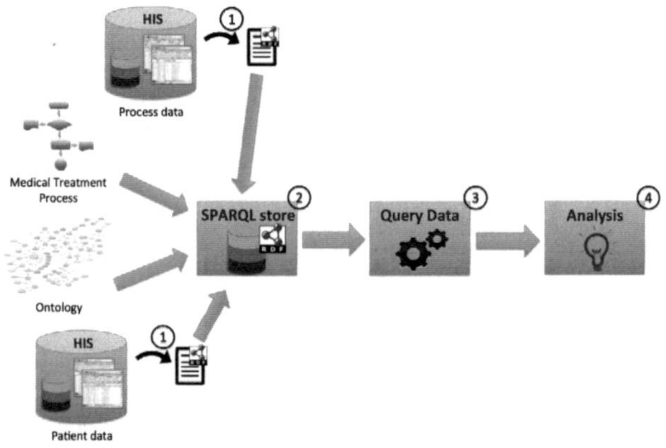

Figure 1. Overview of our proposed approach.

We included semantic information into the SPARQL store, in order to retrieve query results that could not be answered without the new semantic information. Therefore, the knowledge that physicians and nurses are both persons enables to analyse the influence of persons on a process. Retrieving the distinct groups from the raw data sets without semantic is only possible under hard effort. Therefore, the semantic information allow simplified analysis of the data. This kind of knowledge improves the retrieval of data and makes the analysis smarter and therefore more intelligent. The semantic information is machine-readable and can be used by analysis method to comprehend the relations of data for more efficient data analysis.

Another aspect is that the correlations in medical treatment processes are influenced by many different impacts. Thus, the loss of blood during a surgery might depend on the type of surgery, the duration, if complications occurred during the surgery, the age of the patient, and its medical condition. Considering all these impacts in our analysis requires a method to model and query these information.

In addition, the improved retrieval of information allows refined queries. Therefore, we can perform tests for detecting Process-Biomarkers on different abstraction levels on the data. Thus we can use the semantic information and meta-information to refine Process-Biomarkers like e.g the type of surgery does not correlate to the duration of the surgery, but the type of surgery in combination with the surgeon, which performed the surgery, does correlate with the duration of the surgery.

Process-Biomarkers are indicators that help process analysts to comprehend and understand a process and the relations of different process variables and its outcomes in a greater depth. This knowledge is available by the Process-Biomarker, which is a quantified correlation between two performed tasks or events in a medical treatment process. Thus, a process analyst can comprehend the fact that a specific complication during the surgery increases the frequency of blood analysis after the surgery and therefore influences the process. Process-Biomarker also indicates the strength of this coherence. The challenge of finding correlations in processes is the great amount of possible variables might have influences on the process.

In addition, by determining the strength of a coherence, one can state the likelihood and confidence of the Process-Biomarkers. By knowing correlations and confidences of Process-Biomarkers, the prediction of the outcome and the course of a medical treatment process can be improved. Therefore, persons, involved in the medical treatment process, can adapt themselves to possible outcomes and courses. Thus, knowing Process-Biomarkers help process analysts to predict a possible outcome and optimize the likelihood of medical treatment processes to aim a best possible outcome.

Besides predicting future occurrences, Process-Biomarkers can also be used to optimize a process and claim next steps. Therefore, the known correlations and the possible outcome of a medical treatment process can be used to adjust the process for preventing an unwanted outcome. Thus, this knowledge can be used to optimize medical treatment processes according to an established optimization problem.

IV. Semantical Process Correlation Analysis

Our approach is separated into two steps. The first step is the integration of data from multiple sources and the semantic enrichment. This is described in Section IV-A. The second step is the data analysis by exploiting the semantic information, which we integrated into our system. We introduce the methods that we used to identify Process-Biomarkers in Section IV-B.

A. Data Integration and Semantic Enrichment

The first step that we have to tackle is the integration of data from different data sources. We propose a collaborative platform for capturing, annotating and querying process operations, process data, patient data and related process data. Fig. 2 shows a high-level overview of the architecture.

We used a Semantic MediaWiki (SMW) v. 2.3 [26][27] as collaborative platform. This is an extension to MediaWiki [28] that allows for storing information in a structured way and publishes them according to the Linked Data principles [29]. The Semantic MediaWiki performs as the central hub for storing and accessing information. In the backend of the SMW runs an Open Virtuoso Database v. 6.01.3127 that stores the information. Open Virtuoso provides an endpoint that allows

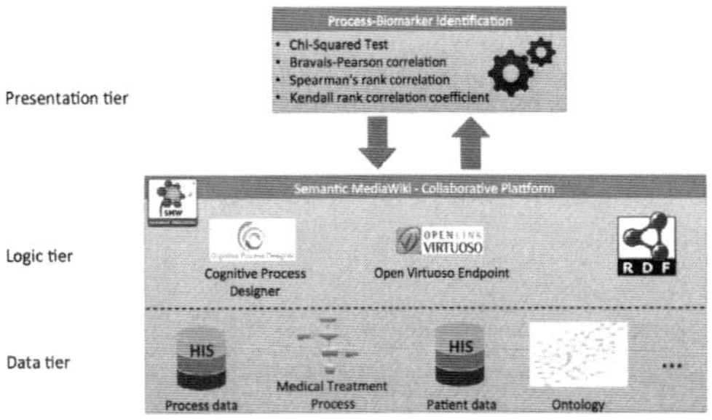

Figure 2. High Level Architecture of the proposed framework.

for querying all available data in the SMW by using SPARQL 1.1 [30]. The advantage of SMW as collaborative platform is the easy access by multiple persons and the easy integration of background knowledge by domain experts through the well-known wiki user interface.

There are two parts of the framework: 1) integrating process data, medical treatment process, patient data and model them with existing ontologies 2) storing and accessing these information semantically in a collaborative platform.

The following data is available for analysis and identifying Process-Biomarkers:

1) Process data from Hospital Information System: The data is stored in a relational database. We exported and structured it according to available ontologies in the medical domain. Available information includes the day of the performed surgery, involved persons, timestamps of each tasks, complications that occurred during the surgery and type of surgery. The data was exported and transformed into RDF.

2) Medical treatment process flows: We modeled the medical treatment process, which shows the sequence of tasks for the considered medical treatment process, by using Business Process Model and Notation (BPMN) as modeling language. The main reason is that BPMN is proposed as a standard by the Object Management Group (OMG) in 2008. The current available version of BPMN is 2.0.2, published in ISO/IEC 19510 [31]. In addition, there are many workflow engines, written in multiple programming languages, available that allows the execution of the processes like, e.g., Oracle Business Process Management Suite [32], Camunda [33] and Sydle [34]. We used an existing ontology from the Data & Knowledge Management (DKM) research unit [17][18]. to structure the information.

3) Patient data from Hospital Information System: This information includes general patient information like gender, weight and age, as well as patient specific information like the habits (e.g. smoker), former diseases (hepatic diseases) and the length of stay in the hospital. It is stored in a relational database. Therefore, we exported and transformed it into a suitable representation according to existing ontologies and standards.

4) Meta-Information: Besides capturing and modeling medical treatment processes and related information, the semantics allow also for including meta-information about the range of values for all parameters in the process. For example, we declared that the parameter *loss of blood* can only take values greater than zero. This knowledge helps to validate data and detect the parameter's scale of measurement.

For the first part of our framework, the process and patient data was exported from the Hospital Information System in spreadsheet format. Afterwards, the data was uploaded via a programmed bot into the SMW. The medical treatment process was captured with the Cognitive Process Designer [35] v.0.6, which is an extension to SMW that allows for modeling processes in BPMN. The integration of an existing BPMN Ontology [17] occurred manually.

An important aspect for identifying Process-Biomarkers is the comprehensive analysis of the data. Different views on the data allows for different analysis and thus revealing refined statements. Providing semantic information on the available data allows for raising enhanced queries and therefore different views. An example of this circumstance is including the information that wound infection, haemorrhage, abscess and burst abdomen are all complications that might occur after a surgery. By including this information, one can retrieve the information if a complication occurred for a patient after the surgery, without defining each of these complications specifically in a query. The advantage is that we can thus check if a Process-Biomarker exists for wound infection. However, we can also generalize the statement and check if a Process-Biomarker for complications that occur after a surgery exists, like, e.g., if the medical condition of a patient influences the fact of having complications after a surgery. Another advantage is that queries do not have to be adapted if additional information about complications are included in the process data but defining them as complication.

We included process specific information, not given by the ontology, in order to specify the tasks in more detail. These semantic information can later be used, in addition to the available data from the HIS, for analysis and identifying Process-Biomarkers.

We considered different scales of measurements of the data, because the used methods to identify Process-Biomarkers cannot be applied to all scales of measurements. We included the knowledge about the scale of measurement of each parameter by using semantic properties. This knowledge was used later in the analysis step automatically to select the appropriate methods for identifying Process-Biomarkers, as well as validating the data.

B. Data Analysis by Exploiting Semantic Information

We introduced knowledge about the cardinal scape in the semantic properties in the previous section. This knowledge is now used to preprocess the data automatically. For characteristics that follow a cardinal scale, we automatically calculated bins by using Scott's normal reference rule [36]. Assigning the values to bins does, on the one hand, represent a coarsement of the data, however, on the other hand, it simplifies calculations and the accompanying coarsement seems acceptable. Scott's normal reference rule calculates the optimal number of bins. After having the number of bins available, we calculated the width of the bins. Scott's normal reference rule is shown in the following.

$$h = \frac{3.5\sigma}{n^{\frac{1}{3}}}$$

After preprocessing the data, we applied methods for identifying Process-Biomarkers. In statistics, the coherence between two or more variables is calculated by using test statistics and correlation analysis. Different correlation test have different characteristics and advantages. Applying multiple methods on the data allows for comparing and validating the results. Furthermore, not every correlation test can be applied to every scale of measurement. Therefore, we used one test statistic and three correlation coefficients to identify Process-Biomarkers that are presented in the following.

Chi-squared [37] is a statistical hypothesis test that allows for chi square test of independence.

Bravais-Pearson correlation coefficient (classical correlation) [38] computes the correlation between two variables. Its range is between $[-1; 1]$. Whereby, -1 implies a perfectly negative correlation between the variables, zero no correlation and 1 a perfectly positive correlation. A negative correlation leads to an increase of a variable if the respective other decreases and vice versa. A positive correlation of a considered variable leads to an increase of the variable, if the respective other increases and vice versa.

Spearman's rank correlation coefficient [39] is a nonparametric measurement of dependence between two variables. Thus, in contrast to Bravais-Pearson correlation coefficient, it does not assume a linear correlation between the two considered variables and can therefore measure the strength of the correlation between two variables on any monotonic function. The range of the Spearman's rank correlation coefficient is $[-1; 1]$. Whereby, the interpretation of the result is same as for the Bravais-Pearson correlation coefficient.

Kendall rank correlation coefficient [40] is, similar to Spearman's rank correlation coefficient, a nonparametric measurement of dependence between two variables and its range, and interpretation, is the same as for Spearman's rank correlation coefficient.

For identifying Process-Biomarkers, we used Chi-Squared Tests, Bravais-Pearson correlation coefficient, Spearman's rank correlation coefficient and Kendall rank correlation coefficient. We used the Apache Commons Mathematics Library [41] for performing the Chi-Squared Test and calculating the coefficients. By having semantic informations an annotations in the data, we can exploit them in our statistical methods and analysis the data in more detail.

V. EXPERIMENTS

For our experiments, we had 1,690 process instances available that describe an intraoperative medical treatment process of a patient including surgical preparation like, e.g., premedication, type of surgery and related process information like the loss of blood during and complications during the surgery. In average are 72 observations for a patient available and at highest 90 distinct observations.

The data set includes all different scales of measurements. Information like the type of the main surgery, which is described by a nominal scale and information if the patient is smoker (true/false), which is an ordinal scale is available, as well as information about the duration of performed activities and the loss of blood during the surgery, which are both described by a cardinal scale.

We performed on these data chi-squared tests, Bravais-Pearson, Spearman's rank and Kendall rank correlation tests. Due to the semantic, we could query and retrieve semantically related information. For instance if in general there was a

TABLE I. SUBSET OF EXAMPLARY RESULTS FROM THE PROCESS-BIOMARKER IDENTIFICATION.

Variable 1	Variable 2	Chi-Square	Pearson	Spearman	Kendall
Operating Room Block-time	Surgical Complication [y/n]	0.005	0.2061	0.2136	0.1751
Start induction - End removal anesthesia	Grade of anastomotic leak	0.0236	0.1496	0.2435	0.1924
Surgical complication [y/n]	Duration of hospitalisation [d]	0	0.4761	0.5322	0.4453
Incision-Suture	Duration of hospitalisation [d]	0	0.3305	0.3876	0.2764
Operating room-time	Operating Room Block-time	0	0.9708	0.9672	0.8569

complication could be queried because of the information that each specific complication is *typeOf* complication. Likewise, we could also retrieve risk factors by including the information which properties belong to this class. On the one hand, we tested all available data on each other, if the scale of measurements allowed it, and on the other hand, we defined own tests, based on the experience and assumptions of physicians. A script queried the data in the SPARQL store. Afterwards, R [42] was used to perform tests on the retrieved data. This workflow was executed fully automatically.

In total, we performed 2,023 tests on the available data. We performed the tests on the available variables but also on own defined variables like, e.g., the ratio of the surgery by the time of anesthesia and looked if a correlation exist. Due to the amount of correlation test, we show in table I a subset that was evaluated by domain experts.

Physicians evaluated the results according to their knowledge and experience. Some of the results are obviously self-explaining such as that operating room-time and the Operating Room Block time does influence each other. So that the time a patient spends in the operating room block depends on the time he spends in the actual operating room. Other identified Process-Biomarkers are also comprehensible like, e.g., if a surgical complication occurs during the surgery, then the length of stay for a patient in the hospital increases. To comprehend the detected Process-Biomarkers, we visualized the created bins and the number of observations for each bin via a chart. Fig. 3 shows the number of observations in the automatically created classes, separated according to the fact if a patient had a surgical complication or not. It illustrates that the length of stays for a patient indeed is increased, if there was a surgical complication. The query for surgical complication could be performed, because we provided the semantic knowledge of each specific surgical complication into the SMW and therefore could retrieve the corresponding information.

Some other Process-Biomarkers like the Start induction - End removal anesthesia influences the Grade of anastomotic leak is surprisingly, although there is only a small correlation. An anastomotic leak is a lack of tightness of a surgically created hollow organ or vascular anastomosis. The fact that Incision-Suture Time effects the duration of hospitalization is also interesting, but more comprehensible. If the operation takes more time, then it might be a more complicated surgery or complication occurred during the surgery and therefore, the length of stay for a patient increases. Therefore, we suppose that the causality is not effected by the operating time, but by a consequent event.

VI. CONCLUSIONS

We applied semantics in the medical domain in order to contribute towards an intelligent data analysis. We integrated

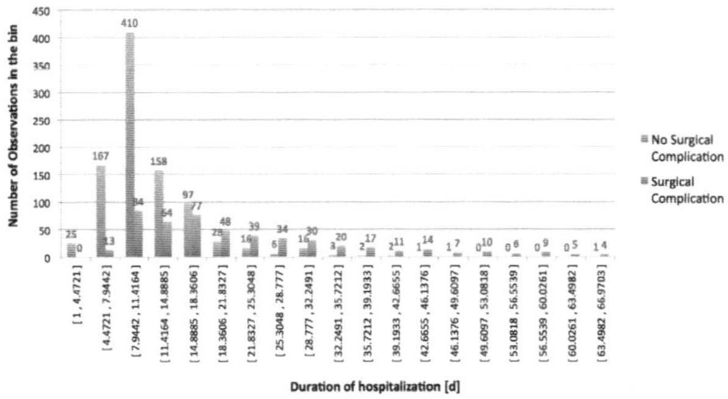

Figure 3. Representation of the bins of the length of stay for a patient, separated if a surgical complication occurred or not.

information from different sources into a collaborative platform and used existing concepts and properties from ontologies to describe the medical treatment process and therefore included background knowledge which could be exploited in the data analysis.

The obtained results from the identified Process-Biomarkers help physicians to comprehend effects during the medical treatment process on specific outcome like, e.g., the length of stay for a patient or the loss of blood during a surgery. In addition, the identified Process-Biomarkers help to adjust the medical treatment processes for preventing an unwanted outcome. Besides the improvement of predictions, one can use Process-Biomarkers to optimize processes, in advance, according to specific endpoints such as length of stay for a patient and the mortality. The result of the statistical optimization is an improved process. Still, the Process-Biomarkers can also be used to adapt proceeding processes to prevent adverse results.

Although, much data was available, we want to extend the considered process and the available data with temporal previous and subsequent processes. Thus, we can make statements with identified Process-Biomarkers that go beyond a single process. We focused in this work on the medical domain, however, our approach is generally applicable. Thus, we can apply the used methods in other domains, for instance to identify Process-Biomarkers in business processes.

In conclusion, we have taken a first step towards a statistical analysis of semantically enriched medical treatment data that allows for identifying Process-Biomarkers. The collaborative platform is well-suited for interdisciplinary work and allows for integrating external knowledge. We will show in a future work, that the detected Process-Biomarkers will help us to improve the prediction of values, relevant for the medical treatment process.

REFERENCES

[1] L. Galárraga, C. Teflioudi, K. Hose, and F. M. Suchanek, "Fast rule mining in ontological knowledge bases with amie," The VLDB Journal, vol. 24, no. 6, 2015, pp. 707–730.

[2] C. J. Matheus, G. Piatetsky-shapiro, and D. McNeill, "20 selecting and reporting what is interesting: The kefir application to healthcare data." AAAI Press/MIT Press, 1996.

[3] A. Wiesner, J. Morbach, and W. Marquardt, "Information integration in chemical process engineering based on semantic technologies," Computers & Chemical Engineering, vol. 35, no. 4, 2011, pp. 692–708.

[4] A. Sheth and C. Ramakrishnan, "Semantic (web) technology in action: Ontology driven information systems for search, integration and analysis," IEEE Data Engineering Bulletin, Special issue: Making the Semantic Web Real, vol. 26, 2003, pp. 40–48.

[5] B. D. W. Group, "Biomarkers and surrogate endpoints: Preferred definitions and conceptual framework," Clinical Pharmacology & Therapeutics, vol. 69, no. 3, 2001, pp. 89–95.

[6] S. Jupp and et al., "The ebi rdf platform: Linked open data for the life sciences," Bioinformatics, 2014.

[7] D. Calvanese, P. Liuzzo, A. Mosca, J. Remesal, M. Rezk, and G. Rull, "Ontology-based data integration in epnet: Production and distribution of food during the roman empire," Engineering Applications of Artificial Intelligence, vol. 51, 2016, pp. 212–229, mining the Humanities: Technologies and Applications.

[8] B. Kämpgen, T. Weller, S. O'Riain, C. Weber, and A. Harth, "Accepting the xbrl challenge with linked data for financial data integration," in The Semantic Web: Trends and Challenges: 11th International Conference, ESWC 2014, Anissaras, Greece, May 25-29, 2014. Proceedings. Springer International Publishing, 2014, pp. 595–610.

[9] B. Kämpgen, "Dc proposal: Online analytical processing of statistical linked data," in The Semantic Web – ISWC 2011: 10th International Semantic Web Conference, Bonn, Germany, October 23-27, 2011, Proceedings, Part II. Springer Berlin, 2011, pp. 301–308.

[10] C. Pasquier, "Biological data integration using semantic web technologies," Biochimie, vol. 90, no. 4, 2008, pp. 584–594, recent advances in complete genome analysis.

[11] T. Katayama and et al., "The 3rd dbcls biohackathon: improving life science data integration with semantic web technologies," Journal of Biomedical Semantics, vol. 4, no. 1, 2013, pp. 1–17.

[12] M. Niinimäki and T. Niemi, "An etl process for olap using rdf/owl ontologies," in Journal on Data Semantics XIII. Springer Berlin, 2009, pp. 97–119.

[13] V. Nebot, R. Berlanga, J. M. Pérez, M. J. Aramburu, and T. B. Pedersen, "Multidimensional integrated ontologies: A framework for designing semantic data warehouses," in Journal on Data Semantics XIII. Springer Berlin, 2009, pp. 1–36.

[14] C. Natschläger, "Towards a bpmn 2.0 ontology," in Business Process Model and Notation: Third International Workshop, BPMN 2011, Lucerne, Switzerland, November 21-22, 2011. Proceedings. Springer Berlin, 2011, pp. 1–15.

[15] J. vom Brocke and M. Rosemann, Eds., BPMN 2.0 for Modeling Business Processes, Handbook on Business Process Management 1: Introduction, Methods, and Information Systems. Springer, 2015, ISBN: 978-3-642-45099-0.

[16] W. Yao and A. Kumar, "Conflexflow: Integrating flexible clinical pathways into clinical decision support systems using context and rules," Decision Support Systems, vol. 55, no. 2, 2013, pp. 499–515, 1. Analytics and Modeling for Better HealthCare 2. Decision Making in Healthcare.

[17] M. Rospocher, C. Ghidini, and L. Serafini, "An ontology for the business process modelling notation formal ontology," in Information Systems – Proceedings of the Eighth International Conference. IOS PRess BV, Sep. 2014, pp. 133–146.

[18] "Data & knowledge management," URL: https://dkm.fbk.eu [accessed: 2016-10-04].

[19] "German institute of medical documentation and information," URL: https://www.dimdi.de/static/en [accessed: 2016-10-04].

[20] M.-C. van de Beek and et al., "C26:0-carnitine is a new biomarker for x-linked adrenoleukodystrophy in mice and man," PLoS ONE, vol. 11, no. 4, April 2016, pp. 1–19.

[21] S. Huang and et al., "Attenuation of microrna-16 derepresses the cyclins d1, d2 and e1 to provoke cardiomyocyte hypertrophy," Journal of Cellular and Molecular Medicine, vol. 19, no. 3, 2015, pp. 608–619.

[22] J. L. et al., "Pkc interacts with {STAT3} and promotes its activation in cardiomyocyte hypertrophy," Journal of Pharmacological Sciences, vol. 132, no. 1, 2016, pp. 15–23.

[23] H.-J. Lee and et al., "Tumor perfusion-related parameter of diffusion-weighted magnetic resonance imaging: Correlation with histological microvessel density," Magnetic Resonance in Medicine, vol. 71, no. 4, 2014, pp. 1554–1558.

[24] I. J. Neeland and et al., "Associations of visceral and abdominal subcutaneous adipose tissue with markers of cardiac and metabolic risk in obese adults," Obesity, vol. 21, no. 9, 2013, pp. E439–E447.

[25] I. Dogan and et al., "Consistent neurodegeneration and its association with clinical progression in huntington's disease: A coordinate-based meta-analysis," Neurodegenerative Diseases, vol. 12, no. 1, 2013, pp. 23–35.

[26] M. Krötzsch, D. Vrandečić, and M. Völkel, "Semantic mediawiki," in The Semantic Web - ISWC 2006: 5th International Semantic Web Conference, ISWC 2006, Athens, USA, November 5-9, 2006. Proceedings. Springer Berlin, 2006, pp. 935–942.

[27] "Semantic mediawiki project," URL: https://www.semantic-mediawiki.org [accessed: 2016-10-04].

[28] "Mediawiki," URL: https://www.mediawiki.org [accessed: 2016-10-04].

[29] "Linked data," URL: https://www.w3.org/DesignIssues/LinkedData.html [accessed: 2016-10-04].

[30] "Sparql," URL: https://www.w3.org/TR/sparql11-overview/ [accessed: 2016-10-04].

[31] "Information technology – object management group business process model and notation," URL: http://www.iso.org/iso/catalogue_detail.htm?csnumber=62652 [accessed: 2016-10-04].

[32] "Oracle," URL: http://www.oracle.com/us/technologies/bpm/suite/overview/index.html [accessed: 2016-10-04].

[33] "Camunda Services GmbH," URL: https://camunda.org [accessed: 2016-10-04].

[34] "Sydle," URL: http://www.sydle.com/en/bpms/ [accessed: 2016-10-04].

[35] T. Weller and M. Maleshkova, "Capturing and annotating processes using a collaborative platform," in Proceedings of the 25th International Conference Companion on World Wide Web, ser. WWW '16 Companion. International World Wide Web Conferences Steering Committee, 2016, pp. 283–284.

[36] D. W. Scott, "On optimal and data-based histograms," Biometrika, vol. 66, no. 3, 1979, pp. 605–610.

[37] K. Pearson, "On the criterion that a given system of derivations from the probable in the case of a correlated system of variables is such that it can be reasonably supposed to have arisen from random sampling," Philosophical Magazine, vol. 50, no. 302, 1900, pp. 157–175.

[38] K. Spearman, "Note on regression and inheritance in the case of two parents," Proceedings of the Royal Society of London, vol. 58, no. 347-352, 1895, pp. 240–242.

[39] C. Spearman, "The proof and measurement of association between two things," The American Journal of Psychology, vol. 15, no. 1, 1904, pp. 72–101.

[40] M. G. Kendall, "A new measure of rank correlation," Biometrika, vol. 30, no. 1/2, 1938, pp. 81–93.

[41] "Commons math: The apache commons mathematics library," URL: https://commons.apache.org/proper/commons-math/ [accessed: 2016-10-04].

[42] "The r project," URL: https://www.r-project.org/ [accessed: 2016-10-04].

Supporting Humanitarian Logistics with Intelligent Applications for Disaster Management

Francesca Fallucchi
University Guglielmo Marconi
Rome, Italy
Email: f.fallucchi@unimarconi.it

Massimiliano Tarquini
Consorzio S3log
Rome, Italy
Email: massimiliano.tarquini@s3log.it

Ernesto William De Luca
Georg Eckert Institute
Brunswick, Germany
Email: deluca@gei.de

Abstract—**The management of humanitarian logistical operations was for many years the weak link in the relief chain. Within the advent of big data, this challenge has been changing life and the way of dealing in the humanitarian field. Data is increasing exponentially due to the growing digitization of modern life and the further evolution of data collection in combination with the digital technology. More and more humanitarian organizations designed numerous system with specific objectives in order to manage the massive amounts of data. Hereby, we propose an intelligent application scenario for disaster management. Here, we use the multi-source information correlation together with the implementation of our own approach based on sudoku principles for supporting humanitarian logistics. This paper aims to show how our system can alert and provide decision support for disaster response and recovery management through the integration of heterogeneous data sources from different organizations.**

Keywords–Data linkage; Disaster Information; Knowledge Base System.

I. INTRODUCTION

The digital evolution of the humanitarian response in disaster relief brings new challenges for the systematic strategy to collect, store and retrieve digital information. These massive data have to be provided in a structured way and should be connected to the experience of humanitarians on the one side and to the experience of logistics experts on the other side. This process could help in distributing the knowledge to those who need it in a timely manner and in a clear structured way. In all stages of disaster relief, the decision makers need a large variety of information to react, such as disaster situation, availability and movement of relief supplies, population displacement, disease surveillance, relief expertise, and meteorological satellite images or maps, etc. In addition to that, during Humanitarian Assistance and Disaster Relief (HADR), it is also required the intervention and aid of various agencies in a concerted and timely manner. As a result, HADR operations involve dynamic information exchange, planning, coordination and all negotiation. The HADR mission goal is to work jointly with other national, UN and Non-governmental organization entities, bringing military speed and scale to the problem in a coordinated planned response as a force for good. The mission is to support military, etc., for planning processes to save lives, relieve suffering, limit damage and initially restore critical services where possible. This includes search and rescue operations, providing supplies such as food, water and shelter, bringing medical care and autonomous critical support facilities, providing planning and tactical coordination services with communications, building shelters, providing vehicles, restoring infrastructure such as power, communications, and transportation. The HADR mission also needs communication support and liaison between military and international government entities. The goal is to provide a rapid tailored response with consideration of all actions including physical, political, legal, and economic impacts on host populations and other supplying nations.

In all humanitarian organizations, there are numerous systems designed with specific tasks. In this paper, we propose objectives and with its own data sources. Each sources, and in general any archive containing information, both structured and unstructured responds and was produced in response to specific needs. What is often missing is a vision that is able to grasp phenomena that go beyond the vision that any single archive can provide. Each source, in general, provides different information of a same entity creating a partial point of view of that entity. Each of these data sources represents a "point of view" of reality, and the sum of these points of view can provide a more complete representation. The combination of multiple views of the same entity could bring out new knowledge. The search for an overview and cross meanings within this growing body of data in HADR, it is currently faced with methods known by the term big data management, namely through tools able to process large volumes of data with the aim of improving research processes or through the application of statistical methods of investigation and representation of financial highlights. The sources were not born either with the purpose to provide a formal semantics of the data, thus making the tools of automatic processing very difficult to apply to. Linked Data is about using the web to connect related data that wasn't previously linked, or using the web to lower the barriers to linking data currently linked using other methods. Structuring Linked Data is to enable a wide range of applications to process the content contained in the datasets. It is extremely difficult to recognize, for example, that two records belonging to different sources are referring to the same logical object to improve the effectiveness and efficiency of the prediction of response for future disasters. Record linkage (RL) usually is used to find records in a data set that refer to the same entity across different data sources. RL is necessary when joining data sets based on entities that may or may not share a common identifier. It should be noted that, being in a multi source environment, the problem doesn't deal only with the comparison of two tables, but the comparison of n tables from m different sources. To reduce the complexity of the RL approach that require to join all table of all sources, we propose correlations between the data directly in the databases of origin (sources), using record linking techniques and statistical algorithms for the identification of common elements between heterogeneous data sources using a approach sudoku. The idea of the proposed approach is to correlate only relevant candidates records of each source that have been produced by sudoku method heuristics. The proposed Records Linkage Approach uses the sudoku principles to reconcile the sources linear method instead of an exponential one because only certain candidates records of each source are compared.

In this paper, we propose a new knowledge management system, that allows to correlate heterogeneous data sources using sudoku approach to reduce record linking computation complexity, for support of the humanitarian logistic response to a natural or man-made disaster. The rest of the paper is organized as in the following: after the presentation of the related work (Section II), we firstly focus on our approach to combining logistics processes with knowledge management (Section III) and then we describe our HL-KMS framework (Section IV). Furthermore, we show a case of study (Section V). Finally, we draw some conclusions and describe shortly the future work (Section VI).

II. Related work

In the following we describe the related work, explaining in more details how humanitarian supply chains (see Section II-A) and Knowledge Management System to support HADR (see Section II-B).

A. Humanitarian supply chains

There are many organizational approaches looking for the best way of coordinating humanitarian supply chains. Humanitarian organizations have acquired an exemplary know-how with their numerous past experiences, but a number of stakeholders poses a problem of coordination, considering that the different actors, often widely different in nature, size and specialization, are also compartmentalized in their operating modes [1]. This coordination is a direct condition for successful aid. In order to improve the monitoring of humanitarian aid, actors will have to learn how to co-elaborate and co-manage relief chains. In other words, an efficient collective strategy will be able to improve the performance of humanitarian supply chains, while a lack of it has dramatic consequences for the stricken populations. Then, it is necessary to better define the logistical coordination difficulties throughout the complexity of humanitarian operations [2]. In a highly uncertain world, where the shortest possible timing will probably save thousands of victims, the issue is not only a matter of money, but also and above all a matter of human life. Saving lives will not be possible without developing a knowledge management approach, in other words learning from previous disasters by capturing, codifying and transferring knowledge about logistics operations [3]. There are systems like SUMA(Supply Management Project) [4], a management tool for post-disaster relief supplies, that use simple software on laptop computers to track and sort incoming donations and their destinations, allowing disaster managers to see what they have and send it where it is needed. Among the works dedicated to humanitarian logistics, we should note the place occupied by research focusing on transportation optimization issues, perhaps to the detriment of a wider reflection on the monitoring of all relief chains. These works tend to modelize the use of transport resources in disaster relief, by referring, for example, to models imported from the military context [5][6]. Although transport management remains a major concern in the literature on humanitarian logistics, it must be admitted that it is no longer the only one.

B. Knowledge Management Systems to support HADR

Today, more and more information technologies have been adopted in support of knowledge management however, Knowledge Management in Humanitarian Assistance and Disaster Relief (KM in HADR) is still in the early stage. KM in HADR is referred to the entire process of acquisition, management, and utilization of disaster information and knowledge for the support of HADR operations [7]. Managing past knowledge for reuse can expedite the process of disaster response and recovery management plays important role. Here we need the most important KMS reference that should be given. KMS is vital for disaster detection, response planning, and efficient and effective disaster response and management [8]. KMS plays important role in gathering and disseminating the natural disaster related information. Murphy and Jennex [9] explore the use of KMS with emergency information system concluded that KMS should be included in more crisis response. Mistilis and Sheldon [10] describe that knowledge is a powerful resource to help governments and organizations in order to plan and to manage disasters and crises. Groups have proposed and created KMS that allow for more efficient use of data and faster response. One example that has been proposed is the Information Management System for Hurricane disasters (IMASH) [11], an information management system based on an object-oriented database design, able to provide data for response to hurricanes. Wolz and Park [12] present another example of knowledge-based system, which serves as an electronic central repository to meet the information needs of the humanitarian relief community. There are other several KMS for the support of specific disaster such as in India [13], in Hurricane Katrina [8], in Malaysia [14], These systems have resulted in a step change in the efficiency and effectiveness of HADR chains, such improvements have the potential to achieve similar advances in humanitarian logistics. Humanitarian logistics is the process of planning, implementing and controlling the efficient, cost-effective flow and storage of goods and materials as well as related information, from the point of origin to the point of consumption for the purpose of meeting the end beneficiarys requirements [15]. A first step towards the development of a broad HLKMS in [16], a conceptual model and an associated taxonomy are given to support the development of a body of knowledge in support of the logistic response to a natural or man-made disaster.

In the next sections we discuss our system that implements Knowledge Management System to support HADR in a logistic scenario.

III. Combining Logistics Processes with Knowledge Management

The humanitarian field has been forever changed by the advent of big data and the attendant challenges of dealing

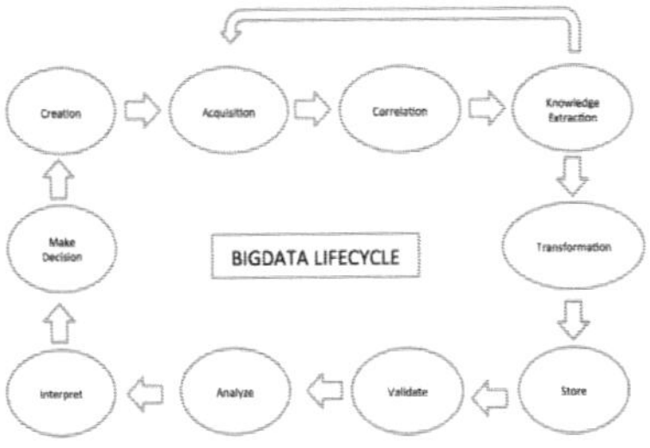

Figure 1. Knowledge lifecycle to support logistic

with it the disaster response. In order to utilize big data in humanitarian logistic organization response, there are multiple steps in the process that must be undertaken before being able to make decisions based on the information. This section tries to identify how big data can be used to support logistics, identify knowledge lifecycles, and assign responsibilities (see Fig. 1). The 10 well-known steps of such a lifecycle have to be developed for addressing 5 relief needs of decision makers:

1) Discover which critical information/knowledge is required by different disaster relief tasks.
2) Identify which organizations or agencies are the major information sources for each particular relief task.
3) Specify the standard structures for each kind of information and knowledge.
4) Determine how to acquire the relevant information from those authorized sources. The organizations that own information sources could submit the newly updated information to the knowledge base as soon as it is available.
5) Examine the acquisition process to make sure that it is manageable and can be aided by information systems and technologies.

In the following section, we presents a linear method to correlate data derived from the game of sudoku: at first certain numbers are entered. This process brings out less certain number. In our method, at first we aggregate certain records and store aggregated data into the KMS, than we use aggregated data into the KMS to aggregate less certain records.

IV. Applying Knowledge Management for Big Data HADR

The humanitarian field has been forever changed by the advent of big data and the attendant challenges of dealing with it the disaster response. In order to utilize big data in humanitarian logistic organization response, there are multiple steps in the process that must be undertaken before being able to make decisions based on the information.

The purpose of our approach is to identify the correct correlations between the data contained in the database. If you make the assumption that sources are able to provide their information in a table, you need an algorithm that is able to join the lines of the various tables sources, taking count of errors and inconsistencies that may occur. Moreover, sources may also be relevant to different moments and then it's necessary managing the execution of the transaction between the current state of knowledge base and the new source. To realize a diachronic multi source RL we propose to correlate only more certain candidates records of each source produced by sudoku method heuristics. The innovation of this reconciliation is also for the return entity and the associated knowledge. There is better accuracy of research. Furthermore there are more reliable results because the knowledge base is more rich and multidimensional.

The proposed solution is the connective substrate to collect and harmonize data coming from heterogeneous sources, thus integrated with business intelligence solutions for graphics and data analysis. In our method, at first we aggregate certain records and store aggregated data into the KMS, than we use aggregated data into the KMS to aggregate less certain records. We propose an Humanitarian Logistics Knowledge Management System (HL-KMS) able to acquire information sources where data coming from different sources are recovered. Our framework performs linkage operation between heterogeneous data from different information sources using a sudoku approach and performs data analysis generating new knowledge. In this way we guarantee validity of the information content by means of keeping a constant trade-off between data quality and the need of human help.

The uniqueness of our approach is the use of a knowledge management system explained by the combination of the following elements:

- "sudoku" approach, in which knowledge is consolidated from simple correlations and increasingly arriving to complex interrelationships.
- diachronicity: it follows the evolution of each source of information over time, recording not only the status of an entity but also all its subsequent changes.
- "Secularism" of the system with respect to the sources: no source is considered primary for data nor free from errors. The information is obtained from the correlation of data, not from a weighted importance scale.
- "Quality control" the module always uses a benchmark to verify the quality of the information produced.
- "cost-quality trade-off" the module is able to predict ex ante which will be the necessary cost to improve the quality of produced information.

HL-KMS framework is structured in 5 modules, as depicted in Fig. 2. Each of these modules populate the Knowledge Base. It provides a layered architecture for data management. The different modules can operate sequentially or independently one from each other. Each module can have one or more components. The first phase of the process consists in the acquisition of the data to solve, given heterogeneity problems, misalignment problems and inconsistency problems all due to the multiplicity of data sources (Data Acquisition module). Once the sources have been suitably normalized, it is possible to understand if two observations refer to the same entity by means of proceeding with an operation of linkage between certain candidate records with the sudoku heuristic (RL-Sudoku module). To discovery new knowledge, the reasoner module browses the relationship between the cross-linked data (Reasoner Relationship module). Validity of the information content (Quality control module) is guaranteed either keeping a constant trade-off between data quality and

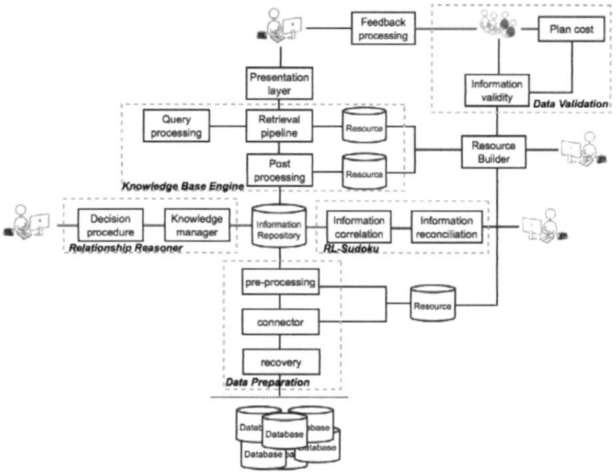

Figure 2. HL-KMS framework Functional Architecture

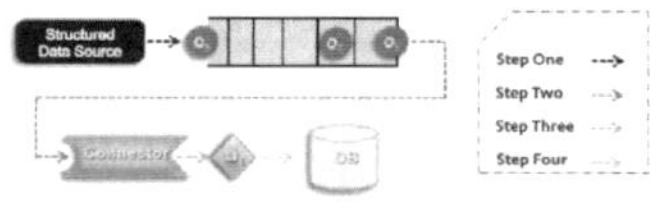

Figure 3. Data preparation module steps.

the need for human help (Cost quality trade-off module). Quality control is a process governed by predictable costs, in accordance to [17]. The HL-KMS framework has a series of dashboards that provide analysis of the data for decision support.

A. Data Acquisition

Before proceeding to entity correlation, Data Acquisition component is responsible of providing connectors to data sources. Each connector is itself responsible of normalizing data and structuring it in a format used by entity correlation component. Connectors do not change data: a connector merely transform input format producing a structured dataset that closely represent the input. We consider datasource to be both structured or unstructured. Data acquisition component and connectors are also responsible of the life cycle of information before data il correlated and imported within the KMS. The proposed system consider a data source as a set of observations relating to a specific phenomenon. An observation is made of records and each record may contains fields of data. These observations may refer to static phenomenon (that do not vary over time) or dynamics phenomenon. A dynamic phenomenon produces new observations or changes in existing ones. How a phenomenon varies over time is also an information. The Data Acquisition is also responsible of representing how diachronically data sources varies over time. Fig. 3 summarizes the steps of the Data Preparation module. In the following we describe them in more details:

- First step: recovery of the observations published by sources;
- Second step: sending observations to the connectors;
- Third step: normalization of the observations;
- Fourth step: normalized observations are submitted to Knowledge Base.

B. RL-Sudoku

This is the component responsible of data reconciliation, correlating data from connectors to the data stored into the KMS. As we said, the process of aggregating data is based upon a function that at first aggregate and store into the kms linked entities, extract the knowledge from newly imported and correlated data, used generated knowledge to aggregate less certain sources record. The RL-Sudoku function has the following features:

1) It is a linear function: each observation to be processed is compared only with a small subset of record from the KMS. This is possible thanks to a component responsible of selecting a small subset of data from the KMS eligible to possible candidate to data aggregation.
2) When comparing entities from the KMS with a new observation, it profit by using all the knowledge previously acquired. It is because entities stored within the KMS are the sum of already linked observation. Comparing to the Sudoku, we are using already entered numbers to enter new ones.
3) The RL-Sudoku method allow the operator (we use to call operator as the Oracle) to train the function to transmit specific knowledge about data sources to be used during data aggregation. This is especially when different data sources may offers different point of view of the same observation: fields that are relevant for a data source to describe an observation, should be insignificant when found in another data source. If it happens, such field should be unverified, affected from errors, aged, etc.
4) For each step of sudoku, the Oracle configures the function assigning weights and thresholds. Weight are used to evaluate how similar are to entities, thresholds are used to determine if similarity is certain. If not, the Sudoku-RL asks to the Oracle to suggest him if two entities can be aggregated. When it happens, the Oracle transfer knowledge to the Sudoku-RL. such knowledge will be used for future entity linking.

C. Relationship Reasoner

This section describes how we represent, extract, store knowledge within the kms. Once sources are reconciled, we can extract the information in the form of data using the the Relationship Reasoner module. Information is used to generate knowledge. We have classified knowledge in three categories:

1) Explicit knowledge: the knowledge clearly written within the source
2) Implicit or tacit knowledge. Tacit knowledge [18] as the kind of knowledge that is difficult to transfer to another person by means of writing it down or verbalizing it. We consider tacit knowledge as the knowledge that cannot be explicated and requires the creation of dedicated structures to be represented.
3) Inferred knowledge: the knowledge derived from the aggregation of the two sources.

Explicit knowledge is represented by linking entities within the KMS using one or more graph. A knowledge graph can be a weighted graph, weighted oriented graph, simple graph depending on the type of relation between entities. It is automatically handled by the Reasoner. Tacit knowledge requires a strategy to be extracted and represented. Our platform provides a programmable interface useful to add capabilities to the reasoner. Inferred knowledge derives from the correlation (Sudoku) and linkage (Reasoner) of entities. Inferred knowledge do not need to be represented. For example, in our experiment, the consequence of correlating data about people per municipalities, health infrastructure, geographical data, gives us a clear representation of the distribution of people per area and per hospital.

D. Data Validation

As highlighted a reconciliation process is difficult to achieve fully automatic and especially not guarantee the reliability that this problem requires. It is therefore necessary to develop a tool for the use of the algorithm by an operator to allow corrections, validations or additions needed to strengthen the process of reconciliation. The cost for manual control of the results of the algorithm must be supported. It should therefore be a tool that keeps a constant trade-off between data quality and the need for human intervention in fact optimizing costs and algorithms. If you accept a loss of performance it could therefore not be necessary to consult the oracle. This process has the following properties:

1) predict and, consequently, to plan the cost of human intervention needed to ensure a quality set;
2) to control, at run time, the cost of human intervention needed to maintain the agreed level of quality;
3) provide the ability to predict the minimum cost necessary to achieve the objectives of guaranteed quality.

According to our previous work done by M. Bianchi et al. [17], we extend the approach involving the identification of a range of indecision determined ex post, in which the performance of the automated systems are not considered appropriate, to identify ex ante the minimum set that must be processed by human intervention. The interval of indecision varies depending on the threshold values obtained ex post to the prediction, control and minimization of the cost of human intervention with a guaranteed quality of service. The proposed approach allows to apply automatic systems in the production chain, for example in industrial processes with constraints of guaranteed quality. In fact, the measurement system reduces costs in a real production chain, limiting the processing to manually necessary to ensure certain performance values taking into account a planned budget to correct errors of the automatic systems.

V. A CASE STUDY: MAPPING OF GEO-POLITICAL AND INFRASTRUCTURAL SITUATION IN ITALY

In this section, we explain how we incorporated and collected Big Data into a HADR framework basing upon a real use case which has been started since 2007. The main goal of the project was to create a Geo-Political and Economical map of Italy, using Big Data as a knowledge base, for future mapping and understanding of other HADR related knowledge domains. Approaching to the problem with a software platform would be restrictive because of multiple related issues (known or unknown). TABLE I lists issues to be addressed:

TABLE I. CRITICAL ITEMS TO BE ADDRESSED GROUPED BY DOMAIN

Data Source related issues
• How to identify data sources? Where the information is? • How to normalize structured and un-structured data-sources? • How to address data linkage? Can I re-use acquired knowledge to improve future data import and linkage? • How often does data need updated/refreshed? • How representative are datasets of a HADR specific domain?
Data Representation related issues
• How will data change over time and how long are datasets valid? • How to represent diachronic variation of data-sources? • What means knowledge? How to represent it?
Data Acquisition related issues
• What is the overall big data strategy? • Can big Data be used preventively?

To address all the items, we created a framework including of software libraries, best practices and strategies. In details:

- A strategy to address the problem of connecting and extracting data from data sources;
- A method together to a software library to approach to data-sources record linkage and a strategy to decide what data-source and when to import;
- A method to address to the problem of extracting explicit knowledge from data-sources and to extract implicit knowledge when two or more data sources are linked;
- A method to design a database suitable to import data and represent knowledge keeping in mind possible future growth and implementations.

In the following, we present some examples of questions that have impact on logistics.

TABLE II. PUBLIC ADMINISTRATION OPEN DATA

—Public Administration Open Data—		
Name	**Type**	**Contents**
IPA	Structured	Index of public administration covering PA, Public Security, Defense.
Ancitel/Ancitada	Structured	Containing data about municipalities in terms of resident population, extension of the territory.
LineAmica	Structured	Index of public administration covering PA, Public Security, Defense.
MinSanita	Structured	Covering health
MISE	Structured	Index of communication and internet service providers.
MIUR	Structured	Covering education.

TABLE III. ITALIAN COMPANIES DATA

—Italian Companies Data—		
Name	**Type**	**Contents**
http://www.guidamonaci.it	Unstructured	Italian Companies grouped by industry sector.
EPO (European Patent Office)	REST services	Information about filed patents per company and market product classification.

TABLE IV. OTHER RELEVANT BIG DATA DATA-SOURCES

—Other relevant big data data-sources—		
Name	**Type**	**Contents**
Google	Unstructured	An entry point to navigate the internet for specific contents.
World Wide Web	Unstructured	Information space where web resources are identified by URLs.
Open Street Map	Structured	Open Geo Data.
ICANN	Text-Unstructured	Index of ISP, domains, ip owners.

For the experimental phase we decided to trace the following scenarios:

- Presence of public administration and coverage area;
- Presence of civil protection and coverage area;
- Presence of infrastructures: barracks, health, education, warehouses, etc.;
- Population distribution and infrastructures coverage;
- Economical ecosystems and distribution of companies per market per area (thin can be also used to define strategies in the domain of cyber security);
- Capacity and independence for the supply of essential goods and technologies;
- Communication Service Providers.

Such knowledge base can be used to extract HADR relevant information and decision support. Knowledge generated can also be used to implement strategies to approach to a real scenario in terms of supporting decision and enhancement of the knowledge base (knowledge can be used to generate knowledge). The following table lists data sources used respectively in Public Administration Open Data TABLE II, in Italian Companies Data TABLE III, and in other relevant big data data-sources TABLE IV.

VI. Conclusion and Future Work

Disaster managers have realized the true potential of KMS to provide a more effective and rapid response in case of disaster. Disaster response requires the intervention and the coordination of a large number of organizations, people, and resources. Accessing to real time information is the key success for a real-time knowledge base decision making.

This paper proposed the implementation of a framework used to generate a KMS to create a Geo-Political and Economical map of Italy as a knowledge base for future mapping and understanding of other HADR related domains. The aim of the framework is to collect and to integrate information resources from different public and private organizations and from other and not institutional sources in order to create situation awareness and support decision maker to make the right decision within the timely manner. In this paper we have also shown how knowledge can be used as the basis for creating new knowledge and providing data analysis for a wide range of HADR scenarios.

References

[1] J. Chandes and G. Pache, "La coordination des chaines logistiques multi-acteurs dans un context humanitaire: quels cadres conceptuels pour amliorer laction?" Logistique & Management, vol. 14, no. 1, 2006, pp. 33–42.

[2] J.Chandes and G.Pache, "Strategizing humanitarian logistics: the challenge of collective action," pp. 104–112, 2010.

[3] T. Rolando and van Wassenhove L N, Humanitarian logistics. Palgrave Macmillan, 2009, vol. INSEAD business press.

[4] C. V. de Goyet, E. Acosta, P. Sabbat, and E. Pluut, Supply Management Project, a management tool for post-disaster relief supplies. World Health Stat Q., 1996, vol. 49.

[5] S. J. Pettit and A. K. C. Beresford, "Emergency relief logistics: an evaluation of military, non-military and composite response models," International Journal of Logistics Research and Applications, vol. 8, no. 4, 2005, pp. 313–331.

[6] M. R. Weeks, "Organizing for disaster: Lessons from the military," Business Horizons, vol. 50, no. 6, 2007, pp. 479 – 489.

[7] D. Zhang, L. Zhou, and J. F. Nunamaker Jr, "A knowledge management framework for the support of decision making in humanitarian assistance/disaster relief," Knowledge and Information Systems, vol. 4, no. 3, 2002, pp. 370–385.

[8] S. Otim, "A case-based knowledge management system for disaster management: fundamental concepts," in Proceedings of the 3rd International ISCRAM Conference, Newark, NJ (USA), 2006, pp. 598–604.

[9] T. Murphy and M. E. Jennex, "Knowledge management, emergency response, and hurricane katrina," International Journal of Intelligent Control Systems, vol. 11, no. 4, 2006, pp. 199–208.

[10] N. Mistilis and P. Sheldon, "Knowledge management for tourism crises and disasters," Tourism Review International, vol. 10, no. 1-2, 2006, pp. 39–46.

[11] E. Iakovou and C. Douligeris, "An information management system for the emergency management of hurricane disasters," International Journal of Risk Assessment and Management, vol. 2, no. 3-4, 2001, pp. 243–262.

[12] C. Wolz and N.-h. Park, "Evaluation of reliefweb," in Office for the Coordination of Humanitarian Affairs, UN, Forum One Communications, 2006.

[13] M.Sujit, P.Biswajit, K.Hermang, and I.Rajeev, "Knowledge management in disaster risk reduction. the indian approach," Ministry of Home Affairs, National Disaster Management Division, Government of India, 2005.

[14] N. A. Hassan, N. Hatiyusuh, and K. Rasha, "The implementation of knowledge management system (kms) for the support of humanitarian assistance/disaster relief (ha/dr) in malaysia," International Journal of Humanities and Social Science, vol. 1, no. 4, 2011, pp. 89–112.

[15] A. Thomas and M. Mizushima, "Logistics training: necessity or luxury," Forced Migration Review, vol. 22, no. 22, 2005, pp. 60–61.

[16] P. Tatham and K. Spens, "Towards a humanitarian logistics knowledge management system," Disaster Prevention and Management: An International Journal, vol. 20, no. 1, 2011, pp. 6–26.

[17] M. Bianchi, M. Draoli, F. Fallucchi, and A. Ligi, "Service level agreement constraints into processes for document classification," in Proceedings of the 16th ICEIS 2014, 2014, pp. 545–550.

[18] I. Nonaka, The knowledge-creating company. Harvard Business Review Press, 2008.

A Multiagent System for Monitoring Health

Leo van Moergestel, Brian van der Bijl,
Erik Puik, Daniël Telgen
Department of Computer science
HU Utrecht University of Applied Sciences
Utrecht, the Netherlands
Email: leo.vanmoergestel@hu.nl

John-Jules Meyer
Intelligent systems group
Utrecht University
Utrecht, the Netherlands
Alan Turing Institute Almere, The Netherlands
Email: J.J.C.Meyer@uu.nl

Abstract—**By using agent technology, a versatile and modular monitoring system can be built. In this paper, such a multiagent-based monitoring system will be described. The system can be trained to detect several conditions in combination and react accordingly. Because of the distributed nature of the system, the concept can be used in many situations, especially when combinations of different sensor inputs are used. Another advantage of the approach presented in this paper is the fact that every monitoring system can be adapted to specific situations. As a case-study, a health monitoring system will be presented.**

Keywords-Multiagent-based health monitoring; learning agent.

I. INTRODUCTION

Monitoring systems are widely used in many situations. Simple systems collect information that can be inspected by humans or other systems. More advanced systems have the capability to react on the data monitored. Smoke detecting systems with an alarm are examples of these systems. Often a situation arises where more than one monitored condition should be taken into account before an action should be performed. Industrial production systems are examples of complicated situations where many sensors are used to control the process [1]. Another example of a complicated situation is the health condition of the human body [2]. Here, alarm conditions may also depend on individual factors, necessitating for the monitoring system to be trained for the specific individual person.

This paper describes a modular agent-based system [3] that can be trained by a medical expert and can monitor the status of a person and react adequately on the conditions encountered. This system has been built using agent technology, resulting in a robust and versatile multiagent-based monitoring system. The concepts presented here can be used in other situations as well [4].

The rest of this paper is organised as follows: Section II will describe the concepts of our approach, the reason for choosing agent technology as well as the architecture of the multiagent system. The section is followed by Section III where the training system will be explained. This training aspect is an important aspect of the system and is treated in detail. The implementation and results are presented in Section IV. Related work will be discussed in Section V and a conclusion will end the paper.

II. AGENT-BASED MONITORING

The first part of this section will show the requirements and explain the use of agent technology, while the second part will focus on the multiagent architecture.

A. *Requirements and technology*

A monitoring system should be built to be capable to handle several input values in combination. Depending on the combined values of the inputs a specific action should be executed. The system should be trained to build a knowledge base and utilise known information to decide on a strategy to react to the current situation. This resulted in the following a list of requirements:

- the system should monitor different inputs simultaneously;
- it should be easy to add extra monitoring inputs;
- the system should be trained in an effective manner;
- the system should have a set of possibilities to react on certain conditions;
- different types of reaction should be possible depending on the input values.

As a case study, a system in the medical domain has been adopted, but the concepts presented here can easily be used in other domains as well.

For the realisation, agent technology has been used [3]. The reasons for choosing agent technology are:

- error resistant. By using separate agents, the failure of an agent responsible for sensor input will not bring down the whole monitoring system. There is now a possibility to fall back on a different solution based on the availablity of sensor inputs.
- clear separation of responsibilities and goals. In our design, the sensors will be tied to separate agents that have a clearly defined goal. This is also true for the

other agents involved, as will be discussed in the next subsection.

- modularity. A multiagent system (MAS) is modular by nature and can be easily expanded with new features and possibilities.

B. *MAS design*

The agents involved have roles and responsibilities. When the different responsibilities are taken into account this will result in the architecture of a multiagent system as depicted in Fig. 1.

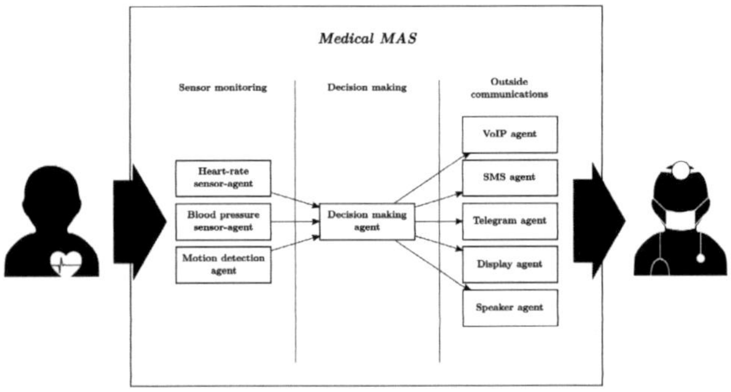

Figure 1. Medical MAS architecture

Three different roles are incorporated in the design resulting in three types of agents.

1) monitoring agents: Monitoring agents are responsible for delivering data to the decision agent. The data is coming from sensors. The agents themselves have a rather simple design. It could be possible to tell the agent at what intervals the data should be presented as well as the format expected by the decision agent.

2) decision making agent: A central role in the system is played by the decision agent. This agent decides what action should be performed under what conditions given by the monitoring agents. To do so, it has to be trained to build a knowledge base on how to react on certain conditions. This training has to be supervised by an expert, in our case a medical expert. A data acquisition system has been developed to help the expert to efficiently add data to the knowledge base. That system will be explained in the next section.

3) communication agent: The system has a set of communication agents that are responsible to communicate with the outside world. These agents are used by the decision agent to send emails, messages for several communication systems, like SMS, and also putting information on a display or generating an audible alarm.

III. DATA AQUISITION FOR AGENT TRAINING

In order to interpret the measurements acquired from the sensors and predict whether the current patient situation constitutes a cause of alarm, the decision agent needs a way to classify potentially high-dimensional data. Each biological factor considered in the model represents an additional dimension for data points. As this information is not guaranteed to be available for various combinations of biological features, it makes sense to explore a way for medical personnel to easily enter such data into the system. Not only does this guarantee the required data can be generated, if not available, it also allows for far greater personalisation, providing the agent with a data-set tailored to its patient. Manual entry, or at least confirmation, also allows an expert intimate knowledge of the agents decision-making process, potentially increasing trust by removing the "black box" aspect of machine learning.

Teaching the system to recognise alarming measurements and differentiate between various levels of threat requires large amounts of information provided by medical personnel, preferably tailored to the patient as thresholds might not be the same for every person. Entering this data can be challenging: as potentially multiple factors need to be taken into account together, it becomes progressively harder for humans to visualise and communicate relevant thresholds. A better way might be to input a set of data-points, together with appropriate assessments of the situation associated with each data-point. These data-points could be used, alone or in conjunction with more general datasets, to train a classification algorithm.

In order to train an agent to make accurate predictions, training data will need to be entered into the system by a medical expert. This should be as easy as possible: the focus should be to quickly train an agent without expending significant time accommodating the system. Unfortunately, entering possibly poly-dimensional data graphically is a difficult task. For one or two dimensional data, clicking points in a scatter plot, as pictured in Fig. 2, can be a quick way to enter points; for three dimensional data this becomes harder: a scatter-plot is still possible for data-visualisation, but entry becomes impossible as a mouse or trackpad and a computer screen are both essentially two-dimensional. For even more simultaneous features, only a subset of the features can be plotted at the same time.

An alternative approach would be to require the expert to manually enter all features, as well as the results that the system should predict. Not only is this rather work-intensive,

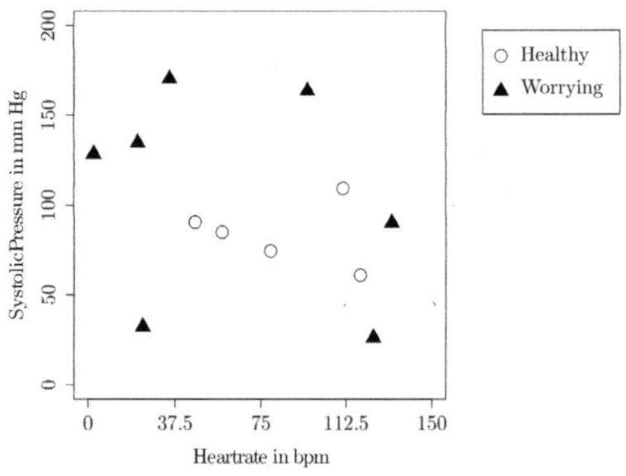

Figure 2. Scatter plot in two dimensions of a small random dataset.

but also prone to omissions: as it is hard for the human mind to visualise all features simultaneously and large gaps are a significant risk.

A better solution would be for the system to dynamically suggest data-points based on the largest knowledge gaps. An expert would then be provided with the parameters for a new datapoint by the algorithm. For this datapoint an assessment of the situation can then be entered. The algorithm continuously updates its collection of datapoints, as well as the model derived from the combination of datapoints and expert assessments, and proceeds to suggest the largest empty areas in its knowledge-continuum as possible locations for new datapoints. This continues until the expert considers the fit of the model to be satisfactory, after which the model is accepted. The expert remains in control of the process of entering datapoints, and can at any time ignore a suggestion or opt to enter the parameters for a new datapoint themself.

This section considers an approach to accomplish this. Each problem will be examined in two dimensions first, as this makes it easier to visualise and demonstrate the applied methods. After the solution has been sufficiently exposed a generalisation can be made in n-dimensions.

To represent gaps in the knowledge-continuum, we create a triangulation of the known datapoints. Each datapoint is considered a vertex in an n-dimensional space, and by triangulating over this set of vertices we can detect sparsely populated areas by the emergence of larger triangles. In contrast, a large amount of datapoints in close proximity will yield a large number of smaller triangles.

Triangles and their higher-dimensional analogues (the tetrahedron in three dimensions, the 5-cell in four, etc.) are collectively referred to as n-simplex or just simplices (singular: simplex). As a triangle (2-simplex) is defined by three vertices of the form (x, y) and and a tetrahedron (3-simplex) is defined by four vertices of the form (x, y, z), an n-simplex is the most basic n-dimensional object defined by $n + 1$ vertices in n-dimensional space.

A. Finding the most valuable points for data-querying

When entering data-points to train an agent, some points are more valuable than others. For example, potential locations completely surrounded by existing data-points all belonging to the same class are unlikely to add any new information to the system. Similarly, points in sparse areas are potentially more valuable, as are points closer to the centre of the point cloud. Fig. 3 shows the same scatter plot as Fig. 2, but adds a decision boundary and three possible locations for new data points marked by numbers. Location 1 does not appear to be a good addition, as it is very close to existing points and is therefore unlikely to add a great deal of information. Location 2 is not a good suggestion either, as it is very far from the decision boundary — it will likely have the same category as the points surrounding it, especially if a large amount of data has been entered. Location 3 is a better spot for a new data point: it is not a near duplicate of another point, and it lies close to the decision boundary. Depending on the category this point will be assigned to it may significantly change the decision boundary in either direction.

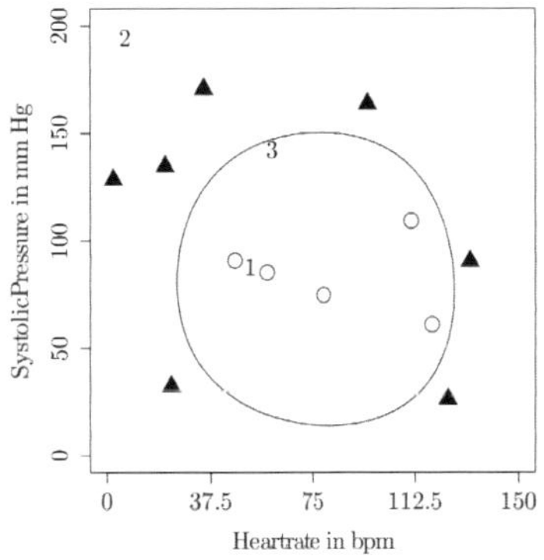

Figure 3. Three possible locations for a new data-point.

B. Data-point-distribution

To find sparsely populated areas to add new data-points, we first create a triangulation containing all data points. For each of these triangles, the circumcentre is calculated, and the collection is ordered based on the area of the triangles. These points can now be evaluated in order to find points close to the current decision-boundary.

C. Triangulating n-dimensional space in simplices

To triangulate a set of points we utilise the Delaunay Triangulation [5]. Most mathematical libraries include a function to quickly get the Delaunay Triangulation of a set of points in n dimensions. Triangulating the example data from Fig. 2 yields the triangulation as shown in Fig. 4.

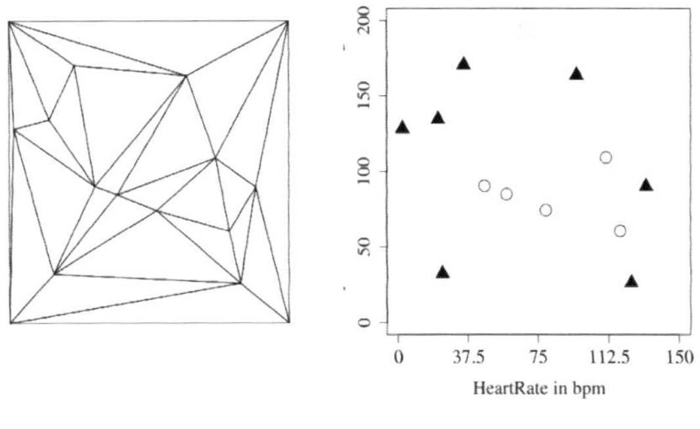

Figure 4. Triangulation and scatter plot in two dimensions

D. Calculating the size of each n-simplex

To find the largest simplex we use the determinant of the matrix constructed by adding each vector representing a vertex as a single column, and adding a final row of ones [6]. For a triangle, the absolute value of the result is equal to two factorial times the triangle's area. For a tetrahedron, the absolute value equals three factorial times the volume. For higher-dimensional shapes, this method continues to yield a scalar multiple of the n-hypervolume of the simplex. As the simplex size is only used for sorting, the scalar multiplication does not influence the ordering and can safely be ignored. As an example, the size of a triangle described by $a = (0, 0)$, $b = (0, 4)$ and $c = (3, 0)$ is given by

$$\text{abs}\left(\begin{vmatrix} 0 & 0 & 3 \\ 0 & 4 & 0 \\ 1 & 1 & 1 \end{vmatrix}\right) = 12 \quad (1)$$

which is twice the area of the triangle.

E. Calculating the circumcentre of each n-simplex

Once the largest data-gap has been found, we want to find its centre to suggest as a new data point. A simplex has multiple definitions of its centre; for this purpose the circumcentre, the point equidistant from all its vertices [7], seems a logical choice. Given a n-simplex defined by vertex $\boldsymbol{v}^{(1)}, \boldsymbol{v}^{(2)}, \ldots \boldsymbol{v}^{(n+1)}$ with a circumcentre c, we know that the distance between any vertex and c must, by definition, be equal. For any two vertices $\boldsymbol{v}^{(a)}$ and $\boldsymbol{v}^{(b)}$, this means:

$$\|\boldsymbol{v}^{(a)} - \boldsymbol{c}\| = \|\boldsymbol{v}^{(b)} - \boldsymbol{c}\|$$
$$\|\boldsymbol{v}^{(a)} - \boldsymbol{c}\|^2 = \|\boldsymbol{v}^{(b)} - \boldsymbol{c}\|^2$$
$$(\boldsymbol{v}^{(a)} - \boldsymbol{c}) \cdot (\boldsymbol{v}^{(a)} - \boldsymbol{c}) = (\boldsymbol{v}^{(b)} - \boldsymbol{c}) \cdot (\boldsymbol{v}^{(b)} - \boldsymbol{c}) \quad (2)$$

We translate each vector by $-\boldsymbol{v}^{(1)}$ so that $\boldsymbol{v}^{(1)}$ becomes the origin (denoted $\boldsymbol{o}$) and equate the distance to $\boldsymbol{c}$ of each remaining vector with the distance of $\boldsymbol{c}$ to $\boldsymbol{o}$, yielding the locus for each translated vertex $\boldsymbol{v}$ and the origin $\boldsymbol{o}$:

$$(\boldsymbol{o} - \boldsymbol{c}) \cdot (\boldsymbol{o} - \boldsymbol{c}) = (\boldsymbol{v} - \boldsymbol{c}) \cdot (\boldsymbol{v} - \boldsymbol{c})$$
$$\boldsymbol{c}^2 = \boldsymbol{v}^2 - 2\boldsymbol{v} \cdot \boldsymbol{c} + \boldsymbol{c}^2$$
$$2\boldsymbol{v} \cdot \boldsymbol{c} = \boldsymbol{v}^2$$
$$\boldsymbol{v} \cdot \boldsymbol{c} = 0.5\boldsymbol{v}^2$$
$$\boldsymbol{v}_1\boldsymbol{c}_1 + \boldsymbol{v}_2\boldsymbol{c}_2 + \cdots + \boldsymbol{v}_n\boldsymbol{c}n = 0.5\|v\|^2 \quad (3)$$

Doing this for every vertex $\boldsymbol{v}^{(2)}$ to $\boldsymbol{v}^{(n+1)}$ gives us n equations, allowing us to find the n-dimensional vector $\mathbf{c}$. We can write these equations in matrix form and solve all equations simultaneously:

Writing

$$S = \begin{pmatrix} v_1^{(2)} - v_1^{(1)} & v_1^{(2)} - v_1^{(1)} & \cdots & v_1^{(2)} - v_1^{(1)} \\ v_2^{(3)} - v_2^{(1)} & v_2^{(3)} - v_2^{(1)} & \cdots & v_2^{(3)} - v_2^{(1)} \\ \vdots & \vdots & \ddots & \vdots \\ v_n^{(n+1)} - v_n^{(1)} & v_n^{(n+1)} - v_n^{(1)} & \cdots & v_n^{(n+1)} - v_n^{(1)} \end{pmatrix}$$

$$\boldsymbol{c} = \begin{pmatrix} c_1 \\ c_2 \\ \vdots \\ c_n \end{pmatrix} \quad \boldsymbol{r} = 0.5 \begin{pmatrix} \|v^{(2)} - v^{(1)}\|^2 \\ \|v^{(3)} - v^{(1)}\|^2 \\ \vdots \\ \|v^{(n+1)} - v^{(1)}\|^2 \end{pmatrix}, \quad (4)$$

we have

$$S\boldsymbol{c} = \boldsymbol{r} \ . \quad (5)$$

Given this, we can multiply both sides by S^{-1} to get

$$\boldsymbol{c} = S^{-1}\boldsymbol{r} \ . \quad (6)$$

As c was translated by $-v^{(1)}$, all that remains is adding $v^{(1)}$ to find the triangle's circumcentre.

F. Avoiding suggesting out-of-bounds points

As shown in Fig. 4, Delaunay triangulations are prone to yielding obtuse simplices, in particular around the edges. This can be a problem because an obtuse simplex has a circumcentre outside itself. On the edges, this will result in the algorithm suggesting points outside the sensor's bounds. As these points are meaningless and only serve to distract the user, we would like to avoid generating obtuse simplices.

We solve this problem by introducing a border of false data-points around the edge. These data-points are only used to determine the Delaunay triangulation, and are not present in the actual training-data being generated. The number of data-points is determined by a variable $\beta \in \mathbb{N}_1$: For $\beta = 1$, only the corners of the graph are added. For larger values of β, each axis is subdivided into β parts. As β becomes larger, out-of-bounds points become increasingly unlikely, and suggestions start to gravitate towards existing data-points.

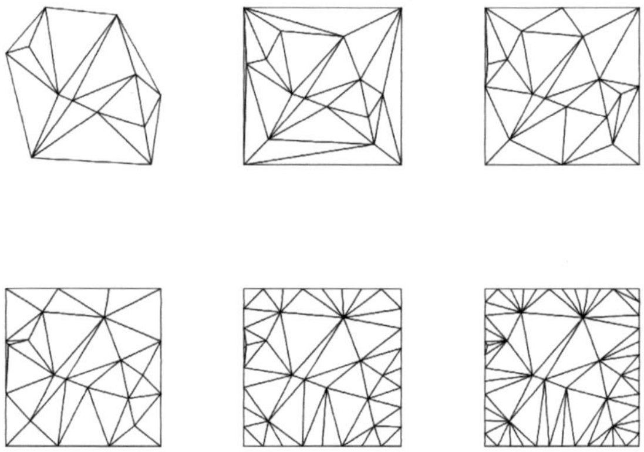

Figure 5. Triangulation for $\beta \in \{1, 2, 3, 8, 12\}$ alongside original triangulation.

As Fig. 5 and Fig. 6 show, too large a value for β makes the algorithm increasingly unlikely to suggest points around the edges. Though more central points are preferred, limiting data-points to a central cluster might not be the way to go. A solution for this could be to gradually decrease β over time.

G. Generating the borders

The set of points to be used as a border constitutes of the following:

- a point for each vertex of the n-cube describing the range of data-points

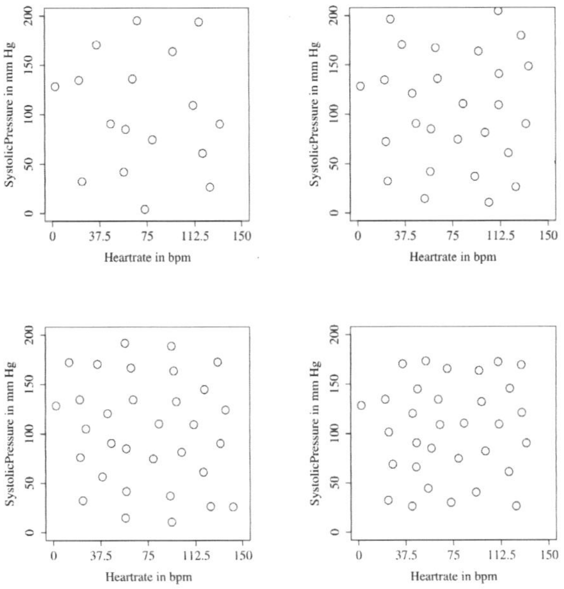

Figure 6. Scatter plot of the first twenty suggestions for $\beta \in \{1, 2, 4, 8\}$. Note that out-of-bounds points are not plotted.

- $(\beta - 1)$ points on each edge (1-face)
- $(\beta - 1)^2$ points on each face (2-face)
- $(\beta - 1)^3$ points on each cell (3-face)
- ...
- $(\beta - 1)^{n-1}$ points on each $(n - 1)$-face

The number of points denoted by $\#P$ needed given a dimensionality n and a border-saturation β can therefore be calculated by

$$\#P(n, \beta) = \sum_{i=0}^{n-1} F(n, i)(\beta - 1)^i \quad (7)$$

where $F(n, i)$ is the number of i-faces on a n-cube [8]:

$$F(n, i) = 2^{n-i}\binom{n}{i} \quad (8)$$

The actual value of $P(n, \beta)$ can intuitively be seen as the Cartesian product of n instances of interval(β), also known as its Cartesian Power, of which only those points for which at least one of its members is equal to -1 or 1 are kept. In other words, for which the infinity norm $\|x\|_\infty$ equals 1.

$$P(n, \beta) = \{x \mid x \in \text{interval}(\beta)^n \wedge \|x\|_\infty = 1\} \quad (9)$$

$$\|x\|_\infty = \max_i |x_i| \quad (10)$$

H. Feature Scaling

The interval-function creates an interval between -1 and 1 in β steps. This is because all features are scaled to lie between -1 and 1, even though the actual measurements might range from 0 to some arbitrary maximum. This fscale is applied to make sure that all features are of the same importance when applying logit later on.

I. Avoiding symmetry

The algorithm presented above tends to favour generating a symmetrical data-set: As the range of values is a perfect n-cube, the first point suggested will be the centre, followed by a group of points equidistant from the first. This is undesirable, as symmetrical data points feature will introduce redundant features when multiplied during the fmap process. It will not help in generating a better hypothesis but will slow down the learning algorithm.

To prevent generating such a duplicate set of data, we will move each suggestion by a small random amount, controlled by a variable δ, that represents the maximal displacement for each point in each dimension. In order to ensure that this displacement will not place points outside the feature boundaries, this displacement will be opposite to the sign of the original location. This results in the data point being moved slightly towards the centre, which generally is the most interesting area to collect data on. We achieve this by replacing each vector element c_i by the weighted mean of $r \cdot 0$ and $(1 - r)c_i$, where $r \sim U([0, \delta])$ is a random variable uniformly distributed on $[0, \delta]$.

IV. Implementation

For the implementatation of the MAS, Java agent development framework (Jade) [9] has been used. The Jade runtime environment implements message-based communication between agents running on different platforms connected by a network. The reasons for choosing Jade are:

- the system presented is a multi-agent-based system. Jade provides the requirements for multiagent systems;
- the agent communication standard "Foundation for Intelligent Physical Agents" (FIPA) [10] is included in Jade;
- Jade is Java-based and it has a low learning curve for Java programmers. Java is a versatile and powerful programming language;
- Jade is developed and supported by an active user community.

The prototype has been developed and implemented on a standard Linux-based laptop. It should be possible to operate the system on any small device capable of running Java such as the Raspberry Pi [11]. Though the Jade-platform was selected for the prototype, this does not preclude development of a medical MAS in another framework or language. The concepts explored here can be implemented in any language, though support for a solid agent-development framework would be a serious asset. Nevertheless, if better performance is needed, the same principles could be implemented in a lower-level language, such as C, reducing much of the overhead at the cost of lower maintainability.

The prototype has been built and the working has been tested. In summary the following results have been achieved:

- The concept of a medical MAS consisting of three types of agents working together to monitor the patient and communicate the result.
- A method of collecting data from medical experts and utilising this knowledge to teach an agent to evaluate readings provided by sensors.
- The beginnings of a generalised framework upon which to build agents for inclusion in a medical MAS.

V. Related work

Agent-based monitoring for computer networks has been proposed and implemented by Burgess. Burgess [12] [13] describes Cfengine that uses agent technology in monitoring computer systems and ICT network infrastructure. In Cfengine, agents will monitor the status and health of software parts of a complex network infrastructure. In [14], an agent-based monitoring system is proposed. A so-called product agent is responsible to monitor the working of a system in several different phases of its lifecycle. The actions performed by the agent are limited to prevent disasters or misuse. The aforementioned concept of a product agent that supports a product during its lifecycle from production to recycling is described in [15].

A lot of literature is available regarding health monitoring systems. Pantelopoulos and Bourbakis [16] give an overview of wearable sensor-based systems for health monitoring and prognosis. Their work focusses on the hardware implementation of the monitoring systems as well as communication technologies that might be used by such systems. The work of Milenkovic [17] is dedicated to wireless sensor networks in personal health monitoring. The system they describe collects data that is transferred to a central monitoring system whereas the system described in our paper aims for autonomous operation. Furthermore, monitoring systems that focus on special health related situations exist, such as the work of Marder e.a [18] where a system for monitoring patients with schizophrenia is described. An agent-based health monitoring as a concept for application of agent technology has been proposed by Jennings and Wooldridge in [19].

VI. Conclusion

In this paper, a complex, expandable and agent-based monitoring system has been proposed and a proof of concept was built. The system turned out to work as expected. Special attention has been given to the way the system builds its knowledge-base, resulting in an efficient system that focusses on the borders of operating space where transitions from one situation to another situation are possible. In the case of the medical monitoring system, this could result in a personal adapted monitoring system that can also be easily changed. Though the system is designed for use in a medical context, the concepts can be used in other domains as well.

References

[1] L. v. Moergestel, J.-J. Meyer, E. Puik, and D. Telgen, "A versatile agile agent-based infrastructure for hybrid production environments," IFAC Modeling in Manufacturing proceedings, Saint Petersburg, pp. 210–215, 2013.

[2] J. T. Parer and T. Ikeda, "A framework for standardized management of intrapartum fetal heart rate patterns," American Journal of Obstetrics and Gynecology, vol. 197, no. 1, pp. 26.e1 – 26.e6, 2007.

[3] M. Wooldridge, An Introduction to MultiAgent Systems, Second Edition. Sussex, UK: Wiley, 2009.

[4] L. v. Moergestel, J.-J. Meyer, E. Puik, and D. Telgen, "Embedded autonomous agents in products supporting repair and recycling," Proceedings of the International Symposium on Autonomous Distributed Systems (ISADS 2013) Mexico City, pp. 67–74, 2013.

[5] Wolfram MathWorld. Delaunay Triangulation. [Online]. Available: http://mathworld.wolfram.com/DelaunayTriangulation.html [retrieved: april, 2016]

[6] P. Stein, "A note on the volume of a simplex," The American Mathematical Monthly, vol. 73, no. 3, pp. 299–301, 1966. [Online]. Available: http://www.jstor.org/stable/2315353 [retrieved: april, 2016]

[7] Wolfram MathWorld. Circumcenter. [Online]. Available: http://mathworld.wolfram.com/Circumcenter.html [retrieved: april, 2016]

[8] R. J. McCann, "Cube face," 2010. [Online]. Available: http://www.math.toronto.edu/mccann/assignments/199S/cubeface.pdf [retrieved: march, 2016]

[9] Telecom Italia. JAVA Agent DEvelopment Framework. [Online]. Available: http://jade.tilab.com/ [retrieved: januari, 2016]

[10] Foundation for Intelligent Physical Agents. FIPA. [Online]. Available: http://www.fipa.org/ [retrieved: januari, 2016]

[11] E. Upton. Oracle Java on Raspberry Pi. [Online]. Available: https://www.raspberrypi.org/blog/oracle-java-on-raspberry-pi/ [retrieved: april, 2016]

[12] M. Burgess, "Cfengine as a component of computer immune-systems,," Proceedings of the Norwegian Informatics Conference, pp. 283–298, 1998.

[13] M. Burgess, H. Hagerud, S. Straumnes, and T. Reitan, "Measuring system normality," ACM Transactions on Computer Systems (TOCS) Volume 20 Issue 2, pp. 125–160, 2002.

[14] L. v. Moergestel, J.-J. Meyer, E. Puik, and D. Telgen, "Monitoring agents in complex products enhancing a discovery robot with an agent for monitoring, maintenance and disaster prevention," ICAART 2013 proceedings, vol. 2, pp. 5–13, 2013.

[15] L. v. Moergestel, J.-J. Meyer, E. Puik, and D. Telgen, "The role of agents in the lifecycle of a product," CMD 2010 proceedings, pp. 28–32, 2010.

[16] A. Pantelopoulos and N. G. Bourbakis, "A survey on wearable sensor-based systems for health monitoring and prognosis," IEEE Transactions on Systems, Man, and Cybernetics, Part C (Applications and Reviews), vol. 40, no. 1, pp. 1–12, 2010.

[17] A. Milenković, C. Otto, and E. Jovanov, "Wireless sensor networks for personal health monitoring: Issues and an implementation," Computer communications, vol. 29, no. 13, pp. 2521–2533, 2006.

[18] S. R. Marder, S. M. Essock, A. L. Miller, R. W. Buchanan, D. E. Casey, J. M. Davis, J. M. Kane, J. A. Lieberman, N. R. Schooler, N. Covell et al., "Physical health monitoring of patients with schizophrenia," American Journal of Psychiatry, vol. 161, no. 8, pp. 1334–1349, 2004.

[19] N. R. Jennings and M. Wooldridge, "Applications of intelligent agents," in Agent technology. Springer, pp. 3–28, 1998.

Agent-Based Modelling And Simulation Of Insulin-Glucose Subsystem

Sebastian Meszyński
Faculty of Physics, Astronomy and Informatics
Nicolaus Copernicus University
Toruń, Poland
email: sebcio@fizyka.umk.pl

Roger G. Nyberg, Siril Yella
School of Technology and Business Studies
Dalarna University
Borlänge, Sweden
email: {rny, sye}@du.se

Abstract— **Mathematical analytical modeling and computer simulation of the physiological system is a complex problem with great number of variables and equations. The objective of this research is to describe the insulin-glucose subsystem using multi-agent modeling based on intelligence agents. Such an approach makes the modeling process easier and clearer to understand; moreover, new agents can be added or removed more easily to any investigations. The Stolwijk-Hardy mathematical model is used in two ways firstly by simulating the analytical model and secondly by dividing up the same model into several agents in a multiagent system. In the proposed approach a multi-agent system was used to build a model for glycemic homeostasis. Agents were used to represent the selected elements of the human body that play an active part in this process. The experiments conducted show that the multi-agent model has good temporal stability with the implemented behaviors, and good reproducibility and stability of the results. It has also shown that no matter what the order of communication between agents, the value of the result of the simulation was not affected. The results obtained from using the framework of multi-agent system actions were consistent with the results obtained with insulin-glucose models using analytical modeling.**

Keywords: ***multi-agent system; normoglycemia; diabetes mellitus; Stolwijk-Hardy model.***

I. Introduction

The purpose of modeling is to obtain an understanding of the actual functioning of biological systems using mathematical models that describe and simulate all or some of the essential features of the biological object. Models may be a useful tool in the structuring of research or for the investigation of relationships between the different parts of biological systems in silico. System models are used to identify key elements in a biological system and to integrate different types of information. In addition, hypotheses about a system can be tested in order to afford a better understanding. The human body can be modelled as an open (biological) system. In the perceived model in this work, we have used differential equations and various methods taken from the artificial intelligence (AI) domain (e.g., fuzzy logic). The ultimate goal is to understand how this system works. We can focus on some of the subsystems or just one of them (see Figure 1. Not only are we looking for a model that helps us to understand how the human body works, but this study also allows us to carry out different virtual experiments.

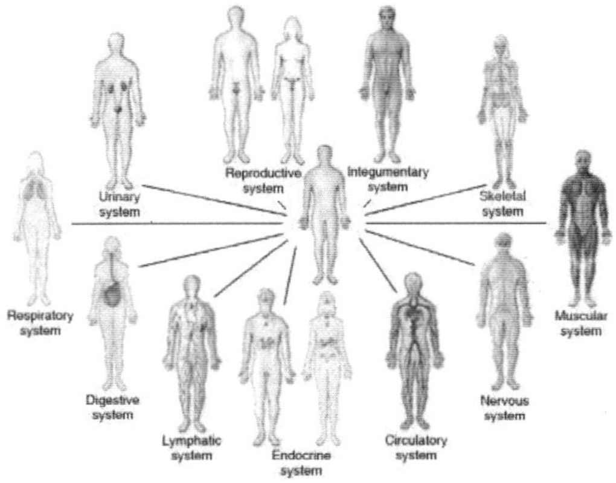

Figure 1. Subsystems of human body.

The main objective of this paper is to show how biological systems can be modeled and analyzed at different levels of complexity with the use of multi-agent systems. We also used a compartment model description in which the agent could be understood as a compartment (i.e., a separate area of the body)[1]. In this paper, we compare the Stolwijk-Hardy model by simulating the analytical model and by dividing the same model into parts in where each part is implemented into an agent as its behavior. The authors are inclined to believe that the multi-agent systems presented in this paper are easier to use and better illustrate the processes that occur in the phenomenon of glucose homeostasis. In addition, the proposed solution enables a comparison of a model description using different simulation environment, in this case by using MATLAB and implemented as a multi-agent system. Furthermore, they provide an easy way to deduce which element of the model represents the body and how it affects the studied process. The authors are aware that this work and the presented model does not reflect all the processes that are actively involved in the metabolism of carbohydrates. It should also be noted that the presented approach largely reflects the processes in a qualitative rather than a quantitative way. Section 2 is devoted to the multiagents systems in medicine. In Section 3 will introduce the main concept of agent-based modelling and briefly describes an implementation of this concept. Section 4 describes results between differential model and our model. The last one, Section 5, describes conclusion of this work.

II. MULTIAGENT SYSTEMS IN MEDICINE.

In computer science, an intelligent agent (IA) is a software agent that exhibits some form of artificial intelligence to assist the user; it acts on their behalf in performing repetitive computer-related tasks. Some scientists characterize agents as initiative and reactive objects, whilst others emphasize, for example, self-learning and communication abilities. In our opinion, the most unifying property of agent models is their decentralization. A good discussion on multi-agent systems can be found in [2][3][4].

The use of multi-agent systems in medicine is related to the resolution of problems of a diagnostic and therapeutic nature. In particular, they feature a large knowledge base and a broad spectrum of cause-and-effect relationships between different states of health in patients and the interaction between treatments [5][6][7], which should simultaneously be taken into account when treating these patients. This rather specific branch of science, which is based on expert knowledge (i.e., the physician) is a good candidate for the use of artificial intelligence systems. These systems would be in addition to traditional methods used to gain a correct disease diagnosis. Likewise, they would be used to carry out the treatment process in order to overcome the disease or reduce complications arising from the disease and for the treatment of advanced stages of disease by many physicians at the same time. For further details, see the following studies [8][9][10][11].

Past study in the area has presented a multi-agent system designed to simulate the tissue at a cellular level [12]. This simulation is designed to help in the understanding of the mechanisms that operate within the cell, and is expected to contribute to our understanding of the development of cancer cells. In this work, the authors have assumed that the most faithful reproduction of biological mechanisms rest in the cell and that by taking this into account, we can assess the impact of external factors on its operations. Another study has described physiological process, namely glucose homeostasis using a multi-agent system [13]. This approach uses a negotiation mechanism between two member regulators: the first portion represents glucose-monitoring for providing nutrition from outside – in this case, in an attempt to reduce the level of glucose in the blood. The second part of his act regulates glucose levels based on the information associated with physical activity - that is to say, its purpose is to maintain glucose levels by lowering insulin levels. Multi-agent systems are also used for the extraction of data from the genotype, even when the data are incomplete [14]. The system also allows data to be managed from different "computing places" and for decisions to be generated that relate to the progression analysis.

III. THE OVERALL CONCEPT OF A MULTI-AGENT MODEL

Below, we describe the concept of a multi-agent system in which the aim is to restore glucose homeostasis. The amount of glucose supplied from the gastrointestinal tract into the blood depends on the amount, composition and frequency of meals. On the other hand, the energy demand by tissues and organs is variable. The concentration of glucose in the blood of a healthy man is maintained within relatively narrow limits of about 4.5 - 9.0 mmol/l (81 - 162 mg/dl). Mechanisms to prevent the lowering of glucose concentration in the blood as well as its excessive growth are extremely important for the proper functioning of the body.

One kind of control mechanism is the hormonal control patch. This mechanism should take into account the most important hormone that lowers blood glucose: insulin. The effect of insulin in the liver mainly involves the stimulation of glycogen synthesis and the inhibition of gluconeogenesis. Muscle and fat insulin affect the glucose transporter proteins across cell membranes, stimulating the uptake of glucose by these tissues, as well as stimulating glucose oxidation and glycogen synthesis [15]. An indirect effect of insulin uptake, oxidation and size of glycogen is the rate it inhibits the effects of lipolysis and the oxidation of fats.

The proposed model consists of three layers:

- Layer 1 - base layer, where agents represent the cell. This layer reflects the basic building blocks of the individual cell structure of the body's organs. This layer also scales the processes of the cell. Layer 1 can be called the cell's layer.
- Layer 2 - layer organ, which enables communication between the layers through biochemical signals. This is the layer at which the actual process of normoglycemia takes place. Layer 2 can also be called the physiological layer.
- Layer 3 - layer representing the selected areas of the brain that are directly involved in the process of the stabilization of nerve glucose. This layer simulates the processes related to the information flow control dynamics of glucose and insulin in the blood and makes it possible to simulate the psychological stimuli that affect blood sugar levels. Layer 3 can be called a psychological layer.

A multi-agent environment is built using the JAVA Agent Development Framework (JADE) [17]. Agents act as the appropriate organ (i.e., pancreas, liver, adipose tissue, the gastrointestinal tract as a source of food, and the kidney as a simple mechanism for glucose utilization). Each agent is assigned its own task in the form of the behavior described by using the tool or knowledge base. The first description applies to a situation in which the agent is the source medium, i.e., food in the form of glucose. This is then treated as an agent that produces its own interior medium, which feeds into the environment that is common to all agents. The second situation applies when the agent mediates a medium; for example, the agent represents the circulatory system, which flows from one side (glucose) to another agent. Specific interactions between agents are shown (in Figure 2). This approach allowed us to carry out a more complex and sophisticated analysis than would have been the case with a model based on differential equations [17].

The use of this type of multi-agent model has many advantages over analytical methods:

- The interactions in the model are clearly described.

- Rules can be easily modified.
- The objective function and the definitions of limitations may be more complex.
- The attributes of individual organs/agents can be more easily defined.
- There are more opportunities to analyze simulation results.

We can also benefit from a new description of glucose metabolism, where each agent represents one organ (see Figure 2). Agents 1 to 5 ask agent 6 for the level of glucose in the blood and check their own knowledge base of what the answer should be. Agent 7 represents an insulin infusion dose. Each of the agents is from a child class and are developed to be able to simulate each vital organ. In the body of each of the agents are coded functions that describe how the authority operates, based on equations formulated by Stolwijk-Hardy (see Figure 3); thus, each of the agents is part of the above equation. This model is characterized by relatively simple mathematical form and however, can generate the results reflecting several important physiological processes occurring during changes in blood

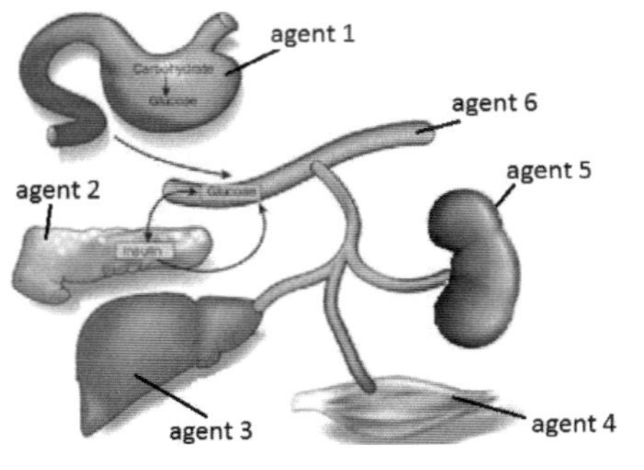

Figure 2. A schema connection between agent and organ.

glucose. Firstly, the increase in postprandial glucose levels is fast - until it reaches a maximum in 30-60 minutes. Secondly, the function of the violence changes after approx. 3 h after eating a meal appears reactive hypoglycemia. This

$$\frac{dg}{dt} = \omega - \nu g i - \lambda g - \mu(g - \Theta) + G$$

agent 3 agent 4 agent 4 agent 5 agent 1

$$\frac{di}{dt} = -\alpha i + \beta(g - \psi) + I$$

agent 3 agent 2 agent 7

agent 6

Figure 3. The Stolwijk-Hardy model.

model takes into account the additional ways of glucose utilization, and its internal production from a glucagon is given constant function ω (endogenous glucose flux). Using a description of the agent, without the need for the formulation of formal numerical coefficients, it is possible to formulate a solid adaptation of a mathematical model to identify actual changes in glucose-insulin levels.

We can describe five types of agents (see Figure 4):

1. The first type (AK) - blood agent (agent 6). This agent is of a higher order, and affects the behavior of other agents. It stores information related to the value of the levels of glucose and insulin, and provides updated information about the level of the individual agents, i.e., bodies. In this paper, this agent is also the environment in which other agents exist. Because of its function, only this agent has the ability to send information to other agents.
2. The second type (AO) – body agent (agents 2, 3, 4, and 5). This type of agent performs specialized functions that depend on the type of body to which it responds. Once implemented, this agent simulates the behavior of the dynamic processes that occur in the real organ. Through two-way communication with a blood agent, this type of agent is able to interpret process and generate feedback, which is then sent to the blood agent.
3. The third type (AKO) - cell agent (agent that exists inside of agent 2). This agent is the lowest type in the described solution. Its function is solely to generate information relevant to the cell. This agent is the simplest of them all: it exhibits two types of behavior, one of which is to be purely reactive. More specifically, it is responsible for generating a value, which is then sent to the master agent. The cell agent is only compatible with the master agent, and only interacts with this type of agent. The cell agent is questioned by an agent of the parent and its reaction to this question is to send the relevant information.
4. The fourth type - dosing agent (agent 1, 7). In this example, there are two agents in this category. The first represents the dosage of insulin infusion in an extravascular and active form. In terms of a simulation model, it is only used for the modeling of a person suffering from diabetes type one. The second type of dosing agent is one that simulates the supply of glucose from the gastrointestinal tract. It can therefore be concluded that this agent represents the entire digestive system through its provision of blood glucose.
5. The fifth type - GUI agent. This is a special agent, which has been developed exclusively for the visualization of the internal states of agents of the first and second type. It is represented by a user interface that allows specific, essential parameters to be set for the simulation.

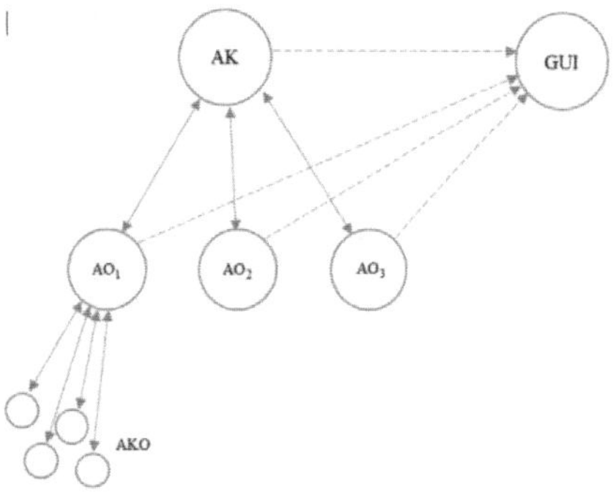

Figure 4. The Stolwijk-Hardy model.

The blood agent, which is a parent agent, representing authority, sends information about the current value of glucose and insulin to agents via an approximate circulation loop. This is characterized by the passing of blood through the capillary network of the stomach, duodenum, and small intestine and colon, followed by the pancreas, before dropping into the portal vein and the liver. Thus, the flow of information between the agents is based on this circulation loop. The blood agent sends information to other agents in the following order: digestive agent, pancreas agent, liver agent, kidneys agent, and finally, the muscle agent.

IV. EXPERIMENTAL RESULTS

We designed a series of four experiments aimed at gaining knowledge about the temporal stability of the model, and the stability of the generated results. We also sought to determine the convergence of the results with the results of the method of analysis of differential equations carried out using MATLAB in experiment 4. The analytical model for multi-agent model was used as a reference and results were compared with it.

A. *Experiment 1*

The first experiment was carried out to determine the temporal stability of the performance of individual agent's behavior for the different numbers of behaviors implemented and the number of agents that communicate with each other. The purpose of this experiment was to determine the temporal stability of a different number of agents' behaviors. Several variants of the experiment were designed:

- One agent
  - Simulation of one behavior.
  - Simulation of two behaviors.
  - Simulation of three behaviors.
  - Simulation of four behaviors.
- Implementation of two agents and, for each one, the agents used to carry out communication with a second agent.
- Implementation of three agents and, for each one, the behaviors used for communicating with other agents.

Each of the experiments was carried out using a specific run-time behavior (jade.core.behaviours.TickerBehaviour) - values were taken from the set [10ms, 20ms, 50ms, 100ms, 250ms, 500ms, 1000ms, 1500ms]. Each of the experiments was performed through 100 cycles. The experiment showed that the best stability was obtained by implementing each of the behaviors of an agent in a separate thread. Particularly good stability was preserved for the following times: 10ms, 20ms and 50ms.

B. *Experiment 2*

The second experiment was designed to check the influence of the communication sequence between the blood agent and other agents on the generated simulation results. This experiment aimed to examine whether or not the sequence of communication between the agent and other blood agents was significant. Simulations were performed for three types of simulated "patient" properties: a healthy patient (i.e., classed as normal), with type 2 diabetes (DM2) and type 1 diabetes with insulin dose (DM1). The simulation was carried out with a dose of glucose measuring 75g and an absorption time of 15 min. For DM1, the simulation used an infusion of Regular insulin. The simulation time for a healthy person and DM2 amounted to four hours, and for a person with DM1, 12 hours. For the purposes of this experiment the following defined order of communication was used:

- K1: digestive, pancreas, liver, muscle, kidneys, insulin.
- K2: digestive, liver, pancreas, muscle, kidneys, insulin.
- K3: muscle, kidneys, liver, pancreas, digestive, insulin.
- K4: pancreas, kidneys, liver, muscle, digestive, insulin.

Figure 5. Definition of measurement points.

In order to determine the repeatability of solutions, we performed an experiment that simulated each of these instances in strictly defined points in time. Three characteristic points of comparison are given in (see Figure 5):

- Point A (upper left) - Its coordinates determine the occurrence of the maximum value for a specific time moment
- Point B (middle) - shows the value of the test function at a time of two hours
- Point C (lower left) - represents the value of the function under examination at the end of the simulation time.

The results are shown on Table I. The experiment shows that the order of communication between agents does not affect the results.

TABLE I. ORDERING OF AGENTS.

	Healthy person		
K1	370,6 ± 1,55	53,7 ± 0,24	59,0 ± 0,18
K2	370,9 ± 1,77	53,7 ± 0,12	59,0 ± 0,18
K3	366,9 ± 0,15	53,5 ± 0,36	58,9 ± 0,13
K4	366,8 ± 0,02	53,7 ± 0,09	58,9 ± 0,01
	DM2		
K1	493,6 ± 1,51	201,5 ± 0,46	110,4 ± 0,18
K2	493,6 ± 1,44	201,9 ± 0,29	110,5 ± 0,25
K3	491,6 ± 0,01	201,6 ± 0,35	110,2 ± 0,27
K4	491,6 ± 0,01	201,5 ± 0,53	110,4 ± 0,00
	DM1		
K1	460,9 ± 1,53	141,4 ± 0,53	122,1 ± 0,01
K2	461,1 ± 1,92	141,7 ± 0,27	122,2 ± 0,18
K3	457,9 ± 1,23	140,9 ± 0,55	122,1 ± 0,17
K4	458,2 ± 0,43	141,3 ± 0,41	122,1 ± 0,00

C. Experiment 3

The third experiment was carried out in order to check the repeatability of the generated simulation results. In other words, we want to check whether or not our simulation will always generate the same results. The test points are the same as those used in experiment 2. This experiment was conducted using three cases (i.e., a normal, DM2, and DM1 person). In all, ten simulations were generated for each case and, in each case, they were subjected to a statistical analysis in order to determine the mean value and standard deviation. As Table II shows, the results are very stable; they have a small standard deviation.

TABLE II. RESULTS OF EXPERIMENT.

	A	B	C
Normal	370,6 ± 1,55	53,7 ± 0,24	59,0 ± 0,18
DM2	493,6 ± 1,51	201,5 ± 0,46	110,4 ± 0.18
DM1	460, 9± 1,53	141,4 ± 0,53	122,1 ± 0,01

D. Experiment 4

The fourth experiment was based on a comparison of the results obtained from the analytical model (see Figure 3) and our proposed multi-agent model. The experiment was performed for the same dose of glucose (75g), and in the case of a patient with type 1 diabetes, using the same dose and type of insulin (Regular). Curves were obtained for each of the cases: normal, DM1, and DM2. These were obtained from a simulation of the analytical model using MATLAB and the proposed multi-agent system (see Figure 6). The same three points (A, B, C) were used to compare the results from the analytical model in MATLAB and the proposed multi-agent system. In this comparison, the results show that they are similar to each other (see Table III).

TABLE III. RESULTS OF MODELING.

(Multi-agent system)	A	B	C
Normal	370,6	53,7	59,0
DM2	493,6	201,5	110,4
DM1	460,9	141,4	122,1

(MATLAB)	A	B	C
Normal	382,2	52,6	57,4
DM2	572,3	265,0	102,5
DM1	531,3	223,4	129,1

V. CONCLUSION

The main objective of the research is to show, in what way, biological systems can be modelled and analysed in various scales of complexity, with the use of advanced programming tools such as multiagent systems. Moreover, the following paper presents the way of transformation from the compartmental description to the description of physiological subsystem, using the multiagent description. According to the authors, the description presented in this paper is easier to use, better illustrates processes taking place in homeostatic phenomena of glucose and furthermore, it allows for an easy deduction which element of a model represents given organ and how it influences examined process. The authors are fully aware that the following research and presented model do not reflect all the processes actively participating in the process of carbohydrate metabolism. It should be mentioned here that presented approach reflects processes in mainly qualitative, not quantitative way. This paper presents a model of glucose homeostasis, which is based on a multi-agent programming paradigm. Using the Stolwijk-Hardy model, a model of multi-agent was used to develop a new tool that allowed us to simulate and analyze the phenomena associated with the regulation of sugar levels in the blood. The experiments carried out show that the multi-agent model has good temporal stability, especially in the short term. In addition, the results are highly reproducible. Our study has also shown that the order of communication between agents does not affect the value of the result of the simulation. The final experiment confirmed the equivalence of the results obtained from the analytical model and the multi-agent model. A discrepancy is visible at some points; we believe that this is a result of the different modes of the model's operation. Thus, during this period of time, there are different dynamics for changes in glucose levels.

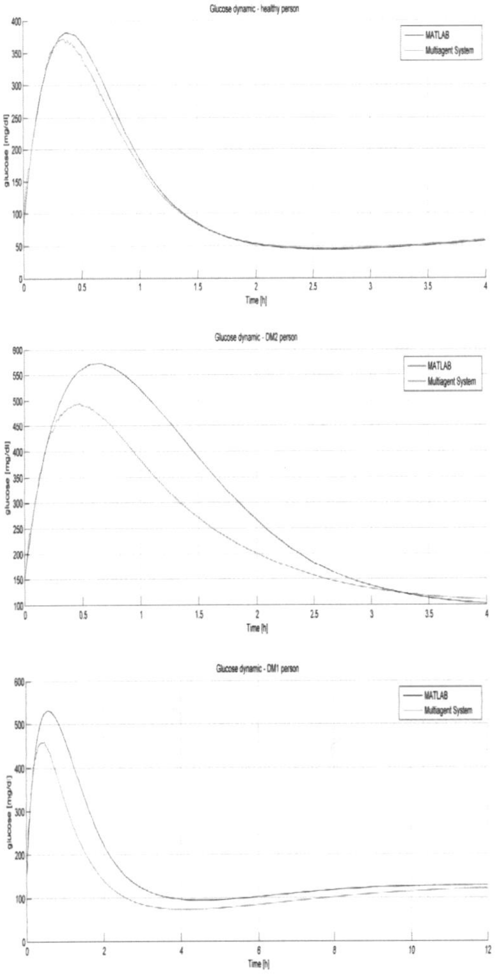

Figure 6. Solutions – validated data from the Multi-agent System and MATLAB.

REFERENCES

[1] S. Meszyński, and O. Sokolov, "Modeling the Dynamics of Insulin-Glucose Subsystem Using a Multi-agent Approach Based on Knowledge Communication."

[2] G. Weiss, "Multiagent systems: a modern approach to distributed artificial intelligence.", MIT press, 1999.

[3] M. Wooldridge, "*An introduction to multiagent systems.*", John Wiley & Sons, 2009.

[4] P. Stone, and M. Veloso, "Multiagent systems: A survey from a machine learning perspective.", *Autonomous Robots* 8.3: pp. 345-383, 2000.

[5] B. Iantovics, "A Novel Mobile Agent Architecture.", Proceedings of the 4-th International Conference on Theory and Applications in Mathematics and Informatics, Acta Universitatis Apulensis, Alba Iulia. Vol. 11. 2005.

[6] B. Iantovics, "Cooperative Medical Diagnosis Elaboration by Physicians and Artificial Agents.", *From System Complexity to Emergent Properties*, Springer Berlin Heidelberg, pp. 315-339, 2009.

[7] R. Unland, "A holonic multi-agent system for robust, flexible, and reliable medical diagnosis.", *OTM Confederated International Conferences" On the Move to Meaningful Internet Systems"*, Springer Berlin Heidelberg, 2003.

[8] A. I. Vesnenko, A. A. Popov, and M. I. Pronenko, "Topo-typology of the structure of full-scaled clinical diagnoses in modern medical information systems and technologies.", *Cybernetics and Systems Analysis,* 38.6: pp. 911-920, 2002.

[9] B. Iantovics, "A novel diagnosis system specialized in difficult medical diagnosis problems solving.", *Emergent Properties in Natural and Artificial Dynamical Systems*, Springer Berlin Heidelberg, pp. 185-195, 2006.

[10] S. Kirn, "Ubiquitous healthcare: The onkonet mobile agents architecture.", Net. ObjectDays: International Conference on Object-Oriented and Internet-Based Technologies, Concepts, and Applications for a Networked World, Springer Berlin Heidelberg, 2002.

[11] J. Huang, N. R. Jennings, and J. Fox, "Agent-based approach to health care management.", *Applied Artificial Intelligence an International Journal* 9.4, pp. 401-420, 1995.

[12] E. E. Santos, D. Guo, E. Santos Jr, and W. Onesty, "A Multi-Agent System Environment for Modelling", Cell and Tissue Biology. In *PDPTA*, pp. 3-9, 2004.

[13] F. Amigoni, M. Dini, N. Gatti, and M. Somalvico, "Anthropic agency: a multiagent system for physiological processes.", *Artificial Intelligence in Medicine 27*(3), pp. 305-334, 2003.

[14] J. W. Keele, and J. E. Wray, "Software agents in molecular computational biology.", *Briefings in bioinformatics* 6.4 pp. 370-379, 2005.

[15] D. Kelley, et al., "Skeletal muscle glycolysis, oxidation, and storage of an oral glucose load.", *Journal of Clinical Investigation*, *81*(5), 1563, 1988.

[16] P. J. Randle, P. B. Garland, C. N. Hales, and E. A. Newsholme, "The glucose fatty-acid cycle its role in insulin sensitivity and the metabolic disturbances of diabetes mellitus.", *The Lancet*, *281*(7285), pp. 785-789, 1963.

[17] JAVA Agent DEvelopment Framework (JADE). Internet. http://jade.tilab.com/ [retrieved: 09, 2016]

A Hybrid Approach for Time series Forecasting using Deep Learning and Nonlinear Autoregressive Neural Network

Sanam Narejo and Eros Pasero
Department of Electronics and Telecommunications
Politecnico Di Torino
Torino, Italy
Email:{sanam.narejo, eros.pasero}@polito.it

Abstract—**During recent decades, several studies have been conducted in the field of weather forecasting providing various promising forecasting models. Nevertheless, the accuracy of the predictions still remains a challenge. In this paper a new forecasting approach is proposed: it implements a deep neural network based on a powerful feature extraction. The model is capable of deducing the irregular structure, non-linear trends and significant representations as features learnt from the data. It is a 6-layered deep architecture with 4 hidden units of Restricted Boltzmann Machine (RBM). The extracts from the last hidden layer are pre-processed, to support the accuracy achieved by the forecaster. The forecaster is a 2-layer ANN model with 35 hidden units for predicting the future intervals. It captures the correlations and regression patterns of the current sample related to the previous terms by using the learnt deep-hierarchal representations of data as an input to the forecaster.**

Keywords-Feature Extraction; Deep Belief Network; Time series; Temperature forecasting.

I. INTRODUCTION

Weather forecasting has a long history and over the centuries it has always been a major topic of interest. It still remains an open issue that has a big impact on daily life. In the past, forecasting was simply based on the observation of weather patterns. In recent years the development of time series models and the increase in computational power have completely changed the approach for forecasting, improving the accuracy of the predictions.

Time series forecasting is based on the use of a model to predict future values based on previously observed values. It is obvious that a massive computational power is required to describe and predict the weather because of the chaotic nature of the atmosphere.

Artificial neural networks (ANNs) are one of the most precise and extensively used forecasting models. They have created dynamic applications in economics, engineering, social, foreign exchange, stock problems, etc. The application of neural networks in time series forecasting is based on the ability of neural networks to predict non-stationary behaviors. Traditional mathematical or statistical models are not suitable for irregular patterns of data which cannot be written explicitly in the form of function, or deduced from a formula, whereas ANNs are able to work with chaotic components.

The present paper deals with a new method for multistep time series forecasting. It consists in combining the feature extraction of the input time series through deep learning approach and a nonlinear autoregressive model for multistep prediction for future intervals. The focus of deep architecture learning is to automatically discover significant abstractions, from simplest level features to higher level complex representations of inputs [1]. This ability of deep architectures, to automatically learn the powerful features without using any hand engineered human effort or statistical approach is becoming increasingly popular as the range of applications in machine learning discipline continues to propagate. Temperature is one of the most common parameters for an accurate weather forecast and it has therefore, been selected as a case study for the current work. However, the methodology must be considered as general and applicable to different and larger sets of meteorological parameters.

A literature review is presented in Section II. The theoretical background is described in Section III. Section IV deals with the explanation of the research methodology while Section V presents the obtained results and discussion. The paper ends with conclusions and suggestions for possible future research specified in Section VI.

II. LITERATURE REVIEW

The fundamental aim of time series modeling is to carefully gather the data and thoroughly anticipate the past perceptions of time series to design a suitable model which depicts the genetic construction of a series. In statistical inference, a related topic is regression analysis, which is used to know how much uncertainty is present in a curve that fits the data observed with random errors. It is apparent that effective time series forecasting relies upon proper model fitting. An appropriate consideration should be given to fitting a satisfactory model to the underlying time series.

The research in the literature shows that Autoregressive Moving Average (ARMA) models provide analysis of time series as a stationary stochastic process in terms of two polynomials one for Autoregression and second for moving average [2]. Autoregressive Integrated Moving Average (ARIMA) models and the Box-Jenkins methodology became highly popular in the 1970s among academics. The traditional approaches to time series prediction, such as the ARIMA or Box Jenkins [3]-[7] undertake the time series as generated from linear methods. However, they may be inappropriate if the underlying mechanism is nonlinear. In fact, the real world systems are often nonlinear. A pretty successful extension of the ARIMA model is the Seasonal ARIMA (SARIMA) [8]. The Seasonality is considered to understand the structure of time series if there exist repeated patterns over known, fixed periods of time within the data set. The restriction of these models is the pre-assumption of the time series in linear practice which is not suitable in real-world scenarios.

A considerable amount of research work has already been accomplished on the application of the neural networks for time series modeling and forecasting. An analysis on the state-of-the-art related to neural networks for time series forecasting is conducted in [9]. ANN is already present in the form of various forecasting models available in the literature [10]-[14]. The most widely recognized and prominent among them are multi-layer perceptrons (MLPs) [4], [9]. Other widely used variations are the Time Lagged Neural Network (TLNN), Recurrent Neural Network (RNN) and its variants.

Recently, the area of Deep Learning has received high attention from the Machine learning researchers. Deep learning has given marvelous performance not only in computer vision, speech recognition, phonetic recognition, natural language processing, semantic classification, but also information and signal processing [15]-[23]. Deep architectures have also shown the state-of-art performance in various benchmark tests [22], [23].

III. THEORETICAL BACKGROUND

In our work, a novel approach is implemented for forecasting the future values of time series data. The work combines the nonlinear feature extraction of input time series through a deep learning approach and nonlinear autoregressive model for multistep prediction for future samples. Meaningful features are extracted from the recorded temperature data series by developing and training Deep Architecture NN, specifically DBN (Deep Belief Network). The extracted features from the hidden layers of DBN form an input set, which is useful for training another model which can foresee future observations and work as a multi step forecaster.

Deep learning belongs to the training of deep architectures, which are composed of multiple levels of non-linear operations, which learn several levels of representation of the input. It is difficult to find the optimal parameter space of deep architectures. Optimization with gradient descent from the random starting point near the origin is not the best way to find a good set of parameters, as random initializations get stuck near poor solutions or local optima [24]. However, the emergence of DBNs holds a great promise to help by addressing the problem of training deep networks with more hidden layers.

DBN deep neural networks are composed of multiple layers of stochastic, unsupervised models such as Restricted Boltzmann Machines (RBMs). These are used to initialize the network in the region of parameter space that finds good minima of the supervised objective. RBMs are well-known probabilistic graphical models. RBMs are constructed on two types of binary units: hidden and visible neurons. The visible units correspond to the components of an observation and constitute the first layer. The hidden units model the dependencies between the components of observations. The layers are constructively added while training one layer at a time, which essentially adds one layer of weights to the network. This retraining of layers follows unsupervised learning at each layer to preserve information from input.

Fine tuning of the whole network is performed specifically, with respect to the subject of interest. The entire procedure is known as greedy layer-wise unsupervised learning to train the network as depicted in Fig. 1. The low level layers extract low level features from raw sensory data, whereas the upper layers of DBN are expected to learn more abstract concepts that explain the input set. The learnt model constructed on the combination of these layers can be used to initialize a deep supervised predictor or a neural network classifier. On the other hand, the learnt representations from the top layers can also be characterized as features that can be used as input for a standard supervised machine learning model.

An RBM with n hidden units and m visible units is a Markov Random field (MRF). Therefore, the joint distribution between hidden variables hi and observed variables vj are given by the Gibbs distribution. Expectations are approximated from the distributions based on Markov chain Monte Carlo (MCMC) technique, i.e., Gibbs sampling. Then the binary states of the hidden units are all computed in parallel using (1). Once binary states are chosen for the hidden units, a "reconstruction" is achieved by setting each vj to 1 with a probability given in (2). Wij is the weight associated between the units vj and hi whereas bj and ci are the bias terms. The change in weight parameter is then given by (3).

$$P(h_{i=1}|v) = sigmoid(\textstyle\sum^{m}_{j=1} w_{ij} v_j + c_i) \quad (1)$$

$$P(v_{j=1}|v) = sigmoid(\textstyle\sum^{n}_{i=1} w_{ij} h_i + b_j) \quad (2)$$

$$\Delta\ wij = 1|v) = \epsilon(<vjhi>_{data} - <vjhi>_{recon}) \quad (3)$$

IV. RESEARCH METHODOLOGY

As stated in the Introduction, our approach depends on following two main aspects: The first step is to create a DBN model which understands the underlying patterns and relations present in the data. This model is capable of producing the abstract features of recorded time series data. Deep learning in our work is achieved through training DBN in a way similar to [22],[23]. The second aspect of our approach is creating a forecasting model which is trained on these highly non-linear hierarchical abstractions. The forecasting model is developed to capture the linear dependencies and the nonlinear Autoregression entity because the time series exist with the natural temporal order of observations. The estimation of future values depends on previous observations available in the record, also including some external effectors and some stochastic term. The work flow of our adapted methodology is illustrated in Fig. 2.

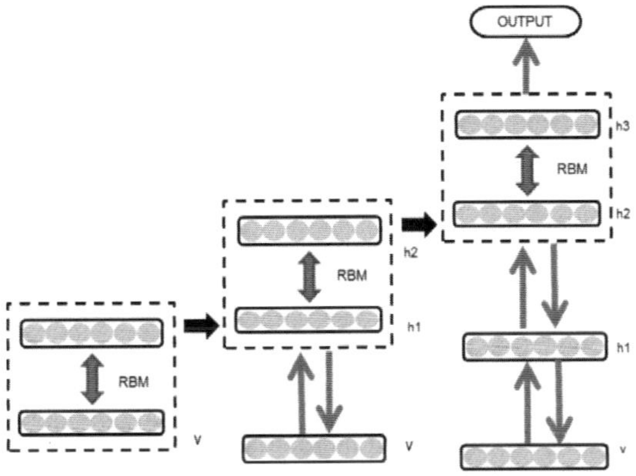

Figure 1. Proposed Research Methodology for Time Series Forecasting.

A. *Data preprocessing*

The data were recorded from Meteo weather station of Neuronica Laboratory at Politecnico di Torino. The samples were taken from 4 October 2010 at 11:45 to 7 August 2015 at 09:15. The temperature was recorded with the frequency of 15 minutes. The data recorded through sensors may include noise, some of missing samples and unwanted frequency fluctuations or outliers. Data was inspected for any outliers prior to the training of the model, because the outliers make it difficult for the neural network to model the true underlying functional form. The missing time steps were replaced by applying a linear interpolation method. Afterwards, the data were filtered with a low pass second order Butterworth filter with a cutoff frequency of 0.11 mHz. Finally, the data was normalized in the range of (0,1). The input set given to the model for extracting the useful features was based on hour, month and a temperature at t-1 and at t-2. Around four years of data upto March 2014 was used to train the DNN. The rest of the data were kept aside to check the performance of the model on unseen samples.

B. *Experimental Setup*

In the first part of our work, a 6-layer DNN architecture was developed with 4 hidden layers, as illustrated in Fig. 3. The last top layer was the output layer which predicts the temperature data. The initial 120000 samples were used to train the DNN. The size of the input layer is 4 in correspondence with the input. The number of units in layers of DNN follows as 4-500-200-100-10-1. The size of each hidden layer was calculated through a Monte Carlo simulation. This section of layers was chosen because it is more efficient to blueprint the structure of DNN while selecting the size of layers either in increasing, decreasing order or keeping the layer size constant throughout the model. The nonlinear hidden units appearing layer-wise in our model are in decreasing order. Each layer was independently trained as RBM with sigmoid activation function. After training the first hidden layer of 500 units, the second hidden layer was added with 200 sigmoid neurons. The input data that used for training the second layer was the outcome from the first layer. The third layer comprising 100 units was trained with the output data from the second layer. Similarly, the last top layer took the abstractions of fourth layer bearing 10 neurons and attempted to predict the temperature as an output. The states of hidden nodes computed by the trained RBM were used as input to the next layer. After unsupervised training, the labels were provided at the output layer for linear mapping. The parameters used for pre-training of each layer are specified in Table I. The pretraining of each layer proceeded with only one epoch. The error and the mean approximations of each layer are presented in Table II.

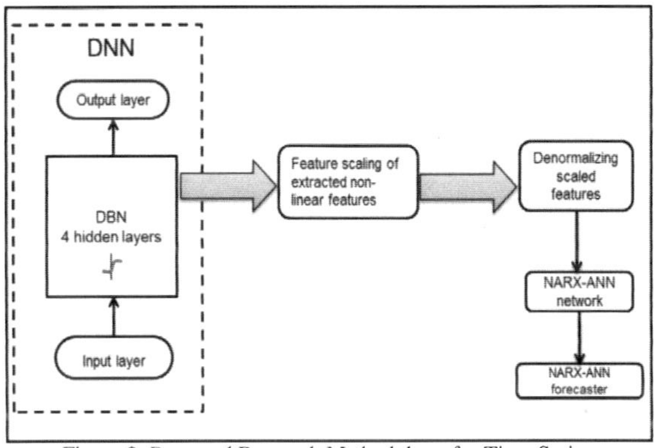

Figure 2. Proposed Research Methodology for Time Series Forecasting.

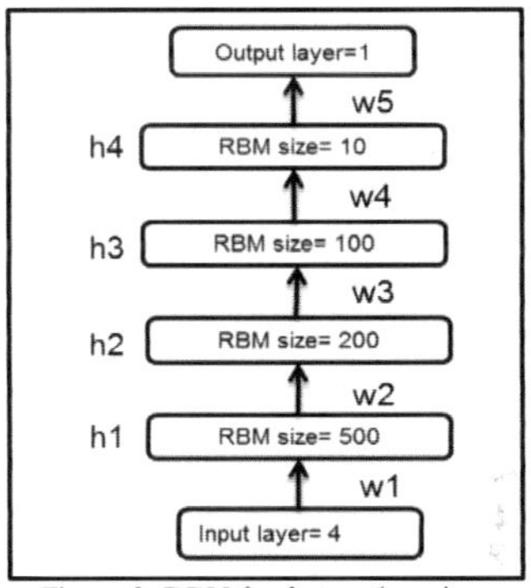

Figure 3. DBN for feature learning.

TABLE I. PARAMETER SETTINGS OF DBN

Parameters	Value
Max Iterations	1
Initial momentum	0.5
Final momentum	0.9
Learning rate	0.1
Batch size	5
Transfer function	Sigmoid

TABLE II. ERROR AND MEAN APPROXIMATION OF PRETRAINING

Layers	RMSE	Mean (hidden units)
Layer 1	0.2744	0.5001
Layer 2	0.0004	0.4986
Layer 3	0.0011	0.4975
Layer 4	0.0024	0.4950
Layer 5	0.0034	0.4992

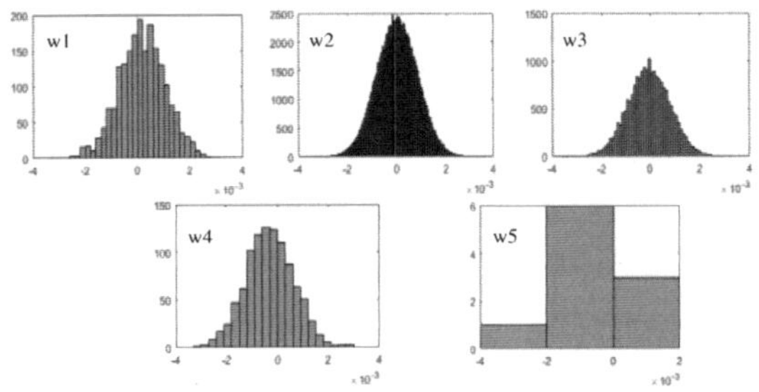

Figure 4. Histograms; Weight Distributions of DBN Layers after pretraining

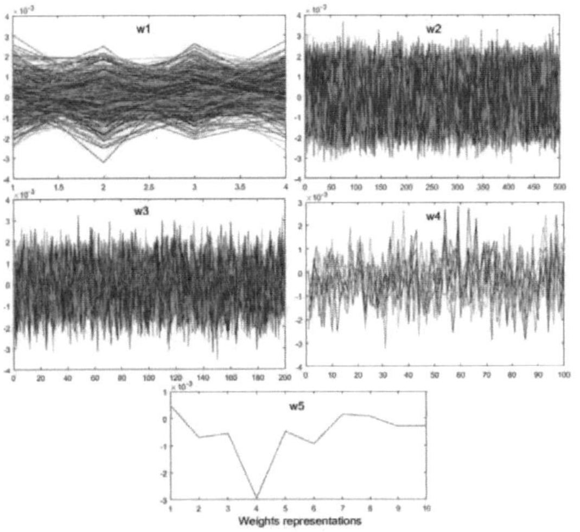

Figure 5. Illustration for weights of DBN after Pretraining

After completing the pretraining, the reformed outcomes as weight distributions associated with each layer are shown in Fig 4. It is clearly perceptible that pretraining initializes the weights and biases of the network to sensible values. The structure of weights connected with each layer as feature detectors of the model is visible in Fig. 5. This parameter initialization with unsupervised greedy layer-wise training expresses that weights linked with each layer are efficient but although not optimal ones. After unsupervised greedy layer-wise training, fine tuning was applied by backpropagation algorithm, training the model with stochastic gradient descent. The pre-training gave a good start to retrain the model by driving the loss function towards its minima.

A total 800 of iterations are used to train the pre initialized DBN model. The weights of model influenced by fine tuning are now modified into different depictions than the earlier ones. The patterns in weight matrices of DNN are illustrated in Fig. 6.

C. *Forecasting*

The task of forecasting temperature on the extracted features from the deep learning architecture was achieved by configuring the Non-linear AutoRegressive model with exogenous inputs i.e. NARX ANN. The literature shows that NARX networks are often much better at discovering long time dependencies than the conventional recurrent neural networks. The NARX feed forward network is created with one hidden layer of 35 neurons and an output layer consisting of one neuron. The size of the hidden layer was selected on the basis of optimal solution given by different models trained in the range of 10 to 40 neurons. The hidden layer activations were processed with a hyperbolic tangent sigmoid transfer function as shown in (4). The output layer was configured with a linear transfer function.

$$tansig(x) = 2/(1+exp(-2*x))-1 \quad (4)$$

The external input set to train the model contained hour, month samples and aggregated learned features from DBN. The preprocessed input was inserted in the network with tapped delay lines to store the previous values of lagged terms for network training. The forecasting model is shown in Fig. 7. Subsequently, once the model is trained to capture the data generation patterns, the model is extrapolated to forecast future values. For forecasting along with the external input another input set is considered, i.e., feedback connection from the network output. This indicates, for predicting multistep samples the predictions of y(t) will be used in place of actual future values of y(t). The architectural view of feedback model is represented in Fig. 8.

The number of previous terms to be used by forecaster can be called as delay terms. The associated delay terms were calculated with Autocorrelation. It describes the correlation between the values of the process at different times, as a function of the two times or of the time lag. By use of autocorrelation the sliding window size of lagged terms is calculated as 4. The data set was divided into training, validation and test set to a ratio of 70, 15 and 15. The network was further trained with Levenberg-Marquardt algorithm with 1000 iterations. The performance of the model was measured by Root Mean Square Error (RMSE) and Mean Square Error (MSE) on training, testing and validation datasets.

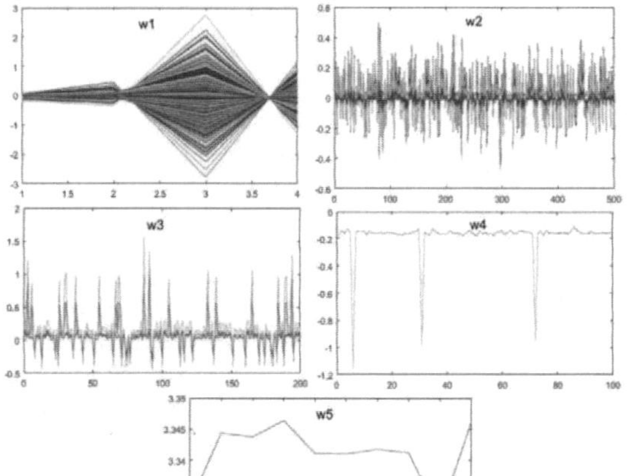

Figure 6. Illustration for weights of DBN-DNN after Fine tunning

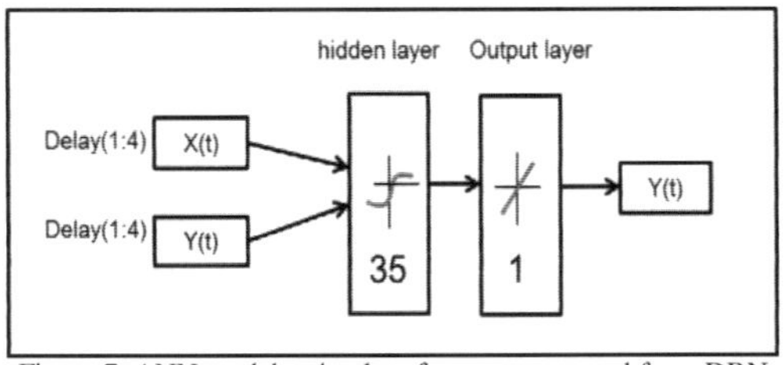

Figure 7. ANN model trained on features extracted from DBN

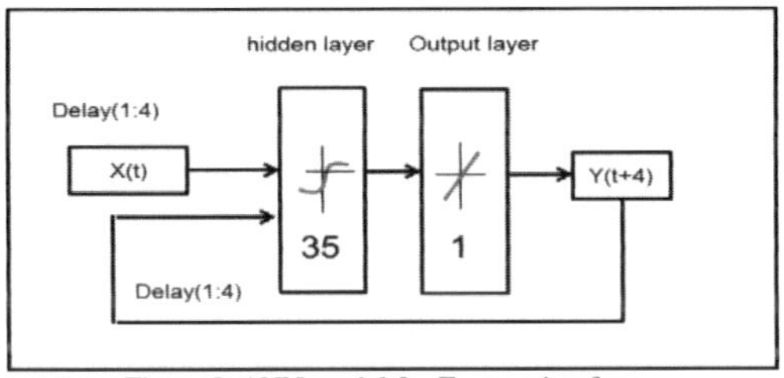

Figure 8. ANN model for Forecasting future

V. RESULTS AND DISCUSSION

A. *Nonlinear Hierarchal Feature Extraction*

The fully trained DNN achieves the error of 8.5e-04 on training data. Further, it results 7.99e-04 on the test set containing 5691 samples. This experiment took more than one day for fine tuning the pretrained model. The simulations were executed on 16 and 32 cores of HPC cluster of AMD Bulldozer CPU. The hierarchal features that are learned with our model are presented in Fig. 9. The graph at the top, shows the abstractions of the top hidden layer. The graph at the bottom, shows the nonlinear relations learned by the first low-level hidden layer. The first hidden layer abstractions are low level attributes that reside in time series of temperature. The top level hidden layer was able to learn the representations as close as possible to the target series which is clearly visible in the figure. Apart from this the top hidden layer extracts 10 valuable features. Along with the property of being significant, the features in the top layer also contained the element of redundancy. Moreover, the features extracted from the top most hidden layer are sent to forecaster for future predictions. These representations give evidence that they are salient for forecasting the future intervals. Several attempts were made to select the appropriate top hidden layer, with the different number of neurons in the range of 1-10. The finest representations learned were with 10 neurons. The prediction of temperature series through DNN is shown in Fig. 10. As seen in the figure, the predicted temperature has accurately replicated the actual temperature records.

B. *Temperature Forecasts*

The performance measurements of the forecasting model for predictions resulted as 0.0010 RMSE on training, 0.0011 on validation and 0.0011 on the test set. After training of the model, it is further extrapolated to forecast next four steps of time interval. As a forecaster for next hour prediction, it provides 0.0068 error performance on the training data while it gives good performance on the test set by achieving 0.0080 as MSE. The statistical analysis for one hour forecasting in the form of error histogram and regression plot is presented in the Fig. 11 and 12. Temperature samples from the test data for next one hour forecasting is shown in Fig. 13. Due to accurate predictions, the actual and forecasted values are almost same. In Fig. 14, only 50 samples are reported to better highlight the difference between actual and forecasted temperature values.

Furthermore, temperature samples from April 2014 to August 2015 to monitor the performance of both models. Feature extraction with DNN resulted in prediction error of 9.8240e-04, which is a good response as compared to the training result of DNN. A useful representations as features are those one, which are significant as an input to a supervised predictor. Henceforth, our model efficiently learned the expressive representations as a feature set for forecasting model. It has the capability to capture possible input configurations which were impossible to identify statistically or mathematically. These findings in our study are highly correlated with [25],[26].

For a comparative analysis of the proposed model with some conventional approaches, the summary of measurements is prescribed in Table III. It presents the relative analysis of our proposed approach with NAR, NARX and MLP. The NAR and NARX belong to the family of dynamic RNNs. The above mentioned models were created and trained by using one hidden layer comprising of 35 neurons, one input layer and one output layer a way similar to the training of Hybrid NARX approach. The rate of training error and test error for the performance of each model is measured in MSE. It is clearly noticeable that the proposed hybrid model outperforms the other models in the form of test error. MLP model is found to be with the least accurate model as compared to the other models.

TABLE III. ERROR RATE COMPARISIONS

Models	Training Error Rate	Test Error Rate
DBN-DNN-NARX	0.0068	0.0080
NAR	0.0056	0.012
NARX	0.069	0.019
MLP	0.045	0.045

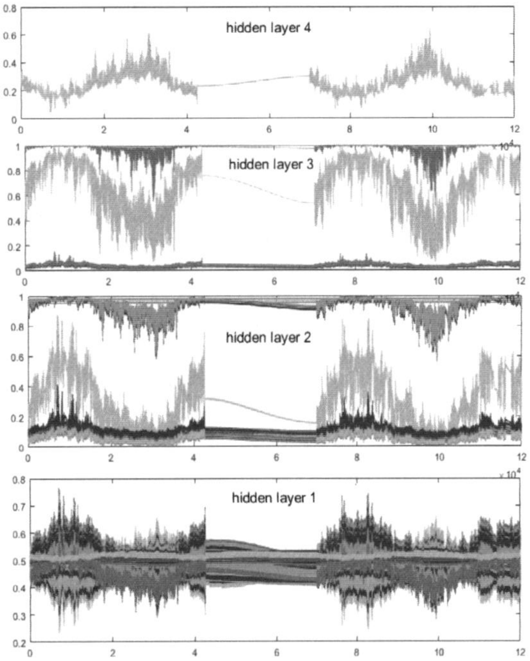

Figure 9. Learnt Nonlinear Representations of data from Hidden layers of DBN.

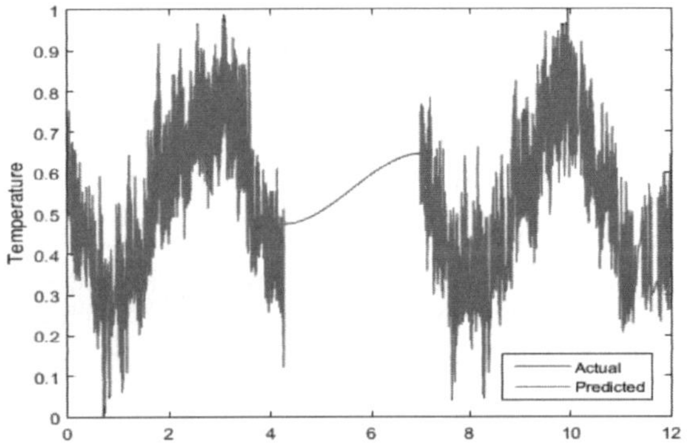

Figure 10. Temperature predictions by output layer of DBN-DNN

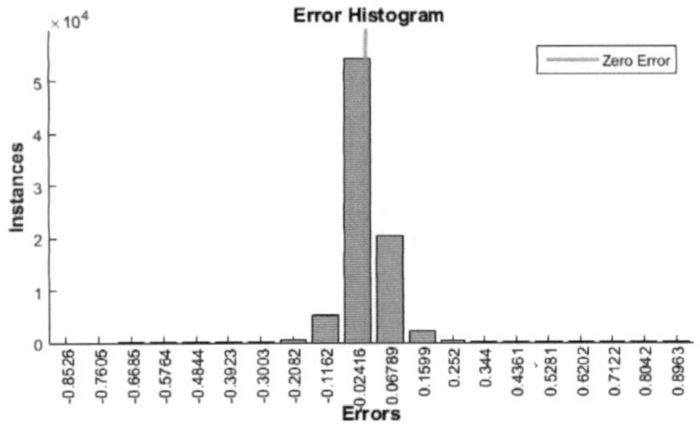

Figure 11. Error Histogram of 1 hour forecast.

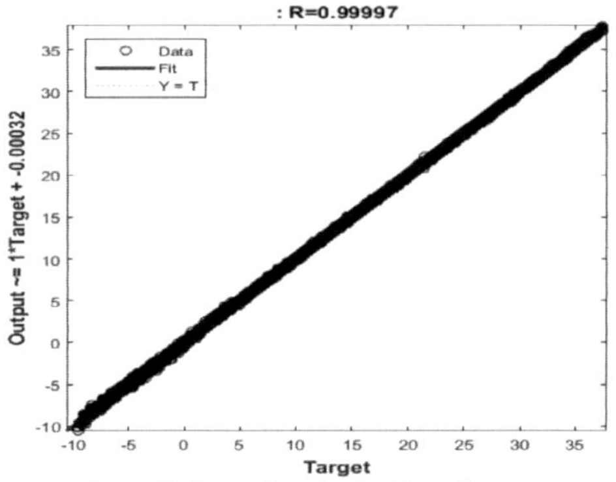

Figure 12. Regression plot for 1 hour forecast.

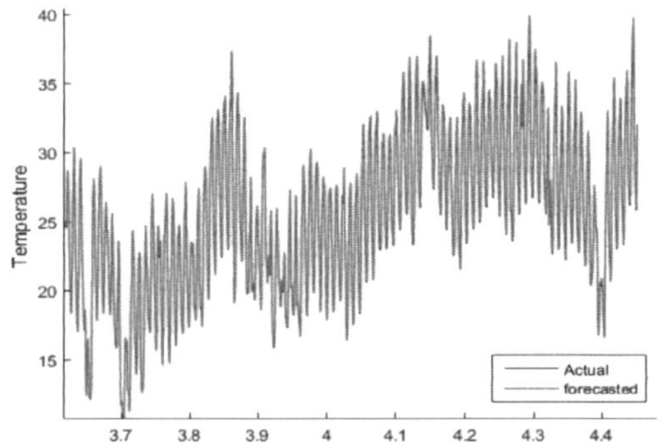

Figure 13. 1 hour Forecasting of Temperature

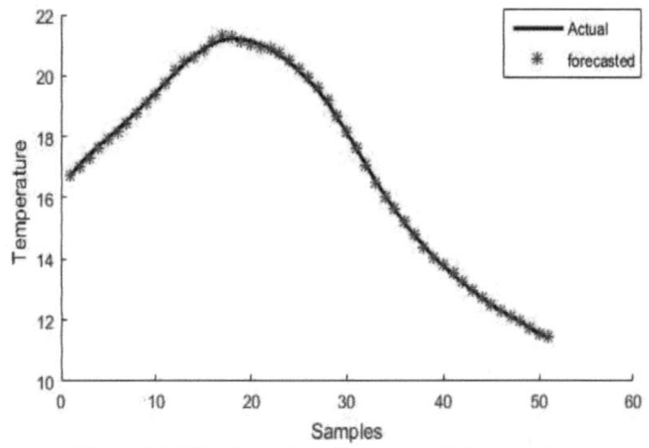

Figure 14. Fifty Samples of Forecasted Temperature.

VI. CONCLUSION

In the paper, a novel approach for temperature forecasting is presented with the aim of improving the prediction accuracy. The main innovation is that the extracted feature set, used for forecasting, is not constructed through statistical feature engineering methods, but it is extracted through the deep learning of a Deep Belief Network. Firstly, the nonlinear hierarchical representations are extracted through the hidden layers of the developed

DBN-DNN model. Subsequently, the raw input series are transformed into gradually higher level of representations as learnt features.These represent more abstract functions of input at the upper level of the layers by implementing a DBN-DNN architecture. The features extracted learnt the complex mapping between input and output, which is observable from the performance of DBN-DNN. The feature extracted are further, used as data to train the forecaster i.e NARX ANN model. The extracted abstractions reinforced the forecaster ANN model to more accurately predict the temperature, achieving outstanding performance against the mentioned approaches. The results obtained over 5 years of data collection demonstrated that the proposed approach is promising and can be further applied to the prediction of a different set of weather parameters.

ACKNOWLEDGMENT

Computational resources were partly provided by HPC@POLITO, (http://www.hpc.polito.it).

This project was partly funded by Italian MIUR OPLON project and supported by the Politecnico of Turin NEC laboratory.

A special thanks to Dr. Suela Ruffa for her precious suggestions.

REFERENCES

[1] Y. Bengio, "Learning deep architectures for AI. Foundations and trends® in Machine Learning, " vol. 2, no. 1, pp. 1-127, 2009.

[2] B. Choi, "ARMA model identification", Springer Science & Business Media, 2012.

[3] G.E. Box, G.M. Jenkins, G.C. Reinsel, and G.M. Ljung, " Time series analysis: forecasting and control. ", Holden-Day, 1976.

[4] G.P. Zhang, " Time series forecasting using a hybrid ARIMA and neural network model.", Neurocomputing, vol. 50, pp. 159-175, 2003.

[5] C. Brooks, "Univariatetime series modelling and forecasting.", Introductory Econometrics for Finance. 2nd Ed. Cambridge University Press. Cambridge, Massachusetts, 2008.

[6] J.H. Cochrane, Time series for macroeconomics and finance. Manuscript, University of Chicago, 2005.

[7] K.W. Hipel, and A.I. McLeod, Time series modelling of water resources and environmental systems, Elsevier. vol. 45, 1994.

[8] B.M. Williams, and L.A. Hoel, "Modeling and forecasting vehicular traffic flow as a seasonal ARIMA process: Theoretical basis and empirical results.", Journal of transportation engineering, vol. 129, no. 6, pp. 664-672, 2003.

[9] Z. Guoqiang, B. E. Patuwo, and M. Y. Hu, "Forecasting with artificial neural networks:: The state of the art.", International journal of forecasting, vol. 14, no. 1, pp. 35-62, 1998.

[10] T. Kolarik, and G. Rudorfer, "Time series forecasting using neural networks. ", In ACM Sigapl Apl Quote Quad vol. 25, no. 1, pp. 86-94, ACM, 1994

[11] G.P, Zhang, "Neural networks for time-series forecasting. ", In Handbook of Natural Computing, Springer Berlin Heidelberg, pp. 461-477, 2012.

[12] J.J.M. Moreno, A.P. Pol, and P.M. Gracia, "Artificial neural networks applied to forecasting time series. ", Psicothema, vol. 23, no. 2, pp. 322-329. 2011.

[13] R.J. Frank, N. Davey, and S.P. Hunt, "Time series prediction and neural networks. ", Journal of intelligent and robotic systems, vol. 31 no. 1-3, pp. 91-103, 2001.

[14] E.G.A. Pasero, and L. Mesin, " Artificial neural networks to forecast air pollution.", pp. 221-240, 2010.

[15] G.E. Hinton, et al, "Deep neural networks for acoustic modeling in speech recognition: The shared views of four research groups". IEEE Signal Processing Magazine, vol. 29, no. 6, pp. 82-97, 2012.

[16] R. Salakhutdinov, A. Mnih, and G.E Hinton, " Restricted Boltzmann machines for collaborative filtering. " In Proceedings of the 24th international conference on Machine learning, pp. 791-798. ACM. 2007.

[17] M.R. Amer, B. Siddiquie, C. Richey, and A. Divakaran, "Emotion detection in speech using deep networks.", IEEE International Conference on Acoustics, Speech and Signal Processing (ICASSP) , pp. 3724-3728, IEEE, 2014.

[18] I. Sutskever, J. Martens, and G.E. Hinton, "Generating text with recurrent neural networks. ", Proceedings of the 28th International Conference on Machine Learning, 2011.

[19] M.D. Zeiler, et al., "Facial expression transfer with input-output temporal restricted boltzmann machines. ",Advances in Neural Information Processing Systems, pp. 1629-1637, 2011.

[20] G.W. Taylor, and G.E. Hinton, "Factored conditional restricted Boltzmann machines for modeling motion style. ", In Proceedings of the 26th annual international conference on machine learning, pp. 1025-1032, ACM, 2009.

[21] G.E. Hinton, and R.R, Salakhutdinov, "Reducing the dimensionality of data with neural networks", Science, vol. 313, no. 5786, pp.504-507, 2006.

[22] G.E Hinton, S. Osindero, and Y.W Teh, " A fast learning algorithm for deep belief nets", Neural computation, vol. 18, no. 7, pp.1527-1554, 2006.

[23] Y. Bengio, P. Lamblin, D. Popovici, and H. Larochelle, "Greedy layer-wise training of deep networks. ", Advances in neural information processing systems, vol 19, p. 153, 2007.

[24] R. Salakhutdinov, and G. E. Hinton. "Deep boltzmann machines.", International Conference on Artificial Intelligence and Statistics, 2009.

[25] D. Erhan, et. Al., "Why does unsupervised pre-training help deep learning?. ", Journal of Machine Learning Research, vol. 11, no. Feb, pp. 625-660, 2010.

[26] H. Larochelle, Y. Bengio, J. Louradour, and P. Lamblin, "Exploring strategies for training deep neural networks. ", Journal of Machine Learning Research, vol. 10, no. Jan, pp. 1-40, 2009.

Lifecycle Ontologies: Background and State-of-the-Art

Alena V. Fedotova, Valery B. Tarassov
CIM Department
Bauman Moscow State Technical University
Moscow, Russia
e-mail: afedotova.bmstu@gmail.com, vbulbov@yahoo.com

Dmitry I. Mouromtsev
National Research University of Information Technologies, Mechanics and Optics
Saint-Petersburg, Russia
e-mail: mouromtsev@mail.ifmo.ru

Irina T. Davydenko
Belarusian State University of Informatics and Radioelectronics
e-mail: davydenko@bsuir.by

***Abstract*—The problems of creating Lifecycle Ontologies are discussed in the paper. The Ontology of Lifecycle (both as domain and upper ontology), in contradistinction to Lifecycle of Ontology, still remains underdeveloped. The interest in these problems is related to the need in various lifecycle representations and coverings for constructing advanced Product Lifecycle Management (PLM) systems. Such PLM-systems are seen as a keystone for Enterprise Engineering (EE). First of all, some definitions and viewpoints on EE are discussed. Authors suggest an original pyramid of disciplines for EE. Moreover, the main goal is to develop a trans-disciplinary, synergistic approach to EE based on the integration of Ontological Engineering, Lifecycle Modeling and Knowledge Management. It requires the modeling and co-ordination of (at least) three lifecycles: product (complex technical system) lifecycle, enterprise lifecycle and knowledge lifecycle. The problems of lifecycle modeling are faced.**

Keywords-Ontological engineering; granular meta-ontology; ontological system; lifecycle ontologies; enterprise engineering.

I. INTRODUCTION

Nowadays the development of Lifecycle Ontologies for EE is of primary concern. Lifecycle specification and ontological modeling is a necessary prerequisite for deploying EE that becomes a fundamental paradigm for building new generation industrial enterprises.

In this paper we suggest a new trans-disciplinary approach to EE that encompasses Ontological Engineering[16][21][24][25], Lifecycle Modeling[8][20] and Knowledge Management[13]. Moreover, lifecycle engineering is based on three lifecycles – Product Lifecycle, Enterprise Lifecycle and Corporate Knowledge Lifecycle.

Among lifecycle ontologies we pay a special attention to granular lifecycle meta-ontology and upper (top-level) ontology. A general representation of lifecycle ontology by a mind map is given. Lifecycle granulation problems are elicited, fine-grained and coarse-grained lifecycle parts are specified. To model them, we use an extended Allen's logic [18]. As a result, both abstract and visualized lifecycle representations are constructed: they encompass circular, sequential, incremental, parallel-sequential, spiral models. Abstract models are based on Maltsev's algebraic system [19], ordinary and fuzzy partitions and coverings, Archimedean and logarithmic spiral equations [20].

The paper is organized as follows.

In Section II, we present various viewpoints on EE. Some basic disciplines of EE are considered and the corresponding pyramid visual representation is depicted.

Section III presents basic ideas of lifecycle engineering and lifecycle ontological modeling is seen as a basic instrument of lifecycle engineering.

In Section IV, the formal prerequisites for spiral representations are given.

The perspectives of developing and using formal ontological granulation models are discussed in the conclusion.

II. INDUSTRIAL ENTERPRISE ENGINEERING: AN ONTOLOGICAL APPROACH

Nowadays, an extremely broad multi-disciplinary area of EE has been developed based on systems engineering, organization theory strategic management, advanced information and communication technologies. The objective of EE is the design and creation of modern networked enterprise as an open sophisticated holistic system by modeling and integrating its products, processes, resources, organization structures, business operations, etc. In other words, EE considers the formation of enterprise as a sort of engineering activities. Moreover, it tends to examine each aspect of the enterprise, including various resources, business processes, information flows, organizational structures.

A conventional consideration of enterprise as a family of business processes may break its systemic integrity; here, some other approaches are needed, such as constructing generalized enterprise architectures with using agent-oriented technologies [1] and organization ontologies for industrial enterprise [2].

Let us discuss some viewpoints on the essence and basic disciplines for EE. EE is defined in [3] as a body of knowledge, principles, and practices having to do with the analysis, design, development, implementation and operation of an enterprise. It means the shift from Data Systems Engineering and Information Systems Engineering to Enterprise Ontological Engineering [2]. In [4], three main goals of EE are mentioned: intellectual manageability, organizational concinnity, social devotion.

In [5], Martin focuses on seven disciplines of EE grouped around value framework: 1) strategic visioning viewed as ongoing cycle of value positioning; 2) enterprise redesign – discontinuous change in the value definition; 3) value stream reinvention – discontinuous change in the value offering; 4) procedure redesign – discontinuous reinvention of value creation; 5) total quality management – continuing change in value creation; 6) organizational and cultural development – continuous value innovation; 7) information technology progress (continuous value enablement).

According to Vernadat [6] EE is the art of understanding, defining, specifying, analyzing and implementing business processes for the enterprise entire life cycle, so that the enterprise can achieve its objectives, be cost-effective, and be more competitive in its market environment. Here, two basic disciplines for EE are enterprise modeling and enterprise integration.

Below, we propose our pyramid of EE Activities (EEA-pyramide; see Fig. 1). Our approach to EE is founded on the integration of System of Systems Concept [7], Ontological Engineering, Lifecycle Modeling and Knowledge Management. It supposes the specification and co-ordination of (at least) three lifecycles: product (complex technical system), enterprise and knowledge lifecycles (Fig. 2).

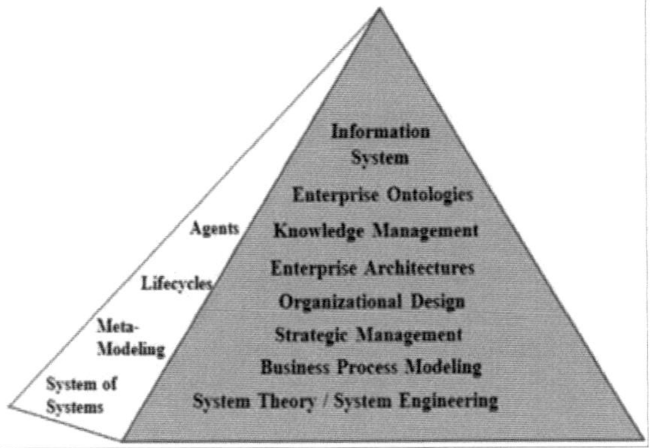

Figure 1. Pyramid of disciplines for EE

On the one hand, a computer-based integration of product lifecycle and knowledge lifecycle leads to the fusion of Product Lifecycle Management (PLM) and Knowledge Management (KM) technologies. The concept of lifecycle represents a basic implementation of systemic approach to complex technical objects that consists in visualizing their state changes for a temporal interval. By the end of XXth century-the beginning of XXIst century the notion of lifecycle has become wider. Now it also encompasses the stage of recycling (getting back used products into a new production process) that underlies the idea of lifecycle conversion [8]. On the other hand, the participation of enterprise at some alliances or consortiums, as well as the formation of extended, virtual or intelligent enterprises [9][10] leads to the prolongation of enterprise lifecycle best stages such as enterprise growth and maturity.

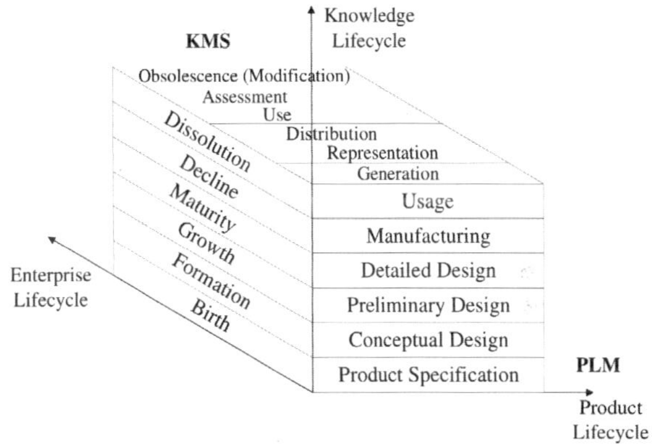

Figure 2. Generalized lifecycle management: towards the integration of PLM and KM

Let us recall that the term «Product Lifecycle» expresses the idea of a circulation of produced artifacts between the fields of design, production and usage (consumption). Product Lifecycle Management is the process of managing the entire lifecycle of a product from its conception, through design and manufacture, to service, disposal and dismantling [11][12]. It integrates data, processes, personnel and organizations to provide product's information backbone for networked enterprises. The development of PLM-systems requires lifecycle modeling and engineering. It means incorporating a variety of key product lifecycle values into the most critical production and usage time intervals.

Knowledge management [13] is often defined as the process of applying a systematic approach to the capture, structuring, dissemination and use of knowledge throughout an organization to work faster, reuse best practices, and reduce costs from project to project. It is evident that KM becomes more and more important for lifecycle knowledge in case of virtual enterprises. Thus, management of industrial enterprise cannot be generally reduced to resource-driven approach, i.e., Enterprise Resource Planning (ERP) systems of 1st or 2nd generations. Here an ontological approach to lifecycle knowledge management and meta-knowledge formation is of special concern, and PLM-systems are more suitable as a core of further IT-

hybrids and synergistic intelligent technologies [22]. Such systems generate and support a united information-knowledge space in the course of product lifecycle (Fig. 2).

III. LIFECYCLE ONTOLOGIES – A KEY TO ENTERPRISE ENGINEERING

Currently, the concept of ontology lifecycle is thoroughly developed, but the problems of lifecycle ontology and lifecycle ontological modeling are still not sufficiently studied (some of them remain open).

The lifecycle concept may be analyzed from various viewpoints; different variants of specifying its phases and activities were suggested. In marketing theory products follow such stages as introduction, growth, maturity, and decline. In industry, all products or systems have a particular life span considered as a sequence of stages, which is called product lifecycle (or complex system lifecycle). The aim of cyclic product definition is to realize both products and processes and economic solutions that are better and more intelligent by integrating lifecycle philosophy into technology and economy.

Our ontological approach to lifecycle knowledge engineering supposes the construction of both visual and formal models of lifecycle ontologies. Here, formal models are based on Maltsev's [19] concept of algebraic system, whereas visual representations encompass linear, circular and spiral models.

In this paper, the main attention is paid to lifecycle ontology viewed as an upper ontology for EE. We also introduce the concept of granular lifecycle meta-ontology; it is based on such concepts as granule, level, hierarchy, relations between levels [14].

The term meta-ontology means «ontology over ontologies». Meta-ontology provides us with both appropriate mathematical specification of ontology and necessary tools for representing and merging various ontologies. The need in granular meta-ontology (opposite to conventional singular one) for lifecycle modeling is obvious [23].

Generally, lifecycle granulation supposes the consideration of such problems as: 1) definition of basic granulation principles and criteria; 2) specification and interpretation of lifecycle granules; 3) analysis of lifecycle granulation approaches and techniques; 4) development of formal granular lifecycle models; 5) construction of mappings between various granularity levels; 6) specification of quantitative parameters of both lifecycle granules and granulation process itself.

It is worth stressing that an optimal granulation level does not exist; granule sizes are problem-oriented and depend on investigation context. Some lifecycle phases can be considered in a more detailed way and other – less thoroughly, with taking into account modeling objectives. We also envisage lifecycle representations with various abstraction degrees: a) rather simple circular representation based on either partition or covering; b) more sophisticated spiral representations showing interrelations between lifecycle phases, as well as between its phases and stages.

Let us focus on various forms of representing lifecycle ontologies. Any cycle, as a whole, is characterized by the presence of finite and repetitive parts on some temporal intervals; here key parameters are durations. In case of complex system's lifecycle, two basic granule types are lifecycle stages and phases. Lifecycle stages are coarse-grained parts that are usually divided into lifecycle phases, fine-grained parts, where each phase corresponds to a specific system's state.

One of fundamental resources for lifecycle management is time. A specific lifecycle feature is its heterochronous character, i.e., irregularity related to the difference of temporal criteria and constraints on various stages. In fact, we try both to accelerate design and manufacturing time and slow down usage time. For instance, during the design stage a basic criterion is to decrease design time, e.g. by using concurrent design strategies [17]. Contrarily, on the usage stage we tend to keep or increase reglamentary period, for example, by improving maintenance system.

Two well-known time metaphors – «time wheel» and «time arrow» – bring about lifecycle circular and consequent time models respectively. On the one hand, consequent linear models express such time properties as course, ordering facility, irreversibility. On the other hand, circular time models make emphasis on alternations, reiterations, rhythms, self-sustaining processes. In our paper, we try to reconcile these opposite models by constructing and analyzing spiral lifecycle models. Basic time theories should be envisaged in the context of lifecycle modeling: substantial and relational, static and dynamic, pointwise and interval time.

First of all, we shall represent lifecycle stages in the framework of set-theoretic approach as granules obtained by partition. Let us introduce natural denotations for complex systems's lifecycle: D – design; M – manufacturing; U – use; R – recycling. Then, we have

$$LC_1 = D \cup M \cup U,\ D \cap M = \varnothing,\ M \cap U = \varnothing,\ U \cap D = \varnothing \quad (1)$$

or $$LC_2 = M \cup U \cup R,\ M \cap U = \varnothing,\ U \cap R = \varnothing,\ R \cap M = \varnothing \quad (2)$$

Here, the structure of LC2 (2) expresses the «ecological imperative» of modern manufacturing being tightly related to above mentioned Kimura's lifecycle inversion concept. The first lifecycle partition LC1 (1) may be depicted by sectors of the circle (Fig. 3).

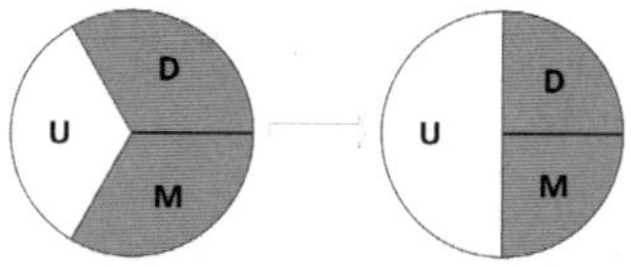

Figure 3. A Circular representation of complex system's lifecycle: an illustration of reducing lead (design and manufacturing) time and increasing period of usage

It is worth noticing that the representation of lifecycle by partition is rather simplistic and does not express many existing interrelations and co-operation links between partially overlapping stages. Moreover, this simultaneous work enables very important functions. For example, the specification is generated by using the information that circulates in both usage and design processes, production technologies ought to be discussed on the edge of design and manufacturing, whereas maintenance requires the collaboration of users and manufacturers. Taking into consideration such factors, we obtain the circular lifecycle model with fuzzy boundaries. For these cases, lifecycle granulation is based on covering (Fig. 4). Here,

$$LC_1 = D \cup M \cup U, \text{ but } D \cap M \neq \emptyset, M \cap U \neq \emptyset, U \cap D \neq \emptyset \quad (3)$$

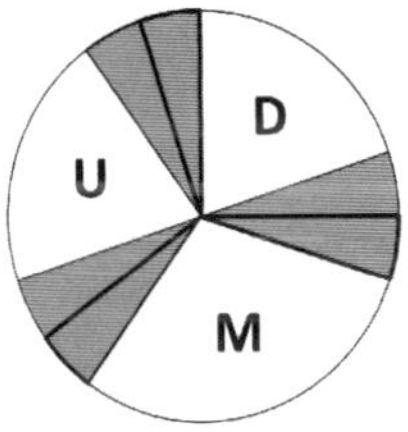

Figure 4. A Circular lifecycle representation on the basis of covering: the presence of collaborative works and fuzzy boundaries between stages

Generally, our approach is based on relational time model and interval time primitives. We use a fuzzy extension of well-known Allen's temporal logic [18] to model the links between lifecycle phases (or lifecycle stages and phases). These are mainly two types of relations: consequence and overlapping relations.

Let us recall that fuzzy quantity is defined as a fuzzy set of the real line. Fuzzy quantities are more suitable to describe flexible requirements on lifecycle parts duration.

We introduce a formal model of lifecycle ontologies ONT_{LC} as a quadruple

$$ONT_{LC} = \langle C_{LC}, R_{LC}, \Omega_{LC}, T_{LC} \rangle, \quad (4)$$

where C_{LC} is the set of concepts related to lifecycle, R_{LC} is the set of relations between these concepts, Ω_{LC} is the set of operations over concepts and/or relations, T_{LC} is the set of temporal characteristics for lifecycle.

Basic concepts for lifecycle are its phases and stages; therefore, the triple below can be taken as lifecycle systemic kernel

$$\text{ONTS} = \langle S, Rs, Os \rangle, \quad (5)$$

where S is the set of lifecycle stages (phases), R_s is the set of relations between these stages (phases), O_s is the set of operations used on these stages (phases).

It is worth noticing that each lifecycle phase may be seen as an interval primitive $s=[a^-, a^+]$, where a^- is the starting point and a^+ is the end point of the interval. A fuzzy interval extending the concept of an interval is a special kind of fuzzy quantity that is represented by a convex fuzzy subset of a real line. As a special case, we have

$$ONT_{S1} = \langle S, <_f, \approx_f \rangle, \quad (6)$$

where $<_f$ is a fuzzy strict linear order relation that is non-reflexive, asymmetric, transitive and linear, $\approx_f$ is a fuzzy simultaneity relation, i.e., fuzzy reflexive, symmetric relation.

More generally, we can use the linguistic variable «Time» with a linguistically ordered term set such as {almost simultaneously, a bit later, later, much later, very much later}.

IV. SPIRAL LIFECYCLE REPRESENTATIONS

The essence of spiral lifecycle model consists in integrating two contrary time models: linear model and circular model. Linear time model expresses such time properties as irreversibility, directional character, ordering facility, course, whereas circular time model makes emphasis on alternations, reiterations, rhythms, self-sustaining processes. Spiral time models tend to reconcile these two contrary cases.

Let us recall that in polar coordinates each point on a plane is determined by a distance from a fixed point r, $r \geq 0$ and an angle $\varphi \in [-\pi, +\pi]$ from a fixed direction: $M = (r, \varphi)$. A spiral is a curve that winds around a fixed center point at a continuously increasing or decreasing distance from the point. Here, we consider two spirals, namely, Archimedean spiral and logarithmic spiral. The first one is the locus of points corresponding to the locations over time of a point moving away from a fixed point with a constant speed along a line which rotates with constant angular velocity. It is given by the equation $r = a + b\varphi$, where modifying the parameter a will turn the spiral, while b controls the distance between successive turnings. In the context of lifecycle, we interpret these spiral parameters in the following way: φ is the time interval, a is the productivity index, b is the level and r is system's state.

The Archimedean spiral has the property that any ray from the origin intersects successive turnings of the spiral in points with a constant separation distance. Hence, such lifecycle features as time acceleration on early phases of lifecycle (for instance, decrease of design time) or time deceleration on later phases (increase of usage period) cannot be taken into account by using the Archimedean spiral (Fig. 5). Oppositely, in a logarithmic spiral these distances, as well as the distances of the intersection points measured from the origin, form a geometric progression (Fig. 6).

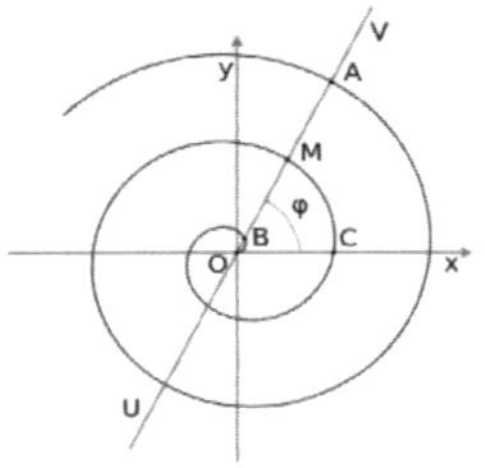

Figure 5. Archimedean spiral

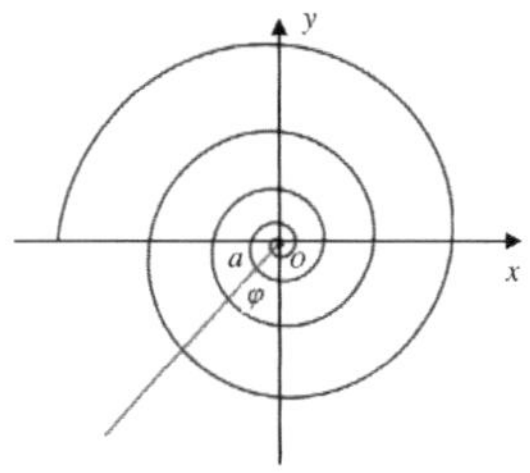

Figure 6. Logarithmic spiral

In particular, the spiral model is the most suitable approach to system's lifecycle knowledge engineering. The amount of knowledge is not equal for different lifecycle phases. One possible pitfall of using the spiral model is the number of rounds needed in developing a complex system (such as an aircraft). The pitfall can be avoided by using as reliable as possible methods in knowledge acquisition and elicitation. Mostly this knowledge representing a level of lifecycle granulation is expressed by a sort of Zadeh's generalized constraints [14] and circulates in a linguistic form, for instance, «to build a more detailed representation of maintenance phase» or «to take into account more knowledge about recycling».

Let us give an example of spiral lifecycle representation (Fig. 7). The starting point in product's evolution is a need formation in the usage (consumption) sector and the final state of the product is its disposal (elimination) interpreted as «a black hole». Spiral model phases are located in three sectors: design, manufacturing, usage.

Let us describe the main lifecycle phases for aircraft. Numbers in the Fig.7 describes the lifecycle phases. At the beginning of the lifecycle we have the identification of social need for a new product and formulation of appropriate product functions (phase 1). This phase is drawn as a circle belonging to the exploitation sector. The second step is the evaluation of production scales (a number of possible users) and the assessment of plausible product's price (phase 2) for the period of design solutions and specification of basic production indices.

Design stage itself starts with forming a specification (phase 3) and performing its analysis to generate feasible design proposal (phase 4). This step is shown by a circle on the boundary between exploitation and design sectors, because basic product's functions and a first draft of specification are given by a customer, whereas these specifications are converted into design proposal by a contractor. To illustrate the importance of this phase let us take the example of aircraft's lifecycle (Fig. 7). Here, basic design characteristics are not reduced to such items as mass, center of mass co-ordinates, aerodynamic surfaces, central tensor of inertia, but also include manufacturability, maintenability, serviceability, etc.

The design proposal ought to contain some technical and technico-economical justification of selected structures, their comparative estimation with taking into account product's structural and maintenance characteristics («Design for Maintenance»).

A preliminary project supposes information search and retrieval concerning available prototypes and analogous systems (phase 5).

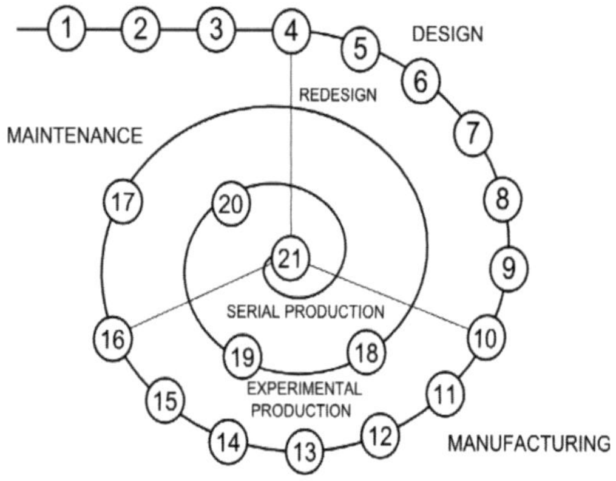

Figure 7. Product lifecycle representation

Phase 1. Formulation of product function;
Phase 2. Evaluation of product scales and product's prices;
Phase 3. Product specification;
Phase 4. Specification analysis and formation of design proposal;
Phase 5. Preliminary project;
Phase 6. Basic project;
Phase 7. Detailed project;
Phase 8. Development of static mockup;
Phase 9. Generation of structural-technological solutions for manufacturing;
Phase 10. Manufacturing pre-planning;
Phase 11. Development of assembly technology;
Phase 12. Design of technological equipment;
Phase 13. Production management design;
Phase 14. Manufacturing of technological equipment, fixtures and tools;
Phase 15. Equipment spatial allocation;
Phase 16. Elaboration of development batch;
Phase 17. Model (ground) tests;
Phase 18. Production management;
Phase 19. Serial production;
Phase 20. Product's maintenance;
Phase 21. Product's disposal

The phase of basic project supposes the justification of conceptual design solutions and specification of basic production indices (phase 6). Here, necessary data arc collected and calculations are made to specify the main product parameters, dimensions and form features. Various types of design analysis are executed: mass analysis, aerodynamic analysis including lift distribution, aerofoil design, aerodynamic performance estimation and confirmation. The construction layout and aerodynamic surfaces may be corrected many times to attain required aircraft properties. As a result, a detailed project is performed to obtain a final structure (phase 7). Here, a working documentation is made such as parts drawings, assembly drawings with appropriate technical solutions and technical requirements. The results of aerodynamic tests permit to fix aircraft form and to perform final strength analysis. Here, given temperatures and efforts on aerodynamic surfaces, so as fight accelerations, on vary possible a materials and reinforcement mode for load-carrying constructions. One specifies all the dimensions and the forms of reinforcement elements, the skin thickness ensuring a necessary strength. The data and knowledge on mechanical loads are widely used to verify forms and dimensions. Here, we deal with an overall construction except some parts such as engine, control system with devices and drives, or transportable parts obtained through plants cooperation. As a result of detailed design, we get final technical solutions with all product parameters and specifications for manufacturing. Then a static mockup (phase 8) is built. The participation of technologists is required to generate complex structural-technological solutions (phase 9) and organize manufacturing pre-planning (phase 10).

The next phases of technological support are assembly technology development (phase 11), technological equipment design (phase 12), and production management design (phase 13). Now, if the production technical-economical indices are satisfactory, then we proceed to manufacturing of technological equipment; fixtures and tools (phase 14), their spatial allocation (phase 15), elaboration and assembly of product's development batch (phase 16).

Because the processes of conceptual design and the enabling production technology and production management have rather approximate than precise nature, it is natural to expect that product's technical-economical indices and performances differ from specifications and requirements. Their correspondence to these preliminary requirements is specified through model (ground) tests (17) in the framework of exploitation sector.

Basing on results of the model tests a comparison with initial specifications is made, and some new local specifications are formulated to correct both the product structure and the production technology and management (18). These steps 3–18 may be repeated on each new spire of lifecycle's diagram (redesign and production modification) until product's performances begin to correspond to general specifications. Later on, a commercialization stage opens with the start of serial production (phase 19), followed by product's usage and maintenance (phase 20) and its disposal (phase 21) due to obsolescence with taking into consideration economic and ecological restrictions.

Such a representation of product's lifecycle by logarithmic spiral simplifies the analysis of concurrent engineering problems and the development and adaptation of appropriate AI methods and tools. The number of spires of life-cycle diagram depend on the level of informational/intelligent support and may be interpreted as a degree of simultaneous engineering.

Uncertain and imprecise knowledge on products' structure and its manufacturing technology, imperfect design and simulation models necessitate a repeated passing of production stages followed by exploitation tests in order to verify how initial specifications are satisfied. According the estimates of Russian experts in aerospace technology [17], the duration of first life-cycle's spire until first exploitation tests is 15% and the cost of this first spire establishes 25% of the integral duration and cost respectively to compare with the whole product' refinement phase until meeting initial specifications/requirements.

V. Conclusion

The new approach to EE centered on various lifecycle models has been proposed. On the one hand, it provides a theoretical background for implementing various lifecycle ontologies to develop advanced knowledge-based PLM systems. On the other hand, a system of lifecycle ontologies seems to be a necessary tool for mutual understanding and join work of all enterprise actors - both human and artificial agents. Here, the main difficulties consist in different ways of information granulation along the whole lifecycle. Lifecycle Ontologies has been considered as a core of EE. Granular lifecycle meta-ontology and upper ontology are of special concern. Both abstract and visualized lifecycle representations have been constructed; they encompass circular, sequential and spiral models. The emphasis has been made on spiral representations with using the Archimedean and logarithmic spirals.

Our future work will be focused on specifying basic indices for granular ontologies and developing an ontological sub-system for intelligent PLM-system.

Acknowledgment

This work has been supported by Russian Foundation for Basic Research (Project No 15-57-04047, 15-07-05623, 16-37-50025).

References

[1] V. B. Tarassov, "From Multi-Agent Systems to Intelligent Organizations", Moscow: Editorial URSS, 2002 (in Russian)

[2] J. Dietz, "Enterprise Ontology–Theory and Methodology", Berlin: Springer-Verlag, 2006.

[3] D. Liles, M. E. Johnson, L. M. Meade, and D. Ryan, "Enterprise Engineering: a Discipline?", Proc. Society for Enterprise Engineering Conference, 1995, vol. 6, pp. 1196-1204.

[4] J. Dietz, et al., "The Discipline of Enterprise Engineering", International Journal of Organisational Design and Engineering, 2013, vol. 3, no. 1, pp. 86-114.

[5] J. Martin, The Great Transition: Using the Seven Principles of Enterprise Engineering to Align People, Technology and Strategy, New York: American Management Association, 1995.

[6] F. Vernadat, Enterprise Modeling and Integration: Principles and Applications, London: Chapman and Hall, 1996.

[7] System of Systems Engineering: Innovations for the Twenty-First Century, Ed. by M. Jamshidi, New York: Wiley, 2008.

[8] F. Kimura and H. Suzuki, "Product Life Cycle Modeling for Inverse Manufacturing", Proc. IFIP WG 5.3 International Conference on Life Cycle Modeling for Innovative Products and Processes (PROLAMAT 95), Ed. by F.L. Krause, H. Hansen, Berlin: Springer-Verlag, 1996, pp. 81-89.

[9] L. M. Camarinha-Matos and H. Afsarmanesh, "A Comprehensive Modeling Framework for Collaborative Networked Organization", Journal of Intelligent Manufacturing, 2007, vol. 18, pp. 529–542.

[10] V. B. Tarassov, "Special Session on Intelligent Agents and Virtual Organizations in Enterprise", Proc. the 2nd IFAC/IFIP/IEEE Conference on Management and Control of Production and Logistics

2000 (MCPL 2000), Ed. by Z.Binder, Amsterdam: Elsevier Science Publishers, 2001, vol. 2, pp. 475-478.

[11] A. Saaksvuory and A. Immonen, Product Lifecycle Management, Berlin: Springer-Verlag, 2008.

[12] J. Stark, Product Lifecycle Management: 21st Century Paradigm for Product Realization, 2nd ed., London: Springer, 2011.

[13] K. Wiig, Knowledge Management Foundations, Arlington, TX: Schema Press, 1993.

[14] L. Zadeh, "Toward a Theory of Fuzzy Information Granulation and its Centrality in Human Reasoning and Fuzzy Logic", Fuzzy Sets and Systems, 1997, vol. 90, pp. 111-127.

[15] A. Bargiela and W. Pedrycz, Granular Computing: an Introduction, Dordrecht: Kluwer Academic Publishers, 2003.

[16] H. S. Pinto, S. Staab, C. Tempich, "DILIGENT: Towards a fine-grained methodology for DIstributed, Loosely-controlled and evolvInG Engineering of oNTologies", Proc. the 16th European Conference on Artificial Intelligence (ECAI), IOS Press, 2004, pp. 393-397.

[17] V. B. Tarassov, L. A. Kashuba, and N. V. Cherepanov, "Concurrent Engineering and AI Methodologies: Opening New Frontiers", Proc. the IFIP International Conference on Feature Modeling and Recognition in Advanced CAD/CAM Systems, vol. 2, May 1994, pp. 869-888.

[18] J.F. Allen, "Maintaining knowledge about temporal intervals", Communications of the ACM, 1983, vol.26, pp. 832-843.

[19] A. Maltsev, Algebraic systems, North-Holland Amsterdam, 1973.

[20] A. V. Fedotova and V. B. Tarasov, "Development and Interpretation of Spiral Lifecycle's Model: a Granular Computing Approach. Part 1. Lifecycle Granulation and Spiral Representation", Proc. Seventh International Conference on Soft Computing, Computing with words and Perceptions in System Analysis, Decision and Control (ICSCCW 13), Sept. 2013, pp. 431-440.

[21] S. F. Mari Carmen, A. Gómez-Pérez, M. Fernández-López, "NeOn Methodology for Building Ontology Networks: Specification, Scheduling and Reuse", Applied Ontology, 2015, vol. 10, no. 2, pp. 107-145

[22] A. V. Fedotova, I. T. Davydenko, and A. Pförtner, "Design Intelligent Lifecycle Management Systems Based on Applying of Semantic Technologies", Proc. the First International Scientific Conference "Intelligent Information Technologies for Industry" (IITI 16), Springer International Publishing Switzerland, vol. 1, May 2016, pp. 251-260, doi: 10.1007/978-3-319-33609-1_22.

[23] V. B. Tarassov, A. V. Fedotova, and B. S. Karabekov "Granular Meta-Ontology, Fuzzy and Linguistic Ontologies: Enabling Mutual Understanding of Cognitive Agents", Proc. the 5th International Conference on Control, Automation and Artificial Intelligence (CAAI 2015), Lancaster PA: DEStech Publications Inc., Aug. 2015, pp. 253-261.

[24] M. Fernández-López, A. Gómez-Pérez, N. Juristo, "Methontology: From Ontological Art Towards Ontological Engineering", Proc. Spring Symposium on Ontological Engineering of AAAI, AAAI Press, 1997, pp. 33-40.

[25] S. Staab, et al., "Knowledge Processes and Ontologies", IEEE Intelligent Systems, Los Alamitos, CA, USA, 2001, vol. 16, no. 1, pp. 26–34.

Intelligent Information System as a Tool to Reach Unaproachable Goals for Inspectors

High-Performance Data Analysis for Reduction of Non-Technical Losses on Smart Grids

Juan I. Guerrero, Antonio Parejo, Enrique Personal, Félix Biscarri, Jesús Biscarri and Carlos León
Department of Electronic Technology
University of Seville
Seville, Spain
e-mail: juaguealo@us.es

Abstract—**The Non-Technical Losses (NTLs) represent the non-billed energy due to faults or illegal manipulations in customer facilities. The objective of the Midas project is the detection of NTL through the application of computational intelligence over the information stored in utility company databases. This project has several research lines. Some of them are pattern recognition, expert systems, big data and High Performance Computing (HPC). This paper proposes module which use statistical techniques to make patterns of correct consumption. This module is integrated with a rule based expert system with other modules as: text mining module and data warehousing module. The correct consumption patterns are generated using rules which will be used in rule based expert system. Two implementations are proposed. Both implementations provided an Intelligent Information System (IIS) to reach unapproachable goals for inspectors.**

Keywords- non-technical losses; pattern recognition; expert system; big data analytics; high performance computing.

I. INTRODUCTION

The information systems have provided a new advantage: the capability to store, manage and analyze great quantities of information, without human supervision. This paper proposes one solution to a very difficult problem: the NTLs reduction.

NTLs represent the non-billed energy due to the abnormalities or illegal manipulations in client power facilities. The objective of Midas project is the detection of NTLs using computational intelligence and Knowledge Based Systems (KBS) over the information stored in Endesa databases. Endesa is the most important utility distribution company in Spain with more than 12 million clients. Initially, this project is tested with information about customers of low voltage. The system uses information of consumers with monthly or bimonthly billing. Although the system can analyze large volume of data, the system has a very high cost in time when there are more than 4 million consumers. Notwithstanding, this information volume will be unapproachable to analyze for an inspector. In order to reduce this cost, a hybrid architecture based on big data and high performance computing is currently applied to create a high-performance data analysis (HPDA). This architecture has been successfully applied in biomedical topics [1], text data classification [2], and other scientific datasets [3]. Smart Grids have provided a new scope of technologies, for example, Advanced Metering Infrastructures (AMI) with smart metering, Advanced Distribution Automation (ADA), etc. These new infrastructures increase the information about consumer, taking hourly or even quarterly measures.

In terms of consumption in utilities, a great spectrum of techniques can be applied; some techniques can be data mining, time series analysis, etc. Basically, it is essential the use of any type of statistical technique to detect anomalous patterns. This idea is not new. Several works usually apply statistical or similar techniques to make analysis of anomalous consumption [4][5][6][7][8]. Some techniques are based on study of consumption of the historical customer consumption; for example, Azadeh et al. [9] made a comparison between the use of time series, neural network and ANOVA, always with reference of the consumption of the same customer. But, these techniques have several problems, the main problem being that it is necessary to have a large historical data about consumption of customer. Other works use different studies to make good patterns of consumption, which compare the consumption of a customer with others who have similar characteristics. For example, Richardson [10] compared both neural networks and statistical techniques; in the tests performed, statistical techniques are 4% more efficient than neural networks. Hand et al. [11] proposed the identification of some characteristic which allow the identification of consumption patterns applying statistical techniques that use them as anomalous patterns. Other methods propose the use of advanced techniques to make other references or patterns of consumption. In this sense, Nagi et al. [12] used support vector machines and [13] applied rough sets, both of them in NTLs detection.

Other applications of advanced techniques, mainly Artificial Neural Network (ANN), which are not used for detection of NTLs, but could be used, are the applications for demand forecasting. In this sense, the forecasting can be made in short [14], medium [15], or long [16] term.

This paper proposes a model which uses statistical technique to detect correct consumption patterns. These patterns are used to generate rules which are applied in a Rule Based Expert System (RBES). The RBES is described in [17][18] and the module of text mining is described in

[19]. In this paper, an increase of functionality of the data mining module is proposed. In Fig. 1 and Fig. 2 the system architecture is shown.

The proposed solution is described in the following sections. In Section II, the architecture and technical characteristics are described. In Section III, the characterization of correct consumption is proposed. In Section IV, the evaluation and experimental results are explained. In Section V, the conclusions are included. Finally, in Section VI, the future research lines are described.

II. ARCHITECTURE AND TECHNICAL CHARACTERISTICS

Initially, the architecture of applications is shown in Fig. 1. This architecture is detailed for Statistical Pattern Generator, showing the different stages of this process. The system was run in a single machine, and it has been successfully tested with four million clients. This volume of analysis forced the system to do partitions in order to analyze more than 4 million customers.

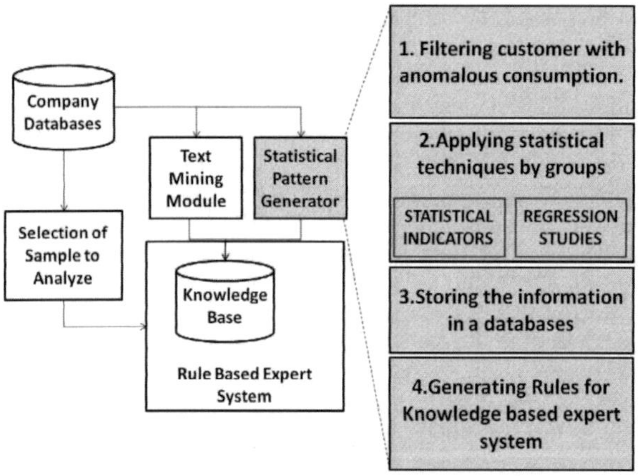

Figure 1. Local Expert System Architecture and Details of Statistical Pattern Generator Module

Currently, the new architecture applies big data and HPC. The big data architecture is based on Apache Spark with a database stored in HBase implemented in Apache Hadoop. The analytics are implemented in MLlib, GraphX, and library to send jobs to Graphics Processor Units (GPUs, based on Compute Unified Device Architecture or CUDA cores). The architecture is shown in Fig. 2.

The architecture is based on Apache Hadoop and Spark, enhanced with a new daemon to take advantage of HPC architectures. This daemon, named *gpulauncher*, is invoked by processes in order to send jobs to GPUs. The processes can be part of a MapReduce or Analytics. Although the system implemented statistical and regression algorithms, the new algorithms will also apply multivariable inference.

The *gpulauncher* daemon implemented several algorithms for analytics, functions for streaming the data to GPUs and functions for synchronization of nodes. These synchronization functions are in development. The main objective is the synchronization between GPUs of different nodes and working in near-real-time (NRT).

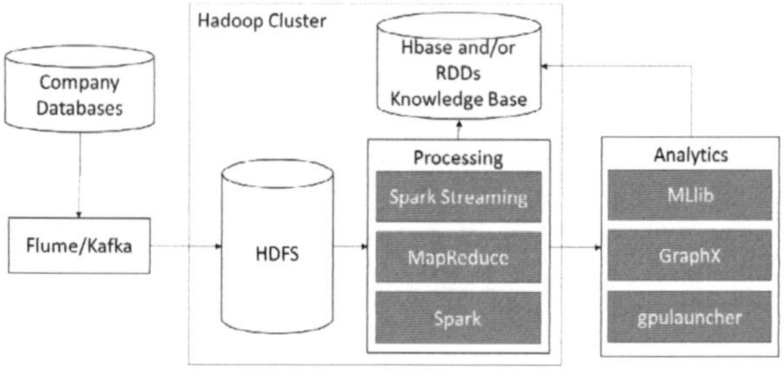

Figure 2. Architecture of Expert System in a High-Performance Data Analysis

The proposed system was not deployed in a real cluster of machines. The cluster was implemented with two virtualized servers. The first server has an Intel i7 (3GHz), 16GB RAM and GTX750 (2GB and 640 CUDA cores). The second server has an Intel Xeon E5 (2GHz), 64GB RAM and Quadro K1200 (4GB and 512 CUDA cores).

III. CONSUMPTION CHARACTERIZATION

To find out which characteristics have more influence in consumption is a very difficult task because there are a lot of consumption information available. An in-depth analysis shows that some characteristics have more influence over the consumption: time, geographical location, postal code, contracted power, measure frequency, economic activity, and time discrimination band. The importance of these characteristics has also been analyzed in other utilities as gas utility. Moreover, the results of these analysis have been compared with the knowledge provided by Endesa inspectors.

Each characteristic by itself is not efficient because the consumption depends on several characteristics at the same time. Thus, grouping characteristics can help find patterns of correct consumption, because these characteristics can determine the consumption with a low level of error rate providing, at least, one consumption pattern. These groups have in common a series of characteristics: Geographical location, time, contracted power, and measure frequency. These are named *Basis Group* because these are the main characteristics. The values for each of these characteristics are wide; therefore, each of them shows great variations of consumption. A description of Basis Group and the other groups are shown in Table I.

TABLE I. GROUPS OF CONSUMPTION CHARACTERISTICS

Consumption Characteristics	Description
Basis Group	This group provides consumption patterns by general geographical location: north, south, islands, etc.

Basis Group and Postal Code	This group provides patterns useful for cities with coastal and interior zones.
Basis Group and Economic activity.	The granularity of geographical location is decreased. In this way, the economic activity takes more importance. Nevertheless, the geographical location cannot be despised because, as for example, a bar has not the same consumption whether it is in interior location or coastline location.
Basis Group and time discrimination band.	There are several time discrimination bands. Each band registers the consumption at a different time range. This group provides consumption patterns in different time discrimination bands. These are usefull because there exists customers who make their consumption in day or night time.

Some characteristics have different granularity because they have continuous values or have a lot of possible values. The granularity is used because there are some problems related with the measures. For example, the proposed framework performs a discretization of contracted power in 40 ranges. In the graph of Fig. 3, the 14th range of contracted power is shown. This range groups the contracted power between 46,852 kW and 55,924 kW in North of Spain. This figure shows an abnormal level of consumption at 2002; this fact represents errors in measures which cannot be filtered.

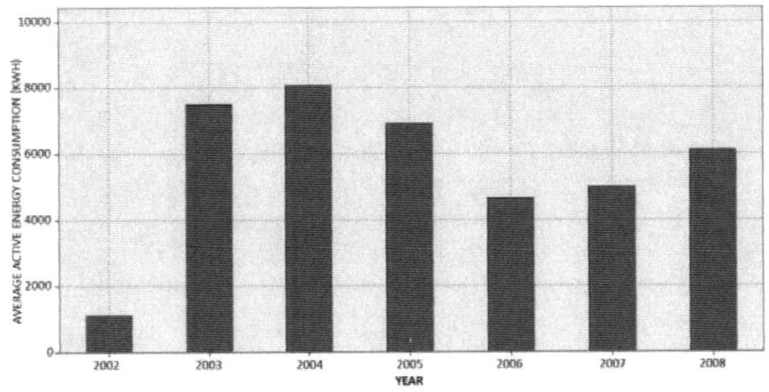

Figure 3. Average yearly consumption graph in different power ranges

In the graph of Fig. 4, the average consumption in monthly periods for the 14th range is shown. In this case, the granularity of time is increased; therefore, it is possible to get another pattern, which is better than the one obtained from the graph of Fig. 3. In this case, the consumption can be analyzed monthly.

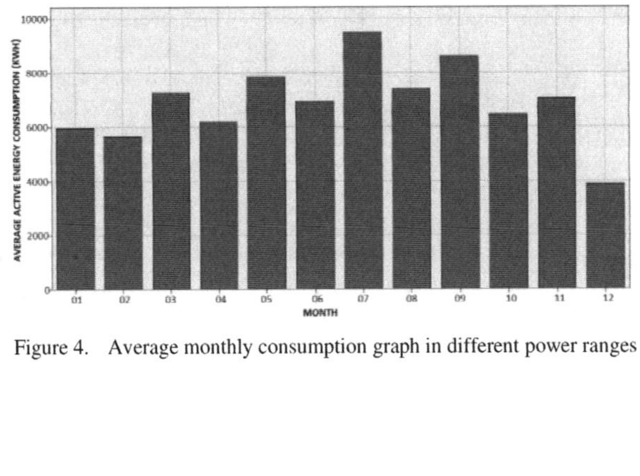

Figure 4. Average monthly consumption graph in different power ranges

Thus, several time ranges are used: absolutely, monthly, yearly and seasonally. For example, the average consumption calculation provides different results: total average consumption (absolutely), twelve/six average, monthly/bimonthly consumption, one average yearly consumption (when the measures are available), and four average seasonally consumption. In the same way, the contracted power has to be discretized in equal consumption ranges. In lower contracted power, the ranges are very narrow because there are a lot of consumers. When the contracted power is higher, the quantity of consumers is smaller, although the consumptions are very different. The reason for aggregating the consumption (of supplies without NTL) in different groups is because there are scenarios in which it is necessary to have other patterns.

These groups provided dynamic patterns, which can be updated according to the time granularity. Once the characteristics are identified, it is necessary to design a process which finds patterns automatically. Initially, these studies were made bimonthly and were applied as a part of an integrated expert system to model correct consumption patterns (Fig. 1). Currently, the process can be performed hourly, through the architecture proposed in Fig. 2. The system applies statistical techniques to get consumption patterns using the process detailed in Fig. 1.

When the rules are created, they are used to analyze the customers in order to determine if there exist any NTLs. There are defined series of rules in RBES which use the information generated by the proposed module. The antecedents of the rules are generated dynamically using the patterns generated in the described process and according to the characteristics of the customer who will be analyzed. In this way, the use of memory resources is minimized because only the necessary antecedents of the rules are generated.

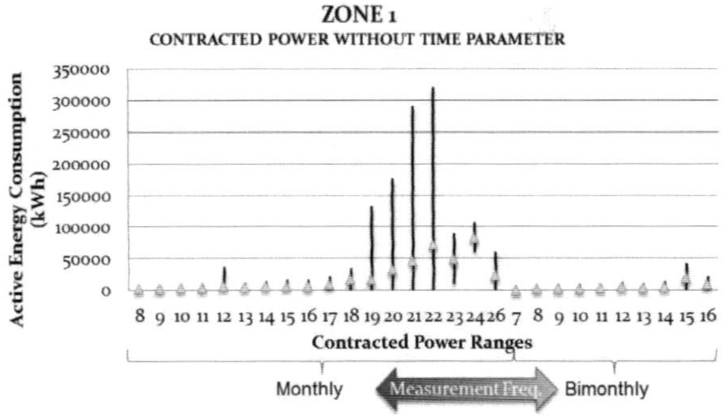

Figure 5. Graph of Active Energy Consumption Ranges vs. contracted power ranges without time parameter for specific geographical zone.

When the consumption of a customer is analyzed, several rules can fit with the characteristics of that customer. Initially, the rules are applied in the most restrictive way; this means, the customer consumption will be correct if it fits in any correct consumption pattern. Moreover, the system notifies if the pattern fails for each customer. For example, the correct consumption ranges of active energy for specific geographic zone, different contracted power ranges, and different measurement frequency (monthly or bimonthly) are shown in Fig. 5.

IV. EVALUATION AND EXPERIMENTAL RESULTS

The proposed module provides patterns of correct customer consumption. The analysis made by the mentioned expert system uses this module to create rules. The customer consumption analysis applies these rules according to the contract attributes: contracted power, economic activity, geographical location, postal code, and time discrimination band. Traditionally, the systems used to detect frauds or abnormalities in utilities make patterns for NTLs detection. But in the proposed system, models of correct consumption ranges and trends are made. The use of these patterns increases the efficiency of the RBES. This module is essential to analyze the customer. The RBES has been applied in real cases getting better results in zones with a lot of clients. The success of the RBES is between 16,67% and 40,66% according to the quantity of clients of the corresponding location. This fact is shown in Fig. 6. The new architecture based on high-performance data analysis allows the application of the expert system in NRT. Thus, this system will be useful in the new Smart Grid infrastructures, based on AMI.

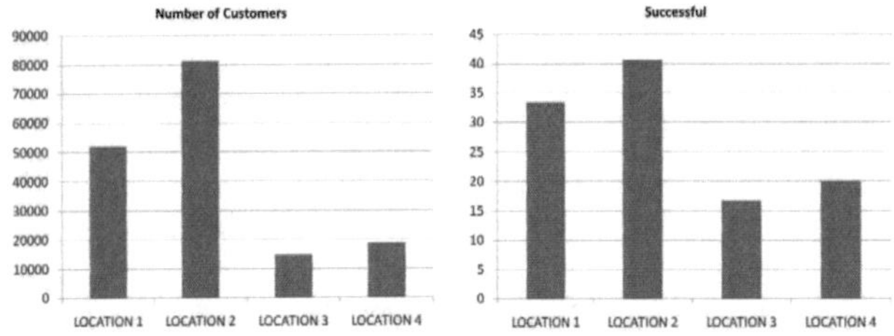

Figure 6. Number of customers vs. successful

V. CONCLUSION AND FUTURE WORK

The proposed framework was implemented, tested and deployed in a real Power Distribution Company. This framework is part of a RBES. This model establishes a series of similarities with other utilities. For example, the utilization of frequency billing, geographical location, and time can be made in all utilities. However, the contracted power can be replaced by the contracted volume of flow in gas or water utilities.

The proposed module can be added to other systems of NTLs detection to increase their efficiency by using rules or a translator of the knowledge generated by the module.

Usually, an inspector takes between 5 to 30 minutes to analyze the information about a customer, in order to confirm whether there exists a NTL. This period depends on the quantity of information to be analyzed; the average time of the analysis process takes 16,3 minutes. This means that the time to analyze 4 million customers (the maximum number of customers in case proposed in Fig. 1) would be 1086666,6 hours of work. In the first case, the proposed system in Fig. 1 takes 22 milliseconds per customer in the analysis process. The HPDA provides the possibility to analyze the information in NRT, without limit in the number of customers. Notwithstanding, the analysis of the inspector will be always better than the machine analysis because inspectors usually work in the same zone and they have additional knowledge of facilities, that is not stored in the system.

Finally, several research lines for improving the efficiency of the proposed framework will be addressed:

- Application of techniques related with Information Retrieval, to increase the information about consumers.
- Test the new approach in a big scenario, based on AMI infrastructure and with hourly measures.
- Application of the proposed framework in other utilities.
- Enhance the analysis with application of multivariable inference.

ACKNOWLEDGMENT

The authors would also like to thank the backing of SIIAM project (Reference Number: TEC2013-40767-R) which is funded by the Ministry of Economy and Competitiveness of Spain.

REFERENCES

[1] E. Elsebakhi et al., "Large-scale machine learning based on functional networks for biomedical big data with high performance computing platforms," *J. Comput. Sci.*, vol. 11, pp. 69–81, Nov. 2015.

[2] A. Rauber, P. Tomsich, and D. Merkl, "parSOM: a parallel implementation of the self-organizing map exploiting cache effects: making the SOM fit for interactive high-performance data analysis," in *IJCNN 2000, Proceedings of the IEEE-INNS-ENNS International Joint Conference on Neural Networks, 2000*, vol. 6, 2000.

[3] J. Liu and Y. Chen, "Improving Data Analysis Performance for High-Performance Computing with Integrating Statistical Metadata in Scientific Datasets," in *High Performance Computing, Networking, Storage and Analysis (SCC), 2012 SC Companion:*, 2012.

[4] I. Monedero et al., "Using regression analysis to identify patterns of non-technical losses on power utilities," in *Knowledge-Based and Intelligent Information and Engineering Systems*, Springer, 2010, pp. 410–419, 2010.

[5] C. C. Ramos, A. N. de Sousa, J. P. Papa, and A. X. Falcão, "A New Approach for Nontechnical Losses Detection Based on Optimum-Path Forest," *IEEE Trans. Power Syst.*, vol. 26, no. 1, pp. 181–189, pp. 181–189, Feb. 2011.

[6] M. E. de Oliveira, D. F. Boson, and A. Padilha-Feltrin, "A statistical analysis of loss factor to determine the energy losses," presented at the Transmission and Distribution Conference and Exposition: Latin America, 2008 IEEE/PES, 2008.

[7] M. Gemignani, C. Tahan, C. Oliveira, and F. Zamora, "Commercial losses estimations through consumers' behavior analysis," presented at the 20th International Conference and Exhibition on Electricity Distribution - Part 1, 2009. CIRED 2009, 2009.

[8] A. H. Nizar and Z. Y. Dong, "Identification and detection of electricity customer behaviour irregularities," presented at the Power Systems Conference and Exposition, 2009. PSCE '09. IEEE/PES, 2009.

[9] A. Azadeh, S. F. Ghaderi, and S. Sohrabkhani, "Forecasting electrical consumption by integration of Neural Network, time series and ANOVA," *Appl. Math. Comput.*, vol. 186, no. 2, pp. 1753–1761, Mar. 2007.

[10] R. Richardson, "Neural networks compared to statistical techniques," presented at the Computational Intelligence for Financial Engineering (CIFEr), 1997., Proceedings of the IEEE/IAFE 1997, 1997.

[11] D. J. Hand and G. Blunt, "Prospecting for gems in credit card data," *IMA J. Manag. Math.*, vol. 12, no. 2, pp. 173–200, Oct. 2001.

[12] J. Nagi, A. M. Mohammad, K. S. Yap, S. K. Tiong, and S. K. Ahmed, "Non-Technical Loss analysis for detection of electricity theft using support vector machines," presented at the Power and Energy Conference, 2008. PECon 2008. IEEE 2nd International, 2008.

[13] J. E. Cabral and E. M. Gontijo, "Fraud detection in electrical energy consumers using rough sets," presented at the 2004 IEEE International Conference on Systems, Man and Cybernetics, vol. 4, 2004.

[14] B. F. Hobbs, U. Helman, S. Jitprapaikulsarn, S. Konda, and D. Maratukulam, "Artificial neural networks for short-term energy forecasting: Accuracy and economic value," *Neurocomputing*, vol. 23, no. 1–3, pp. 71–84, Dec. 1998.

[15] M. Gavrilas, I. Ciutea, and C. Tanasa, "Medium-term load forecasting with artificial neural network models," in *Electricity Distribution, 2001. Part 1: Contributions. CIRED. 16th International Conference and Exhibition on (IEE Conf. Publ No. 482)*, vol. 6, 2001.

[16] K. Padmakumari, K. P. Mohandas, and S. Thiruvengadam, "Long term distribution demand forecasting using neuro fuzzy computations," *Int. J. Electr. Power Energy Syst.*, vol. 21, no. 5, pp. 315–322, pp. 315–322, Jun. 1999.

[17] C. León et al., "Integrated expert system applied to the analysis of non-technical losses in power utilities," *Expert Syst. Appl.*, vol. 38, no. 8, pp. 10274–10285, Agosto 2011.

[18] J. I. G. Alonso et al., "EIS for Consumers Classification and Support Decision Making in a Power Utility Database," *Enterp. Inf. Syst. Implement. IT Infrastruct. Chall. Issues Chall. Issues*, p. 103, 2010.

[19] J. I. Guerrero Alonso et al., "Increasing the efficiency in non-technical losses detection in utility companies," 2010.

Semantic Reasoning Method to Troubleshoot in the Industrial Domain

Antonio Martín, Mauricio Burbano,
Higher Polytechnic School
Seville University
Seville, Spain
toni@us.es, aryburcen@us.es

Iñigo Monedero, Joaquín Luque, C.arlos León
Technical High School of Computer Science
University of Seville
Seville, Spain
cleon@us.es

Abstract—**Currently industrial information provides even more granular information through unit and equipment databases, which provide details about installed equipment, including models, designed capacity, throughput, and start up/shutdown dates for turbines, generators, refining equipment, etc. All these data and information are stored in digital repositories, digital archives, and business Web sites. Access to these collections poses a serious challenge. The present search techniques based on manually annotated metadata and linear replay of the material selected by the user do not scale effectively or efficiently to large collections. This can significantly reduce the accuracy of the search and draw in irrelevant documents. The artificial intelligence and Semantic Web provide a common framework that allows knowledge to be shared and reused in an efficient way. In this paper, we propose a comprehensive approach for discovering information objects in large digital repositories based on analysis of recorded semantic metadata and the application of Case Based Reasoning technique. We suggest a conceptual architecture for a semantic search engine. We have developed a prototype, which suggests a new form of interaction between users and digital enterprise repositories, to support efficient share distributed knowledge.**

Keywords- Case base Reasoning, Ontology, jColibri, Semantic Interoperability, Artificial Intelligence.

I. INTRODUCTION

Nowadays an enormous quantity of heterogeneous and distributed information is stored in BB.DD, Web sites, digital storehouses, etc. Digital Industry Repository (DIRs) are online databases that provide a central location to collect, contribute and share knowledge resources to use in the industrial domain. Mechanisms to retrieval information and knowledge from digital repositories have been particularly important. DIRs present centralized hosting and access to content. DIRs provide the ability to share digital objects or files, the permissions and controls for access to content, the integrity, and intellectual property rights of content owners and creators.

In the traditional search engines, the information stored in DIRs is treated as an ordinary database that manages the contents and positions. Results generated by the current searches are a list of results that contain or treat the pattern. Although search engines have developed increasingly effectively, information overload obstructs precise searches. Thus, it is necessary to develop new intelligent and semantic models that offer more possibilities. Our approach for realizing content-based search and retrieval information implies the application of the Case-Based Reasoning (CBR) technology and ontologies. The objective here is thus to contribute to a better knowledge retrieval in the industrial domain.

There are researchers and related fields works, which include intelligent techniques to share information such as [1] which describes the application of intelligent systems techniques to provide decision support to the condition monitoring of nuclear power plant reactor cores. An intelligent image agent based on soft-computing techniques for color image processing is proposed in [2]. Huang et al. [3] propose an intelligent human-expert forum system to perform more efficient knowledge sharing using fuzzy information retrieval techniques. Yang et al. [4] present a system to collect information through the cooperation of intelligent agent software, in addition to providing warnings after analysis to monitor and predict some possible error indications among controlled objects in the network. Gladun et al. [5] suggest a Semantic Web technologies-based multi-agent system that allows to automatically control students' acquired knowledge in e-learning frameworks.

The meta-concepts have explicit ontological semantics, so that they help to identify domain concepts consistently and structure them systematically. In [6] authors propose a construction safety ontology to formalize the safety management knowledge. Bertola et al. [7] present the building blocks for creating a semantic social space to organize artworks according to an ontology of emotions, which takes into account both the information two ancestral terms share and the probability that they co-occur with their common descendants. In [8] authors present an approach, which allows users to semantically query the BIM design model using a domain vocabulary, capitalizing on building product ontology formalized from construction perspectives. Zhang et al. [9] propose a framework to quantify the similarity measure beneath a term pair, which takes into account both the information two ancestral terms share and the probability that they co-occur with their common descendants. In [10] authors present a method for selecting a semantic similar measure with high similarity calculation accuracy for concepts in two different CAD model data ontologies.

There are a lot of researches on applying Artificial Intelligence (AI) and semantic techniques to share knowledge. In this paper, we present a full integration of AI technologies and semantic methods during the whole life cycle and from the industrial point of view. Our work differs from related projects in that we build ontology-based contextual profiles and we introduce an approaches used metadata-based in ontology search and expert system technologies. This paper describes semantic interoperability problems and presents an intelligent architecture to address them. We concentrate on the critical issue of metadata/ontology-based search and expert system technologies [11]. More specifically, the main objective of this research, is search possible intelligent infrastructures form constructing decentralized public repositories where no global schema exists. For this reason, we are improving representation by incorporating more metadata from within the information. The objective has focused on creating technologically complex environments industrial domain and incorporates Semantic Web and AI technologies to enable precise location of industrial resources.

The contributions are divided into the next sections. The first section reports a short description of important aspects in Industrial domain, the research problems and current work. Next section describes the role of Semantic and artificial intelligence in industrial domain. Next section concerns the design of a prototype system for semantic search framework, in order to verify that our proposed approach is an applicable solution. Finally, we present the results of our on going work on the adaptation of the framework and we outline the future works.

II. Aspects to Reach Efficient Shared Knowledge

Industrial repositories contain a large volume of digital information, generally focusing on making their knowledge resources to improve associate decision-support systems. Within a pool of heterogeneous and distributed information resources, users take site-by-site searching. Quality of search results varies greatly depending on quality of the search query from too limited set of results to a too large number of irrelevant results. For certain cases specifying a couple of keywords can be enough, if they are really specific and no ambiguity is possible [12]. Currently, electronic search is based mainly on matching keywords specified by users with sought information web pages that contain those keywords. Ambiguity of most word-combinations and phrases, which are used for searching web resources, and poor linguistic features of available web-content indexing and matching mechanisms severely affect the results of most internet searchers.

Thus, considerable effort is required in creating meaningful metadata, organizing and annotating digital documents, and making them accessible. This work concerns applications of the semantic technology for improving existing information search systems by adding semantic enabled extensions that enhance information retrieval from information systems. Use of ontologies can provides the following profits:

- Share and common understanding of the knowledge domain that can be communicated among agents and application systems.
- Explicit conceptualization that describes the semantics of the data.

In our work we analyzed the relationship between both factors ontologies and expert systems. We have proposed a method to efficiently search the target information on a digital repository network with multiple independent information sources. The use of AI and ontologies as a knowledge representation formalism offers many advantages in information retrieval. This scheme is based on the principle that knowledge items are abstracted to a characterization by metadata description, which is used for further processing. This characterization is based on a vocabulary/ontology that is shared to ease the access to the relevant information sources. This motivates researchers to look for intelligent information retrieval approach and ontologies that search and/or filter information automatically based on some higher level of understanding that is required. We make an effort in this direction by investigating techniques that attempt to utilize ontologies to improve effectiveness in information retrieval.

To reach these goals we need the capacity of different information systems, applications and services to communicate, share and interchange data, information and knowledge in an effective and precise way, as well as to integrate with other systems, applications and services in order to deliver new electronic products and services.

III. Systems and Services Interoperability Requirements

Connectivity and interoperation among computers, among entities, and among software components can increase the flexibility and agility of industrial systems, thus reducing administrative and software costs for industry. In the business case, expands to include the ability of two or more business processes, or services, to easily or automatically work together [13]. It is clear that the ability to interoperate is key to reducing industrial integration costs and inefficiencies, increasing business agility, and enabling the adoption of new and emerging technologies. Interoperability is the ability of two or more industrial assets like hardware devices, communications devices, or software components, to easily or automatically work together.

ISO/IEC 2382 Information Technology Vocabulary defines interoperability as the capability to communicate, execute programs, or transfer data among various functional units in a manner that requires the user to have little or no knowledge of the unique characteristics of those units. An interoperability framework can be described as a set of standards and guidelines, which describe the way in which organizations have agreed, or should agree, to interact with each other.

In this context, interoperability is the ability of information and communication technology systems and of the business processes they support to exchange data and to enable sharing of information and knowledge. Technical dimension of interoperability includes uniform movement of industrial data, uniform presentation of data, uniform user controls, uniform safeguarding data security and integrity, uniform protection of industrial confidentiality, uniform assurance of a common degree of service quality, Figure 1.

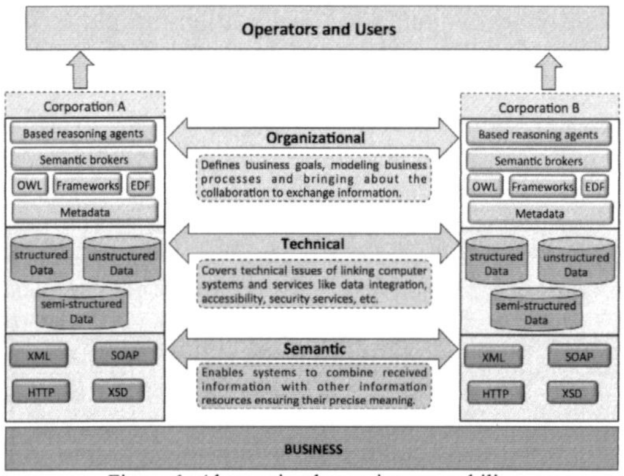

Figure 1. Abstraction layers interoperability

Specifically, the goal of semantic interoperability is to improve communication on industrial related knowledge both among humans and machines. In order to achieve this, a two-pronged approach is necessary: achieving a unified ontology and tackle concrete and clearly delineated issues. Organizational interoperability is defined as the state where the organizational components of the industrial system are able to perform seamlessly together. The vision is an integrated industrial system that provides efficient, effective and holistic. The functional goal is to allow data to be exchanged between different projects in multiple corporations using different equipment's, software etc. From multiple manufacturers or vendors. Technical interoperability consists in being able to communicate and interact between two systems coming from different manufacturers.

Different efforts are being leveraged by many standards efforts to address semantic and organizational interoperability and are proving to be a model for addressing semantic and organizational interoperability like ebXML, RosettaNet, the new UN/CEFACT work on aligning its global business process standards work with Web services, etc. In June 2002, European heads of state adopted the Europe Action Plan 2005 at the Seville summit. They calls on the European Commission to issue an agreed interoperability framework to support the delivery of European Digital services to enterprises. This recommends technical policies and specifications for joining up public administration information systems across the EU. This research is based on open standards and the use of open source software. These aspects are the pillars to support the European delivery of Digital services of the recently adopted European Interoperability Framework (EIF) [14] and its Spanish equivalent (MAP, 2014). This document is a reference for interoperability of the new Interoperable Delivery of Pan-European Digital Services to Public Administrations, Business and Citizens program (IDAbc). Member States Administrations must use the guidance provided by the EIF to supplement their national Interoperability Frameworks with a pan-European dimension and thus enable pan-European interoperability [15].

Furthermore achieving semantic and organizational interoperability requires strictly agreeing on the meaning of information and aligning business processes across enterprises/industries. At one level, general cross-industry frameworks and software infrastructure approaches can be, and are being, developed for semantics and business processes. For example, general semantics for major business transactions, such as purchase orders and invoices, are outlined through standards such as Universal Business Language (UBL), UN/CEFACT Core Components, and Open Applications Group Integration Standard (OAGIS).

IV. System Achitecture and Key Elements

Our system works comparing items that can be retrieved across heterogeneous repositories and capturing a semantic view of the world independent of data representation. The proposed architecture is based on our approach to share information in an efficient way by means of metadata characterizations and domain ontology inclusion. It implies to use ontology as vocabulary to define complex, multi-relational case structures to support the CBR processes [16]. The goal is achieved from a search perspective, with possible intelligent infrastructures to construct decentralized industrial repositories where no global schema exists. This goal implies the application of CBR technique.

In order to support the semantic shared knowledge in industrial repositories, a prototype CBR and ontology based techniques have been development. The architecture of our system is shown in Figure 2, which mainly includes four elements: the acquire engine, ontology, knowledge base, and graphic user interface.

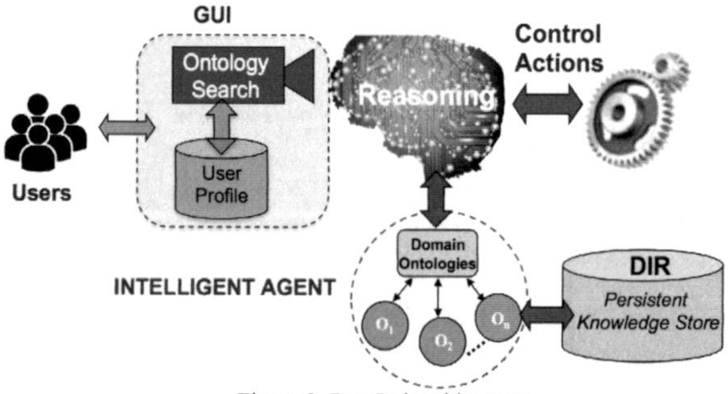

Figure 2. ReasInd architecture

A. *The Acquire Engine - Case Based Reasoning*

CBR is a problem solving archetype that solves a new problem, by remembering a previous similar situation and by reusing knowledge of that state. In CBR application, problems are described by metadata concerning desired characteristics of an industry resource, and the solution to the question is a pointer to a resource described by metadata. A new difficult is solved by retrieving one or more previously experienced cases, reusing the case, revising, and retaining. In our system when a description of the current request is input to the system the reasoning cycle may be described by the following processes [17].

The system retrieves the closest-matching cases stored in the case base. Reuse a complete design, where case-based and slot-based adaptation can be hooked, is provided. If appropriate, the validated solution is added to the case for use in future problem solving. Check out the proposed solution if necessary. Since the proposed result could be inadequate, this process can correct the first proposed solution. Retain the new solution as a part of a new case. This process enables CBR to learn and create a new solution. The solution is validated through feedback from the user or the environment, Figure 3.

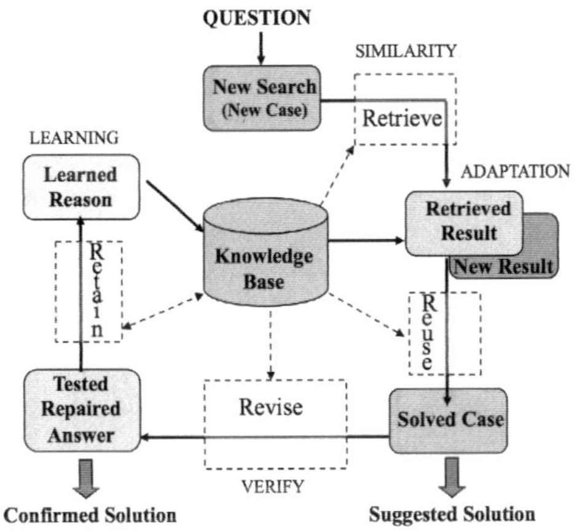

Figure 3. ReasInd Case Based Reasoning Cycle

Implementing a CBR application from scratch remains a time-consuming software engineering process and requires a lot of specific experience beyond pure programming skills. This involves a number of steps, such as: collecting case and background knowledge, modeling a suitable case representation, defining an accurate similarity measure, implementing retrieval functionality and implementing user interfaces. In this work, we have chosen framework jColibri to development the intelligent search.

JColibri is a java-based configuration that supports the development of knowledge intensive CBR applications and helps in the integration of ontology in them [18]. This way the same methods can operate over different types of information repositories. The Open Source JColibri system provides a framework for building CBR systems based on state-of-the-art software engineering techniques. JColibri is an open source framework, which affords the opportunity to connect easily an ontology in the CBR application to use it for case representation and content-based reasoning methods to assess the similarity between them. Nevertheless, at the same time, it ensures enough flexibility to enable expert users to implement advanced CBR applications.

B. *Knowledge Base.*

The understanding provided through semantic models is critical to being able to properly drive the correct insights from the monitored instrumentation, which ultimately can lead to optimizing business processes or, in this case, industry services. As a result, semantic models can greatly enhance the usefulness of the information obtained through operations integration solutions. In the physical world a control point such a valve or temperature sensor is known by its identifier in a particular control system, possibly through a tag name like 103-AA12.

CBR case data could be considered as a portion of the knowledge, i.e. metadata about resources. The metadata descriptions of the resources and objects (cases) are abstracted from the details of their physical representation and are stored in the case base. Every case contains both description problem and the associated solution. The information model provides the ability to abstract different kinds of data and provides an understanding of how the data elements relate. A key value of the semantic model then is to provide access to information in context of the real world in a consistent way.

Semantic models allow users to ask questions about what is happening in a modeled system in a more natural way. As an example, an oil production enterprise might consist of five geographic regions, with each region contains three to five drilling platforms, and each drilling platform monitored by several control systems, each having a different purpose. One of those control systems might monitor the temperature of extracted oil, while another might monitor vibration on a pump. A semantic model will allow a user to ask a question like, "What is the temperature of the oil being extracted on Platform 5?", without having to understand details such as, which specific control system monitors that information or which physical sensor is reporting the oil temperature on that platform. Within a semantic model implementation, this information is identified using "triples" of the form "subject-predicate-object"; for example:

Tank1 <has temperature> Sensor 7
Tank 1 <is part of> Platform 4
Platform 4 <is part of> Plant1

These triples, taken together, make up the ontology for Plant1 and can be stored in the model server. This information, then, can be easily traversed using the model query language more easily than the case without a semantic model to answer questions such as "What is the temperature of tank 1 on Platform 4".

C. *Ontology Development.*

Ontology models can be used to relate the physical world, to the real world, in the line-of-business and decision makers. The objective of our system is to improve the modeling of a semantic coherence for allowing the interoperability of different modules of environments dedicated to the industrial area. We have proposed to use ontology together with CBR in the acquisition of an expert knowledge in the specific domain. We need a vocabulary of concepts, resources and services for our information system described in the scenario, which requires definition about the relationships between objects of discourse and their attributes. The primary information managed in the domain is metadata about industrial resources, such as guides, digital services, alarms, information, etc. ReasInd project contains a collection of codes, visualization tools, computing resources, and data sets distributed across the grids, for which we have developed a well-defined ontology using Resource Description Framework (RDF) language [19].

The total set of entities in our semantic model comprises the taxonomy of classes we use in our model to represent the real world. Together these ideas are represented by an ontology. This provides the semantic makeup of the information model. The vocabulary of the semantic model provides the basis on which user-defined model queries are formed. Our ontology can be regarded as quaternion ReasInd:={caller, resources, properties, relation) where caller represent the user kinds, resources cover different information sources like electronic services, web pages, BB.DD., guides, etc. Also, properties contains all the characteristics of the services and resources and a set of relationships intended primarily for standardization across ontologies. We integrated three essential sources to the system: electronic resources, a catalogue of documents, and personal Data Base, Figure 4.

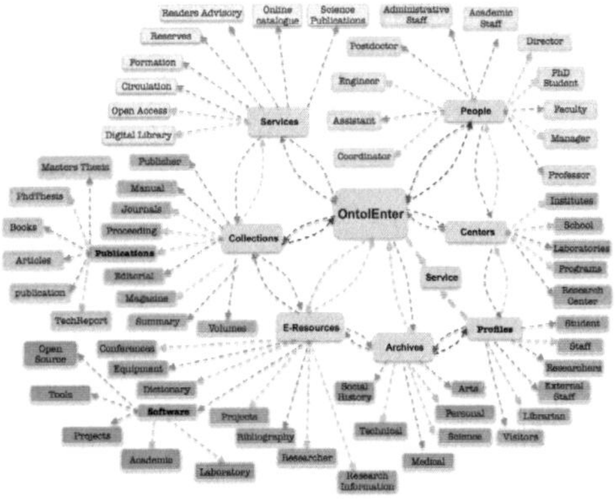

Figure 4. Class hierarchy for the ReasInd ontology

The W3C defines standards that can be used to design the ontology [20]. We wrote the description of these classes and the properties in RDF semantic markup language. We have chosen Protégé as our ontology editor, which supports knowledge acquisition and knowledge base development. Protégé provides an environment for the creation and development of underlying semantic knowledge structures-ontologies and semantically annotated web services. Protégé organizes these elements like a dynamic process workflow [21].

After designing the ontology, we wrote the classes and the properties description of in RDF semantic markup language. Then the domain expert, in this case, administrative staff fills blank units of instance according to the domain knowledge. 13.000 cases were collected for user profiles and their different resources and services. Each case contains a set of attributes concerning both metadata and knowledge.

D. Graphic User Interface.

ReasInd is a platform, which is an intermediate link between users and search engine. Keeping in mind that our final goal is to reformulate requests in the ontology to queries in another with least loss of semantics. We come to a process for addressing complex relations between ontologies. By using ReasInd, the user can tune the query in accordance with his needs, excluding answers from an inappropriate domain and add semantically similar results. Advanced conversational user interface interacts with the users to solve a query, defined as the set of questions selected and answered by the user during the conversation. The real way to get individualized interaction between a user and ReasInd is to present the user with a variety of options and to let the user choose what is of interest at that specific time. In our system, the user interacts with the system to fill in the gaps to retrieve the right cases, Figure 5.

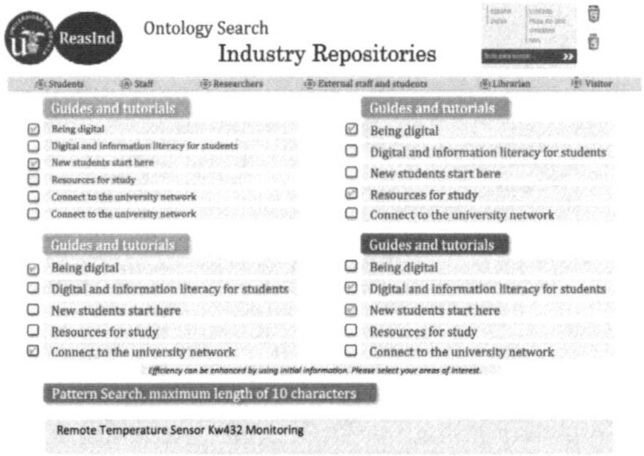

Figure 5. Graphical User interface

Transformation algorithm was implemented in the research prototype as the combined capability of the query transformation agent and the ontology agent of the intelligent multi-agent information retrieval mediator. The system has different users profiles to help to user to build a particular environment, which contains his interest search areas in the industry repositories domain: Plan Managers, Assistants, Operators, and Engineers. In this intelligence profile setting, people are surrounded by intelligent interfaces merged, thus creating a computing-capable environment with intelligent communication and processing available to the user by means of a simple, natural, and effortless human-system interaction. If the information space is designed well, then this choice is easy, and the user achieves optimal information through the use of natural intelligence, that is, the choices are easy to understand so that users know what they will see if they click a link, and what they annul by not following other links.

Profile agents assist to learners with the search, according to the specifications they made. The search parameters in a profile, the start of a search, or the access to the list of retrieved learning objects, can be controlled by invoking appropriate search operations, which extract metadata from learning resources. Ideally, profile agents learn from their experiments, communicate and cooperate with other agents, around in DIRs.

V. EXPERIMENTAL EVALUATION

In order to validate our approach, we have developed an intelligent control architecture in an industrial domain, concretely in an electric power system. This system integrates the management knowledge into the network resources specifications. We study an example of alarm detection and intelligent troubleshooting. We have used a network which belongs to a company in the electrical sector Sevillana-Endesa's (SE) a Spanish power utility. ReasInd is used to optimize the operation of hundreds of connected sensors currently installed. The Spanish power grid company has got a network using wireless on the regional high-tension power grid. These low-cost wireless sensors and accompanying analytics can dramatically improve plant performance, increase safety, and pay for themselves within months. The use of integrating knowledge in agents can help the system administrator in using the maximum capabilities of the intelligent network management platform without having to use another specification language to customize the application.

We have used the SCADA system due to the management limitations of network communication equipment. SCADA consists of the following subsystems, Figure 6:

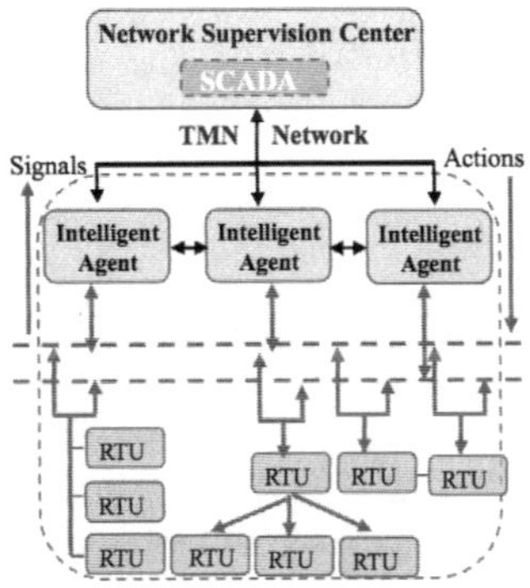

Figure 6. Elements of the prototype

- Remote Terminal Units (RTUs) connecting to sensors in the process, converting sensor signals to digital data and sending digital data to the supervisory system.
- Communication infrastructure connecting the supervisory system to the RTUs.
- A supervisory computer system, gathering acquiring data on the process and sending commands control to the process.

ReasInd monitors in real time, the network's main parameters, making use of the information supplied by the SCADA, placed on the main company building, and the RTUs are installed at different stations. SCADA systems are configured around standard base functions like data acquisition, monitoring and event processing, data storage archiving and analysis, etc. The fundamental role of an RTU is the acquisition of various types of data from the power process, the accumulation, packaging, and conversion of data in a form that can be communicated back to the master, the interpretation and outputting of commands received from the master, and the performance of local filtering, calculation and processes to allow specific functions to be performed locally. The supervision below and RTU includes all network devices and substation and feeder levels like circuit breakers, reclosers, autosectionalizers, the local automation distributed at these devices, and the communications infrastructure.

ReasInd allows the operator to search information, alarms, or digital and analogical parameters of measure, registered on each RTU. Starting from the supplied information, the operator is able to undertake actions in order to solve the failures that could appear or to send a technician to repair the stations equipment. The system has the capability of selecting an agent, which is best suited for satisfying the client's requirement, without the client being aware of the details about the agent. Collaborative agents are useful, especially when a task involves several systems on the network.

VI. Evaluation and Corroborations

Experiments have been carried out in order to evaluate the effectiveness of run-time ontology mapping. The main goal has been to check if the mechanism of query formulation, assisted by an agent, gives a suitable tool for augmenting the number of significant cases, extracted from DIRs, to be stored in the CBR. For our experiments, we considered 15 users with different profiles. So that we could establish a context for the users, they were asked to at least start their essay before issuing any queries to the system. They were also asked to look through all the results returned by the system before clicking on any result. In each experiment, we report the average rank of the user-clicked result for our baseline system, another search engine, and for our system ReasInd [22]. Then we calculated the rank for each retrieval document by combining the various values and comparing the total number of extracted documents and documents consulted by the user, Figure 7.

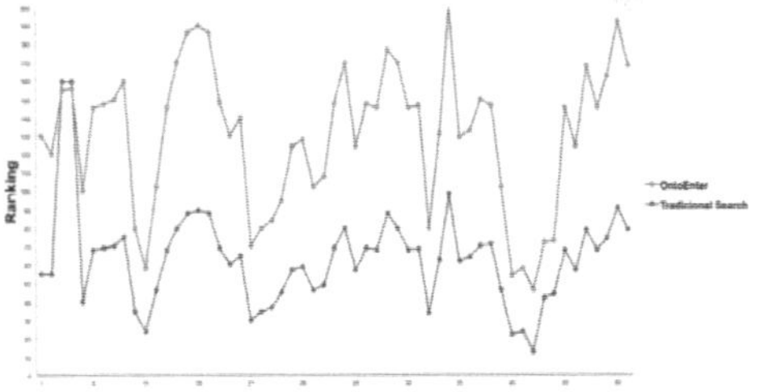

Figure 7. Performance ReasInd & traditional ES

In our study domain, we can observe that the best final ranking was obtained for our prototype and an interesting improvement over the performance of others search engines. Our system performs satisfactorily with about a 98.5 % rate of success in real cases.

During the experimentation, heuristics and measures that are commonly adopted in information retrieval have been used. Statistical analysis has been done to determine the importance values in the results. While the users were performing these searches, an application was continuing running in the background on the server, and capturing the content of queries typed and the results of the searches. We will discuss the issue of response time for five agents associated with transceiver resources. We can establish that ReasInd speed in our domain improves the answer time and the average of the traditional search engine. The results for ReasInd are 25,4 % better than executing time searches/sec in the traditional search engines.

VII. Conclusion and Future Works

Semantic models based on industry standards take that one step further, especially as application vendors adopt those standards, which, as always, will happen more rapidly through pressure from the user community. Semantic models play a key role in the evolving solution architectures that support the business goal of obtaining a complete view of "what is happening" within operations and then deriving business insights from that view. In this paper, we provide different possibilities, which semantic web opens for industry. One important objective is to study appropriate industrial cases, collect arguments, launch industrial projects and develop prototypes for the industrial companies that not only believe together with us but also benefit from the Semantic Web.

We have investigated how the semantic technologies can be used to provide additional semantics from existing resources in industry repositories. We investigated how the semantic technologies can be used to provide additional semantics from existing resources in industrial repositories. For this purpose, we presented ReasInd a system based on ontology and AI architecture for knowledge management in industrial repositories.

This study addresses the main aspects of a semantic and intelligent information retrieval system architecture trying to answer the requirements of the next-generation semantic search engine. We conclude pointing out an important aspect of the obtained integration: improving representation by incorporating more metadata from within the information and intelligent techniques into the retrieval process, the effectiveness of the knowledge retrieval is enhanced. This scheme is based on the principle of the knowledge items that are abstracted to a characterization by metadata description, which is used for further processing. We have proposed to use ontology together with CBR in the acquisition of an expert knowledge in the specific industry domain. The study analyses the implementation results and evaluates the viability of our approaches in enabling search in intelligent-based digital repositories.

Future work will be concerned with the design of distributed and self-managed industry services, which are able to automatically discover, compose, and integrate heterogeneous components, able to manage heterogeneous data/knowledge/intelligence sources, able to create, deploy and exploit linked data, and able to browse and filter information based on semantic similarity and closeness.

REFERENCES

[1] G. M. West, S. D. J. McArthur, and D. Towle, "Industrial implementation of intelligent system techniques for nuclear power plant condition monitoring", Expert Systems with Applications, Volume 39, Issue 8, Pages 7432-7440, 15 June 2012.

[2] S. Guo, C. Lee, and C. Hsu, "An intelligent image agent based on soft-computing techniques for color image processing", Expert Systems with Applications, Volume 28, Issue 3, Pages 483-494, April 2005.

[3] Y. Huang, J. Chen, Y. Kuo, and Y. Jeng, "An intelligent human-expert forum system based on fuzzy information retrieval technique", Expert Systems with Applications, Volume 34, Issue 1, Pages 446-458, January 2008.

[4] S. Yang and Y. Chang, "An active and intelligent network management system with ontology-based and multi-agent techniques", Expert Systems with Applications, Volume 38, Issue 8, Pages 10320-10342, August 2011.

[5] A. Gladun, J. Rogushina, F. Garcia-Sanchez, R. Martínez-Béjar, and J. Fernández-Breis, "An application of intelligent techniques and semantic web technologies in e-learning environments", Expert Systems with Applications, Volume 36, Issue 2, Part 1, Pages 1922-1931, March 2009.

[6] S. Zhang, F. Boukamp, and J. Teizer, "Ontology-based semantic modeling of construction safety knowledge: Towards automated safety planning for job hazard analysis (JHA)", Automation in Construction, Volume 52, Pages 29-41, April 2015.

[7] F. Bertola and V. Patti, "Ontology-based affective models to organize artworks in the social semantic web, Information Processing & Management", Volume 52, Issue 1, Pages 139-162, January 2016.

[8] H. Liu, M. Lu, and M. Al-Hussein, "Ontology-based semantic approach for construction-oriented quantity take-off from BIM models in the light-frame building industry", Advanced Engineering Informatics, Volume 30, Issue 2, Pages 190-207, April 2016.

[9] S. Zhang and J. Lai, "Exploring information from the topology beneath the Gene Ontology terms to improve semantic similarity measures", Gene, Volume 586, Issue 1, Pages 148-157, 15 July 2016.

[10] W. Lu et al., "Selecting a semantic similarity measure for concepts in two different CAD model data ontologies", Advanced Engineering Informatics, Volume 30, Issue 3, Pages 449-466, August 2016.

[11] A. Badii, C. Lallah, M. Zhu, and M. Crouch., "Semi-automatic knowledge extraction, representation and context-sensitive intelligent retrieval of video content using collateral context modelling with scalable ontological networks", Signal Processing: Image Communication, Volume 24, Issue 9, Pages 759-773, 2009.

[12] M. Fernandez. et. Al., [online]. "Semantically enhanced Information Retrieval: An ontology-based approach, Web Semantics: Science, Services and Agents on the World Wide Web", In Press, Corrected Proof, Available online 01 July 2014.

[13] T. Segaran, "Programming Collective Intelligence: Building Smart Web 2.0 Applications", Published by O'Reilly Media, August 23rd 2007.

[14] SEC. Commission Staff Workking Paper: linking up Europe, the importance of interoperability for egovernment services, [Online]. Available from: http://europa.eu.int/ISPO/ida/export/files/en/1523.pdf, July 2016.

[15] EIF. European Interoperability Framework Version 2. [Online]. Available from: http://ec.europa.eu/isa/strategy/doc/annex_ii_eif_en.pdf, Juny 2016.

[16] J. Toussaint and Cheng, K., "Web-based CBR (case-based reasoning) as a tool with the application to tooling selection," International Journal of Advanced Manufacturing Technology, Volume 29, Issue 1, pp 24–34, 2006.

[17] H. Stuckenschmidt and F. V. Harmelen, "Ontology-based metadata generation from semi-structured information", K-CAP, pp. 163–170, ACM, 2011.

[18] GAIA - Group for Artificial Intelligence Applications. jCOLIBRI project, "Distribution of the development environment", [Online]. Available from: http://gaia.fdi.ucm.es/research/colibri/jcolibri/, July 2016.

[19] W3C. "RDF Vocabulary Description Language 1.0: RDF Schema", [Online]. Available from: http://www.w3.org/TR/rdf-schema/, July 2016.

[20] D. Taniar, and J. W Rahayu, "Web semantics and ontology", Hershey, PA: Idea Group, 2006.

[21] PROTÉGÉ. "The Protégé Ontology Editor and Knowledge Acquisition System", [Online], Available from: http://protege.stanford.edu/, July 2016.

[22] D. Amerland, "Google Semantic Search: Search Engine Optimization (SEO) Techniques That Get Your Company More Traffic, Increase Brand Impact and Amplify Your Online Presence", Que Publishing Kindle Edition, July, 2013. Pp. 2013 – 229.

Forecasting the Needs of Users and Systems

A New Approach to Web Service Mining

Juan I. Guerrero, Enrique Personal, Antonio Parejo, Antonio García and Carlos León
Department of Electronic Technology
University of Seville
Seville, Spain
email: juaguealo@us.es

Abstract—**The Smart Grids provides a great scope of new technologies. The new technologies include the integration of heterogeneous systems which perform different task in the Smart Grid ecosystems. These new systems have their own users with different knowledge levels. It is important that the integrated system can assimilate the new systems without a complex implementations and deployments. Additionally, the users of these systems will increase their needs when new systems are integrated. The proposed framework forecasts the needs of new systems make available new Web Services (WSs) to users and systems. The standards related with Smart Grids include specifications for different Web Service Architectures. Thus, the proposed framework is based on Web Service Mining, using different modules, including semantic engine and analytic module, with time series classification and clustering. Finally, the proposed framework was applied in Smart Business Park (SBP), creating new WSs based on the analysis of Web Services activity information, forecasting the needs of users or/and systems.**

Keywords-web service mining; ant colony optimization; smart grids; computational intelligence.

I. INTRODUCTION

There are a lot of examples of technologies that makes our lives more comfortable, since robots with artificial intelligence to make different things (cooking, management, cleaning, etc.), to information technologies to optimize our task and reduce the time. Time is the only thing that you waste and never recover. Additionally, time is a very important asset for any company. Thus, all technologies that let you optimize any task are very important. There are several examples in different economic sectors. In health and e-health sectors, the new technologies related with data mining [1], biomedical imaging and image processing [2] have been reduced the diagnostic time and the quality of health services. In the power distribution sector, the emergent technologies related with Smart Grids (SGs) have provided new functionalities and services for consumers, reducing the restoring power supply time [3] and increasing the supply quality [4]. In information technology sector, the new technologies related with big data [5][6] and high performance computing [7] have improved the capabilities to store and analyze great volumes of information (applied in health, environmental control and monitoring, finance, telecommunication, and other utilities). In particular, Google [8] reduced the searching time using different techniques to rank the results of search requests. Sometimes, these systems are designed to recommend information [9] that could be interesting. This means the systems try to forecast the needs of the users in order to save time and increase the Quality of Service (QoS). Sometimes, some of the previously mentioned technologies could go unnoticed by the final users. There are other technologies as the previously mentioned ones: Web Service Mining.

The Web Service Mining [10] is an emergent technology that deals with the WS in order to discover, check, and improve service behavior, based on service composition, service pattern discovery, managing service registry-repositories, etc. There are several solutions based on process mining [11], pattern usage discovery [12], hypergraph-based matrix representation with a service set mining algorithm [13], constraint satisfaction [14], semantics-based methods [15][16], customer value analysis [17], frequent composite algorithm [18], Heterogeneous Feature Selection [19], etc. for cross-cloud environment [20], RESTful Web Services [21], etc.

This paper proposes a novel web service mining approach based on computational intelligence and data mining framework. This framework creates new WSs based on the usage of existing WSs, in order to forecast functionalities for users and systems. This framework is been researched for a Smart Business Parks (SBPs). The current version has been tested with several systems related to SGs Ecosystem. Thus, the SG ecosystem is formed by several systems to allow the distributed management of power energy, for example, energy management systems, distributed energy resource management, etc. Additionally, the proposed framework could integrate the WSs of the additional system, which may be added to the ecosystem. In this sense, the proposed framework tries to learn the WS usage pattern made by the systems and users, providing the capability to forecast the needs of systems or users creating new WSs that can be useful for them.

The proposed framework is formed by several modules which are described in this paper, each module implies different techniques. In Section II, the overview of proposed framework is included. In Section III, the description of each module is provided. In Section IV, the experimental results are explained. Finally, in Section V, the conclusions and future works are described.

II. FRAMEWORK OVERVIEW

The proposed framework contains several modules, as shown in Fig. 1. Additionally, the architecture of the proposed framework applied in a SBP architecture is shown in Fig. 2.

In this framework, there are several modules to add information to the database of the system. Monitoring Module stored all activity of WSs. Discovery and Check & Test modules are based on Ant Colony Optimization (ACO) Algorithms. Discovery Module performs an ACO in order to discovery new services in the ecosystem. Check & Test Module perform different tests in order to check the new or existing services. The Hybrid Web Service Engine (HWSE) provides to the previously described modules the possibility to interact with different type of services: REST and SOAP.

The Web Service Database (WSDB) stores information about WSs registered in the ecosystem, adding metadata and analytic information, using the Analytic Module and Semantic Engine.

The Analytic Module is based on time series. This module performs an analysis of all available information. The objectives of this module are: establish the importance of service, order the service by importance level and identify the WS groups. Additionally, the module establishes the time usage pattern of each WS and group.

The Web Service Engine (WS Engine or WSE) creates the new WSs by composition of WS groups, registering in Web Service Hybrid Repository (WS Hybrid Repository or WSHR).

The WSHR stores the information of each service in different WS standards.

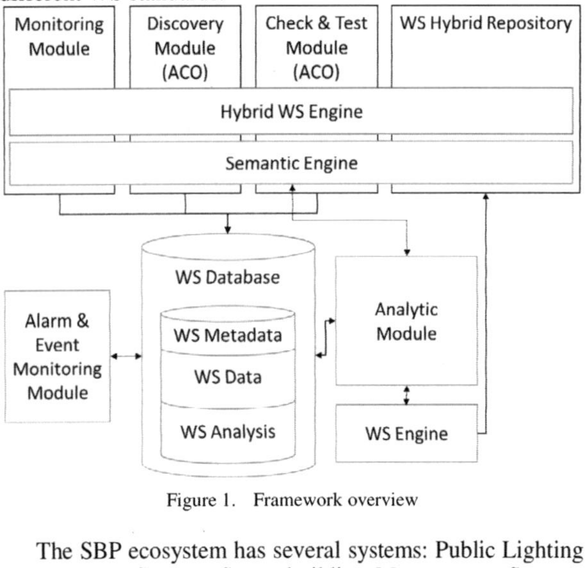

Figure 1. Framework overview

The SBP ecosystem has several systems: Public Lighting Management System, Smart building Management System, KPI Monitoring System, Photovoltaic Management System, and other systems. The ecosystem includes a layer for system integration. This layer is the middleware or gateway to access to Intelligent Electronic Devices (IEDs), which is based on several standards like IEC 61850 and other standards related with SG Standard European Roadmap [22].

In this sense, the Alarm and Event Monitoring Module registers the information of events and alarms generated in the system, at high level in the application layer, and in low level in the IED layer.

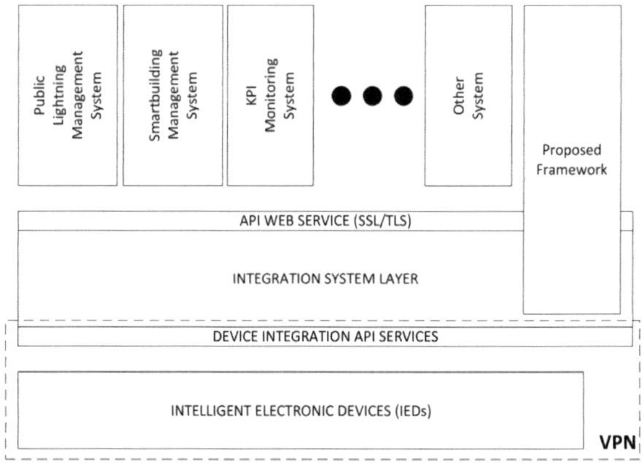

Figure 2. Proposed Framework in SBP Ecosystem

One of the most important requirements of this SBP ecosystem is the capability to assimilate new systems that complains with the established standards. Thus, the proposed framework is an intelligent framework to integrate the services of new systems in the SBP ecosystem.

III. DESCRIPTION OF MODULES

The proposed framework is composed of several modules (see Fig. 1), each of which are responsible of following tasks:

A. *Hybrid WS Engine (HWSE)*

The Hybrid WS Engine is a parser of WSs. This module can extract information from messages in different WS standards: SOAP and REST. The information extracted includes data and metadata.

B. *Monitoring Module*

The Monitoring Module gathers the information of all WS usage, using the HWSE in order to parse the messages. This module is always monitoring and registering the message traffic. The module stores the information of WSs (data and metadata) in the WSDB. Additionally, the module stores information about timestamps, response periods, preconditions, information to calculate frequencies (usage, requester, and provider), results, effects, average size, etc. This information is gathered for Analytic Module.

C. *Discovery Module*

The Discovery Module takes advantage from different WS technologies: Universal Description Discovery and Integration (UDDI), Web-Service discovery (WS-Discovery), electronic business using eXtensible Markup

Language (ebXML), Domain Name System (DNS), etc. Additionally, the Discovery Module uses the information stored in WSDB to improve the WS discovery. This information is loaded in an ACO algorithm. The ACO algorithm has two main objectives: discover the WSs which are not accessible to traditional WS discovery technologies; and extracting the functional information of WS.

D. *Check & Test Module*

The check and test module performs an ACO in order to optimize the created or composed WSs. The non-functional attributes of WS limit the usage of this module. The security level and the critical nature of WS could avoid the WS check or test.

This module has two main objectives:

- Check and test the new WS registered in WSHR.
- Check and test the existing WS registered in other repositories.

This module support SOAP and REST.

E. *Alarm & Event Monitoring Module*

This module was specially designed for SGs ecosystems. The module registers and stores information about any event, warning, or alarm fired in any system or in any device of SG. Alarms, warnings, and events are considered as information entities. These entities are one of the most important sources to improve the web service mining. Entities are usually related with the WS usage in a SG ecosystem. An entity has usually associated several WS usage patterns. The end of pattern is often marked by another entity. Thus, this module stores in WSDB all information about these entities: timestamp, source, etc. This information is gathered for Analytic Module.

F. *Analytic Module*

This Analytic Module applies several data mining techniques to provide additional information about the WSs. This module was implemented in R. This new information is stored in WSDB. The objectives of this module are:

- Composite services according to WS semantic analysis. This analysis is based on the results of Semantic Engine combined with the results of time series classification.
- Analyze services according to the relation between WS invocations, alarms, warnings, and events (from Alarm & Event Module). This analysis is based on time series clustering.

Both objectives are based on time series. Thus, the first step is to translate the data in the same temporal scale. The time series extract and build features from this information. According to the features of the time series and the information stored in WSDB:

- The time series classification applies Support Vector Machine (SVM) and decision tree, in order to aggregate or compose all the WS with similar pattern behavior.
- The time series clustering starts selecting the appropriate distance/similarity metric based on time series features and the results of semantic engine. Then this module applies several clustering techniques: K-means, hierarchical clustering, and density-based clustering, in order to get the best cluster.

This module calculates several Key Performance Indicators (KPI). This KPIs measures the performance and the QoS [23]: throughput, availability, response time, interoperability, accessibility, and cost.

G. *Semantic Engine*

The Semantic Engine provides additional information about WSs. This engine is based on Ontology Web Language – Services (OWL-S) that is a semantic markup for WS. Additionally, Semantic Web Rule Language (SWRL) is used to represent rules.

This module has three main objectives:

- Identification of the service profile, describing the signature of the service in terms of its input, output, parameters, preconditions, service name, service type (stateless, state-based, etc.), provider, business domain, etc.
- Description of the service process model, describing how the service works in terms of the interplay between data and control flow.
- Description of the non-functional service semantics. In this case, the non-functional attributes are related to a QoS model: availability, delivery constraints, etc. Additionally, the semantic engine identifies: the security level, the critical nature of service, the level of service (software, middleware, or hardware), etc.

H. *WS Engine*

This module gathers the information from the analytic module in order to create or composite the new WS. These new WSs are registered in WSHR, in order to start the test & check stage.

I. *WS Database (WSDB)*

The WSDB stores WSs data and metadata. Additionally, the WSDB registers all information about the data and metadata analysis of WSs.

The data model is based on Common Information Model (CIM) from Distributed Management Task Force (DMTF). Nevertheless, some extensions and modifications have been applied in order to store analytic information and speeding up the information exchange.

J. *WS Hybrid Repository (WSHR)*

This module implements several repositories based on ebXML, UDDI, and DNS. The repository stores information of all composed and created WS. Additionally, there is a table in WSDB, which represents the stage of new WSs. There are several stages in the test process: NEW, CHECK, TEST, VALID, NON-VALID, BROADCAST, and USING.

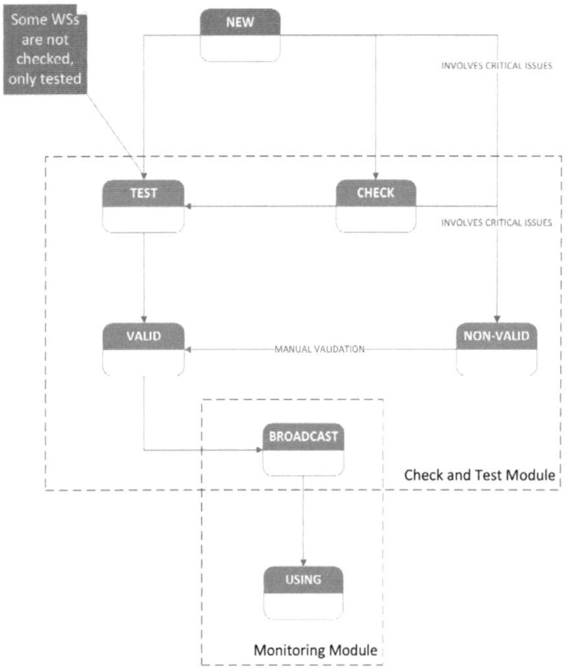

Figure 3. WSs transition status diagram

When the new WS is created the state is NEW. Then the Check and Test Module and the Monitoring Module change the status according to the results of different transitions showed in Fig. 3. Check and Test Module manage the transitions between stages: TEST, CHECK VALID, NON-VALID and BROADCAST. Monitoring Module manages the transitions between stages: BROADCAST and USING. If the WS involves critical services or devices, it will be validated and tested by an expert.

IV. Experimental Results

The first prototype of the proposed framework was developed as part of SBP. The main objective of the proposed framework was to detect the WS usage patterns to create new WS, which makes the system reliable and robust. The second objective was to make easy the integration of new systems in SBP.

The SBP ecosystem has several systems (see Fig. 2). Each system provides its own set of WSs, although the systems have several WSs in common:

- Authentication.
- General services and metadata access.
- Monitoring services.

These systems include services to interact with IEDs, except the KPI monitoring system, which interacts with other systems to extract information for KPIs.

The Monitoring Module of the proposed framework was the first module of the implementation. This module was registering information during two months. The information is stored in a data base according to Distributed Management Task Force (DMTF) Common Information Model (CIM) Standard. This information is applied to test the Analytic Module. Additionally, this information was used to check and test the Semantic Engine and the HWSE.

In case of Analytic Module, this module composed several WSs:

- WSs related with KPI Monitoring System. System were associated with renewable energy resources. The KPI Monitoring System gathered information from different type of renewable energy resources, in order to summarize all consumptions. The system found several cases: photovoltaic farms, wind farms, battery, and electric vehicles. The new WSs reduced time access to information and increased the efficiency.
- Some patterns related with alarms generated by some IEDs in substations. The new WSs involved critical devices. Critical devices can take effect over the continuity of supply. The management of these devices involves important protocols and methodologies designed by companies. The created Adapters for new WSs were successfully evaluated by companies.

However, the systems in the SBP needed an adapter to take advantage from the new WSs created by the proposed framework. The created WSs were manually checked and tested successfully.

V. Conclusion and Future Works

The proposed framework can compose the WSs according to the discovery usage patterns and the relation of WS to alarms, warnings and events on the SBP ecosystem. The lack of adapters to take advantage of these new WSs makes difficult the automatic integration of new systems. Thus, the proposed framework can create composed WS which offers the aggregated functionality of several WSs, reducing the communications and speeding up the final effects. In this way, the system forecasts the needs of users and systems based on the usage data and metadata patterns.

Additionally, the future works to improve the proposed framework are:

- Design and implementation of adapters which takes advantage of the new WS.
- Application of new techniques in the Analytic Module based on multivariable inference.
- Research of new module to composite WS from different WS standards (SOAP, REST, etc.)

Acknowledgment

The authors would like to thank the Smart Business Project (SBP) (Reference Number: P011-13/E24), which provided data sources. Additionally, the authors would like to thank the IDEA Agency for providing the funds for the project.

The authors are also appreciative of the backing of the SIIAM project (Reference Number: TEC2013-40767-R), which is funded by the Ministry of Economy and Competitiveness of Spain.

REFERENCES

[1] H. Yang and Y.-P. P. Chen, "Data mining in lung cancer pathologic staging diagnosis: Correlation between clinical and pathology information," *Expert Syst. Appl.*, vol. 42, no. 15–16, pp. 6168–6176, pp. 6168–6176, Sep. 2015.

[2] M. O. Visscher, S. A. Burkes, R. Randall Wickett, and K. P. Eaton, "Chapter 38 - From Image to Information: Image Processing in Dermatology and Cutaneous Biology A2 - Hamblin, Michael R.," in *Imaging in Dermatology*, P. Avci and G. K. Gupta, Eds. Boston: Academic Press, pp. 519–535, 2016.

[3] F. Mekic, Z. Wang, V. Donde, F. Yang, and J. Stoupis, "Disributed automation for back-feed network power restoration," in *20th International Conference and Exhibition on Electricity Distribution - Part 1, 2009. CIRED 2009*, 2009.

[4] G. Blajszczak, P. Antos, and M. Wasiluk-Hassa, "Smart grid accommodation of distributed generation for more reliable quality of supply," in *2011 11th International Conference on Electrical Power Quality and Utilisation (EPQU)*, 2011.

[5] Y. Demchenko, C. de Laat, and P. Membrey, "Defining architecture components of the Big Data Ecosystem," in *2014 International Conference on Collaboration Technologies and Systems (CTS)*, 2014.

[6] C. Wu, R. Buyya, and K. Ramamohanarao, "Chapter 1 - Big Data Analytics = Machine Learning + Cloud Computing," in *Big Data*, Morgan Kaufmann, pp. 3–38, 2016.

[7] A. Ali and K. S. Syed, "Chapter 3 - An Outlook of High Performance Computing Infrastructures for Scientific Computing," in *Advances in Computers*, vol. 91, A. Memon, Ed. Elsevier, pp. 87–118, 2013.

[8] X. Wang, M. Bendersky, D. Metzler, and M. Najork, "Learning to Rank with Selection Bias in Personal Search," *Proc. SIGIR 2016 ACM*, 2016.

[9] H.-T. Cheng et al., "Wide & Deep Learning for Recommender Systems," *ArXiv160607792 Cs Stat*, Jun. 2016.

[10] G. Zheng and A. Bouguettaya, *Web Service Mining: Application to Discoveries of Biological Pathways*. Boston, MA: Springer Science+Business Media, LLC, 2010.

[11] W. v d Aalst, "Service Mining: Using Process Mining to Discover, Check, and Improve Service Behavior," *IEEE Trans. Serv. Comput.*, vol. 6, no. 4, pp. 525–535, pp. 525–535, Oct. 2013.

[12] Q. A. Liang, J. y Chung, S. Miller, and Y. Ouyang, "Service Pattern Discovery of Web Service Mining in Web Service Registry-Repository," in *2006 IEEE International Conference on e-Business Engineering (ICEBE'06)*, 2006.

[13] A. Zhao, X. Wang, K. Ren, and Y. Qiu, "Semantic Message Link Based Service Set Mining for Service Composition," in *Fifth International Conference on Semantics, Knowledge and Grid, 2009. SKG 2009*, 2009.

[14] Q. A. Liang, S. Miller, and J. Y. Chung, "Service mining for Web service composition," in *IRI -2005 IEEE International Conference on Information Reuse and Integration, Conf, 2005.*, 2005.

[15] H. Luo, L. Liu, and Y. Sun, "Semantics-Based Service Mining Method in Wireless Sensor Networks," in *2011 Seventh International Conference on Mobile Ad-hoc and Sensor Networks (MSN)*, 2011.

[16] A. Zhao, K. Ren, X. Wang, and Y. Qiu, "An approach to service set mining for improving SWS based supply chains coordination," in *2010 International Conference on Logistics Systems and Intelligent Management*, vol. 3, 2010.

[17] W. Hu and Y. Hui, "Service-mining Based on Customer Value Analysis," in *2007 International Conference on Management Science and Engineering*, 2007.

[18] H. Meng, L. Wu, T. Zhang, G. Chen, and D. Li, "Mining Frequent Composite Service Patterns," in *2008 Seventh International Conference on Grid and Cooperative Computing*, 2008.

[19] L. Chen, Q. Yu, P. S. Yu, and J. Wu, "WS-HFS: A Heterogeneous Feature Selection Framework for Web Services Mining," in *2015 IEEE International Conference on Web Services (ICWS)*, 2015.

[20] T. Wu, W. Dou, C. Hu, and J. Chen, "Service Mining for Trusted Service Composition in Cross-Cloud Environment," *IEEE Syst. J.*, vol. PP, no. 99, pp. 1–12, pp. 1–12, 2014.

[21] A. Stroinski, D. Dwornikowski, and J. Brzezinski, "RESTful Web Service Mining: Simple Algorithm Supporting Resource-Oriented Systems," in *2014 IEEE International Conference on Web Services (ICWS)*, 2014.

[22] "SGCG/M490/G_Smart Grid Set of Standards. Version 3.1," CEN-CENELEC-ETSI Smart Grid Coordination Group, SGCG/M490/G-version 3.1, Oct. 2014.

[23] L. K. Goel, S. K. Kottayil, M. Suchithra, and M. Ramakrishnan, "Efficient Discovery and Ranking of Web Services Using Non-functional QoS Requirements for Smart Grid Applications," *Procedia Technol.*, vol. 21, pp. 82–87, pp. 82–87, Jan. 2015.

Cartesian Handling Informal Specifications in Incomplete Frameworks

Marta Franova
LRI, UMR8623 du CNRS & INRIA Saclay
Bât. 660, Orsay, France
email: mf@lri.fr

Yves Kodratoff
LRI, UMR8623 du CNRS & INRIA Saclay
Bât. 660, Orsay, France
email: yvkod@gmail.com

Abstract— **This paper introduces and illustrates a fundamental notion, namely *informal specification*, for creating tools developed as symbiotic recursive pulsating systems (SRPS), in the framework of Inductive Theorem Proving and Intelligent Systems. It illustrates the use of this fundamental notion in scientific systemic creativity relative to theorem proving. We deal simultaneously with the meta-level design of a system that proves theorems automatically.**

Keywords-informal specification; intelligence by design; inductive theorem proving; Cartesian Intuitionism; symbiotic recursive systems; Constructive Matching Methodology.

I. INTRODUCTION

Often, a direct way to achieve a proof requiring the use of the induction principle is not obvious. It might even be impossible to prove a formula within a given framework while an appropriate detour or a switch in interpretation and in the method of thinking may lead to a success. This problem of changing the framework is also relevant to the design of an intelligent inductive theorem proving system.

There is a largely adopted management approach based on so-called "SMART goals," where 'S' in SMART stands for 'specific' and it implicitly means that there is a kind of formal framework and a reproducible or nearly obvious available know-how to reach such a goal. 'T' stands for time-bounded and it means that there is a limit date before which the result is expected. 'M' stands for measurable, 'A' stands for achievable, 'R' stands for realistic.

We shall however see that a systematic use of SMART goals should not always be the way by which invention comes to life. Symbiotic recursive pulsating systems (SRPS) and their corresponding Cartesian paradigm [14] defy this SMART approach, though it is established and today more or less required in Science. Handling or even creating SRPS requires a detour from purely formal thinking expected by exact sciences, a switch from linear synergic interpretations advocated by analysis and synthesis, a switch from observations of 'pure' facts to *creative interpretations*, a switch from use of established know-how to *creating* on-purpose know-how. Handling or even creating SRPS require their own method of thinking that is not as much reproducible as the usual trend of sciences would require. From an immediate-gratification perspective this might lead to the option that the best way to handle them is to ignore them. Hopefully, the rich potential of these systems illustrated in this paper might suggest to adopt a more positive attitude towards these systems.

The problem lies in the fact that SRPS do not rely on a linearly ordered sequence of notions that could be taught in isolated or progressive manner. In a sense, they can be understood only by already using them, which obviously sounds contradictory. In order to dissolve this contradiction, we need accepting to work with loosely specified tools, followed by a patient work of successive try-fail and recover steps. This has to take place until the whole process holds together and leads to the desired solution. When this process is completed, the former loosely defined specifications are transformed into exact ones. We call *symbiotic recursive pulsating thinking* (srp-thinking) this way of thinking.

We have previously introduced the term Cartesian thinking for srp-thinking and Newtonian thinking for the other, more usual, one [14]. Both are useful because they apply to solving different problems. Newtonian thinking allows, by words of Newton himself, "standing upon the shoulders of giants". Newtonian thinking is certainly a SMART approach suitable for solving problems that can be tackled on a modular basis, by analysis and synthesis. Because of the presence of recursion, what we call Cartesian thinking is based on self-justification and self-reference. In terms of deductive systems we can say that Newtonian thinking is a derivation of a knowledge contained implicitly in the given axioms (i.e., these giants' shoulders) while Cartesian thinking focuses on *creating* a relevant axiomatic system for solving a particular problem. In terms of technological development, Newtonian thinking is concerned with innovation (*building* the intended products relying on already existing knowledge; *handling* 'truth') while Cartesian thinking is applied to the cases when the intended product seems utopian or even impossible with respect to the existing available knowledge. It consists in developing new custom-made technologies that were not present so far. Cartesian thinking represents an attempt to *create* a (or *re-create*) 'truth' and a 'desired truth'.

The goal of this paper is to bring introductory insights (via an illustration) concerning one fundamental notion of the SRPS context, namely *informal specification*. This task is not simple in face of prevailing Newtonian paradigm and its particular criteria that are used while evaluating either the process of a scientific research (i.e., how the research should be done) or the final product (i.e., how the result should look-like). Indeed, Newtonian approach requires that research progresses linearly (or modularly) and the results are – in Computer Science – either programs understood in their usual modular sense or proofs about standard properties of these programs. SRPS fail to verify these criteria since they are recursive and symbiotic. Moreover, the results are system-procedures made with sub-procedures (we call them "constructors") that are symbiotic in the same manner as it is the case for Natural Numbers (NAT). NAT are determined (and computed) via the symbiotic constructors 0, successor (*suc*) and NAT themselves. Newtonian thinking often ignores this symbiotic and recursive character of NAT since their representation is possible in seemingly modular form. The same can be said about SRPS. They can be represented in an apparently modular form, but the process of their creation is purely symbiotic and recursive. In NAT the constructors are created via a process that can be described by the informal specifications: Creation(0) = Creation(0,*suc*,NAT), Creation(*suc*) = Creation(0,*suc*,NAT) and Creation(NAT) = Creation(0,*suc*,NAT). This is a symbiotic creation which is analogous to the well-known egg-hen problem: what is created first? Obviously this problem has no known solution. However, a symbiotic solution for this problem is expressed as the simultaneous presence of both hen and egg from the start of the implementation. Let us now describe a visual problem which does have an obvious symbiotic solution. Consider the following well-known picture:

On internet this picture is known as 'young lady and old woman illusion'.

It represents, at the same time, a young lady and an old woman. For some people this is hard to see at once and thus we shall use the following two pictures that help to perceive both women in the above picture:

young woman (yw)

old woman (ow)

The creation of such a picture can be described as a symbiotic creation by which the author before drawing has foreseen the final picture. In other words, the author started with an informal specification "I wish to draw an ambiguous figure and I am almost sure that this will be possible." This is the first step of the creation process. The second step is a *creative preprocessing* by which he foresees the final picture expressed by a formalized specification: Creation(yw) = Creation(yw,ow) and Creation(ow) = Creation(yw,ow). The drawing (implementation) process is the third and last stage of creation. The *creative preprocessing* contains thus research work coming from the informal idea of a symbiotic picture to the presence of the effective tools to give a concrete implementable form to this idea.

We can complete now what has been said above. This paper concerns the introduction of the notion of *informal specification* and brings introductory insights on the *preprocessing stage* in Cartesian design of a particular SRPS. Therefore, it is necessary to be prepared to a non linear symbiotic presentation and to simultaneously consider

- design and meta-design
- action and meta-action
- inseparability of
    - concrete proof
    - abstract overall design.

The paper is organized in the following manner. Section II presents the notion of informal specification and an example of the use of this notion in the domain of Inductive Theorem Proving. Section III presents our fundamental procedure (a *design constructor*) used to reach this goal at the design level. Section IV illustrates this procedure by applying it to the specification of a theorem that will show itself to be, in a particular way, incomplete and thus informal. Section V presents our future research projects.

II. Informal Specifications in Incomplete Frameworks

A. *Informal Specification as a Way of Expressing a Goal*

Due to incompleteness results of Gödel [17], to automate proving theorems by induction (ITP), *ITP-goal*, is unachievable in the context of contemporary mathematics. However, the fact that many apparently unsolvable problems are actually solved when their context or representation are changed has become public knowledge several decades ago when Smullyan [30] started to make game of such transformations. With respect to practical use of ITP for Program Synthesis (via deductive approach pioneered by Manna and Waldinger [23]) and for search of missing axioms in incomplete theories [16], a reasonable implementation of ITP is highly desirable goal (or technological vision). Therefore, in early eighties, building on our previous experience with creating deductive systems and conceptual switches in history of mathematics, we have moved this goal from purely Gödel's mathematical context into 'technological' context by reformulating the above ITP-goal into the following *ITP-system goal*: "Automate ITP as much as possible." The former goal takes into account the underlying Gödel's formal context. Our ITP-system goal leaves some freedom for interpreting and addressing in a non-standard manner not only the problem "How this should be done?" but also the problem "How the solution should look like?" We call *informal specification* a description of any reasonable goal that has this particular property of allowing non-standard criteria for the above two problems (or a description that is in a sense incomplete). We call these problems *pragmatic bias* in contrast to academic bias that expresses, even though implicitly, the necessity for the use of standard criteria for solving these problems.

It must be noted that there can be no 'Impossible!' for an informally specified reasonable goal. The only negative statement can be pronounced and that is "I do not know." It depends only on us if we add "But I will," or not. With respect to the intended applications of our resulting system (Program Synthesis (PS) and completing incomplete theories), we expressed our intention to add this answer when we realized that the best way to tackle the ITP-system goal is to not search for a some clever decision procedure which will in principle face Gödel's incompleteness, but a procedure or system that, in failure cases, will provide sufficient conditions for recovery, i.e., increasing the possibility of proving the intended formula. Our approach is thus very different from academic (or Newtonian) approaches to ITP that consider strictly the framework limited by Gödel's results, such as the system ACL2 [3], the system RRL [22], the system NuPRL [6], the Oyster-Clam system [4], the extensions of ISABELLE [27], the system COQ [26] and Matita Proof Assistant [1].

B. Systemic Background and Guiding Principles for ITP-system goal

We have found that Descartes' method is perfectly suitable for our task. A short systemic description of Descartes' method is given in [14]. More precisions are given in [12].

This systemic Cartesian background allows us to summarize the action-guiding principles used in order to conceive an ITP-system:

- (*GP1*) We welcome incompleteness for practical reasons since it guarantees progress and evolution. Moreover, each missing axiom discovered hints at a more relevant interpretation. Therefore, a unified method of discovery of missing axioms is an asset.
- (*GP2*) We conceive a procedure-system finding sufficient conditions in case of failure and not a decision procedure (see Section III).
- (*GP3*) We conceive an ITP-system as a symbiotic recursive pulsative system (see [14]).
- (*GP4*) Due to the symbiotic character of tools, we develop first a methodology for ITP, which, when its 'practical completeness' will be achieved, a first version of ITP-system will be implemented (this refers to the implemented experimental version 0.3 we presented in [10]).
- (*GP5*) The same methodology is conceived for ITP and PS which implies that we adopt no efficiency criteria for synthesized programs.
- (GP6) Consequence of the previous principles: We create a database of solutions to non-trivial examples obtained with our methodology. These examples often provide informal specifications of tools that must become part of our methodology. The price to pay is that, in contrast to Newtonian approaches, the real implementation may start only when a plateau is reached in building this database. Such a plateau happens when no new informal specifications of missing tools are discovered (see more in Section VI).

Considering the task formulated in (GP2), and using Beth's method of deductive tableaux [2] we understood that the first problem to be dealt with is specified informally as finding a method to prove atomic formulas in such a way that it provides, in case of failure, sufficient conditions for provability of this formula. Our solution to this particular tool-specification is our *CM*-formula construction (recalled in the next Section), where *CM* stands for *Constructive Matching*. Since *CM*-formula construction is the basis (or basic symbiotic constructor) of our methodology (see (GP5)), we call it *Constructive Matching methodology* (*CMM*). *CMM* is thus our intended solution for the ITP-system goal.

In the next Section, we recall *CM*-formula construction so that, in Section IV, we can illustrate its use for solving another example (see (GP6)). This example is interesting since it concerns the proof of the so-called Unwinding Theorem met in the domain of information flow security and developed in [29]. In [15] we present the methodological aspects of this problem. In the present paper we want to illustrate how *CMM*, via *CM*-formula construction, handles informal specification of the given Rushby's theorem. Indeed, as it will become clear, the initial formulation of Rushby's Unwinding Theorem is, in some sense, incomplete.

III. *CM*-FORMULA CONSTRUCTION IN ITP

In this Section we are going to present the basic mechanism for the *CM*-formula construction originally introduced in [7].

For simplicity, let us suppose that the formula to be proven has two arguments, that is to say that we need to prove that $F(t_1,t_2)$ is true, where F is a predicate and t_1, t_2 are terms of the axiomatic theory in use. We introduce a new type of arguments in the atomic formula that has to be proven true. We call them **pivotal arguments**, since focusing on them enables to reduce what is usually called the search space of the proof, and to decompose complex problems (such as strategic aspects of a proof) on conceptually simpler problems (such as a transformation of a term into another, possibly finding a sufficient conditions etc.). These pivotal arguments are denoted by ξ (or ξ' etc.) in the following.

In the first step, the pivotal argument replaces, in a purely syntactical way, one of the arguments of the given formula. The first problem is thus to choose which of the arguments will be replaced by a pivotal argument ξ. A complete algorithmic solution to this problem is not yet proposed, since it will be part of a complete implementation of *CMM* [8]. Nevertheless, a simple informal algorithm is easily obtained in performing a rough analysis of the terms: the most complex one should become the pivot – precisely defining complexity is still left to a human person. Its automation will be tackled with in the final phasis of our research.

In this presentation, let us suppose that we have chosen to work with $F(t_1,\xi)$, the second argument being chosen as the pivotal one. In an artificial, but custom-made manner, we state $C = \{\xi \mid F(t_1,\xi) \text{ is true}\}$. Except the syntactical similarity with the formula to be proven, there is no semantic consideration in saying that $F(t_1,\xi)$ is true. It simply represents a 'quite-precise' purpose of trying to go from $F(t_1,\xi)$ to $F(t_1,t_2)$ while preserving the truth of $F(t_1,\xi)$. We thus propose a detour that will enable us to prove also the theorems that cannot be directly proven by the so-called simplification Newtonian methods, i.e., without this detour.

In the second step, via the definition of F and those involved in the formulation of the term t_1, we look for the features shown by all the ξ such that $F(t_1,\xi)$ is true. Given the axioms defining F and the functions occurring in t_1, we are able to obtain a set C_1 expressing the conditions on the set $\{ \xi \}$ for which $F(t_1,\xi)$ is true. In other words, calling 'cond' these conditions and C_1 the set of the ξ such that cond(ξ) is true, we define C_1 by $C_1 = \{\xi \mid \text{cond}(\xi)\}$. We can also say that, with the help of the given axioms, we build a 'cond' such that the formula: $\forall\xi \in C_1, F(t_1,\xi)$ is true.

In the third step, using the characteristics of C_1 obtained in the second step, the induction hypothesis is applied. Thus, we build a form of ξ such that $F(t_1,\xi)$ is related to $F(t_1,t_2)$ by using the induction hypothesis. For the sake of clarity, let us call ξ_C the result of applying the induction hypothesis to C_1 resulting in its subset $C_2 = \{ \xi_C \mid \text{cond}_2(\xi_C)\}$. C_2 is thus such that $F(t_1,\xi_C)$ is true. We are still left with a work to do: prove that t_2 belongs to C_2. In the case that t_2 does not contain existential quantifiers, this is done by verifying $\text{cond}_2(t_2)$. In the that case t_2 contains existentially quantified variables, this is done by a new detour. In the first step, we try to solve the problem $\text{cond}_2(\xi_C) \Rightarrow \exists\sigma\ (\xi_C = \sigma t_2)$, where σ has to provide a suitable instantiation for the existentially quantified variables in t_2. With such an obtained σ we have then to prove $F(t_1,\sigma t_2)$. In other words, we have to prove that ξ_C and t_2 can be made identical (modulo substitution) when $\text{cond}_2(\xi_C)$ holds.

In the case of the success, this completes the proof. In the case of a failure, a new lemma $\text{cond}_2(\xi_C) \Rightarrow \exists\sigma\ (\xi_C = \sigma t_2)$ with an appropriate quantification of the involved variables is generated. In some cases, an infinite sequence of 'failure formulas', i.e., lemmas or missing axioms, may be generated. *CMM* is conceived in such a way that the obtained sequence is well-behaving (see [7]) so that a human person or an automated tool (in the future) be driven in the choice of a suitable generalization. This formula logically covers the infinite sequence of lemmas or missing axioms and it thus fills the gap that cannot be overcome by a purely deductive formal approach to theorem proving. In the case of generation of missing axioms, the process of completion the initial theory is performed by 'pulsation', i.e., by adding then applying the new axioms to the domain theory. The resulting system is logically coherent by construction. In the future, all the relevant and necessary tools will be designed (with the help of Machine Learning, Big Data and other relevant domains) to eliminate human interaction with the decision of the appropriateness of suggested missing axioms. This is useful for applications where human interaction is impossible. Consider, for instance, space explorations and constructions by robots.

IV. Example : Proof for an Unwinding Theorem

A. *State-based Information Flow Control – Basic Knowledge*

In this Section we present the formal framework for the so-called unwinding theorem presented in [29]. Then, in the next Section, we present the proof of Rushby's unwinding theorem as performed by *CM*-formula construction.

The proof presented is interesting from the man-machine interaction point of view since it illustrates how a human expert of the domain theory is prompted to find a suitable generalization of a potentially infinite sequence of terms without being asked to know the mechanism of *CM*-formula construction. It is known that, in non-trivial cases, academic approaches require from the user to be aware of the proof assistant mechanisms in order to guide it towards success. In our completed system, the generalizations will be performed automatically.

A system M is composed of a set S of states, with an initial state $s_0 \in S$, a set A of actions, and a set O of outputs, together with the functions step and output: *step*: $S \times A \rightarrow S$, *output*: $S \times A \rightarrow O$. We shall use the letters ... s, t, ... to denote states, letters a, b, ... from the front of the alphabet to denote actions, and Greek letters α, β, ... to denote sequences of actions. Actions can be thought of as "inputs" or "instructions" to be performed by the system; *step(s,a)* denotes the state of the system resulting by performing action *a* in state *s*, and *output*(s,*a*) denotes the result returned by the action. In the following, λ denotes an empty sequence and $\circ$ denotes a concatenation. We shall consider an extension of the function *step* to sequence of actions in the form of a function *run*: $S \times A^* \rightarrow S$, defined by

(ax1) $run(s,\lambda) = s$

(ax2) $run(s,a \circ \alpha) = run(step(s,a),\alpha)$

The agents or subjects interacting with the system and observing the results obtained will be grouped into "security domains". Security domains represent clearances in terms of persons and classifications in terms of data. We thus assume a set *d* of security domains, and a function *dom*: $A \rightarrow d$ that associates a security domain with each action. We shall use letters … u, v, w … to denote domains.

Information is said to flow from a domain u to a domain v when some actions submitted by domain u cause the information about the behavior of the system perceived by domain v to be different from that perceived when those actions are not present. We shall consider the flow of information as a reflexive relation $\rightarrowtail$ on d (i.e., u $\rightarrowtail$ u for each domain u.)

A *security policy* will be specified by this relation on d. We use $\not\rightarrowtail$ to denote the complement relation i.e., a closed negation of $\rightarrowtail$ on $d \times d$, that is $\not\rightarrowtail = (d \times d) \setminus \rightarrowtail$, where \ denotes set difference. We speak of $\rightarrowtail$ and $\not\rightarrowtail$ as the *interference* and *noninterference* relations, respectively. A policy is said to be *transitive* if its interference is transitive.

We say that domain u *interferes* with domain v if u $\rightarrowtail$ v. We say that an action *interferes* with domain v if there is *dom*(a) such that *dom*(a) interferes with v, i.e., *dom*(a) $\rightarrowtail$ v.

An action a is said to be required *noninterfering* with domain v if *dom*(a) $\not\rightarrowtail$ v for all action sequences that contain a. The function *purge*: $A^* \times d \rightarrow A^*$ is defined as follows

(ax3) $purge(\lambda, v) = \lambda$

(ax4) $purge(a \circ \alpha, v) = a \circ purge(\alpha, v)$, if $dom(a) \rightarrowtail v$

(ax5) $purge(a \circ \alpha, v) = purge(\alpha, v)$, if $dom(a) \not\rightarrowtail v$.

The machine is *secure* if a given domain v is unable to distinguish between the state of the machine after it has processed a given action sequence, and the state after processing the same sequence purged of actions required to be noninterfering with v.

Formally, the security is identified with the requirement that $output(run(s_0,\alpha),a) = output(run(s_0,purge(\alpha,dom(a))),a)$.

For convenience, we introduce the functions *do*: $A^* \rightarrow S$ and *test*: $A^* \times A \rightarrow O$ to abbreviate the expressions in the last requirement: $do(\alpha) = run(s_0,\alpha)$, and $test(\alpha,a) = output(do(\alpha),a)$. Then we say that system M is secure for the policy $\rightarrowtail$ if

$$test(\alpha,a) = test(purge(\alpha,dom(a)),a) \quad (1)$$

for all actions sequences α and actions a.

The non-interference definition of security is expressed "globally" in (1) in terms of sequences of actions and state transitions. In order to obtain sufficient "local" conditions for verifying the security of systems, Rushby introduces a set of conditions on individual state transitions.

A system M is *view-partitioned* if, for each domain u from d, there is an equivalence relation $\overset{u}{\sim}$ on S. These equivalence relations are said to be *output consistent* if

$$s \overset{dom(a)}{\sim} t \Rightarrow output(s,a) = output(t,a). \quad (2)$$

The following result allows relating the output consistency to security of the system.

Lemma 1:

Let $\rightarrowtail$ be a policy and M a view partitioned, output consistent system such that

$$do(\alpha) \overset{u}{\sim} do(purge(\alpha,u)). \quad (3)$$

Then M is secure for $\rightarrowtail$.

Proof: see [29].

Let M be a view-partitioned system and $\rightarrowtail$ a policy. We say that M *locally respects* $\rightarrowtail$ if

$$dom(a) \not\rightarrowtail u \Rightarrow s \overset{u}{\sim} step(s,a) \quad (4)$$

and that M is *step consistent* if

$$s \overset{u}{\sim} t \Rightarrow step(s,a) \overset{u}{\sim} step(t,a). \quad (5)$$

The following theorem shows that the local conditions formulated are sufficient to guarantee security.

Theorem 1: (Unwinding Theorem)

Let $\rightarrowtail$ be a policy and M a view-partitioned system that is output consistent, step consistent, and locally respects $\rightarrowtail$. Then M is secure for $\rightarrowtail$.

We have thus recalled the basic knowledge formalizing the information needed by an automated theorem prover.

B. CMM Suggests a Generalization Necessary to Prove the Unwinding Theorem

As we said above, we shall suppose that system M is output consistent, step consistent, and locally respects $\rightarrowtail$. To prove this theorem it is sufficient to prove that (3) holds.

Using our above *CM*-formula construction algorithm, we shall study what operations have to be performed in order to prove formula (3) introduced above:

$$do(\alpha) \overset{dom(b)}{\sim} do(purge(\alpha,dom(b))), \quad (3)$$

for arbitrary domain *dom*(b) and state α.

By definition of *do*, $do(\alpha)$ is $run(s_0,\alpha)$ and similarly for $do(purge(\alpha,dom(b)))$. We thus obtain that the goal is to prove the formula (original theorem)

$$run(s_0,\alpha) \overset{dom(b)}{\sim} run(s_0,purge(\alpha,dom(b))). \quad (UTh)$$

Let us consider a proof by induction on α. This means to consider the base step for $\alpha = \lambda$ and the induction step for $\alpha = a \circ \alpha'$, where a is an arbitrary action and α' is a sequence of actions. As the proof for the base step is easy, we focus on the proof of the induction step.

In the induction step, α is $a \circ \alpha'$. The induction hypothesis is

$$run(s_0,\alpha') \overset{dom(b)}{\sim} run(s_0,purge(\alpha',dom(b))). \quad (6)$$

The goal is to prove

$$run(s_0,a \circ \alpha') \overset{dom(b)}{\sim} run(s_0,purge(a \circ \alpha',dom(b))). \quad (7)$$

using the induction hypothesis and the properties of M.

The *CM*-formula construction requires that we replace one of arguments of (7) by pivotal argument. Since the term at the right side is more complex than the term on the left side, we chose to replace this complex term by the pivotal argument ξ. This gives

$$run(s_0, a \circ \alpha') \overset{dom(b)}{\sim} \xi. \quad (8)$$

By definition,

$$run(s_0, a \circ \alpha') = run(step(s_0, a), \alpha')$$

This gives

$$run(step(s_0, a), \alpha') \overset{dom(b)}{\sim} \xi. \quad (9)$$

We would like now to apply the induction hypothesis (6). This means to compare $run(s_0, \alpha')$ in (8) and $run(step(s_0, a), \alpha')$ in the last formula (9). This fails. Therefore, *CM*-formula construction generates a new lemma expressed in terms of the failure formula

$$run(step(s_0, a), \alpha') \overset{dom(b)}{\sim} run(s_0, purge(a \circ \alpha', dom(b))).$$

For simplicity of our presentation here we do not evaluate the term $purge(a \circ \alpha', dom(b))$.

In the last formula, all the variables are universally quantified. The proof is by induction and the variable α' becomes the induction variable. In the base step, $\alpha' = \lambda$ and the induction step for $\alpha' = c \circ \gamma$, where c is an arbitrary action and γ is a sequence of actions.

The base step for this new goal would lead to discovery of a missing precondition. In this paper we would like to insist more on the discovery of a need for a generalization. Therefore, we shall skip the base step and we shall go directly to the induction step.

In the induction step, since $\alpha' = c \circ \gamma$, the induction hypothesis is the formula

$$run(step(s_0, a), \gamma) \overset{dom(b)}{\sim} run(s_0, purge(a \circ \gamma, dom(b))). \quad (10)$$

and the goal to prove is the formula

$$run(step(s_0, a), c \circ \gamma) \overset{dom(b)}{\sim} run(s_0, purge(a \circ c \circ \gamma, dom(b))).$$

The *CM*-formula construction replaces the right hand term by an abstract argument ξ. This yields

$$run(step(s_0, a), c \circ \gamma) \overset{dom(b)}{\sim} \xi.$$

The evaluation of

$$run(step(s_0, a), c \circ \gamma)$$

is $run(step(step(s_0, a), c), \gamma)$, i.e., we have to consider the formula

$$run(step(step(s_0, a), c), \gamma) \overset{dom(b)}{\sim} \xi.$$

CM-construction tries to apply the induction hypothesis (10), but it fails, since there are no axioms that would put into relation the terms $step(s_0, a)$ and $step(step(s_0, a), c)$. This means that a new lemma expressing this relationship is necessary in order to complete the proof. The use of induction on growing terms will, of course, not solve our problem that recurs at each step:

$$run(s_0, \alpha) \overset{dom(b)}{\sim} run(s_0, purge(\alpha, dom(b)))$$

$$run(step(s_0, a), \alpha') \overset{dom(b)}{\sim} run(s_0, purge(a \circ \alpha', dom(b)))$$

$$run(step(s_0, a), c \circ \gamma) \overset{dom(b)}{\sim} run(s_0, purge(a \circ c \circ \gamma, dom(b)))$$

...

Nevertheless, this sequence of failures contains an infinite sequence of 'unprovable' lemmas (in the context of the axioms we use). This 'unprovability' is expressed by means of growing terms. A rather obvious solution is thus to suppose that we miss a lemma in which the sequence of these growing terms is generalized by a variable 's'. This new variable s replaces the following sequence of growing terms:

$$s_0$$
$$step(s_0, a)$$
$$step(step(s_0, a), c)$$

...

Thus the original theorem (UTh) is replaced by the goal to prove a formula into which s_0 is replaced by s in the function 'run' in the non-pivotal argument (i.e., $s_0 \rightarrow s$ in $run(s_0, \alpha)$ of (UTh)). It follows that our task to prove the original theorem (UTh) is replaced by the goal to prove

$$run(s, \alpha) \overset{dom(b)}{\sim} run(s_0, purge(\alpha, dom(b))). \quad \text{(UThG)}$$

Again the proof is by induction on α. In the base step, α is λ. The goal is thus prove

$$run(s, \lambda) \overset{dom(b)}{\sim} run(s_0, purge(\lambda, dom(b))). \quad (11)$$

We introduce the pivotal argument here and thus we have to consider

$$run(s, \lambda) \overset{dom(b)}{\sim} \xi. \quad (12)$$

By definition, $run(s, \lambda)$ is s. This means that (12) changes to $s \overset{dom(b)}{\sim} \xi$. We check now whether ξ can be transformed into the right side of (11), that is $run(s_0, purge(\lambda, dom(b)))$. Because of axioms (ax3) and (ax1), the evaluation of $run(s_0, purge(\lambda, dom(b)))$ is s_0. A pivotal argument can be replaced by s_0. This gives that we are left with checking the formula

$$s \overset{dom(b)}{\sim} s_0. \quad (13)$$

We have no way to prove this and thus this formula becomes a missing precondition to (UThG). In other words, we have to prove the formula (Lm1):

$$s \overset{dom(b)}{\sim} s_0 \Rightarrow run(s, \alpha) \overset{dom(b)}{\sim} run(s_0, purge(\alpha, dom(b))).$$

In order to somewhat shorten this example, we can tell that, if we try to prove (Lm1) following the steps described in Section III, we will again fail and generate yet another infinite sequence of lemmas that leads us to the following generalization (Lm2) in which s_0 is generalized to 't' on both sides of the implication. Note that, at the start of our proof, this generalization is by no means intuitively obvious and it does deserve the effort we put in its discovery (Lm2):

$$s \overset{dom(b)}{\sim} t \Rightarrow run(s,\alpha) \overset{dom(b)}{\sim} run(t, purge(\alpha, dom(b))).$$

In order to prove lemma (Lm2), we again use *CM*-formula construction and this will lead to a success as detailed in Appendix of [15]. The initial formula (UTh) is a particular instance of (Lm2) with $s = s_0 = t$.

This means that initial Rushby's Unwinding Theorem, i.e., the formula (UTh), is in a sense incomplete from the theorem proving point of view. Indeed, the available axioms are not sufficient to prove the given theorem in its original form. It has to be generalized. Note that Rushby's goes directly to proving a generalized formula (Lm2) without explaining the reasons and motivations for this generalization. The above presentation shows that, in our approach, the motivations for this generalization are expressed as a (possibly infinite) sequence of failure formulas that contain a sequence of terms and these terms increase regularly.

A proof of (Lm2) using *CMM* as well as its comparison with Rushby's proof can be found in [15].

Summarizing, our example here shows that the *CM*-formula construction is particularly suited to finding missing preconditions (as we found in formula (13)) and suggesting a need for useful generalizations leading to (Lm2), as we have just shown. In other words, it is particularly effective in recovery from failures. Our paper [16] shows that our approach is able to suggest even missing axioms. As said above, in the future, integration of the suggested axioms will also be automatically handled.

V. FUTURE WORK

Despite our previous success with solving also non-standard problems such as n-queens [9], manipulation of blocks in robotics [16] and unusual reformulation of Ackermann's function [13], the practical completeness of *CMM* is not yet obtained. We need to extend our investigations also to non-atomic formulas, *etc*. This is why we continue in our research in the domain of information flow security that is nowadays important and challenging. As a complementary work to [21] and [20], we plan to help in the search of the necessary extensions of *CMM* in this field by the attempts for mechanized proofs of Unwinding Theorems presented in Mantel's thesis [24] and, among others [18] [28] [19] and [25]. To our best knowledge there is no other existing work related to the automation of the inductive proofs of these theorems. The challenge is here the execution of proofs for theorems that contain non-transitive relations. Our research question is: Do non-transitive relations require specific tools that are not yet present in *CMM*? Are there other problems that we did not meet yet?

We are quite sure that our future investigations concerning also the use of *CMM* for formalizing deductive theories requiring recursion will be very fruitful and will suggest new problems to be handled and new tools to be developed in the field of Machine Learning and Computational Creativity. Mantel's work [24] is our first objective in this direction. Our research question is: Can Mantel's work be enhanced by use of an ITP-system well suited also for proving theorems containing existential quantifiers?

VI. CONCLUSION

Research shows (see [5]) that even a team of super-gifted people is unable to work together if they do not develop, in what we call "research's preliminary phase", a common vocabulary for their already known particular personal tools so that they become able – together – to develop a new custom-made vocabulary for their intended technological vision.

The main contribution of this paper is the introduction of one of fundamental notions for such research preliminary phases of any technological vision made accessible in the framework of SRPS, namely informal specification.

On our example of progressive building the fundamentals of *CMM* for ITP we have illustrated that, due to symbiotic and recursive character of SRPS, the missing tools of *CMM* are informally specified while *by-hand* experimenting challenging examples. The difficulty of this by-hand experimentation lies in the following points:

- All the experiences are performed strictly following *CM*-formula construction and relying on previously informally *on-purpose specified* tools (in our example here: evaluation, generation of induction hypotheses, application of induction hypotheses, terms transformation and generalization), i.e., these experiences are not led by the personal talent of an experimenter.
- Each observation concerns not only specifying (informally) missing tools (in our example here: handling non-recursive formulas as explained in [15]) but also refining informal specifications of already introduced tools (in our example here: some new features of generalization were found; their presentation is out of scope of this paper). This explains and justifies our by-hand research instead of automated experiences in which subtle patterns may be lost.
- The talent (if any) of experimenter is strictly reduced to looking for patterns that either have nothing to do with the semantic of the domain in which ITP is performed or, if this is not the case, the experimenter

must justify their adequate introduction into our Theory of Constructible Domains [11] (this is a particular theory of representation of definitions of recursive functions and predicates suitable for *CMM*); in other words, no domain or problem dependent heuristics are allowed in by-hand experiments.

This means that persistent and relatively humble systemic creativity and goal awareness are the main features of srp-thinking.

This paper explains that there should be no conflict between Newtonian and Cartesian srp-thinking. Both apply to different problems, they are complementary. The problem arises only when the Newtonian criteria are applied to the evaluation of the research on SRPS. This manifests namely by Newtonians rejecting the necessary long term by-hand experimenting and informally specified notion of 'practical completeness'.

ACKNOWLEDGMENTS

Michèle Sebag and Dieter Hutter contributed ideas to improve this paper. This conference referees' feedback is gratefully acknowledged.

REFERENCES

[1] A. Asperti, C. S. Coen, E. Tassi, S. Zacchiroli, "User Interaction with the Matita Proof Assistant," Journal of Automated Reasoning, Vol. 39, Issue 2, pp. 109-139, 2007.

[2] E. Beth,The Foundations of Mathematics; North-Holland,1959.

[3] R. S. Boyer, J S. Moore, A Computational Logic Handbook; Academic Press, Inc., 1988.

[4] A. Bundy, F. Van Harnelen, C. Horn and A. Smaill, "The Oyster–Clam system," in Stickel, M.E. (ed.) 10th International Conference on Automated Deduction, vol. 449 of Lecture Notes in Artificial Intelligence, pp. 647–648. Springer, 1990.

[5] R. Chauvin, Les Surdoués (Super-gifted); Stock, 1975.

[6] R. L. Constable, Implementing Mathematics with the Nuprl proof development system; Prentice-Hall, Inc., Englewood Clifs, New Jersey, 1986.

[7] M. Franova, "CM-strategy : A Methodology for Inductive Theorem Proving or Constructive Well-Generalized Proofs," in A. K. Joshi, (ed), Proceedings of the Ninth International Joint Conference on Artificial Intelligence; Los Angeles, pp. 1214-1220, 1985.

[8] M. Franova, "Fundamentals for a new methodology for inductive theorem proving: CM-construction of atomic formulae," in Y. Kodratoff (ed.), Proceedings of the 8th European Conference on Artificial Intelligence; August 1-5, Pitman, London, United Kingdom, pp. 137-141, 1988.

[9] M. Franova, "An Implementation of Program Synthesis from Formal Specifications," in Y. Kodratoff, (ed.), Proceedings of the 8th European Conference on Artificial Intelligence; August 1-5, Pitman, London, United Kingdom, pp. 559-564, 1988.

[10] M. Franova, "Precomas 0.3 User Guide," Rapport de Recherche No.524, L.R.I., Université de Paris-Sud, Orsay, France, October, 1989.

[11] M. Franova, "A Theory of Constructible Domains - a formalization of inductively defined systems of objects for a user-independent automation of inductive theorem proving, Part I," Rapport de Recherche No.970, L.R.I., Université de Paris-Sud, Orsay, France, Mai, 1995.

[12] M. Franova, Créativité Formelle: méthode et pratique - Conception des systèmes "informatiques" complexes et Brevet Épistémologique (Formal Creativity : method and practice – Design of complex "computational" systems and Epistemological Patent), Publibook, 2008.

[13] M. Franova, "A construction of a definition recursive with respect to the second variable for the Ackermann's function," Rapport de Recherche No.1511, L.R.I., Université de Paris-Sud, Orsay, France, 2009.

[14] M. Franova, "Cartesian versus Newtonian paradigms for recursive program synthesis," International Journal on Advances in Systems and Measurements, vol. 7, no 3&4, pp. 209-222, 2014.

[15] M. Franova, D. Hutter and Y. Kodratoff, "Algorithmic conceptualization of tools for proving by induction « Unwinding » Theorems – A Case Study," Rapport de Recherche N◦ 1587, L.R.I., Université de Paris-Sud, Orsay, France, Mai 2016.

[16] M. Franova and Kooli M., "Recursion Manipulation for Robotics: why and how?"; in R. Trappl, (ed.), Cybernetics and Systems '98; proc. of the Fourteenth Meeting on Cybernetics and Systems Research, Austrian Society for Cybernetic Studies, Vienna, Austria, pp. 836-841, 1998.

[17] K. Gödel, "The completeness of the axioms of the functional calculus of logic", in: J. van Heijenoort, From Frege to Godel, A source book in mathematical logic, 1879-1931, Harvard University Press, pp. 582-592, 1967.

[18] J. Graham-Cumming and J.W. Sanders, "On the refinement of non-interference," Proc. of the IEEE Symposium on Security and Privacy, pp. 11-20, 1982.

[19] J. T. Haigh and W. D. Young, "Extending the noninterference version of MLS for SAT; IEEE Trans. Software Eng. 13(2), pp. 141-150, 1987.

[20] D. Hutter, H. Mantel, I. Schaefer and A. Schairer, "Security of multi-agent systems: A case study on comparison shopping," Journal of Applied Logic, Volume 5, Issue 2, pp. 303-332, June 2007.

[21] D. Hutter, "Automating Proofs of cnwinding conditions," in S. Autexier, H. Mantel (eds.), Workshop Proceedings VERIFY06 at the International Joint Conference on Automated Reasoning, Seattle, 2006.

[22] D. Kapur, "An overview of Rewrite Rule Laboratory (RRL)," J. Comput. Math. Appl. 29(2), pp. 91–114, 1995.

[23] Z. Manna and R.Waldinger, "A Deductive approach to Program Synthesis," in ACM Transactions on Programming Languages and Systems, Vol. 2., No.1, pp. 90-121, 1980.

[24] H. Mantel, "A uniform framework for the formal specification and verification of information flow security," PhD thesis, Universitty of Saarlandes, 2003.

[25] J. K. Millen, "Unwinding Forward Correctability," in Proc. of the 7th IEEE Computer Security Workshop, pp. 35-54, 1994.

[26] C. Paulin-Mohring and B. Werner, Synthesis of ML programs in the system Coq; Journal of Symbolic Computation; Volume 15, Issues 5–6, pp. 607–640, 1993.

[27] L. C. Paulson, "The foundation of a generic theorem prover," Journal of Automated Reasoning, September, Volume 5, Issue 3, pp. 363-397, 1989.

[28] S. Pinsky, "Absorbing covers and intransitive non-interference," in Proceedings of IEEE Symposium on Security and Privacy, pp. 102 - 113, 1995.

[29] J. Rushby, "Noninterference, transitivity, and channel-control security policies," Technical Report CSL-92-02, Computer Science Laboratory SRI International, December, 1992.

[30] R. M. Smullyan, What is the Name of This Book? - The Riddle of Dracula and Other Logical Puzzles; Penguin, 1981.

Deepening Prose Comprehension by Incremental Knowledge Augmentation From References

Amal Babour, Javed I. Khan, and Fatema Nafa
Department of Computer Science, Kent State University
Kent, Ohio, USA
Email: {ababour, javed, fnafa}@kent.edu

Abstract— **Humans read references to gain a better understanding of a topic. In this paper, we propose a system that tries to mimic the human reading process for a given prose. The system can accommodate a deep prose comprehension by discovering the relevant parts from a reference related to the given prose that connect and illuminate a set of learnable concepts from the prose by adding direct meaningful knowledge paths among them. We present an evaluation model to measure the acquired knowledge and the learning process obtained by the system. The analysis of the results verifies that the system succeeded in deepening the prose comprehension.**

Keywords— Prose comprehension; Graph mining; Illuminated Semantic Graph; Knowledge paths; Sub Set Spanning.

I. INTRODUCTION

Prose comprehension is an intriguing cognitive process [1]. Sophisticated prose is often rich with specialized concepts and terminologies that are sensitive and difficult for inexperienced readers to comprehend. This is observed in readings in many domains such as science and technology. Additionally, it is believed that the process of prose comprehension involves the integration of concepts with significant external knowledge, which is often called prior knowledge [2][3]. However, readers have different levels of prior knowledge, or sometimes they might not even have prior knowledge about a specific topic. Therefore, they need help through knowledge of full resources that allows them to compensate for the lack of prior knowledge [4]. However, the extensive number of references might have been a problem in itself. Readers might struggle to keep up with the type and the large amount of references, which can easily be disturbing. Additionally, searching for the relevant needed parts in the references is too extensive and time-consuming.

There is a great deal of work that tried to deepen understanding from prose by explicating the relationship among the text concepts [2][3][5], while there is another group of studies that employs external references to achieve deep comprehension [6][7][1]. The goal of this study is to present a method to develop our previous work [6]. In this paper, we present a method that reads the relevant parts from an external reference related to the given prose and discovers the direct knowledge paths connecting a set of learnable prose concepts. The main contributions of the paper are the following: First, we introduce an algorithm that reads the most appropriate parts from an external reference, such as Wikipedia, Encyclopedia, and textbooks and connects a set of learnable prose concepts by discovering the direct meaningful knowledge paths among them. Second, we present an evaluation model to be used by the system to measure the quantitative insight of the obtained knowledge and the learning process. Finally, we conduct three experiments on three texts of prose to assess and validate the effectiveness of the system.

The rest of the paper is structured as follows. Section II provides an overview of the related work. The main definitions and the overview of the system are presented in Section III. Section IV presents details of the used evaluation model. In Section V, we present the experiment and the evaluation results. The conclusion and the future work are presented in Section VI.

II. REALATED WORK

There has been several interesting studies on text comprehension. Some that focuses on *knowledge-dense* texts has highlighted deepening the understanding from the text itself, while others have focused on deepening the understanding using external consultation. Some of the most influential works on deepening text comprehension were introduced by Hardas and Khan. In [5], they posed the problem as a computational learning model in reading comprehension of natural texts that can mimic the growth of knowledge network as a step-by-step process of classification between recognized and unrecognized concepts during sentence-by-sentence reading. Later, using the computational model, they explored the impact of the concepts sequence on comprehension during reading [2]. Recently, Al Madi and Khan [3] developed the computational model to accommodate both text and multimedia comprehension. In the area of deepening the comprehension using external consultation, Babour and her associates addressed the problem of deepening text comprehension by bringing knowledge from more than one reference [7]. They proposed an automated method that iteratively selects a relevant reference to a given text that illuminates the text concepts by adding new knowledge paths using the selected relevant reference and ontology engine [6][7]. Later, they introduce a novel method that mines the appropriate parts from the relevant reference, which is valuable in deepening the comprehension by discovering the highest familiarity knowledge paths that connect a set of text concepts [1].

It would be relevant to discuss additional studies from graph mining perspective, which are relevant to the technique we have developed. Jin and his associates [8] proposed a graph-based retrieval model to detect a coherent chain between two given concepts across text documents. In [9],

Faloutsos and his associates developed a method that extracts a connected subgraph connecting two given nodes using electrical flow; whereas, Sozio and Gionis [10] proposed a method that extracts a compact subgraph of densely connected nodes by maximizing the minimum degree.

The work in this paper is about the same problem discussed in [1], but the difference is that our method is based on extracting the direct/shortest knowledge paths connecting a set of concepts instead of extracting the highest familiarity knowledge paths connecting them.

III. PROSE COMPREHENSION SYSTEM

The purpose of the system is to mimic the human reading process by creating an automated prose comprehension that discovers the hidden relations among each pair of concepts c_i and c_j in a learnable prose *LTX* and adds knowledge paths *K* among them using the learnable prose itself and a set of related references in an *Illuminated-Semantic-Graph G.*

We define the *Illuminated-Semantic-Graph G* as a graph $G=(C, E)$ that provides a capture of the current state of the learning progress showing the learnable prose concepts C_L and the relationships between them found by reading the learnable prose *LTX*, the relevant parts from a related reference *RTX*, and the ontology engine *OE*, where *C* is a set of concepts $(c_1, c_2, ..., c_n)$ and *E* is a set of edges. The concept is either in *LTX*, *RTX*, or *OE* while the edge between any two concepts represents the relation between them. Each concept c_i can have one or more senses $(s_{i,1}, s_{i,2}, .. s_{i,x})$, where *i* is the concept number and *x* is the sense number. Each edge connects two concepts by a specific sense of each concept and has a label selected from *L'* representing the type of relation between the two concepts, where *L'* is a set of ontology engine and verb relations [1].

We define the *knowledge path K* as a path illuminating the relationship between two concepts, which can be represented as a sequence of edges that connects a concept c_i with a concept c_j in a preserved sense, where c_i and c_j are concepts from *LTX*. The in-between concepts in the path can be external to C_L. The type of the edge between any two concepts in the path is one of the following: Synonym, Hyponym, Hypernym, Meronym, Holonym, Instance or Verbed. The first six types are from the *OE*, and the last type is defined as the verb linked two concepts in the same sentence, where the two concepts are the subject and the object in the sentence [1].

Sometimes reading *LTX* only is not enough to understand, connect and illuminate the relation among the learnable concepts. Thus, there is a need to read a reference or set of references RTX_i to substitute the lack in the understanding. For example, given a specified *LTX* about 'Ethane' for comprehension and a list of five learnable concepts C_L= {ethane, hydrocarbon, hydrogen, gas, petroleum} in *LTX* as shown in Fig. 1 (A). The process of connecting C_L using different recources is shown in Fig. 1 (B).

Ethane, a colourless, odourless, gaseous hydrocarbon (compound of hydrogen and carbon), belonging to the paraffin series; its chemical formula is C_2H_6. Ethane is structurally the simplest hydrocarbon that contains a single carbon-carbon bond. The second most important constituent of natural gas, it also occurs dissolved in petroleum oils and as a by-product of oil refinery operations and of the carbonization of coal.

Figure 1. (A) An example of LTX.

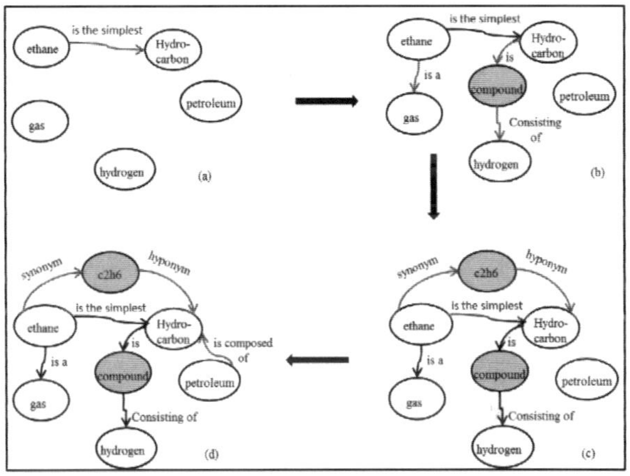

Figure 1. (B). The process of connecting C_L concepts using different resources. (a) Knowledge path K from LTX. (b) Knowledge path K using RTX1. (c) Knowledge path K using Ontology Engine OE. (d) Knowledge path K using RTX2.

Table I lists the symbols and definitions used, sorted by their overall appearance in the paper.

The overall system is applied on two core phases. The input of the first phase is the learnable prose *LTX* and C_L= $\{c_i, ...c_n\}$ in *LTX*. The system performs the ***Verbed-knowledge-paths*** $KP_v(\ )$ ***algorithm*** to generate an initial graph G_{LTX} ($G_{i=0}$) representing the verb relation between each pair of concepts in C_L, which is considered the output of this phase. The input of the second phase is a selected reference RTX_i related to *LTX* and C_L. The system performs the following algorithms in five steps each time it reads a new RTX_i.

1) Verbed-knowledge-paths $KP_v(\ )$ ***algorithm*** generates a graph G_{Ri} representing the verb relation between each pair of concepts in C_L from a RTX_i.

2) Sub-Set-Spanning algorithm SS( ) extracts the M-sub-sets spanning paths from G_{Ri} that connect concepts from C_L with the direct meaningful knowledge paths. The extracted M-sub-sets are represented in G_{Ui} graph.

3) Merge algorithm Gmerge( ) in the third step, generates G_{temp} that merges G_i and G_{Ui} graphs.

4) OE-knowledge-paths $KP_{OE}(\ )$ ***algorithm*** generates G_{Wi} graph representing the *OE* relation between each pair of concepts in G_{temp}.

5) Merge algorithm Gmerge( ) in the fifth step, generates G_{i+1} that merges G_{temp} and G_{Wi}.

TABLE I. SYMBOLS AND DEFINITIONS

Symbol	Definition
LTX	The learnable prose.
$G=(C, E)$	Illuminated-Semantic-Graph.
$C_L= \{c_i, ...c_n\}$	A set of learnable noun concepts in the prose.
$RTX=\{RTX_1,RTX_2,...RTX_n\}$	A set of reference texts.
OE	Ontology Engine.
C	A set of concepts.
$E = \{e_1, e_2, ..,e_q\}$	A set of edges.
$s_{i,x}$	Is the xth sense for concept c_i.
L'	a set of ontology engine and verb relations.
K	A sequence of edges constructing a Knowledge Path.
$KPv(\ )$	Verbed-knowledge-paths algorithm.
G_{LTX}/ G_0	The graph of the learnable prose.
G_{Ri}	A graph for a reference text.
$SS(\ )$	Sub-set-spanning algorithm.
G_{Ui}	The name of the graph extracted by SS( ).
$Gmerg(\ )$	Merge algorithm.
G_{temp}	Temporary graph.
$KP_{OE}(\ )$	OE-knowledge-paths algorithm.
G_{Wi}	The name of the graph created by $KP_{OE}(\ )$
G_{final}	The final graph generated after reading LTX and all RTX.
$v_{i,j}$	A verb connecting two concepts c_i and c_j in a sentence.
Υ	The maximum allowed distance between the concept and the verb in the verb relation in a sentence.
α	The maximum allowed length for K created by $KP_{OE}(\ )$.
β	Cluster Coefficient.
NIC_i	The neighbors interconnections coefficient of concept c_i.
deg_i	Degree of a concept c_i.
δ	Graph Entropy.
p_i	Probability of the concept c_i degree distribution.
$h_i(\Theta)$	Is the illuminated value for concept c_i at a particular phase.
Θ_i	Phase transition.
f_i	The frequency of concept c_i or the relation type extracted from Gutenberg corpus[14].
$H = \{h_i, h_j, ...\}$	Vector of Concepts Illumination Values {a quality between 0 and 1}.
$\|H\|$	Is the summation of h_i for each c_i in C_L.
$a_{i,j}$	An element denoting the association strength between concept c_i and c_j.
A	A matrix with $a_{i,j}$ elements.
$\tilde{N}$	The number of connected concepts.

After reading the whole set of RTX_i, the system generates the G_{final} that includes a set of K, where both ends of each K are from the C_L.

Fig. 2 explains the phases of the system in detail. The bold line in phase 2 shows the iterative process of applying the proposed algorithm with each reading of a new RTX_i for finding the direct meaningful knowledge path among C_L. Both LTX and RTX go through preprocessing. During preprocessing, all stopwords, except negation words, are removed and the remaining words are stemmed using Porter Stemmer [11]. The next section describes each algorithm in detail.

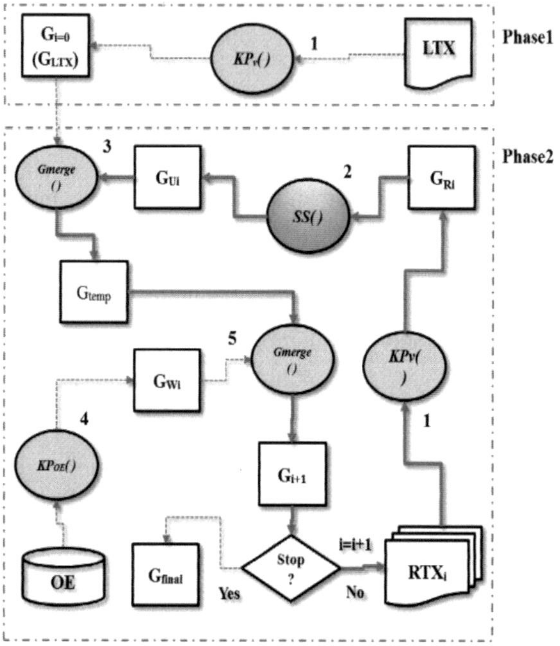

Figure 2. Overview of the system.

A. Verbed-Knowledge-Paths algorithm $KP_v(\ )$

Given a LTX or RTX_i and a C_L, for each sentence *in LTX* or RTX_i, the algorithm searches for any pair of concepts (c_i, c_j) from C_L to see if there is a verb $v_{i,j}$ between them, where the distance between c_i and $v_{i,j}$ and the distance between $v_{i,j}$ and c_j is less than or equal a threshold Υ. If so, it saves them in the form of $[c_i, v_{i,j}, c_j]$ as an edge in the graph representing a verb relation between a pair of concepts c_i and c_j. If $v_{i,j}$ is preceded or followed by a negative word, the negative word is attached to the verb forming one word. The output of the algorithm is a graph that represents the verbed relation between any pair of concepts from C_L.

B. Sub-Set-Spanning algorithm $SS(\ )$

The algorithm in Fig. 3 represents the Sub-Set-Spanning algorithm as follows: The input of the algorithm is G_{Ri} and C_L, where the output is G_{Ui}, which is a subgraph from G_{Ri} that presents the direct paths among C_L. We use the same algorithm used in our previous work [1], but we replace the highest familiarity knowledge paths among the concepts with the direct ones.

The search for a direct knowledge path has been implemented as a breadth-first-search (BFS). For each component *comp* in *G*, the algorithm uses a queue data structure *Queue* to temporarily hold each visited concept in the graph with its neighbors. It picks any concept from C_L as the source *s* for initializing the *Queue*. Then, it initializes the distance *dist* between *s* and each concept *c* in the *comp* to *INFINITY* and initializes the previous concept *prev* of each *c* to *-1*. In the loop iteration, it de-queues the first concept *c* in the queue, marks it as visited, and checks if $c \in C_L$. If so, it updates its *dist* to *0*, adds it to *M* where *M* holds the found C_L

concepts and removes it from C_L. Then, it en-queues all the neighbors c_i*'s* of concept *c* if they are marked as non-visited, assigns *prev* and calculates *dist* for each of them. If the current *dist* of c_i is less than its previous *dist*, that means a shorter knowledge path to c_i is found. The c_i*'s prev* and *dist* are updated to the new less values and the process is repeated till the queue becomes empty. If all *comp* are checked, *getPaths* constructs the M sub-sets spanning from *M* and *prev*. The returned M-sub-sets spanning are represented in G_{Ui}.

Fig. 4 shows an example of the M sub-sets spanning returned by SS( ) algorithm, where C_L ={'ethane', 'carbon', 'petroleum'}. The returned M sub-set spanning is {['ethane', 'chemical', 'carbon', 'constituent', 'petroleum']}.

```
Def Sub-Set-Spanning ( ):
Input: GRi, , CL
Output: M-sub-sets spanning.
  // initialization
  for each comp in G:
   Queue=ϕ
   s= pick any member from CL
   enqueue(Queue,s)
   if CL ≠ ϕ :
     for each concept c in comp
       prev[c]=-1
       dist[c]=INFINITY
       Visited[c]=False
   While Queue ≠ ϕ:
     c= dequeue(Queue)
     Visited[c]=True
     if c in CL:
       dist[c]= 0
       add c to M
       remove c from CL
     for each neighbor ci of c:
       if ci not in Queue and Visited[ci]==False:
         enqueue(Queue,ci)
       alt= dist[c]+ 1
       if alt < dist[ci]
         prev[ci]=c
         // a shorter knowledge path to ci has been found
         dist[ci]=alt
  M-sub-sets = getPaths(M[ ], prev[ ])
  return M-sub-sets
```

Figure 3. Sub-Set-Spanning algorithm.

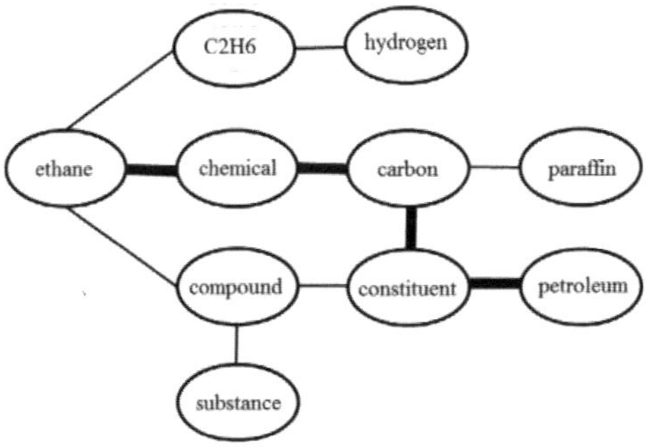

Figure 4. M Sub-Set-Spanning example.

C. Merge algorithm Gmerge( )

The algorithm merges two graphs into a single one.

D. OE-knowledge-paths algorithm KP_{OE}*( )*

The algorithm searches for knowledge paths *K* of a length less than or equal to threshold α connecting each pair of concepts that appear in G_{temp} if found using an ontology engine. The algorithm is presented in detail in our previous work [6].

IV. SYSTEM EVALUATION MODEL

In this section, we present a set of measurements, which are employed to assess the quantitative knowledge gained from *G*, including information content, graph organization, richness of information, concept illumination value, and knowledge paths.

A. Information content

The size of the graph is measured by the whole number of concepts *C* and the associations *E* among them, where the concepts belong to three different sources *LTX*, *RTX*, and *OE*. High size is a good indicator to a wealth of information and therefore deep comprehension. The process of prose comprehension is completed by reading the last RTX_i in which the graph transforms from (G_0, G_1,......,G_{final}). Therefore, the size of *G* is increased and the information is grown respectively.

B. Graph organization quality

The graph organization plays an important role in predicting the performance of the learning progress. A good graph organization gives a clarification about the context of each concept and how each concept is related to other concepts by representing groups of strongly connected concepts each works as constrains on the possible meaning of its concepts, therefore the meaning of the concepts can be greatly clarified. It can be measured by clustering coefficient β, which offers a way to measure how the concepts in the graph tend to form groups of strongly connected concepts. According to [12], we suggest calculating β using (1); the closer to 1 value indicates the higher clustered graph.

$$\beta = \sum_{i=0}^{n} \frac{2NIC_i}{deg_i(deg_i - 1)} \quad (1)$$

C. Richness of Information

Information richness is a measure of how much information a graph contains. High information richness usually indicates a graph rich with information and deep comprehension. It can be measured by entropy δ, which measures the amount of information within the graph. According to [13], we calculate δ using (2):

$$\delta = -\sum_{i=0}^{n} p_i log(p_i) \quad (2)$$

Where p_i is determined by (3):

$$p_i = \frac{deg_i}{2|E|} \quad (3)$$

D. Calculating the concepts illumination values H

The concept illumination value h_i is a way to interpret the level of understanding the concept. It presents the importance of the concepts at each particular phase. The higher the concept illumination value, the more understanding there is in the prose. The initial illumination value of a concept can by calculated using (4). This initial value represents the prior knowledge or the familiarity of the concept, where *h(0)* represents the initial value of concept *i*. The high frequency means the high familiarity of the concept.

$$h_i(0) = -1/\,log\left(\frac{f_i}{10^9}\right) \quad (4)$$

Tracking the growth evolution of the concept illumination value during the learning progress is an interesting approach to measure the deepening of prose comprehension. We calculate the illumination value of each concept at each phase. We consider the phase Θ_i as reading a set of sentences. Then, we estimate how the illumination value varies over the learning process through a set of phases. After a set of phases, the concept illumination value reaches a stable value which is considered its final illuminated value. The learning progress at each phase is assessed by the value of $|H|$ which is the summation of h_i for each c_i in C_L. The higher the $|H|$, the deeper the learning. To calculate h_i for each concept in the graph at each phase, we utilize (5).

$$H(\theta + 1) = transpose(A) * H(\theta) \quad (5)$$

$$\overbrace{\begin{matrix} c_i \\ \cdot\cdot \\ \cdot\cdot \\ \cdot\cdot \\ c_n \end{matrix} \begin{bmatrix} a_{1,1} & a_{1,2} & \cdots & \cdots & a_{1,n} \\ \cdots & \cdots & \cdots & \cdots & \cdots \\ \cdots & \cdots & \cdots & \cdots & \cdots \\ \cdots & \cdots & \cdots & \cdots & \cdot\cdot \\ \cdots & \cdots & \cdots & \cdots & a_{n,n} \end{bmatrix}}^{A:\ c_i \ \ldots\ c_n} * \overbrace{\begin{bmatrix} h_1 \\ h_2 \\ \cdots \\ \cdots \\ h_n \end{bmatrix}}^{H:\ h_i}$$

We will consider the association strength $a_{i,j}$ as the illumination value of the relation type between a pair of concepts (c_i, c_j). The value of $a_{i,j}$ is calculated by (4), f_i here represents the frequency of the relation type extracted from Gutenberg corpus [14], where high frequency means high familiarity of the relation type. The relation between *f* and *h* is a direct relation. This means the higher the frequency, the higher its illumination value. Table II shows different types of relations, which are common between any pair of concepts.

TABLE II. RELATION STRUCTURE BETWEEN ANY PAIR OF CONCEPTS

Relation type	Relation structure	$a_{i,j}$ value
verb relation	**Case#1:** ***single verb:*** c_i – : $s_{i,*}$ – v1 – $s_{j,*}$: – c_j	$h_{v1}(\Theta)$
	Case#2: ***dual verb:*** c_i – : $s_{i,*}$ – v1 v2 – $s_{j,*}$: – c_j	$h_{v1}(\Theta) * h_{v2}(\Theta)$
	Case#3: ***dual paths:*** c_i – : $s_{i,*}$ – v1 v2 – $s_{j,*}$: – c_j c_i – : $s_{i,*}$ – v3 v4 – $s_{j,*}$: – c_j	$h_{v1}(\Theta) * h_{v2}(\Theta)$ + $h_{v3}(\Theta) * h_{v4}(\Theta)$
Wordnet relation	**Case#1:** ***Class/sub-class:*** c_i – : $s_{i,*}$ – Hypernym – $s_{j,*}$: – c_j or c_i – : $s_{i,*}$ – Hyponym – $s_{j,*}$: – c_j	$h_{class}(\Theta)$
	Case#2: ***Part/sub-part:*** c_i – : $s_{i,*}$ – Holonym – $s_{j,*}$: – c_j or c_i – : $s_{i,*}$ – Meronym – $s_{j,*}$: – c_j	$h_{part}(\Theta)$
	Case#3: ***synonym:*** c_i – : $s_{i,*}$ – Synonym – $s_{j,*}$: – c_j	$h_{synonym}(\Theta) = 1$

E. Types of Knowledge Paths

The illumination-semantic-graph is a complex graph of concepts and associations. The graph has many interconnected concepts, ultimately leading to a congested graph. Hence, the information becomes hard to read; for example, it is hard to trace a particular sequence of edges connecting two concepts because the edges overlap. This can be clarified by extracting knowledge paths. A knowledge path is a way to reveal underlying information in the graph tidily. For more clarification, we classified the knowledge paths into seven types described in Table III.

TABLE III. KNOWLEDGE PATHS TYPES

	K types	Description
1.	Genesis-Set	Where each label in the sequence of edges of *K* has either a hyponym or a hypernym relation.
2.	Synonym-Set	Where each label in the sequence of edges of *K* has a synonym relation.
3.	Part-of-Set	Where each label in the sequence of edges of *K* has either a meronym or a holonym relation.
4.	Conceptual-Neighbor-Set	Where the labels in *K* have a combination of hyponym and hypernym relations.
5.	Structural-Neighbor-Set	Where the labels in *K* have a combination of meronym and holonym relations.
6.	Complex-Neighbor-Set	Where the labels in *K* have a combination of hyponym or hypernym and meronym and holonym relations.
7.	Verbed-Set	Where each label in the sequence of edges of *K* has a verb relation.

V. EXPERIMENT AND EVALUATION

In this section, we evaluate the proposed system based on the statistical characteristics of the obtained graphs of three experiments, which indicate the quantitative insight of the amount of comprehension that can be gained by the readers. In the future work, we are going to perform the experiments with actual readers. The selected proses LTX_i used in the experiments, as well as the C_L for each are shown in Table IV.

TABLE IV. LIST OF THE PROSES USDED IN THE EXPEIEMENTS

	LTX	C_L
Experiment1	LTX1: 'Ethane chemical compound' [15]	['Ethane', 'hydrocarbon', 'hydrogen', 'carbon', 'carbon-carbon', 'petroleum', 'carbonization', 'coal']
Experiment2	LTX2: 'New Test for Zika OKed' [16]	['zika', 'infection', 'dengue', 'hikungunya', 'virus', 'aedes', 'mosquito', 'antibody']
Experiment3	LTX3: 'Anesthesia gases are warming the planet' [17]	['Anesthetic', 'carbon', 'climate', 'oxide', 'desflurane', 'isoflurane', 'sevoflurane', 'halothane']

The used *OE* is Wordnet [18] version 1.7 and the used *RTX* is Wikipedia. For each experiment, *RTX* is a set of articles selected from Wikipedia about each concept in C_L. We applied the automated method used in [7] for the selection of the Wikipedia articles. For each experiment, the system goes through eight RTX_i and creates nine *G*, G_0 represents the relation among C_L in *LTX* and eight G_i each represents the relation among the C_L after adding reading a new RTX_i.

A. Graph Analysis

In this section, we present our analysis of the information gained from *G*. The breakdown of the total number of concepts *C* and the number of edges *E* in G_0 and G_{final} are shown in Table V, where the concepts are from *LTX*, *RTX*, and/or *OE*. It is observed that there is a variance in the number of concepts and edges between G_0 and the G_{final}, which is a good indicator to the plentiful information in the G_{final}, hence the depth of prose comprehension.

TABLE V. BREAK DOWN OF THE TOTAL NUMBER OF EDGES AND CONCEPTS IN THE FINAL G

	Experiment1		Experiment2		Experiment3	
	G_0	G_{final}	G_0	G_{final}	G_0	G_{final}
E	3	100	1	76	0	29
Number of *LTX* concepts	8	8	8	8	8	8
Number of *RTX* concepts	0	7	0	8	0	4
Number of *OE* concepts	0	36	0	22	0	9

Furthermore, Fig. 5 shows the number of connected learnable prose concepts C_L in G_i, where (x-axis) refers to the G_i after adding each RTX_i and (y-axis) is the number of connected concepts per G_i. For each experiment, we can observe that the number of connected concepts $\tilde{N}$ is increased when the system reads RTX_i. The concepts become fully connected after reading the 8th *RTX, 2nd RTX, and 1st RTX* for *LTX1, LTX2, and LTX3* consecutively, which verifies the effectiveness of the system for connecting C_L.

Fig. 6 shows the clustering coefficient β observed in each G_i, where (x-axis) is the G_i and (y-axis) is the clustering coefficient β. It is obvious that some of the graphs especially for the first experiment are highly clustered, which signifies that their concepts are highly clustered together.

B. Knowledge Analysis

In this section, we present our analysis of the learning progress on *LTX* comprehension from *G* in the three experiments. Fig. 7 represents the entropy δ per each G_i, where (x-axis) is the G_i and (y-axis) is the entropy δ. It is observed that the δ in the three experiments starts with a low value, then it increases gradually after reading a new RTX_i, which indicates that the graph concepts become more influential each time the system reads a RTX_i.

Moreover, Fig. 8 plots the variance in the concepts illumination values $|H|$ (y-axis) of C_L with the phases of learning progress Θ_i (x-axis) in the G_{final}. We examined 50 phases. We can clearly see from the plot that $|H|$ increases gradually over the phases especially in the first experiment, which indicates the deeper comprehension of the C_L and the *LTX* after each phase Θ_i.

C. Knowledge Paths Classification

The breakdown of *K* types that are found in G_{final} are shown in Table VI.

TABLE VI. BREAKDOWN OF KNOWLEDGE PATHS TYPES

	Experiment 1	Experiment 2	Experiment 3
Genesis-Set	2	0	2
Synonym-Set	0	0	0
Part-of-Set	0	0	0
Conceptual-Neighbor-Set	6	0	2
Structural-Neighbor-Set	0	0	0
Complex-Neighbor-Set	0	0	0
Verbed-Set	17	26	8

VI. CONCLUSION AND FUTURE WORK

In this paper, we presented a computerized human prose comprehension system that discovers relevant parts from a reference that connect and illuminate the learnable concepts by direct meaningful knowledge paths among them. The system is an improved version of our previous work [6]. The statistical results obtained from the graph(s) show that the system succeeds in connecting the learnable concepts by discovering the direct meaningful knowledge paths among them and in achieving a deep prose comprehension. For future work, we are going to compare the results of the used method with the one discussed in [1]. We are also going to test the impact of the system results on the comprehension of actual readers.

REFERENCES

[1] A. Babour, J. I. Khan, and F. Nafa " Deepening Prose Comprehension by Incremental Free text Conceptual Graph Mining and Knowledge," , Cyber-Enabled Distributed Computing and Knowledge Discovery (CyberC), International Conference on. IEEE, 2016 (in press).

[2] I. Khan and M. S. Hardas, "Does sequence of presentation matter in reading comprehension? A model based analysis of semantic concept network growth during reading," IEEE, 2013, pp. 444–452.

[3] N. S. Al Madi and J. I. Khan, "Is learning by reading a book better than watching a movie? A computational analysis of semantic concept network growth during text and multimedia comprehension," IEEE, 2015, pp. 1–8.

[4] J. E. Moravcsik and W. Kintsch, "Writing quality, reading skills, and domain knowledge as factors in text comprehension," Canadian Journal of Experimental Psychology/Revue canadienne de psychologie expérimentale, vol. 47, no. 2, 1993, pp. 360–374.

[5] M. Hardas and J. Khan, "Concept learning in text comprehension," in Lecture Notes in Computer Science. Springer Science + Business Media, 2010, pp. 240–251.

[6] A. Babour, F. Nafa, and J. Khan, "An Iterative Method for Enhancing Text Comprehension by Automatic Reading of References," in ThinkMind(TM) digital library, 2015, pp. 66–73.

[7] A. Babour, F. Nafa, and J. I. Khan, "Connecting the dots in a concept space by Iterative reading of Freetext references with Wordnet," vol. 1, IEEE, 2015, pp. 441–444.

[8] W. Jin, R. K. Srihari, and X. Wu, "Mining concept associations for knowledge discovery through concept chain queries," in Advances in Knowledge Discovery and Data Mining. Springer Science + Business Media, 2007, pp. 555–562.

[9] C. Faloutsos, K. S. McCurley, and A. Tomkins, "Fast discovery of connection subgraphs," ACM, 2004, pp. 118–127.

[10] M. Sozio and A. Gionis, "The community-search problem and how to plan a successful cocktail party," ACM, 2010, pp. 939–948.

[11] M. F. Porter, "An algorithm for suffix stripping," Program: electronic library and information systems, vol. 14, no. 3, 1980, pp. 130–137.

[12] D. G. Bonchev and D. H. Rouvray, "Quantitative measures of network complexity," in Complexity in chemistry, biology, and ecology, Springer US, 2005, pp. 191-235.

[13] R. Navigli and M. Lapata, "Graph Connectivity Measures for Unsupervised Word Sense Disambiguation," IJCAI, 2007, pp. 1683-1688.

[14] M. Hart. Project Gutenberg. 1971.

[15] The Editors of Encyclopædia Britannica. (2016, September 22). Ethane |chemical compound. Retrived from: https://www.britannica.com/science/ethane .

[16] K. Grens. (2016, March 22). New Test for Zika OKed. Reterived from: http://www.the-scientist.com/?articles.view/articleNo/45638/title/New-Test-for-Zika-OKed .

[17] E. DeMarco. (2015, April 7). Anesthesia gases are warming the planet. Retrieved from: http://www.sciencemag.org/news/2015/04/anesthesia-gases-are-warming-planet .

[18] Princeton, "About WordNet - WordNet - about WordNet," Trustees of Princeton University, 2016.

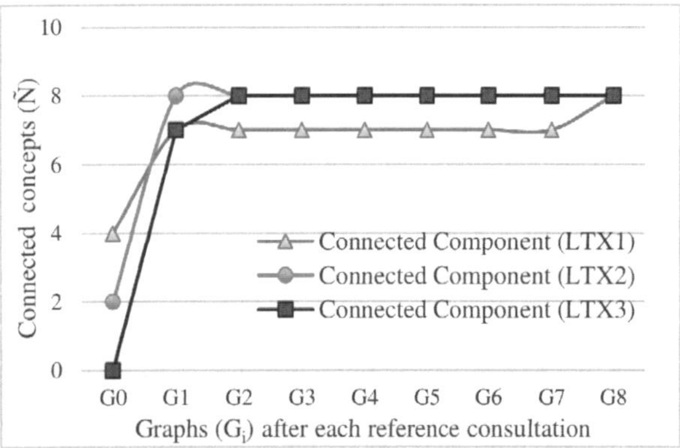

Figure 5. Learnable Prose Concepts connectivity per graphs G_i.

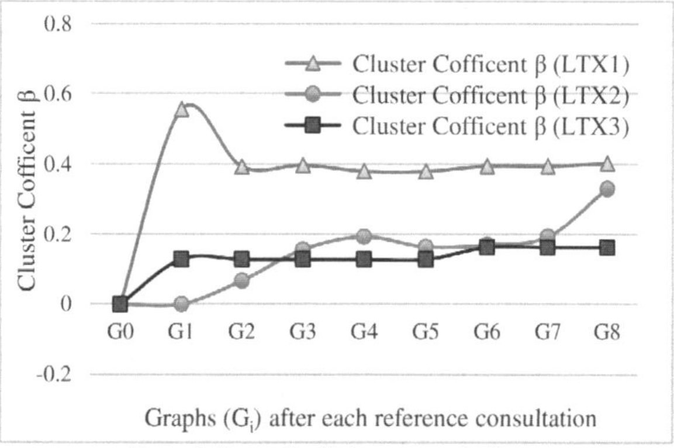

Figure 6. Cluster Coefficient per graphs G_i.

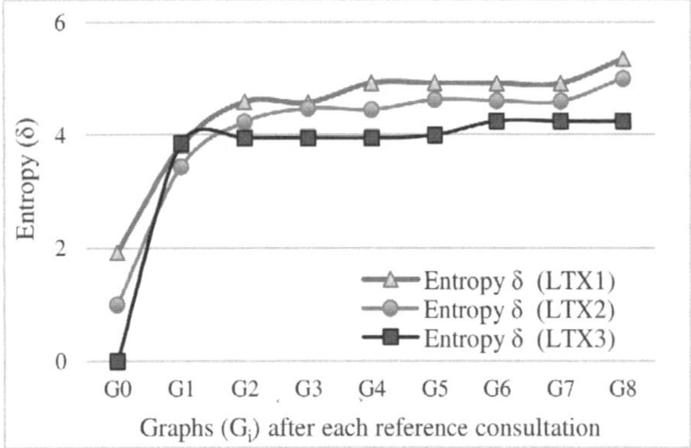

Figure 7. Entropy per graphs G_i.

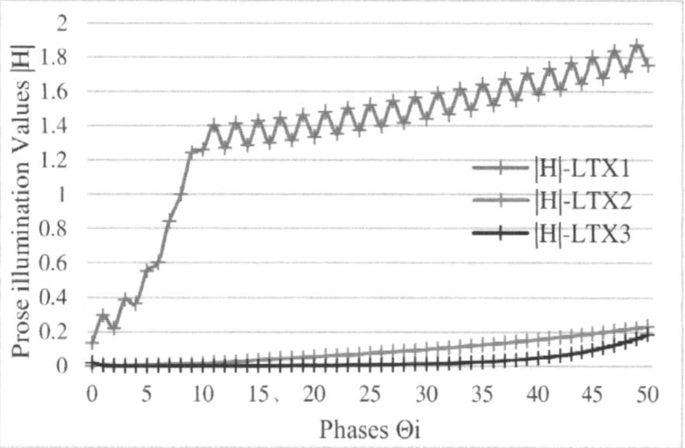

Figure 8. Prose illustration values per phases.

Smart Components for Enabling Intelligent Web of Things Applications

Felix Leif Keppmann, Maria Maleshkova
AIFB, Karlsruhe Institute of Technology
Karlsruhe, Germany
Email: felix.leif.keppmann@kit.edu, maria.maleshkova@kit.edu

***Abstract*—We are currently witnessing an increased use of sensor technologies, abundant availability of mobile devices, and growing popularity of wearables, which enable the direct integration of their data as part of rich client applications in a multitude of different domains. In this context, the Internet of Things (IoT) promises the capability of connecting billions of devices, resources, and things together in an integrated way. However, what we are currently witnessing is the proliferation of isolated islands of custom IoT solutions. A first step towards enabling some interoperability in the IoT is to connect things to the Web and to use the Web stack, thereby conceiving the so-called Web of Things (WoT). However, even when a homogeneous access is reached through Web protocols, a common understanding is still missing, specifically in terms of heterogeneous devices, different programmable interfaces and diverse data formats and structures. Our work focuses on two main aspects: overcoming device and interface heterogeneity as well as enabling adaptable and scalable (i.e., intelligent) decentralised WoT applications. To this end, we present an approach for realising decentralised WoT solutions based on three main building blocks: 1) smart components as an abstraction of a unified approach towards realising the devices' interfaces, communication mechanisms, semantics of the devices' resources and capabilities, and decision logic; 2) adaptability of devices' interfaces and interaction at runtime; 3) adaptability of the devices' data structures and semantics at runtime. We show how our approach can be applied by introducing a reference smart component design, provide a thorough evaluation in terms of a proof-of-concept implementation of an example use case.**

Keywords–Smart Components, decentralised applications, Web of Things, REST, Linked Data

I. INTRODUCTION

Current developments in many domains are characterised by the increased use of mobile devices, wearables, and sensors, which bring the promise of higher digitalisation and rich client applications. In this context, the vision of the Internet of Things (IoT) aims to achieve the capability of connecting billions of devices, resources, and things together in the Internet. Still, what we are currently witnessing is the proliferation of isolated islands of custom IoT solutions, which support a restricted set of protocols and devices and cannot be easily integrated or extended. A first step towards enabling some interoperability in the IoT is to connect things to the Web and to use the Web stack, thereby conceiving the so-called Web of Things (WoT). However, even when a homogeneous access is reached through Web protocols, a common understanding is still missing, specifically in terms of heterogeneous devices, different programmable interfaces, and diverse data. Semantic technologies can be used to describe dataflows on a meta level, capturing the meaning of devices' inputs and outputs, and thus abstracting away from the syntactic structure. However, having the semantics of the data is not enough. While we can describe the exchanged data, the resulting solutions are limited to a specific domain, and the heterogeneous device integration is still lacking.

In this context, our work focuses on two main challenges: 1) overcoming heterogeneity, not only in terms of data but also in terms of devices and interfaces, and 2) enabling intelligent WoT applications. In terms of handling the plenitude of existing devices, we advocate an approach based on providing a unified view on devices and describing them in terms of their programmable interfaces, since this is how their integration as part of applications is realised. The difficulty that we face here is that in multi-stakeholder scenarios, where devices are built by several manufacturers and integrated and used by other parties, it is hardly possible to know all requirements of every possible integration scenario at design time. As a result, we can only provide default interfaces and interaction, thus needing to be able to adapt the component to provide the optimal solution for a specific use case. To this end, we also focus on realising intelligent WoT applications, where the "intelligence" is in terms of being able to adapt to changing requirements, at deployment time, but more importantly at runtime.

In this context, we make the following contributions. First, we present an approach for realising decentralised WoT solutions based on three main building blocks: 1) smart components as an abstraction of a unified approach towards realising the devices' interfaces, communication mechanisms, semantics of the devices' resources and capabilities, and decision logic; 2) adaptability of devices' interfaces and interaction at runtime; 3) adaptability of the devices' data structures and semantics at runtime. Second, we show how our approach can be applied by introducing a reference smart component design, based on Web and Semantic Web paradigms and technologies. We back up the design by a specific implementation. Finally, we provide a thorough evaluation of a proof-of-concept implementation of an example use case.

The remainder of this paper is structured as follows. In Section II, we introduce our motivation scenario, describing the challenges that we are focusing on. Section III describes the requirements for building WoT systems and the preliminaries that we build upon. Furthermore, it provides an architecture to realise this approach, and describes our implementation. For evaluation, in Section IV, we demonstrate the adaptability of our system to update at runtime the devices' interfaces and the controlling logic. We describe related work in Section V and conclude in Section VI.

II. MOTIVATION

In the following, we introduce a scenario that puts our work into context and use it to introduce the specific challenges that we are focusing on.

A. Scenario

To motivate our approach, we choose a generic body tracking component as an example, i.e., "thing". This component is able to track people in front of its video sensor by interpreting the video through algorithmic analysis of the captured video images. The body tracking is provided in the form of coordinates of the different joint points of the skeleton of the tracked people. These coordinates are provided to or send to other components, depending on the specific use case, with the sensor (or a custom point) as the origin of the coordinates.

As typical parts of the body tracking components, we consider a depth video camera, an analysis middleware, and an access layer with network connectivity. The depth video camera provides depth images that are enriched with additional information about the distance from the camera for every pixel. The analysis middleware encapsulates various algorithms, which are required to interpret the stream of depth images. By comparing and classifying the content in a sequence of incoming images, these algorithms calculate and extract different information, e.g., the body tracking data in our case. The access layer provides access to the body tracking data, via an interface to other components, or interacts with the interfaces of other components. Furthermore, the access layer may also enable retrieving data, e.g., modification of configuration settings in our case. An operating system and further common software infrastructure augments these parts, which may be distributed across different hardware devices or embedded in one physical system. In both cases, the body tracking appears as one distinct component to the rest of the network via its access layer.

We explicitly abstract from a particular use case and instead design the "thing" as a generic body tracking component. Thereby, we keep the focus on the specific functionality, i.e., body tracking, which is encapsulated and may be combined with other "things" in a larger integration scenario. This integration scenario may be, for example, safety monitoring in a factory, gesture interaction with technical artefacts, or responsive art installations. By combining and integrating the component with other components, we build distributed applications, which exceed the sum of their parts in functionality.

Our body tracking component is just one example out of a heterogeneous landscape of "things". A multitude of functionalities ranges from simple temperature sensors to complex robots. Different hardware and software requirements range from low-energy embedded systems to processing-intensive calculations, e.g., body tracking. In this market, several stakeholders exist, e.g., different manufacturers of "things", technology integrators, or customers with specific integration scenarios. In this context, there are several challenges that we face while realising the integration of components into a coherent application with a value-added functionality, which is, by design, of distributed nature.

B. Problem Focus

In the following, we focus on two main challenges: 1) the information asymmetry between the design of a component and its use at runtime in different integration scenarios, and 2) the inefficiency that can occur when developing a generic component, which may have several specific use cases.

1) Requirements Asymmetry: In multi-stakeholder scenarios, where components are built by several manufacturers and are integrated and used by others, we hardly know all requirements of every possible integration scenario at design time. As a result, we can only provide default interfaces and interaction but are not able to adapt the component to provide the optimal solution for a specific use case.

2) Development Inefficiency: Even if all integration scenarios would be known, we face an inefficiency issue. Designing and developing the same component in several adapted versions for each and every use case does not only lead to a very complex and inefficient, i.e., time-consuming, development but in consequence may also be inefficient in terms of business requirements, i.e., be unprofitable.

III. Smart Component

In the following, we introduce our approach by clarifying the requirements, presenting the preliminaries, and elaborating on our architecture and implementation.

A. Requirements

As part of the IoT vision, we see applications built upon a number of different components that communicate data to provide a value-added functionality without the necessity of centralised control within the application. While central control is still a valid – thus still to be supported – integration pattern, we must acknowledge integration scenarios, in which distributed control is required, e.g., caused by the scenario itself, or by performance, redundancy, or latency requirements. The requirements for a component's architecture are, with respect to the previously mentioned problems, three-fold:

1) Adaptability of Interfaces and Interaction at Runtime: First, for communication and thus the ability to establish data flows between components, which are required to provide the value-added functionality of an application, components need to interact. This interaction can be supported by a component 1) by – passively – providing an interface for other components, or 2) by – actively – interacting with interfaces of other components. Components must be able to adapt their interfaces and interaction according to the specific situation in the integration scenarios. We derive this requirement from the inability to foresee or consider all possible integration scenarios during the design time of a component.

2) Adaptability of Data Structures and Semantics at Runtime: Second, complementary to the interaction between components, the data, which is communicated, must be handled and processed in an appropriate manner according to both the data structure and semantics. Components must be able to adapt the structure and align the semantic annotation of data to the specific situation in the integration scenarios. We derive this requirement again from the inability to foresee all possible integration scenarios during the design time of a component.

3) Adaptability of Controlling Logic at Runtime: Third, a distributed application, which is composed of several different independently developed components, must be controlled in some way, i.e., a controlling intelligence within the application must exist that coordinates the collaboration of components to achieve the value-added functionality of the application. By default, a central controlling component, custom for the specific integration scenario, actively controls all other components. However, to support scenarios with distributed control, as facilitated by the IoT vision, components must be adaptable in terms of their intelligence by being able to update the controlling logic at runtime.

B. Preliminaries

We build our contribution upon a number of well established paradigms for enabling large heterogeneous distributed systems: Representational State Transfer (REST) for overcoming heterogeneity at interface level and Linked Data (LD) to ease the semantic integration of data.

While paradigm-wise being technology-agnostic, REST [1] is usually realised by utilising the Hypertext Transfer Protocol (HTTP). It incorporates the concept of Uniform Resource Identifier (URI) as unique identifier for resources and provides transport mechanisms for data transfer. HTTP – used as true application protocol – defines a constrained set of methods, e.g., GET, PUT, POST, and DELETE as the most known methods, with standardised semantics, i.e., the protocol defines how clients must interact with resources identified by URIs. Acknowledging the heterogeneous inconsistent nature of large distributed systems with multiple stakeholders, status codes for handling various types of successful and failing communication are part of the protocol.

The architectural paradigm Linked Data introduces shared semantics to data and builds – similar to REST – on URIs as unique identifiers. Technological buildings blocks of Linked Data, that we are taking advantage of, are the Resource Description Framework (RDF) [2], the SPARQL Protocol and RDF Query Language (SPARQL) [3], and the Notation3 (N3) [4] syntax for rule and assertion logic for RDF.

We introduce the notion of a "Smart Component (SC)", when this component is built following our architectural approach: 1) REST for realising interfaces and the communication between components; 2) Linked Data for describing the exchanged data, interface resources, and components' capabilities; and 3) decentralised smartness of each component, described in terms of rules.

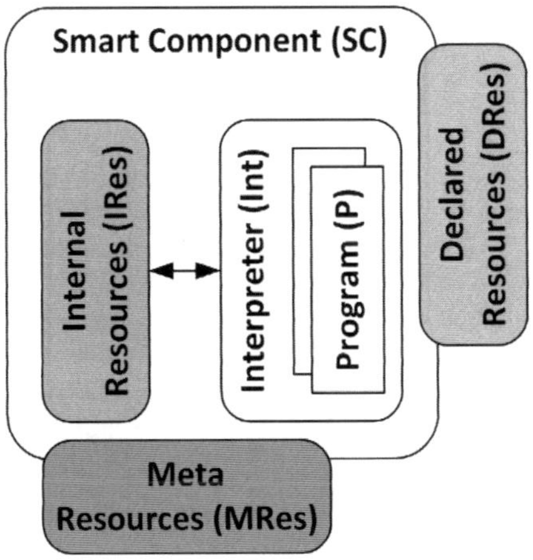

Figure 1. Smart Component Architecture

C. Architecture

Our approach tackles the requirements by combining and extending Web and Semantic Web technologies. In Figure 1, we present the internal architecture of a component that follows our Smart Component approach. It comprises a number of resources providing semantically annotated data, rule programs, which can be interpreted with respect to the data, and an interpreter for interpreting the rule programs.

1) Internal Resources (IRes): Internal resources provide access to the core functionality and data of the component, that distinguishes it from other components. In our motivation scenario, the core comprises depth video recording, image analysis, body tracking, and configuration. Only relevant parts of the core functionality and data are exposed as internal resources, e.g., the complete body tracking data as well as selected configuration parameters. Common to all internal resources is the RDF-conform modelling of data and its integration with the interpreter. The internal resources together form an internal RDF knowledge graph. We do not explicitly prescribe how these resources are integrated with the interpreter to not overly restrict the development of components. Integration can range from programmatic integration, to file-based access, and to HTTP or other communication protocols.

2) Declared Resources (DRes): Declared resources form the Application Programming Interface (API) of the component exposed to the network at runtime. In our motivation scenario, we could, for example, expose the skeleton information of each tracked person as declared resources, or only the distance of specific joint points. These resources conform to the Linked Data and REST paradigms; thus they are identified by URIs, accessible via HTTP, and provide data in RDF serialisation formats. Declared resource are defined as SPARQL CONSTRUCT patterns, which are evaluated against the internal RDF knowledge graph.

3) Program (P): While construct queries are evaluated against the internal RDF knowledge graph, we enable its modification through programs. Programs are written in a declarative N3-based rules language, interpreted by the interpreter, and encode transformation between ontologies, enrichment by reasoning, decisions, and including of data from other components with built-in interaction functions. Optionally, the rule language may provide further built-in functions, e.g., for calculations, to ease the declaration of programs.

4) Interpreter (Int): We introduce the interpreter as a central element of our approach. On the one hand, the interpreter maintains the internal RDF knowledge graph that is build up during each interpreter run by 1) adding data from internal resources, 2) adding data of external resources of other components, if requested by interaction rules in programs, and 3) adding data, which is derived by deduction rules in programs. On the other hand, the interpreter 1) evaluates construct queries of declared resources against the internal RDF knowledge graph and 2) modifies, if requested by interaction rules in programs, external resources. In both cases, external resources are Linked Data REST resources, which belong to other components and are accessible via HTTP to the network. In summary, the task of the interpreter is to negotiate between the private API, the public API, and the interaction with resources of other components.

5) Meta Resources (MRes): With meta resources, we introduce the last type of resources for our design of a Smart Component. These resources are provided by a component as part of the public API, i.e., are Linked Data REST resources accessible by HTTP. In contrast to declared resources, which expose internal data and functionality of the component, meta resources expose the state of the interpreter and declared resources. In other words, they allow to create, update, modify, and delete, rule programs and graph patterns of declared resources. With meta resources, we enable the adaptation of components' behaviour at runtime.

D. Implementation

We implemented a Smart Component based on our motivating scenario to show the feasibly of our architecture and to support our evaluation. Natural Interaction via REST (NIREST) [5] integrates hardware support for depth video cameras, tracking middleware with body tracking algorithms, and, as intelligent access layer, a rule-based data integration framework for Linked Data REST resources. We abstract in the following from actual device manufacturers and software providers, which may change over time.

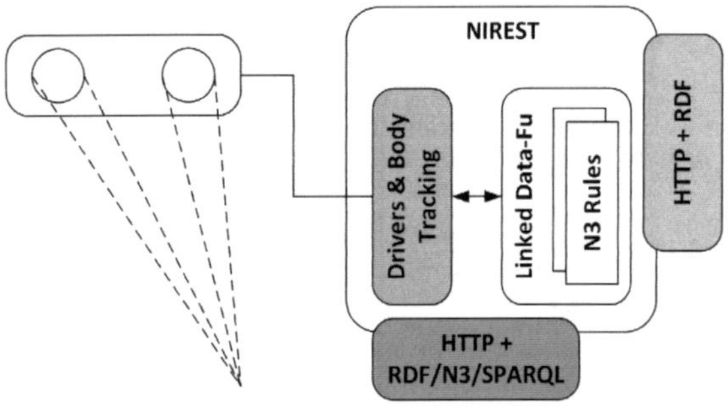

Figure 2. Scenario Component Implementation

In Figure 2, we provide an overview of the implementation that realises all parts of our architecture. The hardware part of our component consists of a separate depth video camera and a computer with appropriate processing power for video analysis. The camera provides raw depth image data and is connected by wire with the computer. Both hardware pieces may be merged in one embedded device. The software part of our component consists of three layers, that we directly integrated in program code. For the two lowest levels, we include third party frameworks, as this functionality is not in the focus of our work. We utilise a low-level framework for device connectivity on the lowest level that provides raw images to a tracking middleware at the second level. The body tracking data, provided by the second level, is then included in the intelligent access layer, which we describe in the following.

To realise the interpreter, programs, and declared resources, we utilize Linked Data-Fu (LD-Fu) [6][7][8]. LD-Fu comprises the LD-Fu rule language based on N3 syntax, the LD-Fu interpreter for execution, and follows a generic approach for the integration of Linked Data REST resources. The rule language supports the declaration of: 1) deductions rules for inferencing new knowledge, 2) interaction rules for encoding of HTTP interaction with built-in functions, and 3) built-in functions to ease decisions and transformations with mathematical calculations. The interpreter maintains an internal RDF graph and is capable of evaluating deduction rules or executing HTTP requests. Both the results of deduction rules and the payload of answers to requests are added to the internal graph and may be subject to further rules, until reaching a fixpoint.

We extended the LD-Fu implementation to support our Smart Component approach by introducing a REST API and enable time-based continuous evaluation of programs. The LD-Fu REST API is closely integrated with the LD-Fu interpreter and supports the creation of interpreter instances, creation and modification of rule programs per instance, as well as the creation and modification of declarative resources per instance. With separate interpreter instances, we support the participation of a component in more than one distributed application, i.e., we may adapt the behaviour of the component per distributed application with a distinct set of interpreter, programs, and declared resources. In addition, we introduced time-base continuous execution of the interpreter.

While LD-Fu supports several ways to include resources, e.g., file-based, pipe-based, or through HTTP requests, we utilise the libraries for direct code-based integration. Therefore, we enable the interpreter to read the body tracking data, annotated in RDF, directly from the tracking middleware and add it during each run to the internally maintained RDF graph. Subsequent, programs declared in the N3-based LD-Fu rule language and declared resources defined as SPARQL CONSTRUCT queries are evaluated against this internal RDF graph.

IV. EVALUATION

We provide an implementation of our approach and a thorough evaluation in terms of: 1) evaluating the deployment and adaptability of decentralised logic within smart components, and 2) evaluating the integration and adaptability of interfaces and interaction.

```
<nirest://user/0>
    nirest:skeleton [
        nirest:jointPoint [
            nirest:coordinate [
                nirest:x "459.8463"^^xsd:float ;
                nirest:y "404.0497"^^xsd:float ;
                nirest:z "2037.2391"^^xsd:float ;
                a nirest:Coordinate ] ;
            a nirest:RightHandJointPoint ] ;
        ...
```

Figure 3. Internal Resources

In Figure 3, we provide a snippet of the RDF graph of internal resources, which is included during every interpreter run of our scenario component. We use the Turtle serialization format and omit, due to space constraints, prefixes in this and following figures. For each person in front of the sensor, the implementation of the component provides – once a person is tracked – an URI as well as a description of the skeleton' joint points, including coordinates. In the figure, we show the description of a right hand joint point, as one of the joint-points described by each skeleton. The unit of measurement for coordinates is millimetres and the descriptions are internally updated with a frequency of approximately 30hz [9] by the sensor.

Prior to the adaptation given in the following, the component has been developed, deployed, and started. With respect to the architecture (Figure 1) and implementation (Figure 2), the component is already tracking bodies in front of the sensor, providing internally access to this tracking data to interpreter instances, and is exposing the generic meta interface for adaptation at the network.

A. Deployment and Adaptability of Decentralised Logic

To integrate the component as part of an application, we need to instantiate and configure the interpreter, i.e., initiate an instance of LD-Fu. In Figure 4, we provide the command used to create an interpreter instance by interacting with the meta interface and to deploy a specific configuration (100ms between interpreter runs), which is shown in the lower part.

```
$ curl -X "PUT" -H "Content-Type: text/turtle" \
    http://localhost:8888/scenario \
    --data-binary @config-scenario.ttl
____
<> ldfu:delay 100 ; a ldfu:Configuration .
```

Figure 4. Instance Configuration

```
$ curl -X "PUT" -H "Content-Type: text/n3" \
    http://localhost:8888/scenario/p/program \
    --data-binary @program-alarm.n3
____
{   ?point nirest:coordinate ?coordinate .
      ?coordinate nirest:x ?x ; nirest:y ?y ; nirest:z ?z .
    (?x "2") math:exponentiation ?x_ex .
    (?y "2") math:exponentiation ?y_ex .
    (?z "2") math:exponentiation ?z_ex .
    (?x_ex ?y_ex ?z_ex) math:sum ?sum .
    ?sum math:sqrt ?square_root .
    ?square_root math:lessThan "1000.0" . } =>
{ ?point scenario:alarm "true" . } .
```

Figure 5. Program Deployment

As already described, programs are interpreted by the interpreter and enrich the RDF of internal resources with inferred knowledge, e.g., triggering of alarms when specific distances become too short. Due to space constrains for figures, we simplify our example to a pure distance-based alarm. As soon as a part of a person's body intrudes the space within one meter of the tracking sensor, an alarm in triggered. In Figure 5, we provide a program containing a single N3 rule, which calculates the euclidean distance to the sensor for each point provided by internal resources. For the calculation, coordinates are matched in the body of this rule, patterns adhering to a built-in ontology, i.e., the "math" prefix, are interpreted, mathematically evaluated, and the calculation results are bound to respective variables. As a consequence, if the condition "distance less than 1000mm" is fulfilled, we enrich the RDF sub-graph of the point with a custom "alarm" property by deriving a respective triple in the rule head.

By deploying this rule, we adapt the component's data structure and semantics at runtime (second requirement; Section III-A2), by triggering an alarm based on the given coordinates, and at the same time, adapt the controlling logic at runtime (third requirement; Section III-A3), by including a distance condition.

```
$ curl -X "PUT" -H "Content-Type: application/sparql-query" \
    http://localhost:8888/scenario/r/shutdown \
    --data-binary @resource-shutdown.rq
____
CONSTRUCT { ?point scenario:shutdown "true" . }
WHERE { ?point scenario:alarm "true" . }
```

Figure 6. Declared Resource

B. Integration and Adaptability of Interfaces and Interaction

We show the integration of the component with other components of a distributed application. As stated before, we can establish this integration either by 1) providing resources for interaction with other components or by 2) actively interacting with resources of other components. In Figure 6, we provide an example for the first case. A SPARQL CONSTRUCT query is deployed as a declared resource at the instance of our scenario's interpreter, by interacting with the meta interface. It constructs a simple "shutdown" triple if an "alarm" triple from the preceding program evaluation is found. The query is evaluated during every interpreter run and the result is accessible as RDF via HTTP by requesting the media type of supported RDF serialization formats.

```
$ curl -X "PUT" -H "Content-Type: text/n3" \
    http://localhost:8888/scenario/p/shutdown \
    --data-binary @program-shutdown.ttl
____
{ ?point scenario:alarm "true" . } =>
{   [] http:mthd http-m:PUT;
        http:requestURI <http://localhost:8889>;
        http:body { <> scenario:shutdown "true" . } . } .
```

Figure 7. Interaction Program

For the second case (actively interacting with resources of other components), we provide and example in Figure 7. Again by interaction with the meta interface, we deploy a second program at the scenario interpreter instance. It contains a single N3 rule that matches to the body of "alarm" triples generated by the first program. In the head of the rule, we use the interaction capabilities of LD-Fu, encoded with respective ontologies, i.e., "http" and "http-m" prefixes. If the condition is fulfilled, i.e., an "alarm" triple was generated before, the interpreter executes a HTTP PUT request at the specified URI, containing our custom "shutdown" triple as payload.

By deploying the declared resource and the rule, we adapt the component's interface and interaction (first requirement; Section III-A1), by passively exposing alarms through a resource to other components at the network and by actively communicating alarms to other components. At the same time, we adapt again the controlling logic at runtime (third requirement; Section III-A3), by including the alarm triple as a condition for the interaction.

V. Related Work

We focus in our related work on three areas: 1) read-write Linked Data (LD), 2) the Web of Things (WoT), and 3) the Semantic Web of Things (SWoT).

Read-write Linked Data is built upon the idea of combining the architectural paradigms of Linked Data (LD) [10] and Representational State Transfer (REST) [1]. This combination has been used in several approaches, e.g., Linked Data Fragments (LDF) [11], Linked APIs (LAPIS) [12], Linked Data Services (LIDS) [13], RESTdesc [14], or Linked Open Services (LOS) [15]. The Linked Data Platform (LDP) [16] standardizes this combination, including RDF and non-RDF resources, containers, and rules for HTTP-based interaction with resources. Our approach aims at the adaptation of components to specific application scenarios, while still being compatible with arbitrary Linked Data REST interfaces.

The IoT [17] paradigm is about connecting every device, application, object, i.e., thing, to the network, in particular the Internet and thus to ensure connectivity. The Web of Things (WoT) [18] builds on top of this paradigm to provide integration not only on the network layer but also on the application layer, i.e., the Web. The goal is to make things part of the Web by providing their capabilities as REST services.

Therefore, common existing Web technologies are introduced, e.g., URIs for identification and HTTP as application protocol for transport and interaction. Integrating these technologies has been, for example, addressed for embedded devices in [19].

The extension of IoT to WoT is primarily focused on the interoperability between things on the application layer. In order to foster horizontal integration and interoperability the Semantic Web of Things (SWoT) [20] focuses a common understanding of multiple capabilities and resources towards a larger ecosystem by introducing Semantic Web technologies to the IoT. Challenges related to SWoT have been, for example, addressed by the SPITFIRE [21] project, or the Micro-Ontology Context-Aware Protocol (MOCAP) [22], both in the area of sensors. We build upon several synergies introduced by a common resource-oriented viewpoint of the Linked Data and REST paradigms. These paradigms also play a key role in WoT and in particular SWoT to cope with heterogeneous data models and interaction mechanisms. However, integrating decentralised components into applications without central control, even with a clear interaction model and semantically powerful data model, requires to distribute the controlling intelligence, at least to some extent, to the components. In this context, our approach aims to enable the adaptation of components to specific application scenarios at runtime, while still being compatible with other approaches based on read-write Linked Data REST interfaces.

VI. Conclusion

The growing use and popularity of mobile devices, wearables and sensors offers new opportunities for the way that products and services are being designed, developed and offered. The IoT and WoT lay the foundation for integrating devices by providing network connectivity and a stack of communication protocols, while SWoT aims to enhance these to address the lack of interoperability. In this context, our work focuses on two main aspects: overcoming not only data but also device and interface heterogeneity as well as enabling adaptable (i.e., intelligent) decentralised WoT applications. To this end, we introduce Smart Components as a unified approach towards realising the devices' interfaces, communication mechanisms, semantics of the devices' resources and capabilities, and controlling logic. We provide support for the adaptability of devices' interfaces and interaction, as well as of devices' data structures and semantics, at runtime. We believe that enabling interoperability but also offering simple mechanisms for adaptability are key for contributing towards the evolution of the Web.

References

[1] R. T. Fielding, "Architectural Styles and the Design of Network-based Software Architectures," Ph.D. dissertation, University of California, Irvine, USA, 2000.

[2] R. Cyganiak, D. Wood, and M. Lanthaler, "RDF 1.1 Concepts and Abstract Syntax," W3C, Recommendation, 2014, http://www.w3.org/TR/2014/REC-rdf11-concepts-20140225/. Latest version available at http://www.w3.org/TR/rdf11-concepts/ [retrieved: 10, 2016].

[3] C. B. Aranda, O. Corby, S. Das, L. Feigenbaum, P. Gearon, B. Glimm, S. Harris, S. Hawke, I. Herman, N. Humfrey, N. Michaelis, C. Ogbuji, M. Perry, A. Passant, A. Polleres, E. Prud'hommeaux, A. Seaborne, and G. T. Williams, "SPARQL 1.1 Overview," W3C, Recommendation, 2013, http://www.w3.org/TR/2013/REC-sparql11-overview-20130321/. Latest version available at http://www.w3.org/TR/sparql11-overview/ [retrieved: 10, 2016].

[4] T. Berners-Lee and D. Connolly, "Notation3 (N3): A readable RDF syntax," W3C, Team Submission, 2011, http://www.w3.org/TeamSubmission/2011/SUBM-n3-20110328/. Latest version available at https://www.w3.org/TeamSubmission/n3/ [retrieved: 10, 2016].

[5] "Natural Interaction via REST (NIREST)," http://github.com/fekepp/nirest/ [retrieved: 10, 2016].

[6] "Linked Data-Fu (LD-Fu)," http://linked-data-fu.github.io/ [retrieved: 10, 2016].

[7] S. Stadtmüller, S. Speiser, A. Harth, and R. Studer, "Data-Fu: A Language and an Interpreter for Interaction with Read/Write Linked Data," in *International World Wide Web Conference*, 2013, pp. 1225–1236.

[8] S. Stadtmüller, "Dynamic Interaction and Manipulation of Web Resources," Ph.D. dissertation, Karlsruhe Institute of Technology, Karlsruhe, Germany, 2016.

[9] F. L. Keppmann and S. Stadtmüller, "Semantic RESTful APIs for Dynamic Data Sources," in *Workshop on Services and Applications over Linked APIs and Data at the European Semantic Web Conference*, 2014, pp. 26–33.

[10] C. Bizer, T. Heath, and T. Berners-Lee, "Linked Data - The Story So Far," *Semantic Web and Information Systems*, vol. 5, pp. 1–22, 2009.

[11] R. Verborgh, O. Hartig, B. De Meester, G. Haesendonck, L. De Vocht, M. Vander Sande, R. Cyganiak, P. Colpaert, E. Mannens, and R. Van de Walle, "Querying Datasets on the Web with High Availability," in *International Semantic Web Conference*, 2014, pp. 180–196.

[12] S. Stadtmüller, S. Speiser, and A. Harth, "Future Challenges for Linked APIs," in *Workshop on Services and Applications over Linked APIs and Data at the European Semantic Web Conference*, 2013, pp. 20–27.

[13] S. Speiser and A. Harth, "Integrating Linked Data and Services with Linked Data Services," in *Extended Semantic Web Conference*, 2011, pp. 170–184.

[14] R. Verborgh, T. Steiner, D. van Deursen, R. van de Walle, and J. Gabarró Vallès, "Efficient Runtime Service Discovery and Consumption with Hyperlinked RESTdesc," in *International Conference on Next Generation Web Services Practices*, 2011, pp. 373–379.

[15] R. Krummenacher, B. Norton, and A. Marte, "Towards Linked Open Services and Processes," in *Future Internet Symposium*, 2010, pp. 68–77.

[16] S. Speicher, J. Arwe, and A. Malhotra, "Linked Data Platform 1.0," W3C, Recommendation, 2015, http://www.w3.org/TR/2015/REC-ldp-20150226/. Latest version available at http://www.w3.org/TR/ldp/ [retrieved: 10, 2016].

[17] L. Atzori, A. Iera, and G. Morabito, "The Internet of Things: A survey," *Computer Networks*, vol. 54, pp. 2787–2805, 2010.

[18] D. Guinard, V. Trifa, F. Mattern, and E. Wilde, "From the Internet of Things to the Web of Things: Resource-oriented Architecture and Best Practices," in *Architecting the Internet of Things*. Springer, 2011, pp. 97–129.

[19] S. Duquennoy, G. Grimaud, and J.-J. Vandewalle, "The Web of Things: interconnecting devices with high usability and performance," in *International Conference on Embedded Software and Systems*, 2009, pp. 323–330.

[20] A. J. Jara, A. C. Olivieri, Y. Bocchi, M. Jung, W. Kastner, and A. F. Skarmeta, "Semantic Web of Things: an analysis of the application semantics for the IoT moving towards the IoT convergence," *Web and Grid Services*, vol. 10, no. 2-3, pp. 244–272, 2014.

[21] D. Pfisterer, K. Romer, D. Bimschas, O. Kleine, R. Mietz, C. Truong, H. Hasemann, A. Kröller, M. Pagel, M. Hauswirth, M. Karnstedt, M. Leggieri, A. Passant, and R. Richardson, "SPITFIRE: Toward a Semantic Web of Things," *Communications Magazine*, vol. 49, no. 11, pp. 40–48, 2011.

[22] K. Sahlmann and T. Schwotzer, "MOCAP: Towards the Semantic Web of Things," in *Posters and Demos at the International Conference on Semantic Systems*, 2015, pp. 59–62.

Semantic Graph Transitivity for Discovering Bloom Taxonomic Relationships between Knowledge Units in a Text

Fatema Nafa, Javed I. Khan, Salem Othman, and Amal Babour
Department of Computer Science, Kent State University
Kent, Ohio, USA
Email : fnafa, Javed, sothman, ababour@kent.edu

***Abstract*— Manual inferring of semantic relationships by domain experts is an expensive and time consuming task; thus, automatic techniques are needed. In this paper, we propose an automatic novel technique for inferring cognitive relationships among concepts and knowledge units in the learning resources by using Graph-transitivity. The cognitive relationships are expressed as Bloom Taxonomy levels. Learning resources are represented as knowledge units in texts. The technique determines significant relationships among knowledge units by utilizing transitivity of knowledge units in the computer science domain. We share an experiment that evaluates and validates the technique from three textbooks. The performance analysis shows that the technique succeeds in discovering the hidden cognitive relationships among knowledge units in learning resources.**

***Keywords*— Cognitive Graph; Graph Transitivity; Knowledge Unit; Graph Mining; Bloom Taxonomy.**

I. INTRODUCTION

Extracting semantic relationships from a text has been widely studied in several research including Natural Language Processing (NLP), Text Mining, Information Retrieval (IR), and others. The goal of the relationships' extraction is different from one task to another and from one resource to another. Learning resources are the most significant repositories of knowledge and information. Discovering hidden interconnections among knowledge units is interesting. Hidden interconnections are represented in different forms. In this paper, the interconnections among knowledge units are represented as a cognitive theory called Bloom Taxonomy(BT). The concept of cognitive theory has crossed the line from psychology and educational theory and has become an important part of computer technology research. The taxonomy idea was first introduced by Benjamin Bloom. Bloom identified three domains of educational activities: the cognitive domain (mental skills), the affective domain (growth in feelings or emotional areas), and the psychomotor domain (physical skills) [1]. The cognitive domain is divided into six levels: 1) knowledge, 2) comprehension, 3) application, 4) analysis, 5) synthesis, and 6) evaluation. The Bloom model was modified in 2001 by Anderson and a team of cognitive psychologists [2]. Significant changes were made to the Bloom's Taxonomy model. The original taxonomy of educational objectives, is referred to as Bloom's Taxonomy and Anderson's work, is known as Revised Bloom's Taxonomy [2]. Revised Bloom's was modified to the Computer Science based Cognitive Domain (CSCD) [3] to make it appropriate for the concept domain in computer science. For this paper, only the cognitive domain is used and we discussed the first sub-task in our previous work [3]. We are going to discuss the second sub-task in this paper.

We introduced an automatic technique to infer the relationships based on CSCD levels among knowledge units using the graph transitivity. The CSCD is used to identify and progressively measure of learner's cognitive level. A learner is not expected to understand the text based on the given ordered knowledge units. Thus, a shared language is needed to provide a highlighted learning map of a text based on cognitive skills.

The rest of the paper is organized as follows. The related work is presented in Section II. The problem definition is discussed in Section III. Section IV describes an overview of the system. Section V describes the transitivity technique as well as a description of the algorithm in detail. Section VI presents the classification of the knowledge units. Section VII shows examples of the technique. The experiment setup and an evaluation of the technique are explained in Section VIII. Section IX presents the conclusion and future work

II. RELATED WORK

The work presented in this paper is situated at the intersection of several areas of related prior work from the linguistics perspective, Graph perspective, and Graph Transitivity Property perspective. We will discuss each of these in turn.

From the *linguistics* perspective, theorists developed three different taxonomies to represent the three domains of learning: a cognitive taxonomy focused on intellectual learning, an effective taxonomy concerned with the learning of values and attitudes, and a psychomotor taxonomy that addresses the motor skills related to learning. One of the cognitive taxonomies [1] is known as Bloom's Taxonomy. Bloom's Taxonomy has been applied in the field of computer science for various purposes such as managing course design [4], measuring the cognitive difficulty levels of computer science materials [4], and structuring assessments [5]. Bloom's Taxonomy has also been used in grading as an alternative to grading on a curve [6]. Additionally, from the mining perspective, there has been some interesting research about extracting relations among concepts. Relations could be replaced by the synonym relationships, or a hypernym, an association, etc. [7] [8]. These relationships are successfully used in different domains and applications [9].

From the *Graph* Perspective, the representation of the extracted relationship is the graph. There has been some research on graphical text representation such as concept graphs [10] and ontology [11]. The authors proposed Concept Graph Learning to present relations among concepts from prerequisite relations among courses.

From the *Graph Transitivity Property* perspective, in the definition of transitivity in graph, two nodes are connected if they share a direct neighbor, so the inferred hidden relationship between those two nodes is based on the transitivity. There has been research on the transitivity in the domain of Biology [12]. In addition, transitivity has been studied in friendship graphs in social networks research [13].

None of the previous work handles the problem of inferring the relationships among knowledge units based on *CSCD* levels in the domain of computer science. Using graph transitivity is a promising way to reach this goal and discover novel cognitive relationships between knowledge units.

This paper presents a technique for mining *CSCD* levels among the knowledge units in a textbook. The technique is based on using graph transitivity to discover relationships between knowledge units. Transitivity technique describes levels of increasing complexity in students understanding of knowledge units. It has the flexibility of giving the new sequential ordering of the knowledge units in a textbook. According to the experimental evaluations, the method can efficiently identify *CSCD* levels among knowledge units. Building an automatic technique to assist in organizing knowledge units based on the level of cognitive skills will provide a new learning trajectory for the learners and will help in circumventing their deficit in understanding any textbook.

III. PROBLEM DEFINITION

In this section let us introduce some definitions, which are used in this paper.

Concepts: are terms that have significant meaning(s) in computer sciences.

Knowledge Unit (KU): is defined as a group of sentences that discuss specific topics in computer sciences and consist of concepts, which are related to the topic.

The Overlap between Knowledge Unit: if a KU consist group of concepts and at least one of these concepts appears in another KU then, we say the two KU's are overlapping.

Given a textbook T^B that contains a set of knowledge units (it could be a topic from a textbook or more) KU = $\{ku_1, ku_2... ku_n\}$ where *n* is the number of knowledge units in T^B. Each knowledge unit is a group of sentences $ku_i= \{s_1, s_2...s_m\}$ and each sentence is composed of a sequence of concepts $s_i= \{c_1,..,c_o\}$; in addition, the Computer Science based Cognitive Domain (*CSCD*) has the levels of (Understanding, Analyzing, Applying-Evaluating, and Creating),which are denoted as $\{B_1, B_2, B_3, B_4\}$ respectively [3]. Each level has a subset of measurable verbs. The contribution of this work is to find transitivity function $f(x)$: KU→βi which maps knowledge units (KU) according to Computer-Science based Cognitive Domain (*CSCD*) using the subset of measurable verbs. To handle this problem, we create a semantic graph G^S from the given textbook T^B in order to find the relationships among concepts in the knowledge unit and subsequently relationships among knowledge units themselves. The transitivity will output the hidden links among knowledge units according to *CSCD* levels. For example, consider that from a textbook three knowledge units (KU #1, KU #2, and KU #3) have been chosen, and we need to find a relationship between knowledge units based on *CSCD* levels using transitivity. As described in the problem definition we have two main problems:

- Converting a textbook to a semantic graph G^S is a directed graph G^S = (C, V) where C (concept) represents nodes, and V (verbs) represents the labels of the relationship among concepts.
- Finding out the relationship (X) among knowledge unit#1, knowledge unit#2 and knowledge unit#3 based on (*CSCD*) $\beta i= \{B_1, B_2, B_3, B_4\}$. Fig. 1 represents the sub-part of G^S for three knowledge units where some of the relationships mainly exist among the KU from the same textbook, or from a textbook of similar topics.

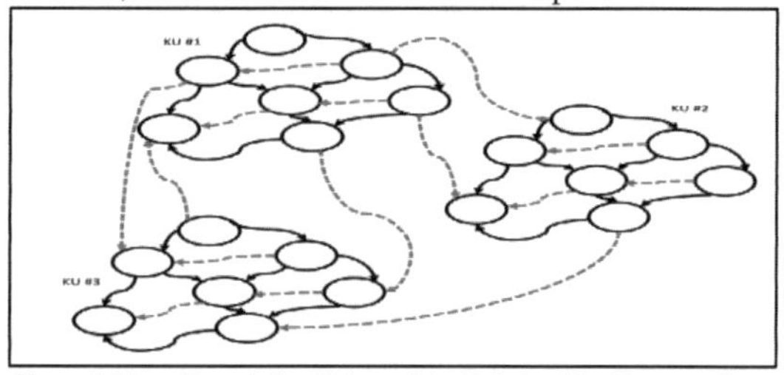

Figure 1. Three Knowledge Units and the Relationships Between them.

IV. OVERVIEW OF THE SYSTEM

The system consists of three main components, called, *System Core, CSCD Engine,* and *Domain Lexicon* as in Fig. 2. The input for the system is a textbook and the output is a cognitive graph G^C classified into *CSCD* levels.

The system *Core* was presented in detailed in our previous work [3]. It includes the following four parts: Text-Preprocessing, Natural Language Processing (NLP), Domain Specific Extraction, and Semantic Relationship Extraction. In the Text-Preprocessing part, the system assumes that the input files are in plain text format. Any other formats are turned into a plain text before it starts the other steps. Then, the Natural Language Processing part incorporates NLP tools, such as splitting each sentence into a sequence of tokens where tokens are unique concepts. Stanford Parser, which is used to parse each sentence to get its part-of-speech (verb, noun, adjective, etc.) will be used to extract semantic relationships between concepts. The Domain Specific Extraction part contains concepts related to the domain of interest, which is computer science. We build the specific stop words list manually, because there is no stop list related to the domain under study. It can also be updated during the process of the system. The Semantic Relationship Extraction part includes extracting the relationships in the form of concept-verb-concept, among concepts in the knowledge unit. The final form of extraction is represented as a semantic graph. Lyons and other [15] structural linguists hold that "words cannot be defined independently from other words. A word's relationship with other words is part of the meaning of the word".

CSCD Engine: The CSCD Engine consists of a graph transitivity based algorithm that extracts CSCD relationships between concepts in the knowledge units. The overall procedure for CSCD Engine is shown in algorithm 1 in Fig. 4.

Domain Lexicon: The Domain Lexicon contains concepts that are related to computer sciences and can save it as base knowledge and update it during the system process.

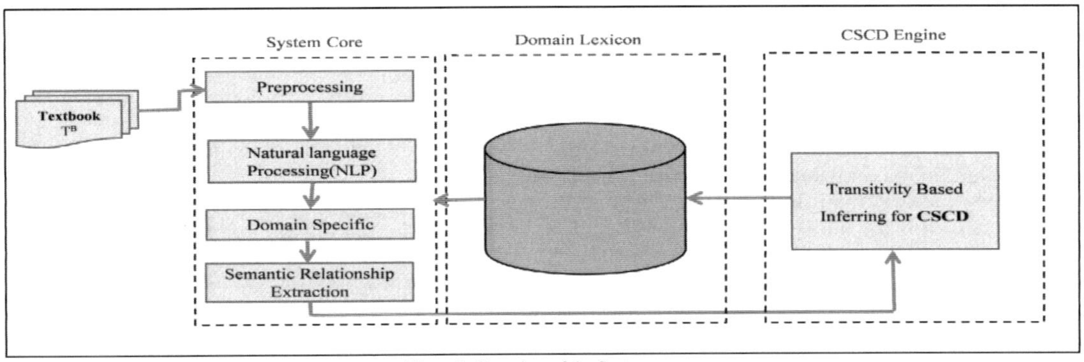

Figure 2. Overview of the System.

V. GRAPH TRANSITIVITY BASED TECHNIQUE

The System Core component plays a very important role in our system. It is the first step for preprocessing the textbook. The output from this component is a semantic graph G^S. In *CSCD* Engine, transitivity based technique used to infer *CSCD* levels from G^S. According to the linguistic view, the connection between words in a sentence is represented by the verb. Verbs, are hypothesized to indicate semantic relations between concepts. In this work the relationships between knowledge units indicated by verbs. We applied the transitivity technique to infer the *CSCD* levels between knowledge units as it is known to us that *CSCD* levels are divided into four levels based on verb majority [14].

The cognitive graph G^c consists of nodes and edges, where nodes are a set of concepts and edges are a set of verbs. Each edge connects two concepts via a specific verb, with each edge having a type (e.g., *CSCD* level). Multiple links between the same pair of concepts are possible. In our cognitive graph, the meaning of an edge between any two nodes is the *CSCD* level. The concept of transitivity between three nodes (c_i, c_j, and c_k) is defined as, if a node c_i has a link to node c_j and node c_j has a link to node c_k, then a measure of transitivity in the graph is the probability that node c_i has a link to node c_k. In general, we refer to c_j as a neighbor of c_i if c_i and c_j are directly connected in the graph. We also refer to the degree of a node as the number of neighbors it has. Fig. 3 shows the transitivity cases.

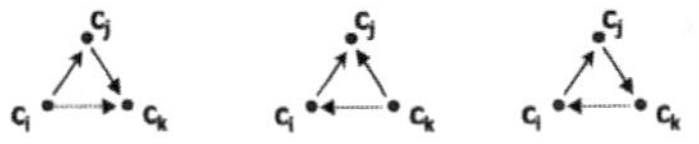

Figure 3. Transitivity Cases.

Based on the assumption that our graph G^S is transitive, we define the transitivity as a path with three hubs length to represent the relationship between two concepts and infer the hidden one. It is represented as three edges that connect a concept ci with a concept cj in the graph, where ci and cj are concepts from a knowledge unit. The edge between any two concepts in the path is one of the *CSCD* levels, which include {Understanding, Analysis, Applying, and Evaluating, and Creating}.

Algorithm 1 in Fig. 4 represents the graph transitivity technique as follows: the algorithm for transitivity has been implemented using Python programming language, providing a solid foundation to use a variety of NLP packages such as NLTK and NetworkX for graph operation. It starts with a source node which represents a knowledge unit (KU) in G^c; the algorithm then initializes the transitivity list and set of concepts or KU.

Algorithm 1: Transitivity Based Technique
Input: Semantic Graph G^S
Output: Transitivity Relationships between C
Def ExtractTransivityFromGraph(self):

```
Transitivity= [ ]
Concepts(C)=set ( )
For each(C) in Graph(self):
C.add(C)
C.Nighbour=set()
Nighbours=set(self. Graph [n])
For Neighbor in Neighbor's:
If Nighbour in Concepts:
continue
Nodes_Nighbour.add(Nighbour)
For Nighbour_of_Nighbour in
Nighbours.intersection( self. Graph [Nighbour]):
Nlist[].append(C[0],count)
If Nighbour_of_Nighbour in Nodes or Nighbour_of_Nighbour
in Nodes_Nighbour:
continue
Transitive. Append((n,Nighbour,Nighbour_of_Nighbour) )
Return Transitivity (G^B)
```

Figure 4. Graph Transitivity Technique.

VI. KNOWLEDGE UNITS CLASSIFICATION

We classify the knowledge units based on the CSCD levels $\beta i = \{B_1, B_2, B_3, B_4\}$ as well as the relations between concepts in knowledge units. The transitivity technique discovers the hidden connections between concepts, and how those concepts are connected to a given knowledge unit, it also investigates the association among knowledge units themselves. The technique presents a strong connectivity between the concepts and knowledge unit.

Transitivity classifications are the sub-graphs extracted from G^C based on the transitivity relationships in the graph. What we have done is try to understand the relationships, which are the prerequisite relationships between concepts, by analyzing the graph. Our classification is divided into four classes as follows:

• C^{ST} (Strong Transitivity): let t denote the target node or knowledge unit, which is shared multi transitivity with their direct neighbors. This class classifies concepts into one of the *CSCD* levels, which is the Creation level. The connectivity between concepts is represented by one of the verbs in Bloom's measurable verbs list [14]. In addition, concepts, which are connected to the knowledge unit are strongly related to it. The concepts must be mastered if the learner needs to learn this knowledge unit. Fig. 5 represents the concepts' transitivity with t i.e., C^{ST}= {tA, tB, tC}.

• C^{MT} (Multi Transitivity): let t denote the target node or knowledge unit; this class consists of the neighbors of t, which shared multi transitivity with t and t's neighbors. The concepts in this class represent another *CSCD* level, which is the Evaluation level. Transitivity relationships among knowledge units in this class overlap and require judgment based on some criteria for some knowledge units. Fig. 5 represents the concepts in this class i.e., C^{MT}= {tE, tD, tW, tZ}.

• C^{WT} (Weak Transitivity): assume t denotes the target node or knowledge unit and it does not share any transitivity relationship with its direct neighbors but their neighbors do share transitivity relationships with other neighbors. Fig. 5 represents the concepts in this class i.e., C^{WC}= {tI, tH, tG}. The concepts in this class represent one of the *CSCD* levels, which is the Applying and Analyzing level. The transitivity relationship inferred combinations of concepts that represent framework to each other.

• C^{DT} (Disconnected Transitivity): concepts in this class are not sharing any transitivity with t or with its neighbors. Actually, the concepts represent the lowest level of *CSCD* levels, which is the Understanding and Remembering level. Most of the concepts are common and not related to the domain under study. Fig. 8 represents the concepts in this class i.e., C^{WC}= {O, P, Q, R, S, V}.

VII. EXAMPLE OF THE PROPOSED TECHNIQUE

The proposed technique goal is to classify the

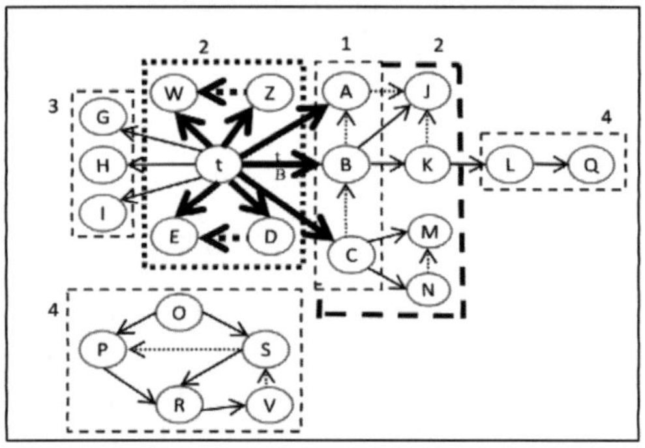

Figure 5. Graph Transitivity Classes.

knowledge units CSCD levels in any given text. For example, consider a knowledge unit (topic) in an Algorithm textbook talking about Quick-Sort Algorithm; we need to classify the knowledge unit into CSCD levels. This section will start explaining our technique through this knowledge unit. Fig. 6 explains the knowledge unit from a textbook.

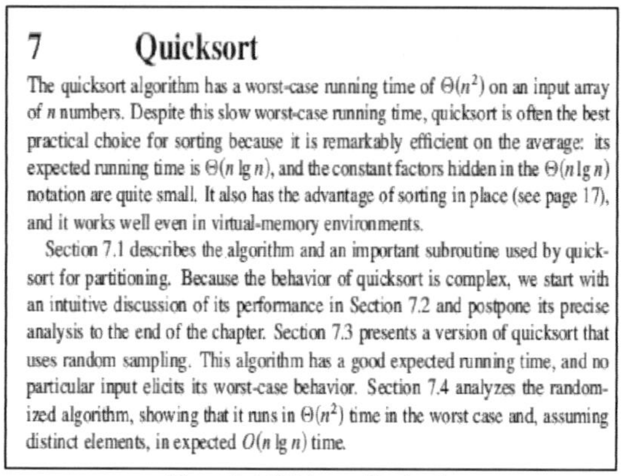

7 Quicksort

The quicksort algorithm has a worst-case running time of $\Theta(n^2)$ on an input array of n numbers. Despite this slow worst-case running time, quicksort is often the best practical choice for sorting because it is remarkably efficient on the average: its expected running time is $\Theta(n \lg n)$, and the constant factors hidden in the $\Theta(n \lg n)$ notation are quite small. It also has the advantage of sorting in place (see page 17), and it works well even in virtual-memory environments.

Section 7.1 describes the algorithm and an important subroutine used by quicksort for partitioning. Because the behavior of quicksort is complex, we start with an intuitive discussion of its performance in Section 7.2 and postpone its precise analysis to the end of the chapter. Section 7.3 presents a version of quicksort that uses random sampling. This algorithm has a good expected running time, and no particular input elicits its worst-case behavior. Section 7.4 analyzes the randomized algorithm, showing that it runs in $\Theta(n^2)$ time in the worst case and, assuming distinct elements, in expected $O(n \lg n)$ time.

Figure 6. A KU from a Textbook.

First, we start with the preprocessing of the given knowledge unit. The output is in Fig. 7; the yellow words which are stop-words were removed from the KU. After that, the *System Core* component extracts the relations among the concepts in a knowledge unit. The output is a semantic graph G^S presented in Fig. 8 where the figure explains all the possible relationships in the given knowledge unit levels for the analyzed knowledge unit, which is a Quick-Sort. It also includes a set of color codes to be used for our classification categories.

In the semantic graph, Fig. 8, we check the transitivity between concepts. First, we checked the relationship type between each two concepts, which is represented by the verb. Based on that, we classified the concepts in each knowledge unit into CSCD levels, and then we classified the knowledge units themselves. Fig. 9 demonstrates all the concepts classified into CSCD levels for the analyzed knowledge unit, which is a Quick-Sort.

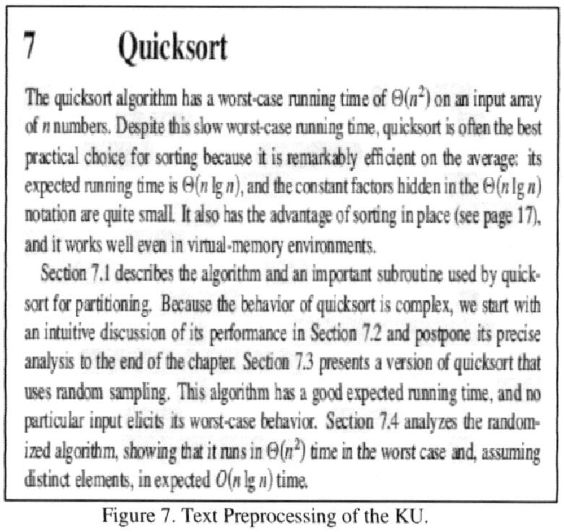

7 Quicksort

The quicksort algorithm has a worst-case running time of $\Theta(n^2)$ on an input array of n numbers. Despite this slow worst-case running time, quicksort is often the best practical choice for sorting because it is remarkably efficient on the average: its expected running time is $\Theta(n \lg n)$, and the constant factors hidden in the $\Theta(n \lg n)$ notation are quite small. It also has the advantage of sorting in place (see page 17), and it works well even in virtual-memory environments.

Section 7.1 describes the algorithm and an important subroutine used by quicksort for partitioning. Because the behavior of quicksort is complex, we start with an intuitive discussion of its performance in Section 7.2 and postpone its precise analysis to the end of the chapter. Section 7.3 presents a version of quicksort that uses random sampling. This algorithm has a good expected running time, and no particular input elicits its worst-case behavior. Section 7.4 analyzes the randomized algorithm, showing that it runs in $\Theta(n^2)$ time in the worst case and, assuming distinct elements, in expected $O(n \lg n)$ time.

Figure 7. Text Preprocessing of the KU.

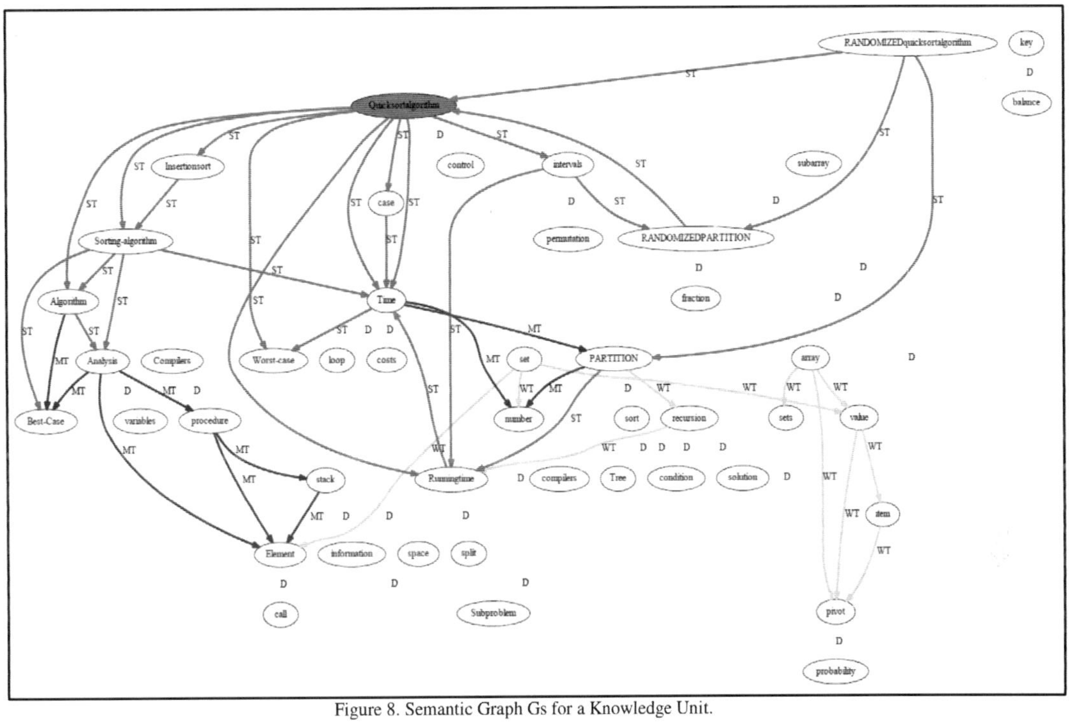

Figure 8. Semantic Graph Gs for a Knowledge Unit.

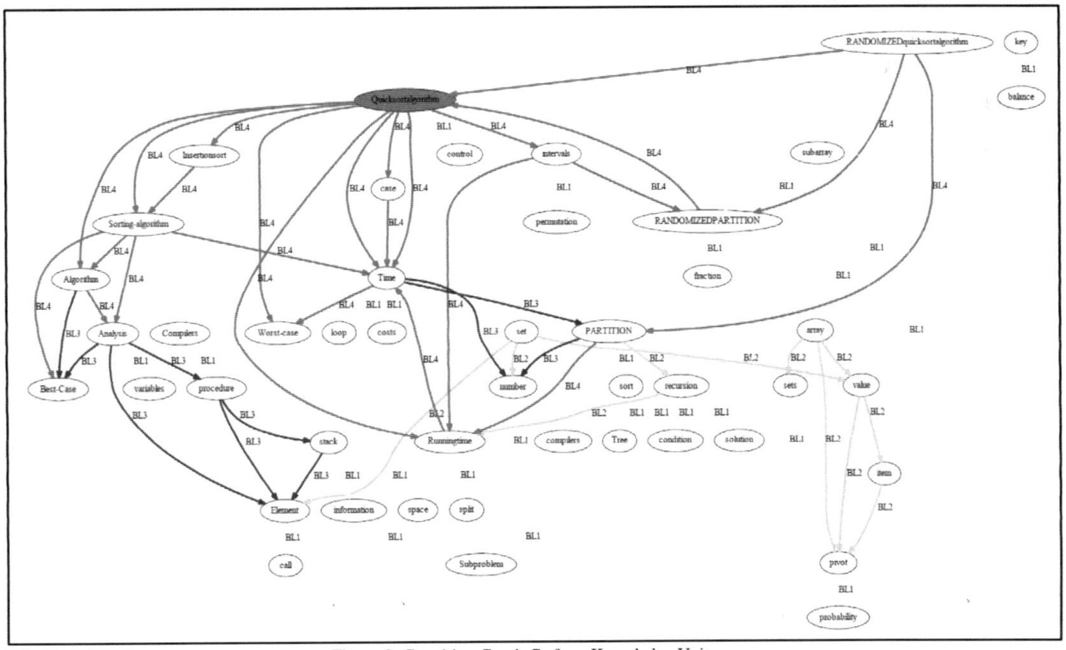

Figure 9. Cognitive Graph Gs for a Knowledge Unit.

VIII. EXPERIMENT SETUP AND EVALUATION

In this section, we first discuss the data set used for testing our system, and then the evaluation metrics will be presented. We used the same data set used in our previous work [3] to see the result from graph transitivity view.

A. Experiment Setup

We test the technique in two ways: locally and globally. Locally means the behavior of the technique using a knowledge unit from the same textbook. Globally means using three high quality textbooks that are used in computer sciences classes as course materials. We apply our technique to see how it performs on textbooks. We obtain three collections of documents from three textbooks on "Introduction to Algorithms" and "Data Structures and Algorithms" and "Algorithms", respectively. The textbooks are used as textbook for computer sciences courses at many universities. Table I shows the statistical information about the three textbooks.

TABLE I. PHYSICAL CHARACTERISTICS OF THE TEXTBOOKS

	Book1	*Book2*	*Book3*
TOC depth	4	3	2
Number of Knowledge unit	120	60	30
Number of extracted Relationships	8500	8200	3000
Number of concepts	1060	1020	950
Number of verbs	610	480	300
Overlaps of Knowledge units	400	300	220

We start with the preprocessing of the text which is the most important step as it includes the stop word filtration, to save only the domain specific concept. Then the semantic relationships extractor is used to extract the semantic graph and we classify all concepts within knowledge units. These knowledge units themselves are classified into CSCD levels which help reorganize the textbook based on the cognitive skills to know at which cognitive level each knowledge unit must be given for learners.

In this experiment, we used Introduction to Algorithm book that includes different knowledge units (topics). Fig. 10 presents the transitivity distribution of concepts in knowledge unit #1 which represented a Heap Sort topic from the textbook. It can be clearly seen that the number of transitivity is high for the concepts which are strongly related to the knowledge unit; the rest of the concepts, which have no transitivity, are common concepts and help knowledge units connect to each other.

Fig. 11 shows the graph connectivity measures which are: *Degree Centrality* ω and *Betweennes Centrality* γ for concepts in KU#1. Both measures prove how strong the concepts related to the knowledge unit are. It means the concepts that appear at the beginning of the chart are concepts related to the domain under study while the common concepts come at the end of the chart.

Additionally, Fig. 11 shows the graph connectivity measures which are: *Clustering Coefficient* (φ) and *Eigenvector Centrality* (μ) for concepts in KU#1. Both measures prove how strongly related the concepts are to the knowledge unit. It means the concepts that appear at the beginning of the chart are concepts related to the domain under study while the common concepts come at the end of the chart.

B. Graph Connectivity Measures

At this step, to measure the concept and knowledge unit connectivity which could be correlated with the graph metrics, we collected and calculated the following success measures:

Clustering Coefficient (φ): it is the measurement that shows the connectivity among knowledge units and the concepts related to them. According to [16] the mathematical formula of **φ** is as follows:

$$\varphi_i = \frac{2e}{k(k-1)} \qquad (1)$$

Where *i* is a knowledge unit with degree *deg (i) = k* in G^T φ_i Takes values as $0 \leq \varphi_i \leq 1$

Degree Centrality (ω): as in [17], it shows that the interactions of a target concept are represented in the knowledge unit with other concepts in G^T. Our result shows the high centrality of the target concept in G^T. ω is defined as in question 2.

$$\omega_i = \text{deg(i)} \qquad (2)$$

Betweenness Centrality (γ) illustrates the connectivity between the target concepts and their neighbors by making a path between concepts; that is calculated as follows [24]:

$$\gamma(w) = \sum_{(i,j)\in V(w)} \frac{\sigma_{ij}(w)}{\sigma_{ij}} \qquad (3)$$

Eigenvector Centrality (μ) as in [17] presents the importance of the target concept's neighbors which measure how well-connected a knowledge unit is to other highly connected concepts in G^T.

C. Evaluation

In order to evaluate the quality of the G^C for each knowledge unit, we are interested in two different measures. The first one expresses the completeness of the set of CSCD relationships, that is, how many valid CSCD relationships are found with respect to the total number of extracted relationships.

The second measure indicates the reliability of the set of CSCD relationships found in the knowledge unit, that is, how many valid Bloom relationships are found with respect to the total number of CSCD in the knowledge units.

To compute the metrics, we compare our system with ground truth by asking Ph.D. students using their own background knowledge and additional resources to classify some knowledge units from a textbook and determine the level of the cognitive skills for each knowledge unit. The students created a semantic graph for each knowledge unit, so for each graph, we perform the ground truth in three knowledge units from the textbook. The purpose is to create a final classification G^C for each knowledge unit as similar as possible to the automatic system.

TABLE iI. PHYSICAL CHARACTERISTICS OF THE TEXTBOOKS

Book Name	# Knowledge Unit	Bloom Trajectory for KU
Introduction to Algorithm	35	90
Algorithms	10	40
Data structure and Algorithms	30	25

IX. CONCLUSION AND FUTURE WORK

In this paper, an automatic technique that finds the relationships between knowledge units according to *CSCD* levels has been presented. The technique is an improved version of our previous work [3]. Discovering relationships based on CSCD levels is a novel and challenging problem. The results show that the relationships between knowledge units are different from one textbook to another. Based on our analytical result, it is possible to conclude that by using CSCD levels we can decide which parts of a textbook to use at which level of learning to match the learner's skills. For future research, we will investigate the use of the method to evaluate online learning resources.

ACKNOWLEDGMENTS

We take this opportunity to thank all the reviewers for this paper for the suggestions that provide helpful tips to improve the paper.

REFRENCES

[1] B. Benjamin Samuel. "Taxonomy of educational objectives". Vol. 2. New York: Longmans, Green, 1964.

[2] A. Lorin W., David R. Krathwohl, and Benjamin Samuel Bloom. "A taxonomy for learning, teaching, and assessing: A revision of Bloom's taxonomy of educational objectives". Allyn & Bacon, 2001.

[3] N. Fatema and Khan J."Conceptualize the Domain Knowledge Space in the Light of Cognitive Skills". In Proceedings of the 7th International Conference on Computer Supported Education. 2015.

[4] P. Machanick,"Experience of applying Bloom's Taxonomy in three courses". In Proc. Southern African Computer Lecturers' Association Conference, 2000.

[5] R .Lister and J .Leaney, "Introductory programming, criterion-referencing, and bloom". In ACM SIGCSE Bulletin.2003

[6] D.Oliver, et al. "This course has a Bloom Rating of 3.9." Proceedings of the Sixth Australasian Conference on Computing Education-Volume 30. Australian Computer Society, Inc., 2004.

[7] H. Marti, "Automatic acquisition of hyponyms from large text corpora." Proceedings of the 14th conference on Computational linguistics-Volume 2. Association for Computational Linguistics, 1992.

[8] R. Alan, S. Soderland, and O. Etzioni. "What Is This, Anyway: Automatic Hypernym Discovery." AAAI Spring Symposium: Learning by Reading and Learning to Read. 2009.

[9] F. Frédéric, and Francky Trichet. "Axiom-based ontology matching." Proceedings of the 3rd international conference on Knowledge capture. ACM, 2005.

[10] R. Kanagasabai, and A. Tan. "Mining semantic networks for knowledge discovery." Data Mining, 2003. ICDM 2003. Third IEEE International Conference on. IEEE, 2003.

[11] N. Roberto, P. Velardi, and A. Gangemi. "Ontology learning and its application to automated terminology translation." IEEE Intelligent systems,2003.

[12] P. Mathew, Snehasis Mukhopadhyay, and Matthew Stephens. "Identification of biological relationships from text documents." Medical Informatics. Springer US, 2005.

[13] A. Mohammad, I. Barjasteh, and H. Radha. "Transitivity matrix of social network graphs." 2012 IEEE Statistical Signal Processing Workshop (SSP). IEEE, 2012.

[14] Bloom's Taxonomy Action Verbs.http://www.clemson.edu/assessment/assessment practices/referencematerials/documents/Blooms%20T axonomy% 20Action%20Verbs.pdf,2011.

[15] L. John, "Linguistic semantics: An introduction." Cambridge University Press, 1995.

[16] M. Newman,"A measure of betweenness centrality based on random walks." Social networks,2005.

[17] A . Réka, H. Jeong, and A. Barabási. "Error and attack tolerance of complex networks." 2000.

[18] H. Thomas, E. Charles, L .Ronald, and C. Stein."Introduction to Algorithms, Third Edition (3rd ed.)". The MIT Press. 2009.

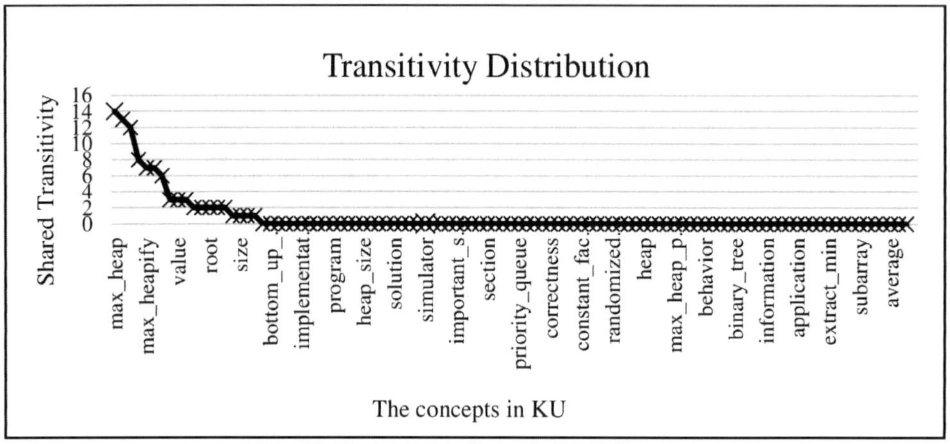

Figure 10. Tringluarity Distribution for KU #1(Heap Sort).

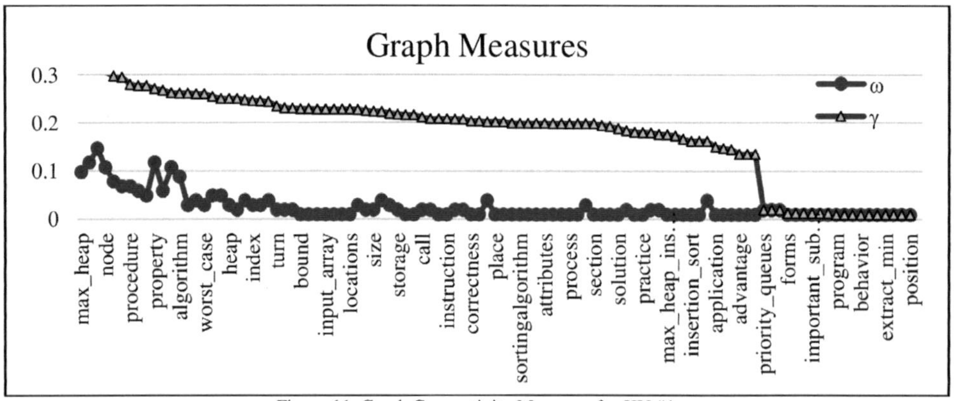

Figure 11. Graph Connectivity Measures for KU #1.

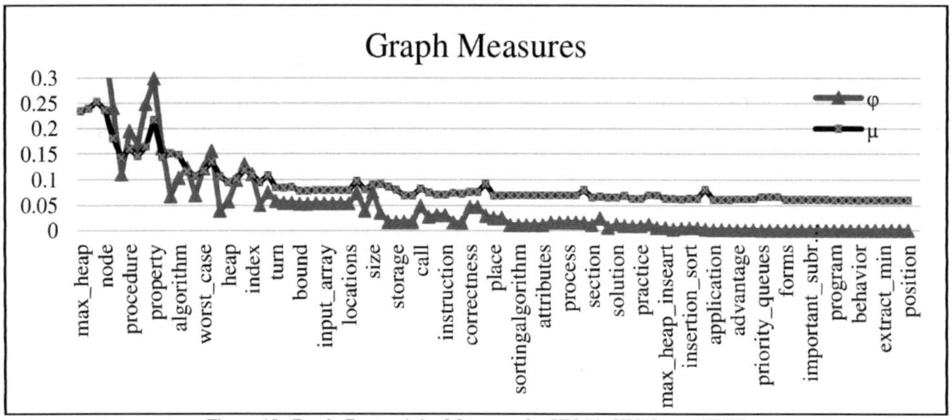

Figure 12. Graph Connectivity Measures for KU #1, KU#2, and KU#3

A Method to Build a Production Process Model prior to a Process Mining Approach

An Illustration through the Detection of Incidents

Britta Feau and Cédric Schaller

Altran Est
Parc d'Innovation,
Boulevard Sebastien Brandt,
67404 Illkirch-Graffenstaden, France

Marion Moliner

Altran Research, MEDIC@
Parc d'Innovation,
Boulevard Sebastien Brandt,
67404 Illkirch-Graffenstaden, France
Email: marion.moliner@altran.com

Abstract—**While manufacturing plants are becoming more digital, the large amount of data they produce remains under-exploited. In particular, event logs generated by production lines are usually monitored only in case of unusual events, such as production incidents. Process mining, a recent research field at the interface between data mining and process modelling, is specialized in extracting knowledge from event logs about the real process followed by a system. While the process model is usually delivered by the provider of the automaton, specific situations can lead to a lack of global view. This adds extra difficulties to carry out a root cause analysis of the incidents. In this short paper, we propose a simple method to overcome that issue. We built an artificial log from the manual root cause analysis performed after series of production incidents and we then applied process mining techniques to recover an accurate view of the process model.**

Keywords–Manufacturing system; incident detection; process model; event logs; process mining.

I. Introduction

Modern manufacturing environments have become more digital, which increases, for example, the accuracy of the tracking of the production batches. This digitization results in a large amount of data being generated by manufacturing plants. While some of these data are monitored and widely used, some other, especially data generated directly by the automatons of the production lines are very little exploited, or even deleted a short time after being generated. Event logs are one particular type of data in which series of actions performed at specific timestamps are described. Event logs generated by manufacturing facilities are usually checked by stakeholders only in case of specific needs, for instance in order to investigate the cause of a production incident. A production process describes the series of steps to perform to transform an initial product or set of products into a final state. Various standard semantics exist to model a process, such as the Unified Modelling Language (UML) [1] or Business Process Model and Notation (BPMN)[2]. The functional documentation supplied by the providers of the industrial automatons is intended to provide the users a mean to visualize the process. However, it is common that in practice the process model is not known accurately. For example, at a macroscopic level, the application of many consecutive customizations can lead to a lack of complete and updated documentation and thus to a loss of the global view of the resulting process. Besides, customizations can lead to unexpected consequences and deviations of the process. As detailed below, at the automatons' level, logs can contain very detailed pieces of information that are not described in the general process model but that are relevant to carry out a root cause analysis of incidents. Building a model out of this content can therefore be helpful for stakeholders to diagnose causes of incidents. Production shut-downs are a major issue for manufacturing plants as they generate losses of productivity, extra costs and often require on-call provided by on-site teams. Reducing the occurrences of incidents is thus a challenging topic that we intend to tackle by using data generated by production lines. A global view of the possible deviations of the process is useful in order to carry out a root cause analysis of production incidents. Investigations are generally carried out "manually" by the production-related teams. Stakeholders collect event logs from the automatons and inspect them directly. This method lacks both efficiency and effectiveness due to the size and dimensionality of the logs. The diagnosis is based on the content the functional documentation and eventually multiples exchanges with the provider of the industrial automatons.

In this short paper, we present a method to build a global view of the process, based on the conclusions of the manual analysis of the event logs. Although our study is tested on data provided by a pharmaceutical manufacturing plant, the method is general and can be applied to other industrial contexts.
In Section II, we present related work of analysing production data from monitoring and control systems, in Section III we introduce the problem considered, in Section IV we introduce process mining and explain how our approach uses this technique. We finally conclude in Section V and give an overview of our roadmap to continue this work.

II. Related work on SCADA log mining

The manufacturing plant that provides us with their data is equipped with a Supervisory Control And Data Acquisition (SCADA) system to control and monitor the production processes. A general SCADA system is organized in layers and consists of components, such as Programmable Logic Controllers (PLCs), Human Machine Interfaces (HMI), Manufacturing Execution Systems (MES), networks, data bases. The first layer of the SCADA system consists in PLCs that are localized at the production level. The data they produce are sent and processed in the second layer, that contains in particular the MESs where we collect the event logs we are interested in. Finally, the third layer consists in work stations, where authorized users can access the information. If accurately tuned, the SCADA logs contain valuable pieces of information about the process to carry out a root cause analysis of unusual events, such as incidents or threats. Since manufacturing plants are becoming more connected, detecting intrusions has become a very relevant subject. Recent research work were published about SCADA log mining in the context of process-related threats [3], [4], [5], [6], [7]. Data mining approaches, based on frequent pattern mining methods [4], [8], [9] or on semantic support [10], were successfully tried to detect intrusions but extensions strongly depend on the manufacturing system. In our use case, root cause analysis of incidents is currently made manually, not only because of the difficulty to put in practice an intelligent reading of the logs, but also because other complementary sources of data provided by the MES need to be taken into account to have a good understanding of the process deviations that result in a incident.

III. Problem statement: System Analysis by Manual Treatment

Let us first describe how we analyse the system by manual inspection. Then, we introduce process mining and present the issues one has to deal with when mining industrial logs. For the purpose of building and testing the method, we focus on a small piece of the full production process.

Two types of users interact with the SCADA system: operators and engineers. Operators monitor the production line and take actions in case of alarm to make sure the process works properly. In case of incident, engineers make a diagnosis and perform additional steps to restart the production. They are also in charge of: carrying out a root cause analysis, documenting the faults and eventually communicating with the provider of the automatons to take action and prevent the same incidents from occurring again. Production incidents have been carefully documented over more than one year. Three types of incidents were clearly identified and the percentage of each type over one year was calculated.

Progressive modifications and customizations of the production line implies that the functional documentation that was originally provided with the automatons might no longer be accurate. Updates should be documented but (i) there might be delays before all concerned teams receive the last version of the documentation (ii) even if specific modifications are documented global views of the processes are not always drawn. Besides, even if the process model is already accurate, automatons' logs can contain information at a finer level of granularity. Consider for example a process in which a rising edge, triggered during step_i, induces step_{i+1} to be performed. Suppose the process allows the rising edge to be repeated n times in case it is not acknowledged directly. If it is acknowledged before the $(n+1)^{\text{th}}$ try, at the lowest level, the process went fine. However, the detail inside the log will indicate that it was not acknowledged directly. Even though this does not lead to an incident, it may be interesting to be informed about recurrence of such events in the context of root cause analysis (for instance to study eventual slowness of the network). The manual investigation of the process is based on a careful analysis of the events logs after production incidents combined with the knowledge of the process model, as described by the provider of the automaton. The SCADA system, together with additional devices, records events at different places in the network. Accessing these logs allows the on-site teams to diagnose the incidents and decide what actions to take to restart the production. This approach has many disadvantages:

1) The large size of the files.
2) Some data are missing because files are deleted due to their large sizes and to the lack of use.
3) The search for patterns is biased. Manual inspection is based on searching for particular strings, which can be improved with small scripts. However, unusual patterns one is not explicitly looking for will not be found. The choice of patterns to look for is guided by some idea of what should be a possible cause of incident. If this pre-diagnosis is not correct, the real cause of incident might not be found.

All these motivate our research on intelligent methods to obtain a global view of the process. Process mining is a very promising option that we introduce in the next subsection.

IV. Solution Approach via Process Mining

In this work, our objective is to restore a model of the process based on the manual system analysis, in order to have an accurate theoretical description to compare with. In order to obtain this global view, we are using a process mining approach. Process mining [11], [12] is an emerging field at the interface between data mining and model-driven approaches. It allows to get a global, complete and objective view of the processes that were actually performed by the system. It aims to discover automatically processes from the events logs, check their conformance by monitoring the deviations between the model and the event logs, analyse the performance (e.g., find bottlenecks), make predictions and eventually improve the processes by making recommendations. In this work, we apply a process mining approach to the logs provided by the full SCADA system in order to diagnose faster and with more accuracy the incidents. We expect to discover new types of incidents that were not correctly diagnosed due to the difficulty for a human to read the logs. To the best of our knowledge, very few research work are dedicated to the application of process mining techniques to fault detection in industrial context [13], [14], [15]. In order to be treated by a process mining tool, a log needs to contain specific categories of information: a case ID (e.g., a batch number), timestamps and descriptions of the activities performed within one case. Extra information, such as the resources that realize each activity and their role also allows to extract valuable information (graphs of interactions, etc.).

SCADA log mining is however a long term task for various reasons:

1) The format of the SCADA logs is not suited for process mining. Major data cleansing is necessary [16]. Even after that step, the eventual lack of case ID (i.e., batch number not printed) makes it impossible to use the content of the log with a process mining tool. A possible cure to that issue consists in making recommendations to the stakeholders. After showing the added value of process mining to support root cause analysis, one can recommend modifications of the content of the logs.
2) One needs to mine more than one type of log. Events collected from various sources then need to be properly connected which is a complex task. A possible solution we are investigating is applying frequent patterns mining techniques, as performed in [4].

3) In relation with the previous point, the network introduces delays from one log to another, even within the same activity.
4) Data is missing. Examples of causes are: data are deleted after a short time or data are erased after a reboot. Stakeholders could take action on the first point by providing suitable servers.

While applying process mining techniques directly from the SCADA logs is still under investigation, we built an artificial log to replay the process, such as understood from the manual inspection. Applying process mining software to this log allows us to mimic process incidents.

1) Building a process model from the manual analysis: In order to build an artificial log, iterations together with the engineers who know about the process and investigate the incidents are required. Preparation of the model is done after manual investigation of the process. We proceeded the following way:

1) Identify what are the steps of the regular process. This matches the functional documentation and can be checked in logs outside unusual events.
2) For each incident, get a picture of the different activities that were performed. This task is crucial but very cumbersome due to the fact that one need to read more than one source of data, those sources are large files and they were not designed to be user-friendly.
3) Classify incidents and try to see if categories can be found. In our case, three types of incidents were identified.
4) Document over a long time (in our case over the full year 2015) and keep record of incidents to get a picture of the percentage of occurrences.

From this manual study, we built an artificial log that describes reality. For this, we wrote a programming code able to generate series of cases that include incidents with the same proportion as the one observed in reality. A case is defined by a series of activities. For example in our case, the regular case (i.e., no incident) contains six activities all of them are performed within seconds. Each type of incidents involves either new activities or unusual repetitions of a given activity. Moreover, bottlenecks appear, they are due to complex necessary intervention, such as rebooting the system in order to restart the production line. While the percentage of incidents cases is known, we want them to take place at random time. For the moment an uniform random sorting is performed to spread these unusual case within the log. In case the manual study finds out that some correlations seem to exist, this sorting could easily be improved to mimic reality better.

After an artificial log containing n events is generated, it can be used directly in a process mining tool. We used an evaluation licence of the Disco process discovery software [17], developed by Fluxicon. Fig. 1 shows results highlighting frequency (top chart) and performance (bottom chart) performed with a fuzzy miner algorithm [18]. In the top chart (frequency), thick paths correspond to the most frequent paths, i.e., the regular process. We clearly see the six activities (dark blue boxes) and three extra activities (clear blue boxes) that take place only during incidents (acknowledgement failure that leads to either SCADA reboot or manual acknowledgement).

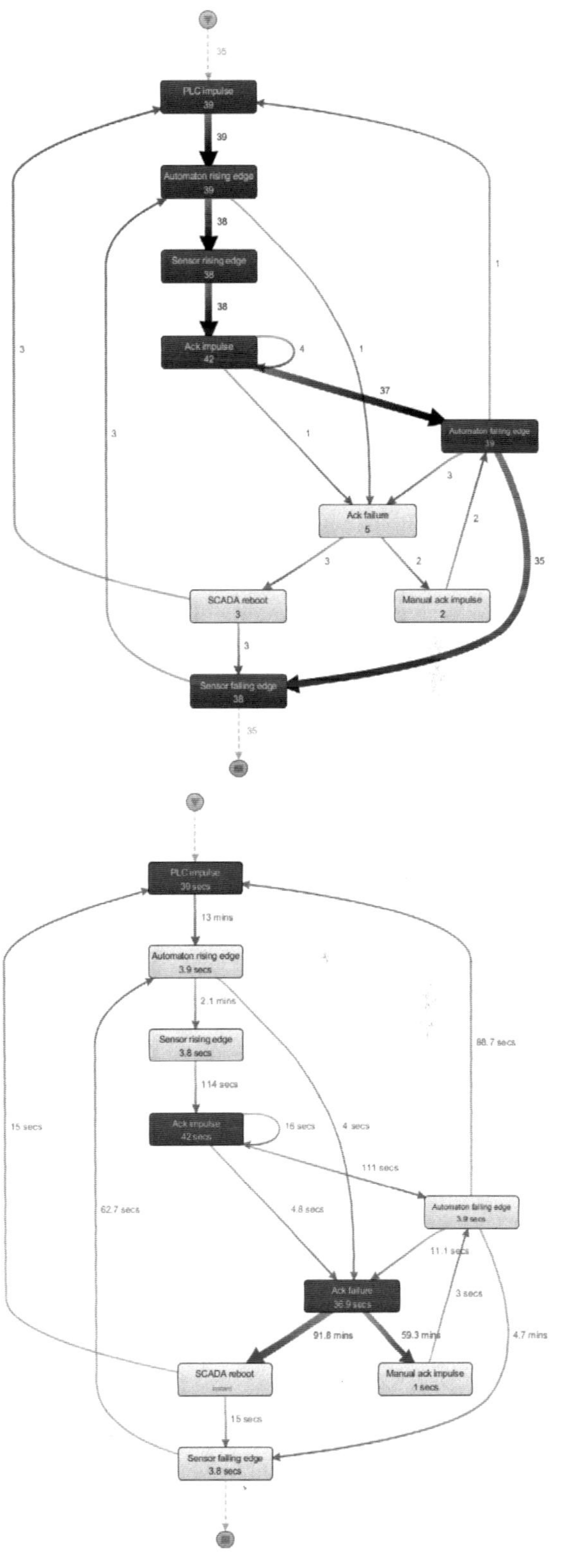

Figure 1. Model of the process and its deviations obtained by the fuzzy miner algorithm from the Disco software [17].

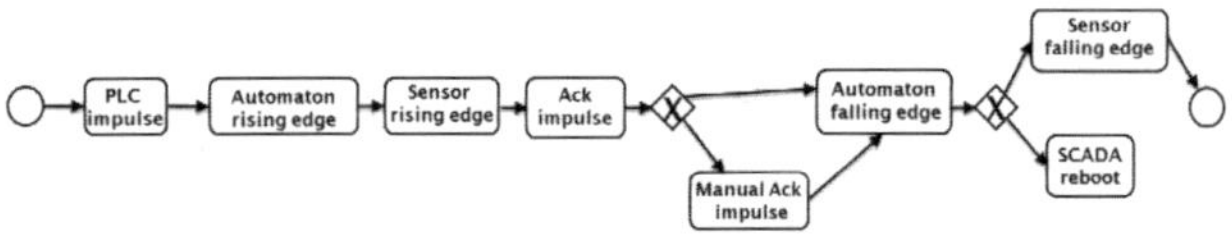

Figure 2. BPMN model corresponding to the process from Fig. 1 extracted automatically with ProM [19] from the artificial log.

The bottom chart (performance) shows the durations of the transitions between activities. The thick red lines correspond to the manual operations, i.e., when an engineer needs to act on the production line. These are the most time-consuming tasks, i.e., the bottlenecks of the process.
Note that, due to confidentiality issues, the names of the activities were anonymized. Of course, no unknown process deviation is to be found since all the deviations were implemented from the understanding we got from the manual approach. This view of the process however offers a better visualization of the outcome of the manual study for stakeholders who need a global picture of the various types of productions incidents. We then used another process mining tool, ProM [19], to extract a process diagram. Fig. 2 shows the BPMN representation [2].

V. Conclusion and Future Research

We are working on an automatic approach to support root cause analysis for production shut-downs. The data used are production event logs. Process mining seems to be a very promising approach to tackle these issues. We have identified barriers that prevent us from using process mining straight forward with our data:

- Major and complex data preprocessing: cleansing, formatting, merging various logs to get the complete required information.
- Missing data: all the process information is not recorded in the logs, logs are erased after a very short time.
- Lack of case ID number and network delays that make it difficult to connect properly the activities within one case.

Solving these issues is still on-going work and requires iterations with the stakeholders.

Before being able to drawn a process diagram directly from the logs, we have presented in this paper a method to build a process model from the manual approach that is performed to support root cause analysis of the incidents. Our method allowed us to provide a global view of the identified process deviations. If the manual analysis is correct, the artificial log that we have built to mimic reality should match quite accurately the real logs with a similar proportion of incidents. In this case, a conformance analysis will thus evaluate the accuracy of the manual analysis.

Acknowledgment

The authors would like to thank the on-site teams for providing data and for fruitful discussions about the system analysis.
This work is supported by Altran Est.

References

[1] Unified Modeling Language, Object Management Group Std. [Online]. Available: http://www.uml.org

[2] Business Process Model and Notation, Object Management Group Std. [Online]. Available: http://www.bpmn.org/

[3] D. Hadziosmanovic, "The process matters: cyber security in industrial control systems," Ph.D. dissertation, Enschede, the Netherlands, January 2014, iPA Dissertation Series No. 2014-02. [Online]. Available: http://doc.utwente.nl/88730/

[4] D. Hadziosmanovic, D. Bolzoni, and P. H. Hartel, "A log mining approach for process monitoring in scada," International Journal of Information Security, vol. 11, no. 4, 2012, pp. 231–251. [Online]. Available: http://dx.doi.org/10.1007/s10207-012-0163-8

[5] R. E. Kondo, E. de F. R. Loures, and E. A. P. Santos, "Process mining for alarm rationalization and fault patterns identification," in Proceedings of 2012 IEEE 17th International Conference on Emerging Technologies Factory Automation (ETFA 2012), Sept 2012, pp. 1–4.

[6] M. Ficco, A. Daidone, L. Coppolino, L. Romano, and A. Bondavalli, "An event correlation approach for fault diagnosis in scada infrastructures," in Proceedings of the 13th European Workshop on Dependable Computing, ser. EWDC '11, 2011, pp. 15–20. [Online]. Available: http://dl.acm.org/citation.cfm?doid=1978582.1978586

[7] B. Lamas, A. Soury, B. Saadallah, A. Lahmadi, and O. Festor, "An experimental testbed and methodology for security analysis of scada systems," INRIA, Technical Report RT-0443, Dec. 2013. [Online]. Available: https://hal.inria.fr/hal-00920828

[8] D. Hadiosmanovic, D. Bolzoni, P. Hartel, and S. Etalle, "Melissa: Towards automated detection of undesirable user actions in critical infrastructures," in Computer Network Defense (EC2ND), 2011 Seventh European Conference on, Sept 2011, pp. 41–48.

[9] G. Grahne and J. Zhu, "Fast algorithms for frequent itemset mining using fp-trees," IEEE Transactions on Knowledge and Data Engineering, vol. 17, no. 10, Oct 2005, pp. 1347–1362.

[10] A. Venticinque, N. Mazzocca, S. Venticinque, and M. Ficco, "Semantic support for log analysis of safety-critical embedded systems," in Tenth European Dependable Computing Conference - EDCC 2014, 2014. [Online]. Available: http://arxiv.org/abs/1405.2986

[11] W. van der Aalst, Process Mining: Discovery, Conformance and Enhancement of Business Processes, S.-V. Berlin and Heidelberg, Eds., 2011.

[12] W. van der Aalst et al., "Process mining manifesto," in Business Process Management Workshops (BPM 2011), Lecture Notes in Business Information Processing, Springer-Verlag, Ed., vol. 99, 2011, pp. 169–194.

[13] N. Khajehzadeh, "Data and process mining applications on a multicell factory automation testbed," Master's thesis, Tampere University of Technology, 2012.

[14] S. Dasani, "Developing industrial workflows from process data," Master's thesis, University of Alberta, 2013.

[15] S. Dasani, S. L. Shah, T. Chen, and J. F. R. W. Pollard, "Monitoring safety of process operations using industrial workflows," in Preprints of the 9th International Symposium on Advanced Control of Chemical Processes, 2015, pp. 451–456.

[16] L. T. Ly, C. Indiono, J. Mangler, and S. Rinderle-Ma, "Data transformation and semantic log purging for process mining," in Proceedings of the 24th international conference on Advanced Information Systems Engineering (CAISE 12), S.-V. Berlin, Ed., 2012, p. 238.

[17] Disco, Fluxicon. [Online]. Available: https://fluxicon.com/disco/

[18] C. W. Günther and W. M. P. Van Der Aalst, "Fuzzy mining: Adaptive process simplification based on multi-perspective metrics," in Proceedings of the 5th International Conference on Business Process Management, ser. BPM'07. Berlin, Heidelberg: Springer-Verlag, 2007, pp. 328–343. [Online]. Available: http://dl.acm.org/citation.cfm?id=1793114.1793145

[19] Prom, process mining workbench, Process Mining Group, Eindhoven Technical University. [Online]. Available: http://www.promtools.org/doku.php

CPS-based Model-Driven Approach to Smart Manufacturing Systems

Jaeho Jeon[1], Sungjoo Kang[2], Ingeol Chun[3]
Embedded SW Research Department
Electronics and Telecommunications Research Institute
Daejeon, Republic of Korea
Email: {jeonjaeho11[1], sjkang[2], igchun[3]} @etri.re.kr

***Abstract*—With advent of new technologies such as Cyber-Physical Systems (CPS), Internet of Things (IoT) and BigData, the technologies have led to the new concept of "Smart Factory" in the field of manufacturing. Several challenges have been raised up on how to handle flexibility, optimization, and interoperability in production life-cycle. This paper proposes a model-driven approach by ETRI CPS Modeling Language (ECML) to solve the challenges and presents a case study of Smart Factory by implementing from the facility design to virtualization.**

Keywords-cpps; smart factory; industry 4.0; modeling and simulation

I. INTRODUCTION

Manufacturing industry is now transforming into the fourth industrial revolution, called Industry 4.0. This transformation has the meaning of embracing a number of contemporary automation, data exchange and manufacturing technologies such as CPS, IoT, Big Data [1]. Nowadays, the assembly of these new technologies has led to the new concept, "Smart Factory", in the field of manufacturing and the entire value chain from product design to delivery is digitalized and integrated.

Manufacturing competitors have used many technologies to solve the issues regarding the complexity of the manufacturing system, and Model-Driven Engineering (MDE) technique [7] becomes one of the solutions to handle the complexity. In this paper we propose a model-driven approach by ECML to solve the challenges in constructing a smart factory and present a "multiple-product production by process control system (MPPCS)" as an implementation for a smart factory. The rest of the paper is structured as follows: in Section 2, the background of smart factory regarding Industry 4.0 and related challenges are examined. Section 3 introduces a modeling and simulation technique described in ECML. Section 4 describes a case study and the paper concludes with a summarization in Section 5.

II. SMART FACTORY

This section describes how the fourth industrial revolution came up with in German and US, and it also explains about a CPPS architecture which plays an important role in a smart factory.

A. *Industrie 4.0, Industrial Internet and Challenges*

Manufacturing industry is currently changing to a new paradigm, targeting innovation, lower costs, better responses to customer needs, and alternatives towards on-demand production [2]. Along with the change, German government has been promoting "High-Tech Strategy 2020 Action Plan" since 2013 and mentioned "4th industrial revolution" or "Industrie 4.0" [3]. The "Industrial Internet" is first introduced by General Electric in US in its visionary paper [6]. Even though both nations use different terms, several key challenges are addressed in common:

- Flexibility: flexible adaptation of the production chain to changing requirements,
- Optimization: production optimization due to IoT, CPS, and BigData
- Interoperability: interoperable data exchange between cyber and physical entities

B. *CPPS Architecture*

CPS refers to the convergence of the physical and computing (cyber) systems over the network. When applied to production, CPS is specialized in Cyber-Physical Production Systems (CPPS) [6]. CPPS consists of autonomous and cooperative elements and sub-systems that connect with each other in situation dependent ways, on and across all levels of production [10]. Fig. 1 illustrates an architecture of CPPS.

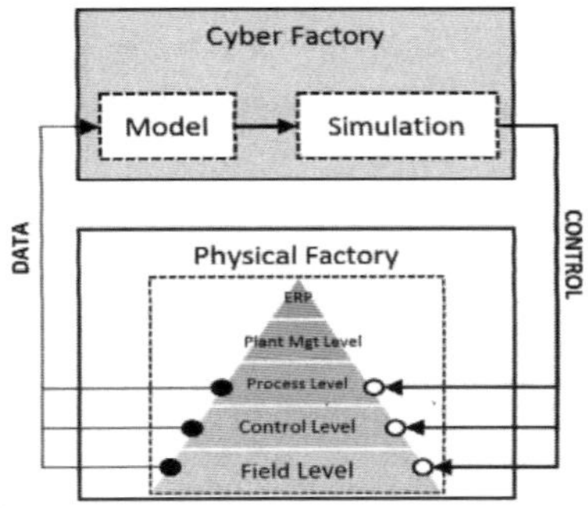

Figure 1. CPPS architecture

CPPS architecture refers to that the cyber and the physical factory are synchronized in time by exchanging data and control messages between them. The simulation in the cyber factory takes data in real-time from the physical factory so that the accurate model (the physical factory model) can be defined. Once the simulation is done, the simulator generates control messages and sends back to the actuators in the physical factory so that the flexible adaptation of the production chain and the production optimization are possible.

III. MODELING AND SIMULATION

For handling the flexible adaptation of manufacturing processes and the production optimization by a model-driven approach, it is very important to define the physical elements in a modeling language which enables modeling the factory as a whole in terms of processes, dependencies and interrelations, data and material flows [8]. ECML can be a possible candidate for it. Fig. 2 illustrates a representation of the physical factory in ECML.

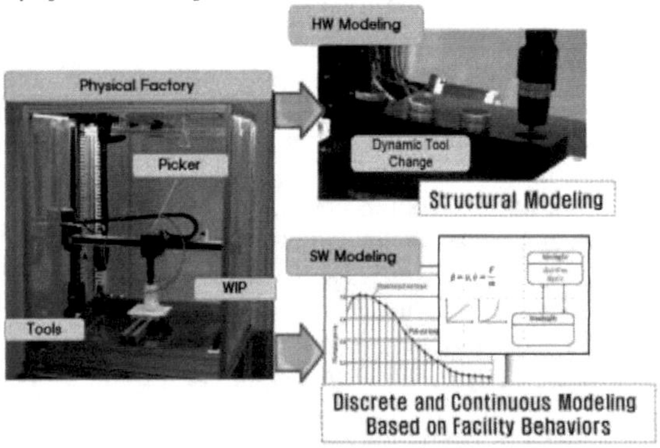

Figure 2. Physical factory modeling

ECML is a hybrid system modeling language as a basis of DEV&DESS formalism [5][10] and Meta Object Facility (MOF) [4]. It is a modular, hierarchical and graphical language for modeling and simulation of systems that can be a discrete event systems described by state transition rules and a continuous systems described by differential equations. It also supports an encapsulation of models, model reuse, and multi-resolution modeling. ECML enables to define, design, and verify the manufacturing resources such as 4M (Man, Material, Method and Machine) related to processes, products and physical resources in the plants.

Once the factory model is defined in ECML, the next step is to do simulation for constructing a virtual factory. Generally precise simulations depend on how closely and directly the models are associated with the target systems. CPS-based simulation takes models with real-time data from the physical factory. Once the simulation is done, the models can be represented as 3D models, as shown in Fig. 3, in a virtual environment on a third-party application.

IV. CASE STUDY

MPPCS, as a case study, is a conceptual facility to support the flexible adaptation of systematic processes according to CPS-based simulation. The goal of CPS-based simulation is to propose an optimized process regarding the resources, such as semi-finished products and parts, and to produce final products in the most effective way in terms of cost and time.

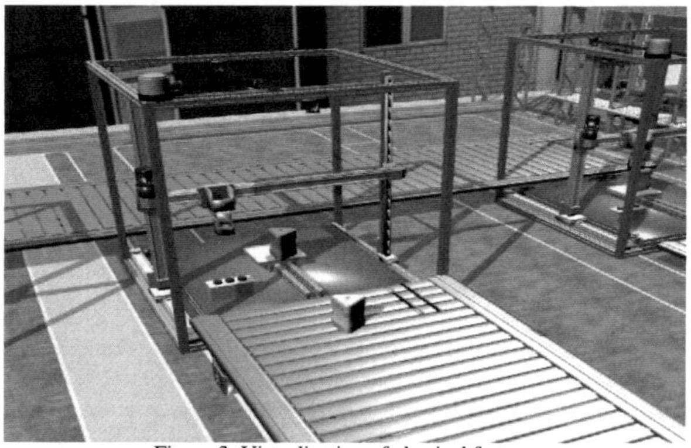

Figure 3. Virtualization of physical factory

First of all, MPPCS is defined in ECML according to the specification in terms of structures and behaviors. For example a picker and a lift of the facility are considered as structural parts, and dynamic movements of the picker are considered as behavioral parts. The facility receives a set of operating schedules from the CPS-based simulation. These schedules are generated by CPS-based simulation by receiving real-time data from sensors of the facility regarding whether the facility is in idle status or how much progress its facility has been done. If any congestions occur in a certain facility, the simulator will regenerate optimal operating schedules, and the resources will be redistributed to the other facilities according to the schedules.

V. CONCLUSION

This paper proposed a CPS based model-driven approach using ECML and presented a case study to test an optimal process generation which can be a solution to the challenges about smart manufacturing systems. Our future research will focus on covering other challenges such as a self-awareness of products and a human-machine interaction (HMI).

ACKNOWLEDGMENT

This work was supported by the ICT R&D program of MSIP/IITP. [R-20150505-000691, IoT-based CPS platform technology for the integration of virtual-real manufacturing facility]

REFERENCES

[1] D. Lucke, C. Constaninescu, and E. Westkämper, “Smart Factory A Step towards the Next Generation of Manufacturing,” Proceedings of the 41st CIRP Conference on Manufacturing Systems, Tokyo, Japan, pp. 115-118, 2008.

[2] A. A. F. Saldivar, Y. Li, W. n. Chen, Z. h. Zhan, J. Zhang and L. Y. Chen, "Industry 4.0 with cyber-physical integration: A design and manufacture perspective," Automation and Computing (ICAC), 2015 21st International Conference on, Glasgow, pp. 1-6, 2015.

[3] W. MacDougall, "Industrie 4.0 Smart Manufacturing for the Future," Mechanical & Electronic Tehcnologies, Germany Trade & Invest(4) 40, 2014.

[4] OMG, ISO/IEC 19502:2005(E). "Meta Object Facility (MOF) Specification", Version 1.4.1.

[5] B. P. Zeigler, H. Praehofer, and T.G. Kim, "Theory of Modeling and Simulation," Academic Press, 2000.

[6] J. Posada et al., "Visual Computing as a Key Enabling Technology for Industrie 4.0 and Industrial Internet," in IEEE Computer Graphics and Applications, vol. 35, no. 2, pp. 26-40, Mar.-Apr. 2015.

[7] M. Brambilla, J. Cabot, and M. Wimmer. "Model-Driven Software Engineering in Practice," Synthesis Lectures on Software Engineering, Morgan & Claypool Publishers, pp. 30, 2012.

[8] M. Sacco, P. Pedrazzoli, W. Terkaj, "VFF: Virtual Factory Framework: Key Enabler for Future manufacturing," In Proceedings of ICE – 16th International Confernce on Concurrent Enterprising, Lugano, Svizzera, pp. 83-90, 2010.

[9] L. Monostori, "Cyber-physical Production Systems: Roots, Expectations and R&D Challenges," Procedia CIRP, vol. 17, pp. 9-13, 2014, ISSN 2212-8271

[10] J. Jaeho, C. Ingeol, and K. Wontae, "Metamodel-based CPS Modeling Tool," Lecture Notes in Electrical Engineering (LNEE), vol. 181, pp.285–291, 2015.

The ReBorn Marketplace: an Application Store for Industrial Smart Components

Renato Fonseca, Susana Aguiar, Michael Peschl, Gil Gonçalves

Institute for Systems and Robotics
Faculty of Engineering of University of Porto
Porto, Portugal
Email: {ee10264, saguiar, gil}@fe.up.pt
Harms&Wende
Germany
Email: michael.peschl@hwh-karlsruhe.de

Abstract—**Rapid changing product portfolios and continuously evolving process technologies require manufacturing systems that are themselves easily upgradeable and into which new technologies and functions can be readily integrated. This new context creates the need for novel manufacturing equipment and control systems able to cope with the increased complexity, required to manage product and production variability in mass customized manufacturing. To achieve this agility modern manufacturing environments need to encapsulate knowledge into sensors and machines, turning them into Smart Components. Based on the concept of logical encapsulation of manufacturing industrial equipment, this paper proposes the creation of a marketplace for Smart Components. This marketplace organises and stores information of industrial machines, not only for potential customers to check and compare different devices, but essentially to allow for (semi)automatic update of the industrial equipment controllers and functionalities on the fly.**

***Keywords*—Smart Components; Smart Components Application Store; Intelligent Manufacturing Environments; Manufacturing Systems; Industrial Equipment Re-usability; ReBorn Paradigm.**

I. Introduction

Increasingly, traditional top-down and centralized process planning, scheduling and control mechanisms are becoming insufficient to respond to the constant variability in high-mix low-volume production environments. These traditional centralized hierarchical approaches limit the adaptability, contributing to a reduced resilience of the system, as well as to reduced flexibility in planning and longer response times. The ability of manufacturing system, on all the functional and organizational levels, to reconfigure itself in order to quickly adjust production capabilities and capacities in response to sudden changes in the market or in the regulatory environment is nowadays a major requirement.

In order to respond to the current industrial environment requirements, the development of a **Marketplace for Smart Components** is proposed. The proposed marketplace organises and stores information of industrial machines, so potential customers can check and compare different devices from a broad perspective, as well as providing a web interface that allows users to insert and change equipment information. Additionally, the marketplace provides tools for integrating interfaces and systems used by the equipment manufacturers to easily update controllers firmware and equipment functionalities.

The concept of the Marketplace for Smart Components was first introduced and discussed within the scope of the European project **ReBorn**. The vision of ReBorn is to demonstrate strategies and technologies that support a new paradigm for the re-use of production equipment in factories. This re-use will give new life to decommissioned production systems and equipment, helping them to be reborn in new production lines. Such new strategies will contribute to sustainable, resource-friendly green manufacturing and, at the same time, deliver economic and competitive advantages for the manufacturing sector. ReBorn will make significant step towards 100% re-use of equipment focusing its approach on three main areas: modular Plug&Produce equipment, in-line adaptive manufacturing, innovative factory layout design techniques and adaptive (re)configuration, flexible and low-cost mechanical systems for fast and easy assembly and disassembly.

This paper is organized as follows. In section II, a literature review is presented, with a discussion regarding the current state of the art in manufacturing systems, electronic platforms and services. Section III, presents the needs and problem definition, followed by the concept and solution in Section IV. Section V describes a sample implementation of the proposed solution and section VI concludes the paper by exposing some final remarks about the implemented solution and next steps for future work are identified.

II. State of the Art and Related Work

This section presents a short overview of the state of the art in areas related with the work described in this paper. Related work is reported from the areas of manufacturing systems, platforms and services.

A. Manufacturing Systems

The manufacturing enterprises of the 21st century are in an environment in which market demand is frequently changing, new technologies are continuously emerging, and competition is global. Manufacturing strategies should therefore shift to support global competitiveness, new product innovation and customization, and rapid market responsiveness. The next generation manufacturing systems will thus be more strongly time-oriented (or highly responsive), while still focusing on cost and quality.

Such manufacturing systems will need to satisfy a number of fundamental requirements [1], including amongst other: full integration of heterogeneous software and hardware systems; capacity to accommodate new subsystems (software, hardware, peopleware) or dismantle existing subsystems on the fly.

Next, a few approaches that intend to fulfill these requirements are described.

*1) **Networked Factories**:* Modern Industries have a continuous need to satisfy their markets at better costs in order to keep competitive. This simple fact creates the continuous need for new products, new production lines and new control methodologies. The XPRESS (FleXible PRoduction Experts for reconfigurable aSSembly technology) project [4], a cooperative European project involving industry and academia studied this issue in order to define a new flexible production concept. This concept, based on specialized intelligent process units, is able to integrate a complete process chain, and includes support for production configuration, multi-variant production lines and 100% quality monitoring.

*2) **Reconfigurable Manufacturing Systems**:* Reconfigurability has been an issue in computing and robotics for many years. In general, reconfigurability is the ability to repeatedly change and rearrange the components of a system in a cost-effective way.

According to [5] it is possible to define a Reconfigurable Manufacturing Systems **(RMS)** as being designed at the outset far rapid change in structure, as well as in hardware and software components, in order to quickly adjust production capacity and functionality in response to sudden changes in market or in regulatory requirements.

Furthermore, Merhabi *et al.* [6] complement this definition with the notion that reconfiguration allows adding, as well as removing or modifying specific process capabilities, controls, software, or machine structure. This reconfiguration aims at improving or upgrading the existing manufacturing systems or its components, rather than promoting its replacement.

RMS are seen as a cost-effective response to market changes, that tries to combine the high throughput of dedicated production with the flexibility of flexible manufacturing systems **(FMS)**, and is also able to react to changes quickly and efficiently. For this to be accomplished, the system and its machines have to be adapted for an adjustable structure that enables system scalability in response to market demands and system/machine adaptability to new products. RMS are composed of reconfigurable machines and open architecture reconfigurable control systems to produce variety of parts with family relationships. Structure may be adjusted at the system level (e.g., adding/removing machines) and at the machine level (changing machine hardware, control software or parameters).

Intelligent Reconfigurable Machines, Smart Plug&Produce and the extensive integration of sensors - in line with the Cyber Physical Systems (CPS) and Internet of Things (IoT) concepts - are becoming more and more present in the industrial shopfloor [11] [12]. Monitoring the current machines process state, and increasing shop-floor analysis, enables rapid decision making according to the production system demands.

B. Platforms

According to Smedlund and Faghankhani [2], it is possible to define a platform as:

Definition 1: Any physical or virtual space where different participants compose a market and a platform that participants orchestrate can be defined as a platform.

Platforms are composed of onion-like multilayered structures in which the technological core element is necessary for complementary technologies that in turn provide ground for software. It is possible to identify a wide range of different types of platforms based on the nature of interactions between its participants. There are, for instance, platforms that aim to help members of some participant group find a match in another group, platforms that bring sellers and buyers together, platforms that measure transactions between participants, and platforms where participants share their input with other participants.

Definition 2: Any virtual or physical venue that enables all participating groups to co-create and co-capture value by interactions which result in offering a system of products, services or both.

Depending on the number of participating groups, platforms make a one-sided, two-sided or multi-sided market possible. In n-sided platforms, which include social media platforms and smartphone ecosystems, the users connect to each other, communicate and co-create value for themselves and for the other users and participants. The user is no longer a passive recipient and object of value delivery, but active co-creator of value. This means that in order to fully benefit from platform offering, the end-user must give something back to the platform.

Platforms are evolving systems capable of adaptation. They can be expanded by either building upon new components or connecting to other systems, or other platforms. After reaching a certain threshold of momentum in the number of participants and relationships between them, platforms develop in an evolutionary manner (i.e. random variation, selection and retention processes). An evolutionary attribute is necessary because it allows the platform to maintain its current participants and simultaneously attract new ones.

Platforms create a network of relationships among the participants. Smedlund and Faghankhan describe and identify two different trajectories on which networks are formed: **Goal-Directedness** and **Serendipity**. In goal-directed networks, the participants see themselves as a part of network committed to some common goal. The network is formed to achieve this goal. In serendipitous networking, there is no preexisting goal, and the network develops in an evolutionary manner.

1) Platform Participants: Platform participant groups include **End-Users**, **Platform Owners**, **Platform Providers**, **Complementors** and **Orchestrators**. For instance, when taking a look at a generic social media network model, Smedlund *et. al* proceeds to describe and identify the mentioned participant groups. The user account holders are the **End-Users**, which can also be called the demand side. **Platform Owners** are the entity which in turn owns the social media network, they can be easily differentiated from the other participant groups as they hold the technological solution for the system that defines its evolution. **Platform Providers** can be exemplified as Internet access providers. Their role is to play the part of an intermediary between a user and the platform, by doing so they become the primary contact points of the platforms end-users. **Complementors** are a platform participant with the ability to add value to the platform itself, they offer complementary services or products to the value proposition of the platform, and they comprise the supply side of the platform. Complementors can be labeled according to the complement they provide to the platform, by doing so its then possible to differentiate them in different segments. Regarding social media networks, a complementor might be an application developer or for instance an advertiser.

It is then important to identify a focal actor, who strives to uphold the platform standards, as well as maintaining its integrity and its evolution according to the industry vision. This focal actor, has been referred to by different terms in different studies, as stated by Smedlund *et. al* it is possible to define this central role as the platform **Orchestrator**.

C. Services

Service activities across industries are now widely recognized. Information and Communication Technology **(ICT)** powered evolution of services is one of the main sources of modern economic growth. Business logic has evolved from the product-dominant logic into service-dominant logic [3]. According to this new business logic, services are conceptualized as processes (rather than something that produces a unit output) and its dynamics are driven by resources, such as knowledge and skills. In this new mindset, value is now understood as a collaborative process between providers and consumers.

The mobile phone industry has revolutionized the way consumers look at a simple phone. Mobile phones have transcended their original form, and through mobile information and communication technology, they have long past surpassed the form of a telephone. Instead, it is now evolving into a platform like format, where it is possible to develop a broad variety of complementary innovations. These surges of platform-like services have now imprinted a heavy mark on todays society and completely changed the recent social interaction format as well as affecting a broad variety of business models and approaches. Mobile internet, e-mail, personal productivity tools, entertainment services, such as games, music, and mobile TV, are all examples of platform oriented services.

Platform as a Service **(PaaS)**, are continuously gaining importance as n-sided markets, offering Software as a Service **(SaaS)** to the respective platform participants. PaaS are bound to co-habit ecosystems with users and autonomous SaaS suppliers. In order to be successful an attempt is made to shape the ecosystems form according to the platforms basic value proposition, and control the service quality according to the users requirements.

III. ReBorn Marketplace Concept & Solution

This section describes the ReBorn Marketplace **(RBM)**. Starting from a motivation example from an industrial component supplier, the concept for the marketplace and its requirements are elicited. The proposed solution is also discussed in this section.

A. Component Supplier Needs & Problem Definition

Component Suppliers play an important part of in the deployment of any production line. They feature control and monitoring systems for all kinds of operations and processes, as well as specialized individual process solutions. Harms&Wende **(HWH)** is a component supplier specialized in welding control systems for various sectors. Harms&Wende customers often are welding machines manufacturers who use the Harms&Wende welding control units. They offer resistance welding equipment in form of control devices, quality assurance systems and complete packages to well-known machine construction companies. Once these components are integrated in a production line, they face however a major implication.

Nowadays production line systems, thanks to the highly competitive industrial environment, are required to be highly flexible. Flexibility directly translates into production systems that need to be easy to update, and in which new technologies and new functions can be quickly integrated. However, that is not the case in the current industrial standard, from a component supplier perspective, offering additional component features and technologies in the form of services is not yet the usual practice.

B. The ReBorn Marketplace Concept

RBM will offer its services in an online platform format, as a platform as a system (PaaS). PaaS enables the creation of an evolving market between actors who would not connect on their own without the platform. PaaS comprises different participant groups, making a multi-sided market possible.

Fig. 1, depicts the RBM platform participants.

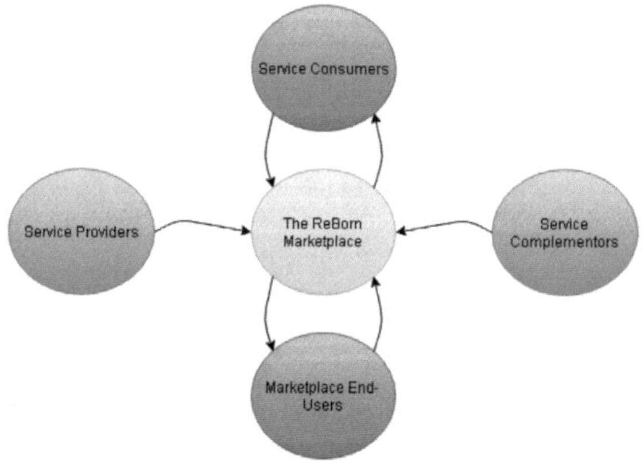

Fig. 1. The ReBorn Marketplace Platform Participants

The RBM is a n-sided market, with service providers on one end and service consumers on the other. This will attract service suppliers in order to respond to the demand side of the platform. The demand side, in the marketplace, is comprised of any potential **End-User** to the platform offerings. **Service Consumers** comprise the marketplace participants which mainly relate to the RBM service offerings. The Marketplace **Service Suppliers** can normally be instantiated by any entity capable of offering its services to the platform while altogether adding value to the platforms base proposition. Service Suppliers are industrial machine builders who provide equipment, as well as equipment information, functionalities (software), and operations. Entities capable of providing complementing services to the platform, in order to co-create value, are labelled as **Complementors**. These can be for instance independent software developers that provide additional equipment functionalities.

1) RBM Case Application: Original Equipment Manufacturers **(OEM)**, constitute a major segment of the marketplaces end-users. When considering OEM as a potential platform end-user, some forethought is needed. As stated previously, the RBM attempts to implement a marketplace solution that is adequate to a wide spectrum of platform end-users. As such, it must be able to cope with multiple application scenarios for any type of production system and factory environment.

When considering that each major OEM entity in the industrial market potentially has a different set amount of production facilities, each of them having a varied amount of production lines, the marketplace when offering its services must satisfy a huge variety of needs and requirements. Also, production facilities from the same OEM can differ greatly. Although they fall under the same company, they can possibly follow different business model approaches, quality inspection guidelines, and for instance factory floor communications protocols. Todays industrial environment is characterised by a lack of business models standardization, which means that each production facility acts uniquely and in independently of each other, while altogether engaging in a highly competitive environment.

In order to test the ReBorns online marketplace on a factory floor, its necessary to take some considerations into account. Usually production lines equipments are closed off to outside networks, which in turn makes any information flow from the inside of the factory plant to the outside an impossibility. Fig. 2 depicts the RBM OEM Case Application.

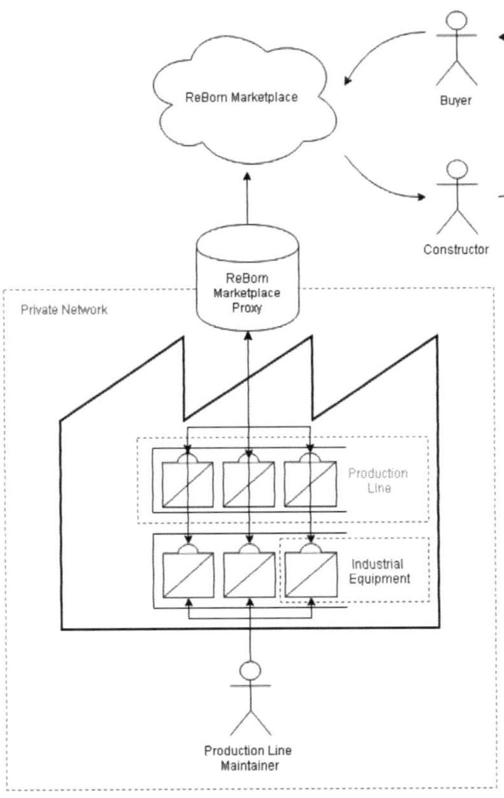

Fig. 2. The ReBorn Marketplace OEM Case Application

The local marketplace attempts to act as an exact copy of the ReBorns marketplace online solution, but instead of being hosted online it is instead hosted on a private network, accessible only to its participants. The local marketplace would employ all the features and available services provided by the original ReBorn online platform. The local marketplace acts as a proxy of the ReBorn marketplace. The local marketplace from a platform perspective acts as a two dimensional platform. Serving in one side each industrial equipment from the factory floor, and on the other side the online ReBorn marketplace. Having identified the local marketplace participants, it is important to discuss how the local marketplace interacts with the online platform.

One could consider the local marketplace to possess direct communication with the online platform, serving as a bridge between the industrial equipments private network and the ReBorn marketplace. On the other hand if the information flow between the local marketplace and the ReBorn marketplace to an outside environment will be strictly enforced the local marketplace can consider being manually updated, in order to have the latest software content made available by the online platform.

The later approach requires the local marketplace to be managed locally. The update batch is made available by the ReBorn marketplace, and then needs to be manually inserted into the local marketplace. The two approaches have very different results, whilst the first approach instantly updates the local marketplace with new content, the second approach requires that the local marketplace manager is notified of the available update batch. Only then he is able to proceed with the update operation. This means that industrial equipment would continue to work with out of date software for a longer period of time, which might be critical for the production line. In the worst case scenario, if a defect is found in an industrial equipment software version and the only available solution refers to a new solution contained by a software update batch yet to be implemented on the local market, this could possibly mean that the production would have to be put on hold until the solution is implemented.

C. Problem Solution

The solution of the problem stated above is framed in the scope of the **ReBorn European project** - Innovative Reuse of modular knowledge Based devices and technologies for Old, Renewed and New factories - and its main purpose is study and implement a **Marketplace for Smart Components**, where the information related to industrial equipment is provided in a standardized way in order to make its use in the planning process of production lines easier and promote the re-use of equipment.

The main features to be developed in this project include also the creation of a solution to integrate the virtualization of the shop-floor equipment directly into the Marketplace. This integration must provide different information access control levels, as well as organize all the information at the cloud level.

The RBM aims to provide a pioneering service that is yet to be seen in the current industrial environment. One of the marketplace services key features is providing interfaces with tools and systems used by the industry, in an application format. From an industrial environment perspective, equipment update or actualization is mainly done at a software level.

Each production equipment is represented by a cyber-physical entity called **Verson**. Versons act as logical encapsulation entities, which store and analyse information, enabling industrial equipment to perform dynamic and highly specialized tasks. It is through specific applications stored in the Verson, that these highly specialized tasks are made possible. The Versons modular architecture allows for individual component management at shop floor level, with a modular plug in and plug out application format. The Verson like product equipment is accompanied by a functional platform. The **Verson Platform** acts as an interface for the integration of the applications provided by the RBM, as well as a service handler for its requests.

An **Open-Source E-commerce Shopping Cart Solution** is used as the RBM platform base. Additionally, the RBM provides the Verson product equipment all the required application content, through a series of **Web Services** which follow a **RESTful Architecture**.

The RBM makes application management at a Verson level possible, as it provides the Verson with a broad variety of applications which feature a wide range of functionalities. By offering industrial equipment update on production runtime, the RBM makes industrial equipment monitoring, upgrading and refurbishment a reality.

IV. SOLUTION IMPLEMENTATION & VALIDATION

The RBM includes a key set of features that are aligned with the new ReBorn paradigm. These features are directly related to the application management services implemented by the Versons and by the RBM. The application management service, as stated previously, aims to locally manage the application content of each equipment's Verson, while the equipment is installed in a production line. In the following section, the implementation process and the validation scenario of the marketplace application management services are described.

The communication between a Verson device and the ReBorn Marketplace online platform was developed to demonstrate the application management service offered by the RBM. A Verson product was provided for requirement validation and testing. Fig. 3 depicts the applied test setup.

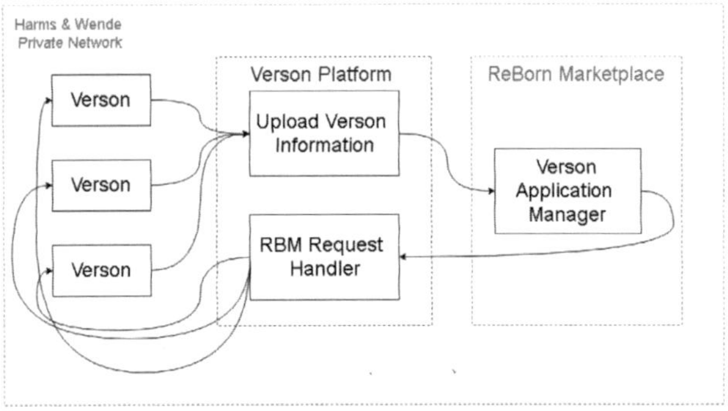

Fig. 3. REST Service Testing with HWH

The Verson acts as a logical encapsulation entity of the production lines equipment, which is responsible for collecting, storing and analysing information. The Verson extension of production equipment is realized on a dedicated hardware platform to enable an easy implementation of the concept. A **RaspBerry Pi** SBC was used for this purpose in the sample implementation.

By means of the Verson platform it is possible to see the Verson's currently installed device applications. The same platform allows to initiate a request, which portrays an application update nature, to the RBM. The Verson's applications serve a multipurpose nature. Through them it was possible to display the equipment status, information and statistics, alongside the current conditions on which the equipment is working. The applications developed by the ReBorn project were developed in **PHP**. Each application consisted of two PHP files and a .dat file. The RBM in turn is responsible to provide all the application content necessary to each request performed by the Verson through the Verson Platform.

In order to establish communication between the Verson and the RBM, the project solution was published on the HWH local server as the provided Verson equipment is restricted to the local private network.

In accordance to the system requirements, the Verson acts as a mediator between the industrial equipment and the ReBorn Marketplace. Requests made to the ReBorn platform are handled by a REST based web service. The ReBorn Marketplace is in turn responsible for providing the latest application content on demand to the Verson equipment.

V. CONCLUSION & FUTURE WORK

The work presented in this paper only scratches the surface of a vast subject. By describing and demonstrating the solution for run-time (software) update and reconfiguration of industrial equipment, it highlights the underlining conditions of a real life application of the RBM.

The ReBorn Marketplace concept discussed in the paper is a potential solution adequate to different types of production systems. By managing the Versons application content, through the ReBorn Marketplace services, it is possible to integrate new technologies and functionalities in industrial equipment on the fly.

The Versons modular architecture allows for plug-in and plug-out application management. However, some considerations have to be made in order to apply it to a real industrial scenario. Applications can be easily installed and removed from a Verson like equipment, but it is necessary to understand if they are independent within the system architecture. Cross dependencies between applications further increase the complexity and create new challenges for the platforms application content management services.

Business and service models are also important for the industrial uptake of such a solution. One of the crucial points relates to the identification of the liable subject. The currently implemented solution, when considering the platforms application management service offerings, requires the Production Line Maintainer to individually access each industrial equipment in order to perform requests to the ReBorn Marketplace platform: application update, install, and remove. In this case, the Production Line Maintainer takes full liability of the newly integrated (or removed) application content, in case the application features are not up to the production lines standards and requirements. This approach when applied to a standard OEM production line, which might contain hundreds of Versons, is unpractical. Individually accessing each Verson in order to proceed with maintenance operations is not a viable approach.

Considering automated application maintenance operations at the Verson individual level, whenever new software content is released and or whenever the new application licenses are made available, sets new requirements for the RBM.

Further developments of the RBM include offering automated maintenance services as well as system restore service, that cover possible unpredictable outcomes of upgrading and installing new software content.

ACKNOWLEDGMENT

This research was partially supported by the ReBORN project (FoF.NMP.2013-2) Innovative Reuse of modular knowledge Based devices and technologies for Old, Renewed and New factories funded by the European Commission under the Seventh Framework Program for Research and Technological Development. We would like to thank all partners for their support and discussions that contributed to these results.

REFERENCES

[1] W. Shen, Q. Hao, H. J. Yoon, and D. H. Norrie. "Applications of agent-based systems in intelligent manufacturing: An updated review." Advanced engineering Informatics, vol. 20, no. 4, pp. 415–431, 2006.

[2] A. Smedlund and H. Faghankhani. "Platform orchestration for efficiency, development, and innovation." 48th IEEE Hawaii International Conference on System Sciences (HICSS), pp 1380–1388, 2015.

[3] V. K. Tuunainen and T. Tuunanen. "Iisin-a model for analyzing ICT intensive service innovations in n-sided markets." 44th IEEE Hawaii International Conference on System Sciences (HICSS), pages 1–10, 2011.

[4] F. Almeida, P. Dias, G. Gonçalves, M. Peschl, and M. Hoffmeister. "A proposition of a manufactronic network approach for intelligent and flexible manufacturing systems." International Journal of Industrial Engineering Computations, vol. 2, no. 4, pp. 873–890, 2011.

[5] Y. Koren, U. Heisel, F. Jovane, T. Moriwaki, G. Pritschow, G. Ulsoy, and H. Van Brussel. "Reconfigurable Manufacturing Systems." CIRP Annals-Manufacturing Technology, vol. 48, no. 2, pp. 527–540, 1999.

[6] M. Mehrabi, A. Ulsoy, Y. Koren, and P. Heytler. "Trends and perspectives in flexible and reconfigurable manufacturing systems." Journal of Intelligent manufacturing, vol. 13, no. 2, pp. 135–146, 2002.

[7] N. A. Duffie and R. S. Piper. "Non-hierarchical control of a flexible manufacturing cell." "Robotics and computer-integrated manufacturing", vol. 3, no. 2, pp. 175–179, 1987.

[8] H. Parunak, A. D. Baker, and S. J. Clark. "The AARIA agent architecture: From manufacturing requirements to agent-based system design." Integrated Computer-Aided Engineering, vol. 8, no. 1, pp. 45–58, 2001.

[9] H. Parunak, J. F. White, P. W. Lozo, R. Judd, B. W. Irish, and J. Kindrick. "An architecture for heuristic factory control." IEEE American Control Conference, pp. 548–558, 1986.

[10] H. V. Brussel, J. Wyns, P. Valckenaers, L. Bongaerts, and P. Peeters. "Reference architecture for holonic manufacturing systems: PROSA." Computers in industry, vol. 37, no. 3, pp. 255–274, 1998.

[11] G. Gonçalves, J. Reis, R. Pinto, M. Alves, and J. Correia. "A step forward on Intelligent Factories: A Smart Sensor-oriented approach." IEEE Emerging Technology and Factory Automation (ETFA), pp. 1–8, 2014

[12] M. Peschl, N. Link, M. Hoffmeister, G. Gonçalves, F. Almeida. "Designing and implementation of an intelligent manufacturing system." Journal of Industrial Engineering and Management, vol. 4, no. 4, pp. 718–745, 2011.

Optimizing Network Calls by Minimizing Variance in Data Availability Times

Luis Neto[1], Henrique Lopes Cardoso[2], Carlos Soares[3], Gil Gonçalves[4]
{lcneto, hlc, csoares, gil}@fe.up.pt
Faculdade de Engenharia, Universidade do Porto, Porto, Portugal
[14]ISR-P, Instituto de Sistemas e Robótica - Porto, Portugal
[2]LIACC, Laboratório de Inteligência Artificial e Ciência de Computadores, Porto, Portugal
[3]INESC TEC, Instituto de Engenharia de Sistemas e Computadores, Tecnologia e Ciência, Porto, Portugal

***Abstract*—Smart Nodes are intelligent components of sensor networks that perform data acquisition and treatment, by the virtualization of sensor instances. Smart Factories are an application domain in which dozens of these cyber-physical components are used, flooding the network with messages. In this work, we present a methodology to reduce the number of calls a Smart Node makes to the network. We propose grouping individual communications within a Smart Node to reduce the number of calls is important to improve the efficiency of the process. The paper exposes and explains the Smart Node internal structure, formally describing the problem of minimizing the number of calls Smart Nodes make to Cloud Services, by means of a combinatorial *Constraint Optimization Problem*. Using two *Constraint Satisfaction Solvers*, we have addressed the problem using distinct approaches. Optimal and sub-optimal solutions for an actual problem instance have been found with both approaches. Furthermore, we present a comparison between both solvers in terms of computational efficiency and show the solution is feasible to apply in a real case scenario.**

Keywords–Sensor Simulation; Combinatorial Optimization; Time Synchronization; Smart Nodes; Industrial Wireless Sensor Networks.

I. INTRODUCTION

Wireless Sensor Networks (WSN) consist of sensors sparsely distributed over a given area to sense physical properties, such as luminosity, temperature, current, etc. They are composed of sensor nodes which pass data until a destination gateway is reached. Common applications are industrial and environment sensing, where they can be used to perceive the state of a machine and prevent natural disasters, respectively. Gateways in WSN play a preponderant role, since they acquire data from the sensors, do pre-processing and in more advanced cases are responsible to send the data to cloud systems for advanced processing. A Smart Node is a gateway that has enhanced data processing, reconfiguration and collaborative capabilities [1]. These components are nodes in Industrial Cyber Physical Systems, wich operate and control *Industrial Wireless Sensor Networks*. Considering a scenario that comprises a reasonable number of these components, in which:

- Gateways are in constant synchronization with Intra/Inter Enterprise Cloud systems.
- Gateways perform collaborative tasks by talking over the network.
- Human Machine Interface devices proceed to on demand requests to the Smart Nodes.

A large number of messages is expected generated by a large number of devices and services.

Gateways collect data from different sensor types (eg: humidity, current, pressure). These cyber-physical components are coupled to industrial machines, along with several sensors, which collect data about the operation of machines; finally, the data collected is treated and synchronized with Cloud systems for multiple purposes. The majority of sensors coupled to industrial machines sample data at very different rates and synchronize the collected data with the Smart Node, in the respective sampling frequency. A Smart Node can embed a set of different data treatment modules. These modules can be instantiated to provide different ways of treating sensor data in a way that can be represented as a graph (Fig. 1). A gateway internal logic arrangement is represented using a *directed acyclic graph (DAG)*. The graph structure in Fig. 1 can be divided into three levels, each with a different label and color assignment: the Sensor Level includes sensor instances (bottom level), providing data to the gateway; the data treatment level (middle level), includes nodes representing instances of algorithms embedded at the gateway that can treat information in several ways (eg: aggregate data using mean or other functions, perform trend analysis); the Network Level (top level) includes nodes where the flow resulting from the lower level nodes can be redirected to subscribing hosts in the network. This internal structure can be dynamically rearranged: new sensors and data modules can be loaded into the Smart Node; the connections between nodes can be reformulated to synchronize and treat data in new ways.

A problem of efficiency emerges due to the different rates at which the data is gathered from the different sensors. When the data reaches the Network Level nodes, it is immediately sent to the subscriber, a network Cloud service. Slight time differences in the availability of data lead the Network Level nodes to perform new and individual calls. If those time differences were eliminated, Network Level nodes would be synchronized and data from the different nodes could be packed together, reducing the total number of calls made and reducing the network traffic heavily. To accomplish synchronization among Network Level nodes, data buffers for all the

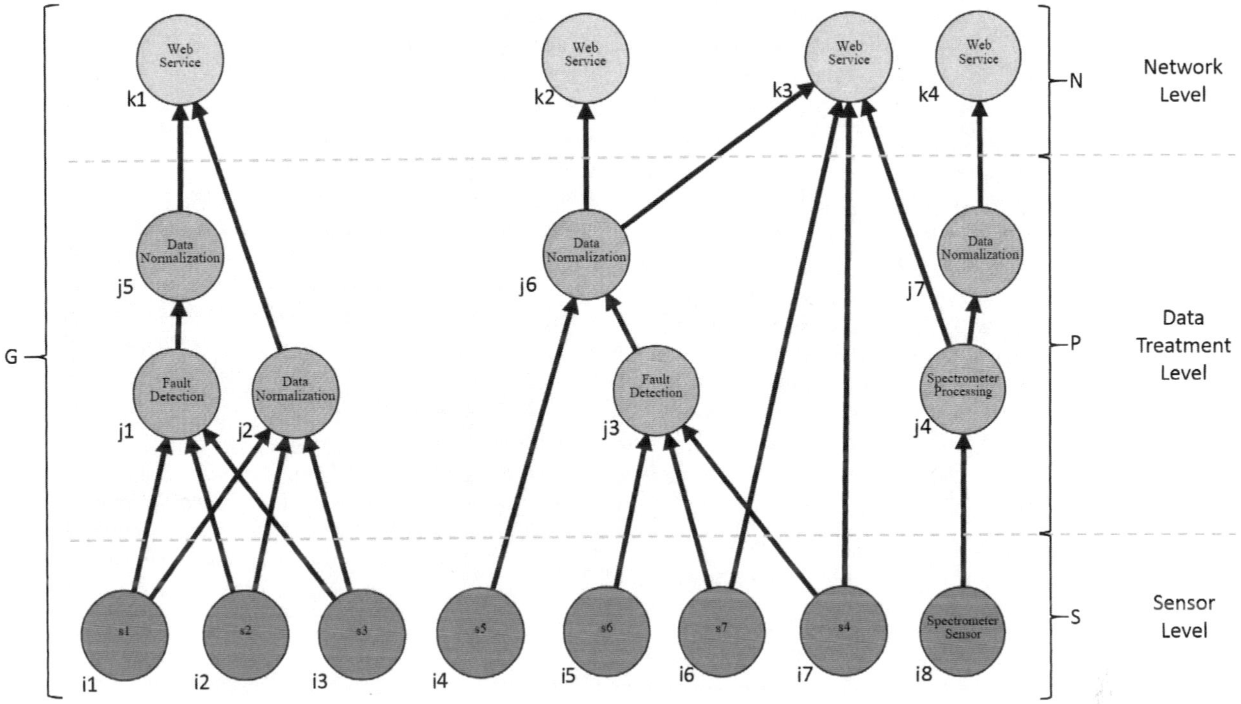

Figure 1. Internal Gateway configuration.

edges connecting nodes previous to a particular Network node must be resized to compensate: (1) different time to process data by Data Treatment level nodes, since each module takes different time to process data; (2) different sampling rates of sensors, a same number of samples is accumulated at different times.

Taking advantage of the DAG representation of the gateway, we formulate and propose a solution to the problem as a combinatorial *Constraint Optimization Problem.*

In Section II, a formal definition of the problem is presented. Section III shows literature review, the problem formulation basis. In Section IV, the solving process is detailed along with assumptions, constraints and technology that has been used. In Sections IV and V, respectively, collected results and conclusions are presented.

II. PROBLEM DEFINITION

Each arc in the graph (see Fig. 1) has an associated buffer $b_{n,m}$. Given the fact that sensors are sampling at different frequencies $freq$, these buffers are filled at different rates. We define G as the set of nodes in a particular Gateway instance; three subsets of nodes are contained in $G : N \subset G$ is the subset of Network Nodes (index k nodes); $P \subset G$ is the subset of data Processing Nodes (index j nodes); $S \subset G$ is the subset of Sensor Nodes (index i nodes). The subsets obey to the following conditions:

$$G = N \cup P \cup S; N \cap P = \emptyset; P \cap S = \emptyset; N \cap S = \emptyset \quad (1)$$

Nodes in N can be classified as consumers; nodes in S are exclusively producers; nodes in P are both producers and consumers. Edges between nodes can be defined as:

$$e_{n,m} = \begin{cases} 1 \text{ if } n \text{ is consumer of } m : n \neq m; \\ \quad m \in P \cup S \text{ and } n \in N \cup P \\ \quad 0 \text{ otherwise} \end{cases} \quad (2)$$

As an example, we can observe in Fig. 1 that node j_6 consumes from i_4 (Sensor Level) and j_3 which is in same level (Processing Level) and all the k nodes (Network Level) only consume from inferior levels. To help in the definition of this problem, two additional subsets of nodes, containing the connections of a given node, are defined as follows:

$$W_n = \{j : j \in P \wedge e_{n,j} = 1\}, n \in N \cup P \quad (3)$$

Equation 3 defines a subset of nodes in P, which are producers for the given node $n \in N \cup P$. As an example (Fig. 1), for $n = j_6 : W_{j_6} = \{j_3\}$; for $n = k_3 : W_{k_3} = \{j_6, j_4\}$; and for $n = j_3 : W_{j_3} = \emptyset$ since it does not consume from any Data Processing nodes.

$$X_n = \{i : i \in S \wedge x_{n,i} = 1\}, n \in N \cup P \quad (4)$$

Equation 4 defines a subset of nodes in S, which are producers for the given node $n \in N \cup P$. In Fig. 1, these are the nodes i in the Sensor Level, from which Processing Level nodes and Network Level nodes consume. As an example (Fig. 1), for

$n = k_3 : X_{k_3} = \{i_6, i_7\}$; for $n = k_1 : W_{k_1} = \emptyset$ since it does not consume from any Sensor Level node and for $n = j_6$: $W_{j_6} = \{i_4\}$.
A processing node in P applies an algorithm to transform the data coming from its associated producers. The data generated at the sensor level is delivered to the processing nodes as a batch, which contains the number of samples equal to the size of the buffer for the corresponding edge.

In order to the processing to be possible, the number of elements in each collection must be the same. This constraint must be applied to the subsets W_n and X_n of a given node n in $N \cup P$, respectively; for that constraint to be respected, the size of every buffer associated to each element in $W_n \cup X_n$ must be the same. Formally this constraint can be represented as:

$$\forall n \in N \cup P, \forall m \in W_n \cup X_n : |b_{n,m}| = f(n) \quad (5)$$

Where $|b_{n,m}|$ represents the size of the given buffer for the given edge $e_{n,m}$ and $f(n)$ is the size of any buffer from which node n consumes.
The size of the buffer is adjustable and can vary from 1 to 1000. The objective of this problem is to arrange a combination of values to parameterize the size of every buffer $|b|$, for every arc in the graph, that minimizes the differences between times at the Network Nodes in which data is available to be sent to the network. To calculate the time that it takes data to be available at every node $k \in N$, the times for all its providers in the graph must be calculated. As data comes in collections (sets of single values), let us define *burst* as the exact time at which data is sent from one provider node to a consumer node and represent the *burst* of a node n as B_n.
The *burst* of a Sensor Node i, is defined by the product of its sampling frequency and the size of the buffer associated to the edge $e_{n,i}$ we are assuming. That way, every time a sample from a sensor is collected, that sample is sent to all consumers of that sensor. A *burst* of a Sensor Node to an adjacent consumer node m occurs when the buffer for the edge $e_{i,m}$ is completely filled, and is formally represented by the expression:

$$B_{i,m} = freq(i) \times |b_{i,m}| \times e_{i,m} = 1; \forall i \in S \wedge m \in P \cup N \quad (6)$$

For a Data Processing Node, the burst time must contemplate all the burst times from its providers, the time that it takes the associated function $T(f(n))$ to treat one data sample and the size of the buffer associated to the edge $e_{n,m}$ we are assuming. The expression which determines burst time for a Data Processing Node j to a consumer node m is defined as:

$$B_{j,m} = (\max_{i \in W_j \cup X_j}(B_{i,j}) + T(f_j) \times (|W_j| + |X_j|)) \times |b_{j,m}|; e_{j,m} = 1 \quad (7)$$

We assume that the growth in time complexity of the function $T(f_n) : n \in P$ is linear with the number of samples to process. Since the size of each producer buffer is equal, we multiply the total number of producers of j by the cost of treating a single sample. To calculate the *burst* for j_1 (see Fig. 1), we take the max *burst* of X_{j_1} and sum the product of $T(f_{j_1})$ (time to process one sensor sample) with the number of elements in X_{j_1} (which corresponds to the producers i_1, i_2 and i_3).
Finally, to calculate the *burst* of a Network Node $k \in N$:

$$B_k = \max_{i \in X_k \cup W_k} (B_{i,k}) \quad (8)$$

Using the expression to calculate the *burst* for each Network Node, the objective is to minimize the variance of *burst* for all the Network Nodes and minimize buffer sizes. By varying the size of the buffers in the graph, the variance of all burst times for Network Nodes and the summation of all buffer sizes are minimized. With a variance of zero or closer, data from different Network Nodes can be packed in the same payload and sent to the subscribers in the network. Even if the quantity of data exceeds the maximum payload size for the protocol or the physical link being used, the number of connections needed is far less than it is in independent calls. The number of buffers $|P \cup N|$, times an upper bound buffer size of 1000 is multiplyed by the variance. This way, the variance has more impact in the search of an optimal solution than the summation of all buffer sizes.

$$\hat{V}(B_k) \times 1000 \times |P \cup N| + \sum_{n \in |P \cup N|} \sum_{m \in W_n \cup X_n} |bn, m| \quad (9)$$

As follows from Equation 9, minimizing variance of burst times for network nodes is the major concern. To reflect this, variance is multiplied by the maximum possible size for a buffer (1000, which is a reasonable number of samples for a sensor), times the number of Processing and Network nodes. This will drive the solver to focus on a solution with less variance, and break ties by considering the minimal buffer sizes (as these incur a cost). With a variance of 0 for the bursts at the Network Level nodes, all data produced can be sent to the cloud using the same call. If variance is higher than 0, a threshold must be used to decide the maximum reasonable time to wait between bursts. In comparison with individual calls strategy – a call made every time a burst at the Network Level occurs – the number of calls to the cloud is minimized as a consequence. The theoretical search space of the problem is E^n, where E represents the total number of edges in the graph and $n = 1000$ is the *Buffer Size* domain upper bound. The real search space, imposed by the constraint of the Equation 5, can be determined by F^n, where $F = |P| + |N|$ is the total number of Processing and Network nodes in the graph.

III. Related Work

The theoretical background behind this problem has a large spectrum of application. The problem of modeling buffer sizes is mostly applied to network routing, where the works [2],[3] and [4] are examples. As we are not interested in dealing with networks intrinsic characteristics, those buffer optimization problems can hardly be extrapolated to this work. The domain of Wireless Sensor Networks (WSN) is another scope of application of buffer modeling optimization, with relevant literature in this domain; the section of *Routing* problems in [5] covers a great number of important works regarding Flow Based optimization models, for data aggregation and routing problems. WSN optimization models care with constraints that this problem modulation does not cover, such as: residual energy of nodes, link properties, network lifetime, network organization and routing strategies.

A relevant work in WSN revealed to be of the major interest for this work. The authors presented and solved the problem of removing inconsistent time offsets, in time synchronization protocols for WSN [6]. The problem presented has an high degree of similarity with the case we are dealing. The problem is represented by a *Time Difference Graph (TDG)*, each node is a sensor, every sensor has local time and every arc has an associated cost time given by a function. The solution to the problem is given by a Constraint Satisfaction Problem (CSP approach. For every arc in the graph there exists an *adjustment variable* (analogous to the buffer size in this case), assignments are made to the variables to find the largest consistent subgraph, ie. a sub-graph in which inconsistent time offsets are eliminated.

Focusing the search in the literature domain of CSP problems, several works were revealed in the sub-domain of balancing, planning and scheduling activities that can be related to this application [7][8][9][10][11]. Namely, models of combinatorial optimization for minimizing the maximum/total lateness/tardiness of directed graphs of tasks with precedence and time constraints [7][11]. These problems are analogous to this work, and due to a simplified formulation with the same constraints (precedences and time between nodes), can be easily extrapolated to our case.

IV. Implementing and Testing

This section starts by stating the assumptions made and introducing the constraint satisfaction solvers used. The last part of this section describes in detail how tests were performed and the implementation of the solution in both solvers.

A. Problem Assumptions

The Smart Node application has several interfaces for real sensors, ranging from radio frequency to cable protocols. By testing this model with simulated scenarios, we assume no interference or noise of any type can cause disturbance in the sampling frequency. In a real case scenario, a sensor could enter in an idle state for a variety of reasons. In that case, data would not be transmitted at all, causing the transmission of data to the Cloud to be postponed for undefined time, waiting for the Network Level node burst depending on the idle sensor. For simplification, we assume a sensor never enters an idle state. Also, it is assumed that the time that takes to treat one collection of data will increase linearly for more than one collection, as mentioned for $T(f_j)$ when introducing Equation 7.

B. Constraint Satisfaction Problem Solvers

For comparison of performance purposes we implemented the problem using both *OptaPlanner* and *SICStus Prolog*. As the Smart Node is implemented in Java we can take advantage of a direct integration with *OptaPlanner* in future. On the other hand, we expected that *SICStus Prolog* would produce the same results with better computation times because of the lightweight implementation and optimized constraint library. Using this premises and the results presented in the next section a grounded decision about what solver to use in future implementations of the Smart Node can be made.

C. Tests

To validate the problem solutions several graph configurations were tested using the two implemented versions, based on *OptaPlanner* and *SICStus Prolog*, as described in Section IV. To test the implementations an algorithm to generate instances of the problem was built. The script generates instances of the Smart Node internal structure, DAG's, with a given number of Processing and Network nodes. Algorithm 1 briefly illustrates the approach:

Data: $G \leftarrow S \cup P \cup N$
Result: Smart Node internal configuration G
$notVisitedNodes \leftarrow G$;
$Pnodes \leftarrow randomInteger(\frac{|P \cup N|}{2}, |P \cup N| - 2)$;
$Nnodes \leftarrow nNodes - Pnodes$;
$Snodes \leftarrow$
  $randomInteger(\frac{nNodes}{2}, nNodes + \frac{nNodes}{2})$;
$G \leftarrow S, P, N \leftarrow$
  $generateNodes(Snodes, Pnodes, Nnodes)$;
$remainingEdges \leftarrow Pnodes \times 2 + Nnodes + Snodes$;
while $remainingEdges > 0$ **do**
  if $node \leftarrow notVisitedNodes.nextNode()$ **then**
    $notVisitedNodes.remove(node)$;
  else
    $node \leftarrow G.randomNode()$;
  end
  if *node is S* **then**
    connect to a random P or S node, disconnected nodes first;
    $remainingEdges --$;
  else if *node is P* **then**
    get connection from a random P or S node, disconnected nodes first;
    connect to a random P or S node, disconnected nodes first;
    $remainingEdges --$;
    $remainingEdges --$;
  else
    get connection from random a P or S node, disconnected nodes first;
    $remainingEdges --$;
  end
end

Algorithm 1: Smart Node instance generation.

Real scenarios generally have a higher number of Sensor Nodes, followed by a small number of Processing Nodes and an even smaller number of Network Nodes. Typically the total number of nodes does not exceed the 30 per operation. The generator picks aleatory numbers for the nodes bounded by a real case scenario application. Sampling frequencies for the sensors are assumed to vary from 400 to 2000 milliseconds. Functions to treat data in Processing Nodes are not typically complex. We measured the real case scenario functions to treat the minimum amount of data (1 sample) and we got values ranging from 0.19 to 0.38 milliseconds. To cover the buffer size domain, we need to take the worst case, 1000 samples. Given best and worst cases, the values attributed to cost of Processing Nodes ($T(f_j)$ in Equation 7) are between 1 and 40 milliseconds.

1) OptaPlanner: This solver [12] is a pure *Java* constraint satisfaction *API* and solver that is maintained by the *RedHat* community, and it can be embedded with the Smart Node application to execute and provide on demand solutions to our optimization problem. Because of the reconfigurable property of the Smart Node internal structure, each time the structure is rearranged, the solution obtained to the problem instance prior to the reconfiguration becomes infeasible. The integration (see Fig. 3) between the two technologies is accomplished by defining the problem in the OptaPlanner notation: (1) *Buffer Size* class corresponds to the *Planning Variable*, during the solving process it will be assigned by the different solver configurations; (2) *Edge* class is the *Planning Entity*, the object of the problem that holds the *Planning Variable*; (3) *SmartNodeGraph* class is the *Planning Solution*, the object that holds the problem instance along with a class that allows to calculate the score of problem instance. The score is given by implementing Equation 9; the best hard score is 0, which corresponds to null variance between the Network Levels nodes. The soft score correspond to the minimization of the summation of all buffer sizes and does not weight as much as hard score in search phase.
Since the search space is exponential, heuristics can be implemented to help the *OptaPlanner* solver to determine the easiest buffers to change. The implemented heuristic sorts the buffers from the easiest to the hardest. The sorting values are given by the number of ancestors of a given edge, an edge with a greater number of ancestors is more difficult to plan. Also, if an edge leads to a Network Node, it is considered more difficult to plan. *OptaPlanner* offers a great variety of algorithms to avoid the huge search space of most *CSPs*. These algorithms can be consulted in the documentation [13] and configured to achieve best search performances. For a correct comparison we used the *Branch and Bound* algorithm, which is the same algorithm that *SICStus Prolog* uses by default, without heuristics.

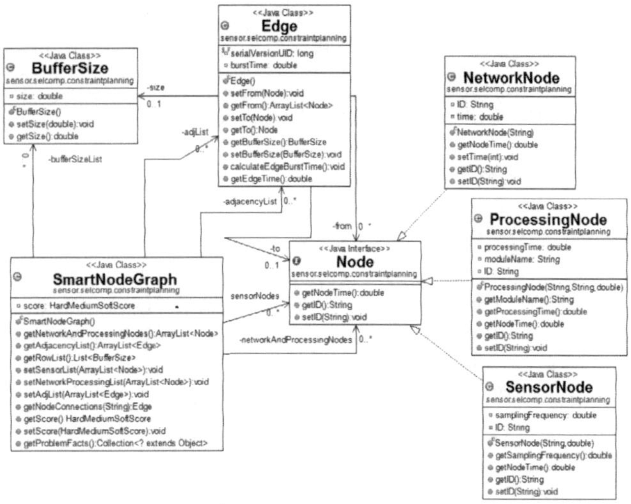

Figure 2. UML for Smart Node and OptaPlanner integration.

The UML diagram in Fig. 3 shows the modeling of the problem using the *OptaPlanner* methodology.

2) SICStus Prolog: SICStus Prolog [14] provides several libraries of constraints that allow to model constraint satisfaction problems much more naturally than the *OptaPlanner* approach, which follows from the fact that modeling a problem in *SICStus Prolog* takes advantage of the declarative nature of logic programming. The problem modeling involved four types of facts (to represent N, P and S nodes, and to represent edges) and six predicates (to gather variables, express domain and constraints). The *clpfd* (Constraint Logic Programming over Finite Domains) [15] library was used to model and solve the problem. This library contains several options of modeling that can be used to optimize the labeling process. In our case the labeling process takes as objective the minimization of the difference between the Network Node with the maximum burst time and the one with the lowest burst time (Equation 9). The variables of the problem are given by a list of all the facts *edge(from,to,buffer_size).*, where *buffer_size* are the variables to solve in a finite domain from 1 to 1000. In future implementations of the problem, global constraints and labeling options must be analyzed to ensure the modulation is the most optimized.

V. RESULTS

For both implementations the results are shown in Tables I and II. The results shown, are a mean of 5 different problem instances, for each problem size (which is determined by $|P \cup N|$, see Section II. To gather results, the generator was used to generate 5 instances of the problem for each row. Then, both solvers were used in the same machine (Intel(R) Core(TM) i7-4710HQ CPU @ 2.50GHz (8 CPUs), 2.5GHz, 16384MB RAM), with the same conditions (Windows 10 Home 64-bit), to run the tests. Considering that the solution will run online (in idle CPU time), and that a suboptimnal solution will also reduce heavilly the network trafic, by introducing a time window to compensate residual variance. We established a limit of 60s, which was considered acceptable for the solvers to find a feasible solution in a real case. Another limit was the number of nodes used in the experiences. With a number of nodes in the order of 100, and a time window of 8 hours, both solvers were unable to give a response to most cases. Given the complexity stated, and given the fact that in real cases the number of nodes normally does not exceed 30, 50 nodes was the limit used for the tests.

The quality of the solutions found is mostly given by the second column, which represents the constraint of minimizing the burst times at the Network Level. As we can see (Table II), the *SICStus Prolog* implementation shows the best results for the most relevant quality factor. In the third column, the summation of all the buffer sizes is lower in the *OptaPlanner* implementation (Table I). During the tests, we observed in the logs that the *OptaPlanner* was much more slower walking the search tree. Regarding all the columns, a clear tendency to worst results is obvious along the table, but in the last line of both tables, a sudden improvement in the variance occurs. This behavior enforces the NP-Completeness nature of this kind of problems. In every row of both tables in which a *Solution time* of 60 seconds is found, that row matches a sub-optimal solution. Since both solvers were programmed to stop at 60 seconds, mostly the solutions are not optimal. The sub-optimal solutions found are feasible in a real case, even if the variance between call times is not zero, because the gap is heavilly

TABLE I. OPTAPLANNER RESULTS

OptaPlanner			
|P ∪ S|	$\Delta V(B_k)$(ms)	$\sum \|b_{n,m}\|$	*Solution time(s)*
5	15.600	264.400	48.133
10	82.200	30.600	60.000
15	205.800	241.400	48.037
20	637.600	189.800	60.000
25	1494.000	56.600	60.000
30	1218.600	128.800	60.000
35	979.000	74.400	60.000
40	1434.400	74.600	60.000
45	1138.200	89.000	60.000
50	646.600	118.600	60.000

TABLE II. SICSTUS RESULTS

SICStus			
|P ∪ S|	$\Delta V(B_k)$(ms)	$\sum \|b_{n,m}\|$	*Solution time(s)*
5	0.400	731.800	38.022
10	1.800	738.000	48.894
15	73.000	1738.600	60.000
20	102.400	4912.600	60.000
25	600.000	8210.800	60.000
30	457.800	6214.800	60.000
35	351.800	7986.200	60.000
40	564.000	5792.200	60.000
45	630.000	10457.000	60.000
50	321.200	14706.400	60.000

reduced. Theoretically, every reduction in the variance is a better solution, in practice, a minimum acceptable value for variance needs to be defined. The Smart Component can define a time window with the size of the variance, and this way, include all results in the same call.

VI. CONCLUSION AND FUTURE WORK

Despite the search space of the problem, both solvers reached an optimal solutions in cases that are feasible to real application. In the future, tuning options of the solvers must be explored. Another additional constraint to this problem could be the introduction of a case in which a single or several sensors are producing data with an higher priority. The problem can be easily reformulated to embrace that kind of situation modifying the objective function Equation 9. *SICStus Prolog* shows a clear advantage in computation time. That difference can be the reflex of the number of lines of code needed to model the problem. *SICStus Prolog* required eight procedures (predicates), against 10 classes and 1 *XML* configuration file for the *OptaPlanner* implementation. The difference in modeling complexity possibly causes an additional overhead. Another important remark is that, given the experience of implementing the problem and playing with the solvers options, two contrasts can be highlighted: (1) *SICStus Prolog* is very intuitive at the problem modeling phase, on the other hand, *OptaPlanner* required more effort, both in implementing an perceiving the methodology; (2) tuning the solvers, for example the time out feature that allows to stop the solver in the desired time, is more intuitive in the *OptaPlanner* approach. Considering all pros and cons, *SICStus Prolog* most probably will be chosen to integrate the Smart Node in future work. This experiments were made offline, as future work, the Smart Component can embedd the optimization code and adopt a strategy to optimize the variance in idle CPU time until an optimal solution is found online. Although the time limit used was short, in a continuous operation environment, even if running in idle CPU time, the solvers will gradually converge to an optiomal solution.

REFERENCES

[1] L. Neto, J. Reis, D. Guimaraes, and G. Goncalves, "Sensor cloud: Smartcomponent framework for reconfigurable diagnostics in intelligent manufacturing environments," in Industrial Informatics (INDIN), 2015 IEEE 13th International Conference on. IEEE, 2015, pp. 1706–1711.

[2] I. Ioachim, J. Desrosiers, F. Soumis, and N. Bélanger, "Fleet assignment and routing with schedule synchronization constraints," European Journal of Operational Research, vol. 119, no. 1, 1999, pp. 75–90.

[3] K. Avrachenkov, U. Ayesta, E. Altman, P. Nain, and C. Barakat, "The effect of router buffer size on the tcp performance," in In Proceedings of the LONIIS Workshop on Telecommunication Networks and Teletraffic Theory. Citeseer, 2001.

[4] K. Avrachenkov, U. Ayesta, and A. Piunovskiy, "Optimal choice of the buffer size in the internet routers," in Decision and Control, 2005 and 2005 European Control Conference. CDC-ECC'05. 44th IEEE Conference on. IEEE, 2005, pp. 1143–1148.

[5] A. Gogu, D. Nace, A. Dilo, and N. Meratnia, Review of optimization problems in wireless sensor networks. InTech, 2012.

[6] M. Jadliwala, Q. Duan, S. Upadhyaya, and J. Xu, "On the hardness of eliminating cheating behavior in time synchronization protocols for sensor networks," Technical Report 2008-08, State University of New York at Buffalo, Tech. Rep., 2008.

[7] J. Błażewicz, W. Kubiak, and S. Martello, "Algorithms for minimizing maximum lateness with unit length tasks and resource constraints," Discrete applied mathematics, vol. 42, no. 2, 1993, pp. 123–138.

[8] B. Gacias, C. Artigues, and P. Lopez, "Parallel machine scheduling with precedence constraints and setup times," Computers & Operations Research, vol. 37, no. 12, 2010, pp. 2141–2151.

[9] K. Rustogi et al., "Machine scheduling with changing processing times and rate-modifying activities," Ph.D. dissertation, University of Greenwich, 2013.

[10] A. Malapert, C. Guéret, and L.-M. Rousseau, "A constraint programming approach for a batch processing problem with non-identical job sizes," European Journal of Operational Research, vol. 221, no. 3, 2012, pp. 533–545.

[11] J. H. Patterson and J. J. Albracht, "Technical noteassembly-line balancing: Zero-one programming with fibonacci search," Operations Research, vol. 23, no. 1, 1975, pp. 166–172.

[12] O. Team, OptaPlanne - Constraint Satisfaction Solver, Red Hat. [Online]. Available: http://www.optaplanner.org/

[13] ——, OptaPlanner User Guide, Red Hat. [Online]. Available: http://docs.jboss.org/optaplanner/release/6.3.0.Final/optaplanner-docs/pdf/optaplanner-docs.pdf

[14] M. Carlsson, J. Widen, J. Andersson, S. Andersson, K. Boortz, H. Nilsson, and T. Sjöland, SICStus Prolog user's manual. Swedish Institute of Computer Science Kista, Sweden, 1988, vol. 3, no. 1.

[15] M. Carlsson, G. Ottosson, and B. Carlson, "An open-ended finite domain constraint solver," in Programming Languages: Implementations, Logics, and Programs. Springer, 1997, pp. 191–206.

Life-cycle Approach to Extend Equipment Re-use in Flexible Manufacturing

Susana Aguiar, Rui Pinto, João Reis, Gil Gonçalves

Institute for Systems and Robotics
Faculty of Engineering of University of Porto
Porto, Portugal
Email: {saguiar, rpinto, jpcreis, gil}@fe.up.pt

***Abstract*—Nowadays, manufacturing industry has to adapt quickly, with minimum effort, to constant changes on customer demand. On the other hand, concerns regarding the environmental and social impacts of industrial processes is growing. These are ideas behind the project Innovative Reuse of modular knowledge Based devices and technologies for Old, Renewed and New factories (ReBORN). This paper presents the System Assessment Tool, a software application developed in ReBORN, which is used for assessing the sustainability of highly adaptive production systems. The main objective of this evaluation tool is to provide methods and algorithms for assessing the various (re)configuration possibilities and the corresponding effect on the overall system cost, performance and status throughout the entire life-cycle(s) of the manufacturing system. In order to help the system designer to make more informed decisions, different factors relating the life-long assessment of the concerned system and device were taken into account. This results in the optimum utilization of the manufacturing equipment throughout their life-cycle.**

Keywords–Smart factories; Life-cycle assessment; Re-use; Production systems.

I. INTRODUCTION

The ReBORN project - Innovative Reuse of modular knowledge Based devices and technologies for Old, Renewed and New factories - is a project co-funded by the European Commission, which intends to demonstrate strategies and technologies that enable the re-use of production equipment in old, renewed and new factories. The idea is to save valuable resources by re-cycling equipment and use it in a different application, instead of discarding it after one way use. Currently, there is a lack of versatile and modular, task-driven plug&produce devices with built-in capabilities for self-assessment and optimal re-use. This requires new concepts and strategies for repair and upgrade of equipment, the (re-) design of factory layouts and flexible, adaptable and ready to plug-in modules. Such new strategies will contribute to sustainable, resource-friendly and greener manufacturing and, at the same time, deliver economic and competitive advantages for the manufacturing sector.

During its life-cycle, manufacturing equipment passes throw several stages, starting at initial incorporation into the production line, operation, maintenance/upgrade to end-of-use and disassemble. Throughout these stages there are a number of critical intersections, which can potentially cause costly machine downtime or even downtime in the entire production system. Usually, decisions regarding equipment operation are made by engineers and shop-floor operators, which are most of the times based on the experience of these individuals. Sometimes the individuals know-how and gained knowledge by experience is hard to be transferred to other individuals and may be lost [1]. In order to tackle this problem, a support to decision making must exist, combining simulations with the process data history gathered on equipment level. A System Assessment Tool (SAT) was implemented, allowing the analysis and comparison of industrial equipment, based on reliability metrics, Life Cycle Cost (LCC) and Life Cycle Assessment (LCA).

This paper is organized in four more sections. In section II, a brief overview of the ReBORN project is presented, along with a discussion regarding the current state of the art of the metrics used for equipment analysis. In section III, the System Assessment Tool is analyzed and described, followed by a demonstration scenario in Section IV. Section V concludes the paper by exposing some final remarks about the implemented software and next steps for future work are identified.

II. LIFE-CYCLE COST ASSESSMENT

The vision of ReBORN is to demonstrate strategies and technologies that support a new paradigm for the re-use of production equipment in factories. This re-use will give new life to decommissioned production systems and equipment, helping them to be reborn in new production lines. Such new strategies will contribute to a more sustainable and resource-friendly and, at the same time, deliver economic and competitive advantages for the manufacturing sector.

ReBORN efforts are towards 100% re-use of equipment, focusing its approaches on four main areas: 1) modular Plug and Produce equipment, 2) in-line adaptive manufacturing, 3) innovative factory layout design techniques and adaptive (re)configuration, 4) flexible and low-cost mechanical systems for fast and easy assembly and disassemble. All the developments of the four areas together accumulate manufacturing knowledge for a 360 factory equipment life-cycle. These developments will give rise to self-aware and knowledge based equipment, with functionalities to collect and manage information regarding their capabilities. Through its approach and planned activities, ReBORN addresses industrial needs hitherto neglected and contributes to unleash the full potential of sustainable, green and smart factories, by empowering the industry to produce components and assembly systems, which can address fast changing requirements.

In ReBORN, several efforts are being done on the life-cycle cost assessment for adaptive system reconfiguration and change. The system reconfiguration and change is performed through the assessment of various reconfiguration possibilities, such as change, upgrade, reuse, dismantle and disposal, and the corresponding effect on the overall system cost, performance and status throughout the life-cycle. This is accomplished by what-if simulation scenarios on the virtual agents representation of the equipment in the virtual design environment, in order to estimate the likely impact on the physical system before making a change recommendation.

Over the years several models, tools, and standards have been developed for reliability [2] [3], LCC [4]–[8], and LCA [9]–[12]. These three areas are usually treated as separate fields, where each one of them have their own metrics, tools, and standards. Some attempts to bring them closer have been made [13]–[15], where the relation between different sustainability assessment tools is presented, and the central concept is life cycle assessment for sustainability [16]. Several surveys of existing the methodologies and tools on all the three fields have been performed [7], [15]–[18].

Cerria, Taisch and Terzi on [19], proposed an integrated, structured and robust model to support and help the activity of designers and engineers to create and identify the optimal life cycle oriented solution. This solution takes into account some of the LCC, LCA, and technical constraints and/or performances methodologies. This work presented some results of the tests that were performed with an industrial case that look promising. Unfortunately the metrics used were not described and no further details were provided.

Although some steps have being made in order to correlate reliability, LCC, and LCA, there is still work to be done. This is what motivated us to develop our System Assessment tool.

III. System Assessment Tool

The SAT integrates reliability and life cycle status information during the early design phases. This tool is a web based application that allows users to use it directly or through a REST web service.

The life-long cost assessment of the system is accomplished through the collection of the system performances data throughout its life cycle. Based on this performance data, the SAT performs the life cycle cost assessment and analyses the effect on the overall reconfigured system, by comparing machines and production lines. According to the requirements of the ReBORN consortium, this comparison is done based on three different metrics: 1) reliability (Fig. 4), such as failure rate, Mean Time Between Failure (MTBF), Mean Time To Repair (MTTR), reliability, availability, performance, quality, and Overall Equipment Effectiveness (OEE); 2) LCC (Fig. 6), such as Future Value (FV), Present Value (PV), Net Present Cost (NPC), and Net Present Value (NPV) with initial costs; 3) LCA (Fig. 7), such as life cycle emissions.

A. Architecture

The SAT is a tool that has two main objectives: 1) provide an easy and intuitive way for the user to compare machines or production lines through a web application; 2) provide a web API service, able to receive requests and communicate the results with other modules in the project, or other future applications.

Both the web application and the web API service provide the same functionalities, which are depicted, at a high level, in Fig. 1.

The tool has four main groups, namely the Reliability metrics, LCC metrics, LCA metrics, and Machine Label. These functionalities are further described in the next sections.

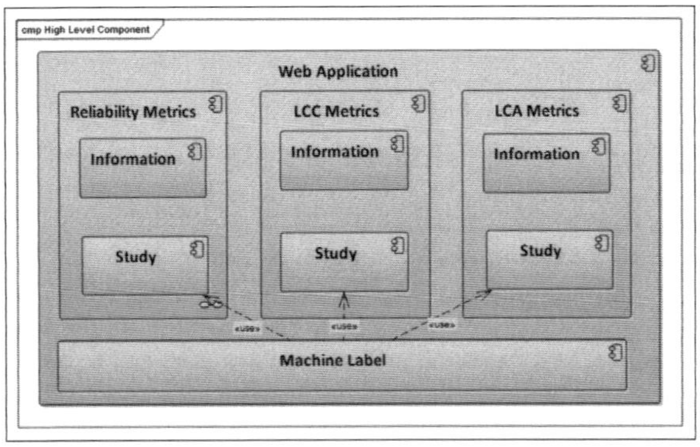

Figure 1. System Assessment Tool Overall Architecture

B. Reliability Metrics Functionality

The SAT can calculate the following parameters related to the reliability of operation of the machines or production lines:

- Failure rate, which can be defined as the frequency which an engineered system or component fails, expressed in failures per unit of time.

$$Failurerate = \frac{\text{\#failures per unit of time}}{\text{Operating Hours per unit of time}} \quad (1)$$

- MTBF is defined as the predicted elapsed time between inherent failures of a system during operation.

$$MTBF = \frac{\text{Operating Hours per unit of time}}{\text{\#failures per unit of time}} \quad (2)$$

- MTTR is a basic measure of the maintainability of repairable items. It represents the average time required to repair a failed component or device.

$$MTTR = \frac{\sum(\text{breakdown times per unit of time})}{\text{\#failures per unit of time}} \quad (3)$$

- Reliability is the probability that the equipment will complete a mission of length t without failure. It is an exponential function.

$$Reliability = e^{\text{-failureRate*time}} \quad (4)$$

- Availability is defined as the ratio between the actual run time and the scheduled run time.

$$Availability = \frac{\text{Operating Hours Year}}{\text{Planned Production Time}} \quad (5)$$

- Performance is the ratio between the actual number of units produced and the number of unit that theoretically can be produced. It is based on the standard rate, which is the rate the equipment is designed for.

$$Performance = \frac{(\text{Total Pieces} * \text{Ideal Cycle Time})}{\text{Operating Hours Year}} \quad (6)$$

- Quality is the ratio between good units produced and the total units that were produced.

$$Quality = \frac{\text{Good Pieces}}{\text{Total Pieces}} \quad (7)$$

- OEE is the ratio between the theoretical maximum good output during the loading time vs. the actual good output.

$$OEE = \text{Availability} * \text{Performance} * \text{Quality} \quad (8)$$

C. LCC Metrics Functionality

In the area of LCC metrics, the following parameters are calculated by the SAT:

- Capital Cost Unit Over Service Life, which is the cost of producing a unit over the machine expected service life.

$$\begin{aligned} CC = {} & (\text{Hardware Acquisition} + \text{Software Acquisition} \\ & + \text{Service Contracts} + \text{Administrative} \\ & + \text{Set Up Installation} + \text{Other Inicial Costs}) \\ & + ((\text{Training Maintenance Support} \\ & + \text{Materials Costs} + \text{Equipment Upgrade} \\ & + \text{Other Operations Maintenance}) \\ & + ((\text{Default Annual Energy Consumption} \\ & * \text{Eletricity Rate}) * \text{Machine Expected Service Life})) \\ & + \text{Disposition Cost} \quad (9) \end{aligned}$$

- Capital Annualized Cost Unit is the cost of producing a unit per year.

$$CA = \frac{\text{Capital Cost Unit Over Service Life}}{\text{Machine Expected Service Life}} \quad (10)$$

- FV, which is the value of an asset or cash at a specified date in the future that is equivalent in value to a specified sum today. The idea is that an amount today is worth a different amount at a future time (this is based on the time value of money).

$$\begin{aligned} FV = {} & (\text{Hardware Acquisition} + \text{Software Acquisition} \\ & + \text{Service Contracts} + \text{Administrative} \\ & + \text{Set Up Installation} + \text{Other Inicial Costs}) \\ & * (1 + (\frac{\text{Interest Rate}}{100}) * \text{Years to be analysed}) \quad (11) \end{aligned}$$

- PV is the present day value of an amount that is received at a future date.

$$PV = \frac{\text{Future Value Over Period Review}}{(1 + \frac{DiscountRate}{100})^{\text{Years to be analysed}}} \quad (12)$$

- NPC is the sum of all costs, such as capital investment, non-fuel operation and maintenance costs, replacement costs, energy costs (fuel cost plus any associated costs), any other costs, such as legal fees, etc. If a number of options are being considered then the option with the lowest NPC will be the most favorable financial option.

$$\begin{aligned} NPC = {} & \text{PV OverPeriodReview} + (\frac{\text{Discount Rate}}{100}) \\ & * (\text{total Cash Flows}) \quad (13) \end{aligned}$$

- NPV is used to determine the present value of an investment by the discounted sum of all cash flows received from the project and discounting the initial costs.

$$\begin{aligned} NPV = {} & \sum (\text{cash Flow} * \frac{1}{1 + \frac{\text{Discount Rate}}{100}^{\text{Period Review}}} \\ & - \text{Initial Costs} \quad (14) \end{aligned}$$

D. LCA Metrics Functionality

Life cycle assessment is a cradle-to-grave approach for assessing industrial systems. Cradle-to-grave begins with the gathering of raw materials from the earth to create the product and ends at the point when all materials are returned to the earth [10] [11].

According to [9] LCA had its beginnings in the 1960s due to concerns over the limitations of raw materials and energy resources. One of the first publications of its kind was done by Harold Smith, who reported his calculation of cumulative energy requirements for the production of chemical intermediates and products at the World Energy Conference in 1963.

The realization of an LCA study is a complex process that needs a large amount of different data that usually is not commonly available. Due to that fact, simpler metrics related to the environmental impacts were considered. The following commonly study impacts were considered: Global Warming, Stratospheric Ozone Depletion, and Human Health. Each one of these impacts has a characterization factor associated to it:

- Global Warming factor has as characterization factor the Global Warming Potential. To calculate this impact, several types of flows must be taken into account, such as Carbon Dioxide (CO2), Nitrogen Dioxide (NO2), Methane (CH4), Chlorofluorocarbons (CFCs), Hydrochlorofluorocarbons (HCFCs), and Methyl Bromide (CH3Br).

$$\begin{aligned} GWP = {} & (\text{CO2*1})+(\text{CH4*25})+(\text{CH3Br*5}) \\ & +(\text{N2O*298})+(\text{SF6*22800})*(\text{NF3*17200}) \quad (15) \end{aligned}$$

- Stratospheric Ozone Depletion has as characterization factor the Ozone Depleting Potential. To calculate this impact, several types of flows must be taking into account, such as: Chlorofluorocarbons (CFCs), Hydrochlorofluorocarbons (HCFCs), and Halons Methyl Bromide (CH3Br).

$$\begin{aligned} ODP = {} & (\text{CCl3F(CFC11)*1})+(\text{CCl2F (CFC12)*1}) \\ & +(\text{C2Cl3F3(CFC113)*1.07})+(\text{C2F4Cl (CFC114)*0.8}) \\ & +(\text{C2ClF5(CFC115)*0.5})+(\text{HClFC2 HCFC22)*0.055}) \\ & +(\text{CH3CCl3(HC140a)*0.12})+(\text{CF3Br(Halon1301)*16}) \\ & +(\text{CF2BrCl(Halon1211)*4}) \\ & +(\text{CCl4(Tetrachloromethane)*1.08}) \quad (16) \end{aligned}$$

- Human Health has as characterization factor the LC50. To calculate this impact, several types of flows must be taking into account, such as Carbon Monoxide (CO), Oxides of Nitrogen (NOx), and Sulphur Dioxide (SO2).

$$HH = (\text{CO*0.012})+(\text{NOx*0.78})+(\text{SO2*1.2}) \quad (17)$$

E. Machine Label

The Machine Label main objective is to attribute a grade from A to F to the machines, based on the metrics calculated and represented on Table I. The basic idea is to attribute weights to selected metrics and determine the grade based on these weights. The goal is to have an equipment label similar to the European Union energy label [20].

TABLE I. LABEL SCALE

Grade	*Range (%)*
A	100-90
B	89-70
C	69-50
D	49-30
E	29-10
F	10-0

As a first approach, this grade is defined using (1), represented by a few metrics and identical weights. Label is the grade, R and Rw are the reliability and reliability weight, OEE and OEEw are the overall equipment effectiveness and respective weight, Oc, Ic and DOc are the operational cost, the initial cost and dispose off cost, EC and ECw are the energy consumption and respective weight, PR and PRw are the percentage reusable and the corresponding weight. Sensitivities studies to determine a more robust metric to determine the attribution of the machine label are ongoing.

$$Label = R*Rw + OEE*OEEw + ((Oc)/((Ic+DOc)*Weight) + EC*ECw + PR*PRw \quad (18)$$

IV. DEMONSTRATION SCENARIO

As mentioned before, the ReBORN aims to develop a general design methodology for manufacturing systems, building on the availability of great amounts of data and knowledge of life and use of production equipment collected by the devices, with the purpose of enabling new system design methods with extensive re-use of production equipment.

The design methodology is based on the concept of component-based agent representation of modular manufacturing equipment [21] [22], where every piece of equipment is controlled through an intelligent agent that continuously captures knowledge about the current status of the equipment. This information about the task-related efforts, the prospective lifetime, maintenance- and refurbishment-related needs as well as enhancement-related needs allows for the formulation of an overall cost function and for the optimum choice of new, re-use, refurbished or enhanced production equipment.

In order to implement the defined methodology, several software applications where developed by the ReBORN consortium, which are integrated in a workbench developed by Critical Manufacturing company [23], as shown in Fig. 2. This workbench application manages links to the set of tools that will allow a user to build the best possible layout and configuration for a factory, given a set of requirements, constraints and goals.

The SAT can be used inside of the ReBORN workbench or it can be used as an independent software application.

The SAT web application main page is shown in Fig. 3.

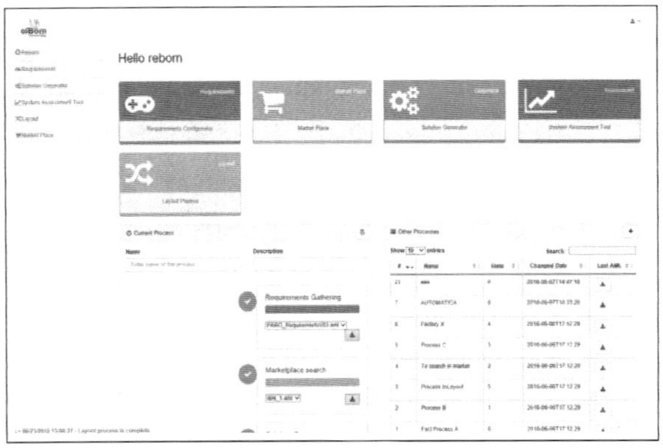

Figure 2. ReBORN Workbench

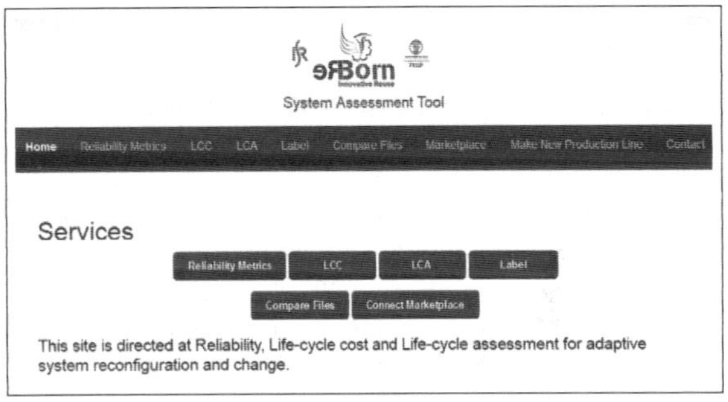

Figure 3. System Assessment tool main web page

As shown on Fig. 3, SATs main tab presents the core functionalities described in the previous sections, namely Reliability, LCC, LCA, Label, and Compare files.

Each of the functionalities has two main sub-functionalities: 1) Information, which deals with all the operations related to adding a new machine or production line, changing them or deleting them; 2) Study, which performs the comparison between several machines or production lines.

The following images show all the possible functionalities and how the results of the studies are shown. As mentioned before, the information can be introduced through the web pages or through an XML file. This applies to both Information and Study. After a Study is executed, the results can also be stored in a XML file.

Fig. 4 presents the graphics view that represents the result of comparing equipments or production lines.

In the LCC study, besides choosing the machines or production lines to be compared, other information must be selected or provided, such as review periods in years, country to be considered, machines or production lines to be compared, and finally the cash flows values for the years, up to the maximum review period, for the machines or production lines under comparison. The LCC study steps are represented in Fig. 5.

Fig. 6 presents the charts generated after the selected equipment or production lines are compared.

Fig. 7 shows the result charts of the comparison of equip-

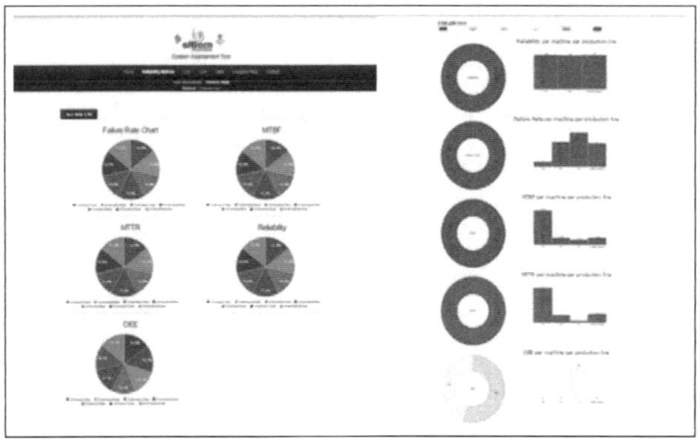

Figure 4. Reliability Study Views

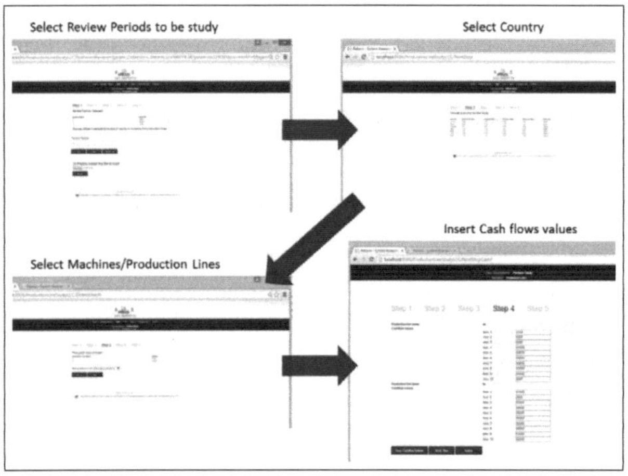

Figure 5. LCC Study steps

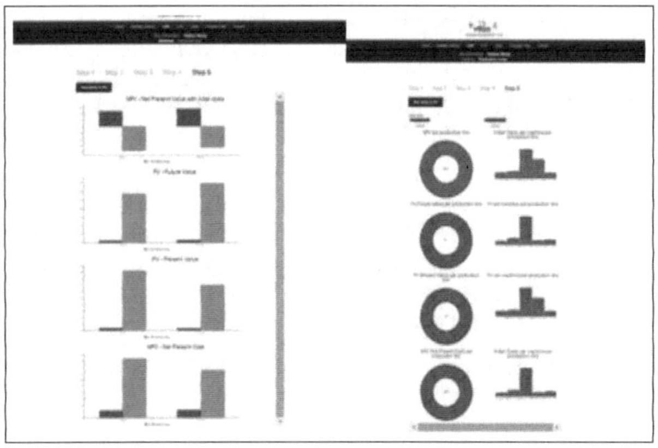

Figure 6. LCC Study results Views

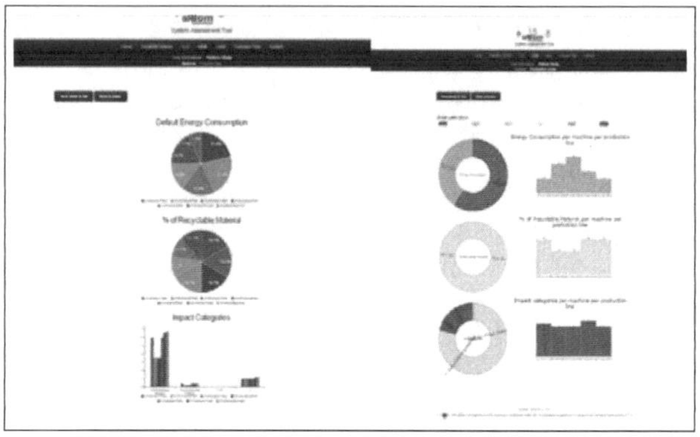

Figure 7. LCA Study Views

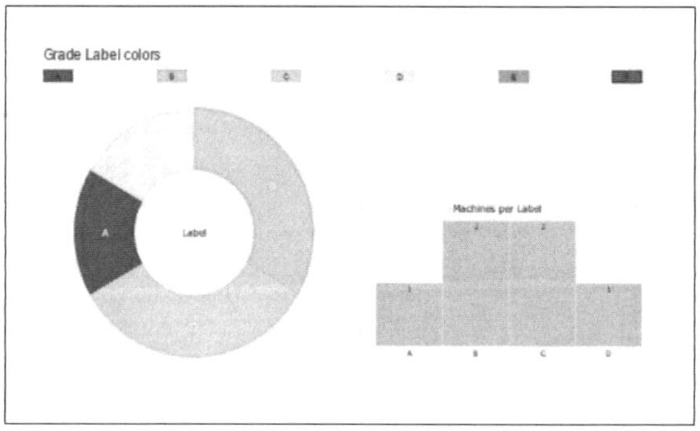

Figure 8. Label View

ment and production lines in terms of LCA metrics.

Fig. 8 presents the charts showing the result of calculating the equipment label.

As mentioned before, the System Assessment tool can be used through the upload of XML files or through the Web API service, allowing flexibility and easy collaboration with other software tools, such as simulators. For example, a simulation tool, such as the FlexSim [24], can be used to simulate the production line, and collect different data. This data can be exported and feed into the SAT.

As a practical example let us assume that a company, in our case one of the industrial partners in the ReBorn project, such as Fagor Automation, PARO, or Harms & Wende, needs to change or acquire an equipment. Using the SAT, new and used equipments can be easily compared. For example, if the idea is to compare them in terms of financial advantage, the SAT allows to compare, for several periods of time, the equipments (or production lines). The result is presented in a straightforward way through the use of circular or bar charts, as shown in Fig. 5. A visual comparison of the charts, allows the industrial partners to realize that if the equipment that they need is going to be used for a short period of time, it makes sense to buy a used equipment. On the other hand if the equipment is going to be used for a long period of time it is reasonable to buy the new equipment.

This type of comparison can be performed considering other aspects besides the financial ones, such as operational factors (reliability, MTTB, MTTR, OEE) or environmental factors (Global Warming, Stratospheric Ozone Depletion, Human Health). The results are also presented visually as in the financial related case (Fig. 7).

As mentioned before, there are several tools that calculate the metrics used in the SAT, but most of the tools concentrate on a specific area, operational, financial, or environmental. One of the advantages of the SAT is the ability to have all these metrics in just one tool. The SAT also proposes a way of easily comparing equipments through the use of a Label, much like the energy label used to classify other equipments, such as refrigerators, TVs, etc.

Always keeping in mind the easy usability of the application, all the information needed to perform the metrics can be introduced through the web interface or through a file. Two types of files are so far supported: XML or AutomationML (AML). The SAT also has a compare files functionality. This functionality purpose is to enable the user to compare several machines or several production lines. This comparison will be able to perform all the metrics of the SAT, namely reliability, LCC, LCA, and Label. The information of the several machines or the several production lines to be compared will be supplied in XML or AML files.

V. CONCLUSION

A System Assessment tool was developed. This is a software web application that allows the comparison of several machines or several production lines in terms of different metrics, such as reliability, LCC and LCA. A System Assessment Web API was also developed. This is a web service based on REST, which can receive requests to calculate the metrics specified in the previous sections.

The purpose of this System Assessment tool is to support the decision making during the planning and running phase of complex manufacturing systems.

As future work a sensitivity analysis on the metrics used and of the parameters available, will be executed. This analysis will provide a clear view of what metrics and parameters really influence and are important when comparing machines.

ACKNOWLEDGMENT

This research was partially supported by the ReBORN project (FoF.NMP.2013-2) Innovative Reuse of modular knowledge Based devices and technologies for Old, Renewed and New factories funded by the European Commission under the Seventh Framework Program for Research and Technological Development. We would like to thank all partners for their support and discussions that contributed to these results.

REFERENCES

[1] M. Oppelt, M. Barth, and L. Urbas, "The Role of Simulation within the Life-Cycle of a Process Plant. Results of a global online survey," 2014, URL: https://www.researchgate.net/ [accessed: 2016-06-01].

[2] V. Cesarotti, A. Giuiusa, and V. Introna, Using Overall Equipment Effectiveness for Manufacturing System Design. INTECH Open Access Publisher, 2013.

[3] K. Muthiah and S. Huang, "Overall throughput effectiveness (ote) metric for factory-level performance monitoring and bottleneck detection," International Journal of Production Research, vol. 45, no. 20, pp. 4753–4769, 2007.

[4] "Standard practice for measuring life-cycle costs of buildings and building systems," 2002, URL: https://www.astm.org/Standards/E917.htm [accessed: 2016-06-01].

[5] F. Bromilow and M. Pawsey, "Life cycle cost of university buildings," Construction Management and Economics, vol. 5, no. 4, pp. S3–S22, 1987.

[6] D. Elmakis and A. Lisnianski, "Life cycle cost analysis: actual problem in industrial management," Journal of Business Economics and Management, vol. 7, no. 1, pp. 5–8, 2006.

[7] D. Langdon, "Literature review of life cycle costing (lcc) and life cycle assessment (lca)," 2006, URL: http://www.tmb.org.tr/arastirma_yayinlar/LCC_Literature_Review_Report.pdf [accessed: 2016-06-01].

[8] "Life cycle costing guideline," 2004, URL: https://www.astm.org/Standards/E917.htm [accessed: 2016-06-01].

[9] M. A. Curran, "Life cycle assessment: Principles and practice," 2006, URL: http://19-659-fall-2011.wiki.uml.edu/ [accessed: 2016-06-01].

[10] G. Rebitzer and et al., "Life cycle assessment: Part 1: Framework, goal and scope definition, inventory analysis, and applications," Environment international, vol. 30, no. 5, pp. 701–720, 2004.

[11] D. Pennington, J. Potting, G. Finnveden, E. Lindeijer, O. Jolliet, T. Rydberg, and G. Rebitzer, "Life cycle assessment part 2: Current impact assessment practice," Environment international, vol. 30, no. 5, pp. 721–739, 2004.

[12] R. A. Filleti, D. A. Silva, E. J. Silva, and A. R. Ometto, "Dynamic system for life cycle inventory and impact assessment of manufacturing processes," Procedia CIRP, vol. 15, pp. 531–536, 2014.

[13] R. Hoogmartens, S. Van Passel, K. Van Acker, and M. Dubois, "Bridging the gap between lca, lcc and cba as sustainability assessment tools," Environmental Impact Assessment Review, vol. 48, pp. 27–33, 2014.

[14] R. Heijungs, G. Huppes, and J. B. Guinée, "Life cycle assessment and sustainability analysis of products, materials and technologies. toward a scientific framework for sustainability life cycle analysis," Polymer degradation and stability, vol. 95, no. 3, pp. 422–428, 2010.

[15] B. Ness, E. Urbel-Piirsalu, S. Anderberg, and L. Olsson, "Categorising tools for sustainability assessment," Ecological economics, vol. 60, no. 3, pp. 498–508, 2007.

[16] R. K. Singh, H. R. Murty, S. K. Gupta, and A. K. Dikshit, "An overview of sustainability assessment methodologies," Ecological indicators, vol. 9, no. 2, pp. 189–212, 2009.

[17] C. Böhringer and P. E. Jochem, "Measuring the immeasurablea survey of sustainability indices," Ecological economics, vol. 63, no. 1, pp. 1–8, 2007.

[18] I. T. Cameron and G. Ingram, "A survey of industrial process modelling across the product and process lifecycle," Computers & Chemical Engineering, vol. 32, no. 3, pp. 420–438, 2008.

[19] D. Cerri, M. Taisch, and S. Terzi, "Proposal of a model for life cycle optimization of industrial equipment," Procedia CIRP, vol. 15, pp. 479–483, 2014.

[20] "Energy Efficient," URL: http://ec.europa.eu/energy/en/topics/energy-efficiency/energy-efficient-products [accessed: 2016-06-01].

[21] M. Peschl, N. Link, M. Hoffmeister, G. Gonçalves, and F. L. Almeida, "Designing and implementation of an intelligent manufacturing system," Journal of Industrial Engineering and Management, vol. 4, no. 4, pp. 718–745, 2011.

[22] G. Gonçalves, J. Reis, R. Pinto, M. Alves, and J. Correia, "A step forward on intelligent factories: A smart sensor-oriented approach," in Proceedings of the 2014 IEEE Emerging Technology and Factory Automation (ETFA). IEEE, pp. 1–8, 2014.

[23] "Critical Manufacturing," URL: http://www.criticalmanufacturing.com [accessed: 2016-06-01].

[24] "Flexsim," URL: https://www.flexsim.com/ [accessed: 2016-06-01].

Concept for Finding Process Models for New Classes of Industrial Production Processes

Norbert Link, Jürgen Pollak, Alireza Sarveniazi
Intelligent Systems Research Group
Hochschule Karlsruhe - Technik und Wirtschaft
Karlsruhe, Germany
e-mail: Norbert.Link@hs-karlsruhe.de, Juergen.Pollak@hs-karlsruhe.de

Abstract— **The required knowledge about relations between quantities governing the control and quality estimation of production processes is represented in so-called process models. Such models may relate process parameters and process goals allowing to find appropriate parameter values for given goals. Other models allow the derivation of the process state from observable quantities. Controls based on Markov Decision Processes require a state transition model and a cost function model of subsequent states. The functional relationships between the quantities of a model are usually represented by a dedicated combination of some base functions with given, fixed parameter values. In many cases, this is a linear combination of Kernel functions, where the parameters are determined by fitting known experimental data, such as in Support Vector Regression methods. The process models always refer only to a dedicated process class with given conditions (e.g., parts materials and geometries or machine properties). There are model populations in most industrial process domains, such as laser metal sheet welding, representing several metal alloys in combination with sheet thicknesses and welding equipment. In this paper, we propose novel methods on how to make use of this already existing model knowledge, which is used for the derivation of models of new process classes in the same process domain. For this purpose, the formation of a common model representation is derived from the individual models of the domain. The parameters of the individual models in this common representation form a model space, in which a model of the models can be formed: the hyper-model. General ideas of hyper-model formation are presented and approaches are discussed how dedicated models for specific, new process classes (e.g., with different conditions) can be derived from it.**

Keywords: machine learning; data modeling; hyper-model; process model; welding.

I. INTRODUCTION

Mathematical models represent the mapping of adjustable quantities on resulting phenomena, such as process parameters on process results. Models of processes can represent many dependencies of process quantities, depending on the purpose of model exploitation. In the case of simple controlled processes, the model might describe the relation of process parameter values with quality measures to be achieved (goal values). In the case of a Markov Decision Process the model might represent the state transition probability depending on present state and control action [2].

In simple controlled processes the process parameters describe the variable control quantities, which can be represented by a vector $\boldsymbol{p}$ and which determine the actions. All fixed quantities otherwise governing the process are the process conditions, which are represented in a vector $\boldsymbol{c}$. They are fixed externally and independently from process execution. The desired end state of the process ("goal") is described by goal quantities forming the goal vector $\boldsymbol{g}$. For example, in car seat manufacturing metal sheets are joined by laser welding seams. The process parameters are laser power, laser focus and welding speed. The variable conditions are the material thicknesses of the two sheets. The goal is a certain seam width and seam depth, which have to be obtained. The welding task is then given by the combination of the goals and the conditions $\boldsymbol{t} = [\boldsymbol{g}, \boldsymbol{c}]$. At least one method (consisting of process parameters $\boldsymbol{p}$) has to be found, fulfilling a given task $\boldsymbol{t}$. In other words, a mapping from $\boldsymbol{t}$ to $\boldsymbol{p}$ has to be performed. We call this the task-to-method transform (T2MT) which is the inverse process model. The process model itself in the simple case is the functional relationship $\boldsymbol{g} = f(\boldsymbol{p}, \boldsymbol{c})$ of the goal quantities with the condition and control quantities $\boldsymbol{c}$ and $\boldsymbol{p}$. It is used to find the suitable control quantities or process parameters by solving the equation for $\boldsymbol{p}$ at given $\boldsymbol{c}$.

A process model can be built from experimental data where a variety of process conditions is explored. For each specific condition, a set of methods $\boldsymbol{p}$ is applied and the resulting goal values $\boldsymbol{g}$ are measured. Each single experiment gives a vector triple $[\boldsymbol{g}, \boldsymbol{p}, \boldsymbol{c}]$ and the available experimental series give a set of such triples. We build an abstraction of the experimental data by the formation of a goal function $g(\boldsymbol{p}, \boldsymbol{c})$ [1]. It represents the knowledge contained in the experimental data: the model. The model function $\boldsymbol{g}$ is representative in our example of a class of processes, where the thicknesses of the two metal sheets may vary within the bounds covered by the experimental sample.

In this formulation of the model formation, we have implicitly assumed that many other external conditions have been controlled and kept constant during all experiments for setting up the sample to learn the abstraction. In our example case above these are the material types of the metal sheets and the welding laser head type for instance. Laser welding manufacturers usually set up process models as described above for the common materials and welding heads as required by their customers by creating full, independent experimental samples in each case. The possible relationships between models are not exploited. On the other hand side, the "implicit" conditions can be represented by numerical quantities ς as well (such as orientation density function and grain size distribution in poly-crystalline metal sheets or optical parameters of the laser head), forming a vector $\boldsymbol{\varsigma}$.

Then, each model function is in correspondence to a point in the space of vectors $\boldsymbol{\varsigma}$. The relations between models could be exploited if it would be known how a model of some $\boldsymbol{\varsigma}^*$ transforms into the model of some other $\boldsymbol{\varsigma}'$, when moving from $\boldsymbol{\varsigma}^*$ to $\boldsymbol{\varsigma}'$. The knowledge of such a transformation

$$g(p, c|\varsigma') = h[g(p, c|\varsigma^*)] \qquad (1)$$

is called a hyper-model. Once such a hyper-model is set up, it can be exploited to derive estimates of process models for new process classes.

The paper is organized as follows:

We first review some common modelling approaches in Section II to create the basis for hyper-models. Then in Section III we propose the novel hyper-model approach which consists of a method to derive a hyper-model from a set of existing process models and a method to derive a new process model from the hyper-model for a given $\boldsymbol{\varsigma}$. Finally, we show in Section IV how this approach might be applied to our laser welding example. The acknowledgement and conclusions close the article.

II. MODELLING PROCESSES AND MODEL EXPLOITATION

In process state tracking (following the state evolution during processing) and quality estimation (properties of the final state) and in control (determining the process-governing control quantities or process parameters) various models are required. These models map available or given quantities $\boldsymbol{x}$ (such as observable measurement values) to other quantities $\mathbf{z}$ bearing the information required to decide upon actions. This mapping is usually represented as mathematical transformation, which is specified as a dedicated transformation function $\mathbf{z} = f(\boldsymbol{x})$ between the corresponding vector spaces of vectors $\boldsymbol{x}$ and $\boldsymbol{z}$ where the vector components are assumed to be real-valued. This function has to be determined in order to represent the required knowledge. Due to the complexity of real-world production processes it is almost always impossible to determine the model form analytically from physical principles. The common way of arriving at models is a generalization of the relations encountered in experimental data, which are supposed to represent the process. This is performed by specifying a quite general function with a set of parameters, the values of which are determined to optimally fit the data. For this purpose many machine-learning methods, such as Support-Vector-Regression [3], Artificial Neural Networks [7], Symbolic Regression [8] or Levenberg-Marquart fitting of parameters of dedicated functions derived from physical considerations [9] are used.

In many cases, it is the inverse of the desired transformation, which is captured by the experiments. An example of this is the goal function, where experiments yield the process result, induced by the selected process parameters. The process is sampled by varying the process parameters and recording the respective results. Now the functional dependency of the result quantities on the process parameters (the goal function) can be fitted, while in the process control the parameter values required for a given process result are required. For this purpose the goal function must be used to find the set of solutions resulting in the desired goal value.

The process of model formation is depicted in Fig. 1.

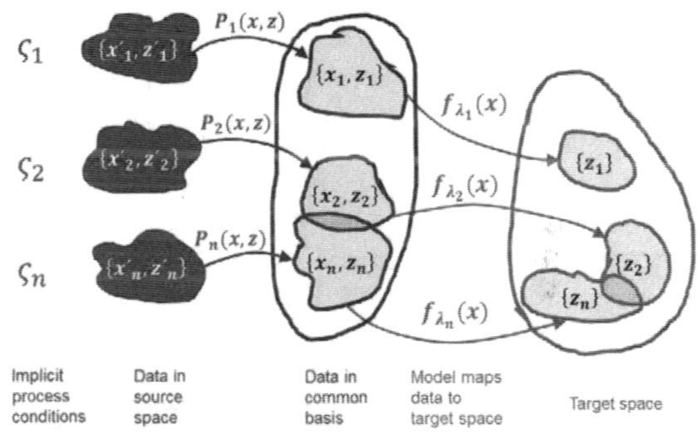

Figure 1. Data from experiments under different implicit conditions serve to form process models.

A model is a function (parametrized by a vector $\boldsymbol{\lambda}$) which describes the target value $\mathbf{z}$ depending on a variable $\boldsymbol{x}$. In general, the input variable $\boldsymbol{x}$ is a vector of quantities, which are controlled by the user to generate the target quantity. The generation of a model from given data corresponds to the determination of $\boldsymbol{\lambda}$. Available data always depends implicitly on other conditions not covered by $\boldsymbol{\varsigma}$. This implicit dependency is retained in $\boldsymbol{\lambda}$ and the corresponding model $f_{\boldsymbol{\lambda}}$ is only valid under these implicit conditions. The first step after the experimental acquisition of the sample data set $\{\boldsymbol{x}'_n, \boldsymbol{z}'_n\}$ under a certain condition $\boldsymbol{\varsigma}_n$ is to bring the data into a common representation basis via a "normalizing" transformation $\boldsymbol{P}_n(\boldsymbol{x}, \boldsymbol{z})$. This allows to operate on the data with the same functional representation of model functions. With these "normalized" data $\{\boldsymbol{x}, \boldsymbol{z}\}$ the parameters $\boldsymbol{\lambda}$ of a transformation function are estimated to optimally represent the mapping $\boldsymbol{z} = f_{\boldsymbol{\lambda}}(\boldsymbol{x})$ with methods as mentioned above. This results in dedicated models

$$\mathbf{z}_n = f_{\lambda_n}(\mathbf{x}) \qquad (2)$$

for each of the implicit process conditions $\boldsymbol{\varsigma}_n$. The model functions can be linear combinations of some base functions

$$f_{\lambda_n}(\mathbf{x}) = \sum_{i=1}^{N} \lambda_i \boldsymbol{\phi}_i(\mathbf{x}). \qquad (3)$$

If the model functions obtained this way represent the required mapping, they can be directly used to retrieve the desired quantity value of $\boldsymbol{z}$ by inserting the given value $\boldsymbol{x}$ and evaluating the formula.

If –on contrary- the data and the derived model function represent the inverse transformation, and $\boldsymbol{x}$ is the quantity to be retrieved for a given instance of $\tilde{\mathbf{z}}$, then the solution set $\tilde{\boldsymbol{x}}$ of values $\boldsymbol{x}$ has to be found which satisfies

$$\tilde{\mathbf{z}} = \mathrm{f}_{\lambda}(\mathbf{x}). \quad (4)$$

The target function $\boldsymbol{z} = f_{\lambda}(\boldsymbol{x})$ represents a surface embedded into a high-dimensional space spanned by the given quantities $\boldsymbol{x}$ (e.g., process parameters and process conditions). A specific, desired value $\tilde{\mathbf{z}}$ of the quantity $\boldsymbol{z}$ defines a parallel hyperplane over the space of vectors $\boldsymbol{x}$ at constant height $\tilde{\mathbf{z}}$, which intersects with the curved target function $\boldsymbol{z} = f_{\lambda}(\boldsymbol{x})$. The intersection hyper-curve is then the sought-after solution set, which is called the level set:

$$\{\tilde{\boldsymbol{x}}\} = \{\boldsymbol{x} \mid \tilde{\mathbf{z}} = \mathrm{f}_{\lambda}(\mathbf{x})\}. \quad (5)$$

The level set can be found by meshing the $\boldsymbol{x}$ space if the dimension is not too high. The mesh is refined by incrementally subdividing cells, which are intersected by $\tilde{\mathbf{z}} = f_{\lambda}(\boldsymbol{x})$, until the desired accuracy is reached. The level set is afterwards given by a discrete set of solutions.

The final level set is then a list of $\tilde{\boldsymbol{x}}$ vectors. Each of them will produce the result $\tilde{\mathbf{z}}$ as requested by the task. Every solution in the found level set is associated with some cost such as energy, wear of tools, production cycle time and so on, which is used to select a best solution.

III. Hyper-Model Approach

If there exist several process models $\boldsymbol{z}_n = f_{\lambda_n}(\boldsymbol{x})$, each representing a different process class under dedicated, different implicit process conditions ς_n, these models can be considered as a sample of models over the space of ς. The dependencies of the models on the implicit process conditions ς_n are implicitly reflected by the values of the model parameters $\boldsymbol{\lambda}_n$. Finding a model corresponding to new conditions ς^* means finding the corresponding parameter values $\boldsymbol{\lambda}^*$. The new model can then be applied for its usual purpose (task-to-method transform, quality estimation, state prediction, etc.) in the new situation. If a valid functional relation between $\boldsymbol{\lambda}$ and ς can be established, based on existing models, it is possible to derive new models from the generalization represented by this functional relation. We call such a relation

$$\varsigma = \mathrm{g}_{\beta}(\boldsymbol{\lambda}) \quad (6)$$

a hyper-model, e.g., a sum of weighted base functions Ψ_k,

$$\mathrm{g}_{\beta}(\boldsymbol{\lambda}) = \textstyle\sum_k \beta_k \boldsymbol{\Psi}_k(\boldsymbol{\lambda}). \quad (7)$$

A hyper- model is a function (parametrized by a vector $\boldsymbol{\beta}$) which describes the connection between the implicit conditions ς and the models represented by $\boldsymbol{\lambda}$. The hyper-model operates on model parameters and represents the differences between models.

Another point of view on a hyper model is that of a transformation between models. The transformation operator T_{ς} depends on the implicit conditions ς and maps a model $f_{\lambda'}$ to f_{λ}.

$$\mathrm{T}_{\varsigma}\, \mathrm{f}_{\lambda'}(\mathbf{x}) = \mathrm{f}_{\lambda}(\mathbf{x}) \quad (8)$$

This is equivalent to another transformation operator T'_{ς} which maps the model parameters $\boldsymbol{\lambda}'$ to $\boldsymbol{\lambda}$.

The operator T'_{ς} can be represented by a function G' depending on model differences ς and model parameters $\boldsymbol{\lambda}$.

$$\mathrm{G}'(\varsigma, \boldsymbol{\lambda}') = \boldsymbol{\lambda} \quad (9)$$

If $\boldsymbol{\lambda}'$ represents a fixed standard reference model (derived under standard conditions), then $\boldsymbol{\lambda}'$ can be absorbed completely in the function leading to

$$\mathrm{G}(\varsigma) = \boldsymbol{\lambda} \quad (10)$$

This formulation of a hyper model brings us back to the previous definition of a hyper-model. The two points of view are equivalent if the hyper-model g_{β} is invertible:

$$\varsigma = \mathrm{g}_{\beta}(\boldsymbol{\lambda}) \Rightarrow \mathrm{G} = \mathrm{g}_{\beta}{}^{-1} \quad (11)$$

This way, the hyper-model can be considered either as a transformation between models or as a generating function, which relates model parameters to situations ς.

The hyper-model $\varsigma = g_{\beta}(\boldsymbol{\lambda})$ can be determined as a generalizing function from sample models, since each model, belonging to a condition ς is then represented by a point in the space of vectors $\boldsymbol{\lambda}$. A set of models corresponds to a set of points in $\boldsymbol{\lambda}$ –space with associated condition values. This can be considered as a set of sample points of a (eventually vector-valued) condition (ς-)surface over the space of $\boldsymbol{\lambda}$. This surface can be represented by the function $g_{\beta}(\boldsymbol{\lambda})$, which is a generalization of the sample points (models). A hyper-model must not necessarily represent conditions which are associated with the models but can represent any quantifiable semantic information.

IV. Laser Welding Example

An application of the T2MT to laser welding is described in [4]. In order to weld metal sheets by laser, the sheets are held in fixed positions. The laser head is delivering the radiation power of the laser to a focal area, where the metal sheets are molten by the absorbed energy. When the focus is moving on, the energy delivery to the previous area ceases and the metal solidifies again after cooling off. A robot moves the laser head along the intended seam, while the head adjusts angle and distance of the laser focus relative to the sheet surface. Three parameters determine the process: "focal distance" z_f (in the range of ±10 mm), "laser power" P (up to 6 kW) and translational speed of the focus ("speed") v (up to 200 mm/s). The resulting welding seam can be described by weld width w and penetration depth d (Fig. 2), which are usually specified by the customer as w_0 and d_0. The required parameter values of z_f, P and v are derived by inversion of the process model $w_0 = w(z_f, P, v)$ and $d_0 = d(z_f, P, v)$ via T2MT, as described in Section II. The process model is built via machine learning from a large set of experimental data with width and depth measurements in the lab. It represents the functional dependency of the customer goal on the parameters under the present conditions (e.g., initial laser head h_{init}) as $w(z_f, P, v|h_{init})$.

Under new conditions (e.g., new laser head) the process will behave differently and the model no longer be valid. As long as the physics of the process has not changed, the new process model can be most likely derived by a transformation of the initial model as in equation (8).

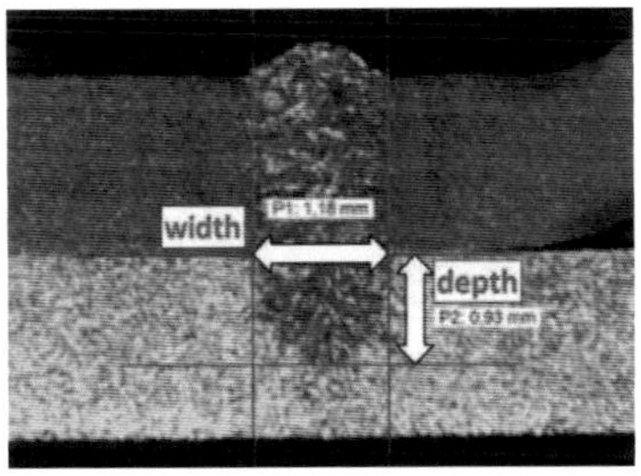

Figure 2. Cross section of two metal sheets joined by a welding seam from laser seam welding. With kind permission of AWL-Techniek B.V [5]

The initial model and only a few new experimental data with an exchanged laser head h_{exch} were used to estimate such transformation as depicted on the right column of Fig. 3. Just an affine mapping was required to transform the process model for capturing the new condition with sufficient accuracy (middle column of Fig. 3).

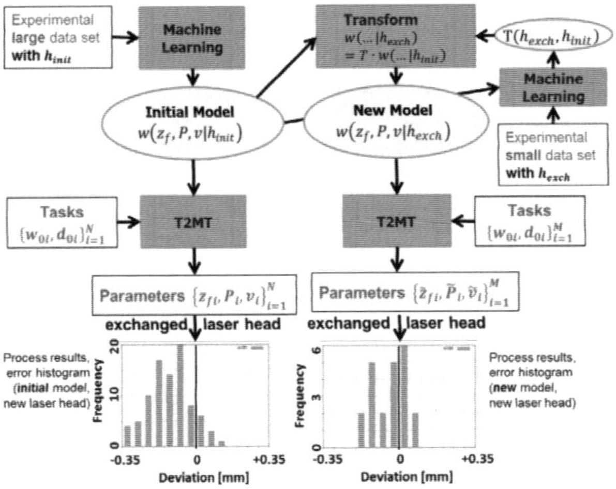

Figure 3. Transformation of laser seam welding process model from the initial laser head to an exchanged laser head.

The left column shows the large deviation of the process results with parameters derived from the initial model.

CONCLUSION

Instead of having to set-up a new model from hundreds of lab experiments, it is sufficient to estimate the transformation from only very few experiments. This can be generalized to a more generic hyper-model as in Section III to also include other conditions such as sheet material.

This way, hyper-modelling is enabling the re-use of existing models and minimizing efforts to explore and represent processes under new conditions. It is also an embedding of process-induced condition relations in the hyper-parameter space, which can be explored and exploited for the prediction of processes under modified conditions.

ACKNOWLEDGMENT

The authors would like to thank the German Federal Ministry of Education and Research (BMBF) for funding the presented research under grant # 03FH061PX5. [6]

REFERENCES

[1] J. Pollak, A. Sarveniazi, and N. Link, "Retrieval of process methods from task descriptions and generalized data representations," The International Journal of Advanced Manufacturing Technology, vol. 53, no. 5, pp. 829–840, 2011. [Online]. Available: http://dx.doi.org/10.1007/s00170-010-2874-1

[2] M. Senn, N. Link, J. Pollak, and J. H. Lee, "Reducing the computational effort of optimal process controllers for continuous state spaces by using incremental learning and post-decision state formulations," Journal of Process Control, vol. 24, no. 3, pp. 133 – 143, 2014. [Online]. Available: http://www.sciencedirect.com/science/article/pii/S0959152414000055 [retrieved: July, 2016].

[3] V. Vapnik, "The Nature of Statistical Learning Theory". Berlin: Springer, 1995.

[4] J. Pollak, "Application of task-to-method transform to laser seam welding" in INTELLI 2015: The Fourth International Conference on Intelligent Systems and Applications. IARIA, p. 128 – 133, 2015. [Online]. Available: https://www.thinkmind.org/download.php?articleid=intelli2015_7_20_95016 [retrieved: June, 2016].

[5] AWL-Techniek B.V., Nobelstraat 37, NL-3846 CE Harderwijk, (postal address: P.O. Box 245, NL-3840 AE Harderwijk), The Netherlands, Web: http://www.awl.nl [retrieved: June, 2016].

[6] Project HyperMod, funded by German BMBF, "Generalization of mathematical models of physical objects and processes: Hyper-Models for the generic description of a set of phenomena classes from single models and their exemplary use in intelligent manufacturing"

[7] M. Senn, K. Jöchen, T. Phan Van, T. Böhlke, and N. Link, "In-depth online monitoring of the sheet metal process state derived from multi-scale simulations". The International Journal of Advanced Manufacturing Technology, Volume 68(9-12), pp 2625-2636, 2013.

[8] S. Fischer, "Process State Observation using Artificial Networks and Symbolic Regression", (INTELLI2015), ISBN: 978-1-61208-437-4, pp 142-147, 2015.

[9] M. Senn and N. Link, "A Universal Model for Hidden State Observation in Adaptive Process Controls", International Journal on Advances in Intelligent Systems, 4(3&4), pp 245-255, 2011.